THE CAMBRIDGE ILLUSTRATED HISTORY OF
Ancient Greece

edited by Paul Cartledge

D0001735

CAMBRIDGE
UNIVERSITY PRESS

CAMBRIDGE UNIVERSITY PRESS
Cambridge, New York, Melbourne, Madrid, Cape Town, Singapore, São Paulo

Cambridge University Press
The Edinburgh Building, Cambridge CB2 8RU, UK

Published in the United States of America by Cambridge University Press, New York

www.cambridge.org
Information on this title: www.cambridge.org/9780521521000

First published 1998
Paperback edition published 2002
Reprinted 2004, 2007

Printed in Italy at Rotolito Lombarda

Typeset in Berkeley 10.25/14 pt

Layout: David Seabourne, Erlestoke SN10 5TZ
Picture research: Callie Kendall, Cambridge CB3 7HR
Artwork: European Map Graphics Limited, Finchampstead RG11 4RF
and Malcolm Forbes, Cambridge CB1 2PD
Imagesetting by Hilo Offset, Colchester CO4 4PQ

A catalogue record for this book is available from the British Library

Library of Congress Cataloguing in Publication data

The Cambridge illustred history of ancient Greece / edited by Paul Cartledge.
p.   cm. — (Cambridge illustrated histories)
Included bibliographical references and index.
ISBN 0-521-48196-1 (hb)
1. Greece—Civilization.
I. Cartledge, Paul.   II. Series: Cambridge illustrated history.
DF77.C32   1998
938—dc21   96-51545
CIP

Half-title: The Sun god, Helios
(see also p. 330).

ISBN-13 978-0521-48196-0 hardback

Title Page: 'Phidias and the
Frieze of the Parthenon' (1869)
by Lawrence Alma-Tadema
(see also p. 278-9).

ISBN-13 978-0-521-52100-0 paperback

Contents

Mt Pangaeum

Amphipolis

Thasos   Aegospotami
                Alopece   Lampsacus
Aegae   Samothrace
Pella
        Stagira
Verghina Methone
        Olynthus   DARDANELLES
                          (HELLESPONT)   Troy (Hissarlik)

Mt Olympus
        Dium

                          Lesbos

Mt Pelion   Mytilene
Pherae   Elea
                                          Cyme

AEGEAN

Corcyra   SEA
(Corfu)   Dodona   Clazomenae
                                              Chios   Colophon
        GULF OF   Notium
        AMBRACIA Mt   Thermopylae   R. Maeander
                  Parnassus   Opus   Lefkandi   Ephesus
        Orchomenus   Chalcis   Samos   Priene
Thermum Chaeronea Mt   Aulis   Eretria   Mt Pentelicum (Pendele) Miletus   Heraclea
        Delphi Cithaeron Thebes   Didyma
Naupactus   Leuctra Marathon
Ithaca   Plataea   Athens   Carystus
                Eleusis Sphettus
        Sicyon Megara Piraeus Brauron   Mykonos
        Corinth Isthmia Myrrhinous   Halicarnassus
Mycenae Nemea Aegina Ceos Laurium   Delos
Olympia Mantinea Argos Epidaurus Anavyssus   Paros   Cos   Cnidus
        Tegea Tiryns Halieis   Naxos
Bassae   Argive Mt Hymettus
Mt Lycaeum Heraeum
        Megalopolis   Siphnos
Mt Ithome Sparta
Messene
Pylos
Methone   Thera

        Chania   Drerus
              Cnossus

                                    ETRURIA
                                       Caere   ILLYRIA
                                                  LATIUM   Taras
                                                  (Tarentum)
                                       Pithecousae
                                       (Ischia)   Paestum   Heraclea
                                       BAY OF   Elea
                                       NAPLES   Thurii
                                                  Croto

MEDITER
                                          Segesta
                                          Acragas   Gela   SICILY
                                          Camarina   Syracuse
                            Carthage   R

0   300 km
0   200 miles

Acknowledgements

The Editor wishes to thank most warmly, on his own behalf and on behalf of all his contributors, professors Pat Easterling (University of Cambridge) and Mike Jameson (Stanford University), who have selflessly read through the entire manuscript and acted as the wisest of academic advisers. Also the tireless and keen-eyed picture researcher, Callie Kendall, and above all others the series editor, Pauline Graham, a versatile modern Penelope.

Acknowledgements for paperback reprint

The volume Editor wishes to offer thanks to all those readers, including reviewers, who kindly pointed out errors or shortcomings of one sort or another in the original hardback edition, especially Mark Greenstock and Alan Griffiths. As far as possible, these have been corrected in this paperback reprint. On behalf of the contributors, the Editor also wishes to thank Kevin Taylor, series editor in succession to Pauline Graham, for seeing the reprint through to publication so efficiently.

(*Opposite top*) **The oldest of the three 'classic' tragedians, Aeschylus died aged around seventy at Gela in Sicily in 456. His epitaph concentrated exclusively on his feats as a patriotic Athenian soldier fighting the Persians, specifically mentioning the 'grove of Marathon'. But to posterity he is known for his tragic dramas, above all the** *Oresteia* **trilogy of 458.**

(*Opposite bottom*) **Born in Athens around 445, Aristophanes wrote over forty comedies, performed between 427 and the mid-380s, of which eleven survive today. Like Aeschylus' tragedies, they were first staged at the two main Athenian religious play-festivals in honour of Dionysus.**

The Glory that was Greece?

Whatever, in fact, is modern in our life we owe to the Greeks. Whatever is an anachronism is due to medievalism.
                                                                    Oscar Wilde

Suppose you could book passage on a time-machine and have yourself transported back to ancient Greece during the fifth century BCE (499–400). There, in the Agora (the civic centre) of Athens you might have encountered any one of the following people: Aeschylus, Alcibiades, Anaxagoras, Aristophanes, Aspasia, Callias, Cleon, Cleophon, Cratinus, Cresilas, Ephialtes, Eupolis, Euripides, Gorgias, Herodotus, Hippodamus, Ictinus, Isocrates, Miltiades, Parrhasius, Pericles, Phidias, Plato, Polygnotus, Protagoras, Socrates, Sophocles, Thucydides, Xenophon, and Zeuxis. They were not all native Athenians, but all of them were somehow stimulated by and contributed to the enormous energy released in this small hothouse of culture and politics.

Not all of these figures are household names today. But what is really striking is how many of them still *are*, despite constant attempts to downgrade – and downsize – the study of the ancient Greek and Roman Classics as a going educational concern.

Between them they helped to lay the political, artistic, cultural, educational, philosophical and scientific groundwork on which so much of subsequent Western civilization and culture has since been based. Small wonder that Plato, himself an Athenian born in the late fifth century, styled the glorious Athens of his youth as the 'City Hall of Sophia' (*sophia* being both theoretical and practical wisdom). Small wonder too that the Athenians themselves liked to hear praise of their 'violet-crowned' Athens in the works of praise-singers, such as Pindar of Thebes, and tragic poets, such as Euripides. Small wonder, even, that in the nineteenth century and the early part of the twentieth, classically educated Europeans and Americans should have found it natural to hymn – in the famous phrase of Edgar Allan Poe's *Ode to Helen* – the 'glory that was Greece'.

'WE ARE ALL GREEKS...'

But is Shelley's claim true? Are we, all of us, really? This illustrated history aims to capture the multifariousness and greatness of ancient Greece, but also to set that undoubted glory firmly in its proper historical perspective, in its widest context, even at the cost of tarnishing the halo a little. In some cases – the treatment of women, or of slaves, above all – tarnishing it more than a little. Here, surely, we can fairly claim to have made some significant advances on the achievement of our Greek predecessors?

We will also seek to do justice to the unspectacular, relatively immobile history of the countryside in which a multitude of anonymous peasants and slaves laboured to make possible the brilliant urban civilization with which the ancient Greeks are now primarily identified. George Orwell once likened the coal miners of Britain to a sort of grimy caryatid on which was supported everything that was *not* filthy and dirty in British life. In this vein we hope to view the Greek achievement, as far as possible, from the bottom up; from the perspective of those unsung heroes and heroines who made the famous deeds and words possible.

THE GREEK ALPHABET

By the fifth century BCE Greek civilization and culture were long established. Thanks to the brilliant amateur detective work of the architect Michael Ventris, allied to the patient philological scholarship of, among others, John Chadwick (see Chapter 1), we now know that the unromantically named Linear B syllabary encoded an early form of the Greek language (see Chapter 3). Through it 'Greek' civilization and culture can be traced back at least to the latter half of the second millennium BCE. Linear B archival tablets of clay, recording the incomings and out-goings of centralized palace economies, have been discovered at Pylos, Tiryns and Mycenae in the Peloponnese; at Thebes in central Greece; and at Chania and Cnos-sus in Crete. Other sites have yielded oil-jars marked with Linear B symbols.

Thanks also to the remarkable efforts of archaeologists from many countries, not least modern Greece itself, we now know a great deal about the earliest Greek civilization of the late Bronze Age or 'Mycenaean' era (roughly 1600–1100). Enough, for example, to be able to state confidently that it was this civilization which provided the background and original inspiration of the tales of heroic derring-do preserved in the earliest works – and masterpieces – of European literature: Homer's *Iliad* and *Odyssey*.

However, archaeology has also taught us that between the world of the Mycenaean palace, in which the literary figures of Agamemnon and Achilles held sway, and the world of the historic Greek *polis* or city, in which the Homeric epics were created and received, there yawns a huge cultural as well as chronological gap. For instance, the script eventually used to write down the orally transmitted Homeric poems was not Linear B, a script so ill-adapted to transcribing Greek that the written symbols had to be supplemented by explanatory ideograms, or picture-symbols. Instead, an alphabet was used, the idea of which had been borrowed from the Semitic Phoeni-cians of modern Lebanon, though it was brilliantly adapted so as to be capable of fully representing all Greek sounds, including vowels. Whereas Linear B was a scribal script, invented and used solely for keeping records, the alphabet was poten-

Byron, Shelley and Wilde

Three of the greatest poets writing in English in the nineteenth century were also passionate helleno-philes – and in the case of Byron also a philhel-lene, who did not merely pay money or lip-service to the cause of Greek independence but died for it, at Missolonghi in 1826. His younger friend Shelley was a brilliant classicist, who perhaps over-identified modern Western culture with its ultimate Greek roots but enriched the Western cultural tradition by his reworkings of the Prometheus myth and his pioneering translation of Plato's *Symposium* – not excluding the controversial passages cele-brating male homosexual love. Wilde, who studied Classics at both Dublin and Oxford universities, never lost touch with the ancient Greek world that inspired his life as well as his writings. His best poetry and his one novel, *The Picture of Dorian Gray*, managed both to be utterly of their own late Victorian times and to remain visibly connected to their Greek sources.

(Left) **Wilde**
(Top right) **Byron**

tially open for use by almost everyone, male or female, high or low, rich or poor, free or slave. Whereas the Linear B scribes were palace functionaries, the alphabet could be used for the whole range of written expression, from works of literature such as Homer, through public laws and treaties, to personal correspondence.

The Greek alphabet was devised in a number of local variants probably some time during the eighth century BCE (799–700). It was eventually transmitted to us via the Romans, who themselves received and adapted it from two Italian sources: the Etruscans of modern Tuscany, who for a period in the sixth century BCE may even have controlled the city of Rome; and the Greek cities of what came to be known as Great Greece – that is, the cities lying around the bay of Naples and the coast to the south around Italy's 'foot'. Our word for the Greeks is in fact a version of the Romans' originally rather derogatory term *Graeci*; the Greeks as far as we know have always called themselves Hellenes, although the term is not attested before the poetry of Archilochus of Paros (and later Thasos) in the seventh century BCE.

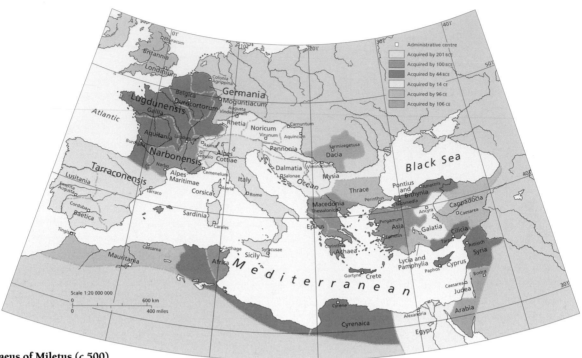

Hecataeus of Miletus (*c.*500) was credited with making the first ancient Greek map of 'the world' (see p. 300) – but it would have looked nothing like this map of the Roman Empire; modern map projections go back only to 'Mercator' (the sixteenth-century Flemish cartographer Gerhard Kremer). And the world known to Hecataeus and the classical Greeks did not extend far beyond the shores of the Mediterranean and Black Sea.

HELLAS

Before the establishment of the modern Greek state in the early nineteenth century, *Hellas* was a cultural rather than a strictly political entity; something like 'Christendom' in the Middle Ages, or 'the Arab world' today. It was defined by common descent (sometimes genuine, sometimes invented); by common language (all those who did not speak Greek were labelled 'barbarians' because their languages were an unintelligible babble of 'bar-bar' sounds); and by common customs – not least those of shared religious ritual.

By 500 BCE Hellas in this cultural, not political, sense stretched from the 'Pillars of Hercules' (Straits of Gibraltar) in the west to Colchis (in modern Georgia, at the far end of the Black Sea) in the east (see pp. vi–vii). Greeks, as Plato's Socrates put it, lived 'like frogs or ants around a pond' – that is, around the Mediterranean Sea and its north-easterly extension the Black Sea. But only limited areas of this huge world achieved – or had thrust upon them – any semblance of political unification, and then only for limited periods. Examples include much of the Aegean Greek area (embracing also the western coast of modern Turkey) during the second half of the fifth century, thanks to the anti-Persian empire dominated by Athens; or most of the Greek mainland and adjacent islands following their conquest in the fourth century by Philip and his son Alexander the Great of Macedon and their Hellenistic successors. But when their territory was in its turn conquered by the Romans, they followed their usual 'divide and rule' strategy and broke it into two separately administered provinces: Achaea and Macedonia. The Romans also absorbed the remainder of the Greek-speaking world, which formed the eastern half of their massive world empire and gave rise eventually to the separate Byzantine empire based on Constantinople – though the Byzantines called themselves Romans. Formerly Byzantium, founded originally from mainland Greek Megara in the seventh century BCE, Constantinople was renamed after its second founder Constantine the Great (d. 337). Conquest by the Ottoman Turks in 1453 led to a further change of name, but even the Turkish Istanbul stubbornly contains a Greek linguistic trace (-bul from polis).

THE GREEK LEGACY

Political

Some modern students of ancient Greece, especially since the rise of international bodies such as the League of Nations and United Nations, have been dismayed by the classical Greeks' inability to forge lasting inter-city bonds of unity on the basis of their common culture, and have pointed out that this political disunity made their conquest and subjugation from outside that much easier. Alternatively, and on the contrary, it might be more plausibly argued that it was precisely the cities' jealous independence of each other that made possible their extraordinarily fertile experiments in citizen self-government; most notably of course their invention of democracy.

It has been estimated that there were well over 1000 separate and radically self-differentiated Greek communities scattered across the Greek world. In the time of Aristotle, during the fourth century, the vast majority of these communities enjoyed some form of democratic or oligarchic government – that is, versions of self-rule in which power was vested primarily in the hands of either the poor majority (*demos*) or the rich minority of the adult, male citizens. Following Aristotle's death in 322, however, democracy virtually disappeared, or rather was suppressed, throughout the ancient world. It reappeared – in very different guise – only during the sixteenth century. Nevertheless, when the idea of popular self-government was once again mooted as a serious, if at first revolutionary, political system, it was given the Greek-derived word *democracy*.

(*Previous page*) **A native of Stagira in northern Greece, with strong connections to the Macedonian royal court, Aristotle spent most of his adult life as a resident alien in Athens. In the mid-330s, in imitation and rivalry of his master Plato, he founded his own philosophical school in a grove sacred to Apollo Lyceius, whence its name, the Lyceum. In early 1997 the Greek Archaeological Service triumphantly proclaimed the discovery and excavation of the school's remains. Aristotle and his pupils between them covered and codified practically all the then recognized branches of learning. Tradition had it that Aristotle's personal library formed the basis of the famous Library founded at Alexandria in the third century by the ruling Ptolemy dynasty of Egypt.**

Linguistic

The word 'democracy' is just one example of our linguistic heritage from the ancient Greeks. No less than a third or so of English vocabulary, it is estimated, has Greek etymological roots. According to the Greek Alexandra Fiada's consciously self-deprecatory *Xenophobe's Guide to the Greeks*, without them nothing and no one could be European, mysterious, ethereal, patriotic, phlegmatic, tragic, diplomatic, automatic, nostalgic, magnetic, tropical, aromatic, hysterical, ironic, or even anonymous ... not to mention democratic (or oligarchic or tyrannical). There would be no strategy, tactics, politicians, ethics, aristocrats, nymphomaniacs, anarchists, technocrats, schizophrenics, heroes, history, schools, organizations, symbols, pirates, climates, paper, thermos, or diets. The arts would have to do without poets, dramatists, scenes, theatres, comedy, cinema, acrobats, melodies, guitars, chords, symphonies, orchestras, programmes, critics, and photographs. Science and technology would lack ideas, architects, physicians, metal, discs, hydraulics, electrics, lamps, polyurethane, and atoms.

And that is deliberately to omit mention of the whole raft of words associated with Christianity, the dominant religious tradition of Europe and the West since the birth of Christ (Greek for 'the anointed one'). These include words such as Christmas, bible, prophets, angels, paradise (a Greek borrowing from old Persian), apostles, martyrs, hymns, cemeteries, idols, exorcists, heretics, atheists, blasphemers, demons, and dogmas. However, one legacy we do not owe to the pre-Christian Greeks, with whom this book is principally concerned, is their religion.

Chronographic

Which is the main reason why, rather than the more familiar BC/AD system of universal time-reckoning devised by the Greek Dionysius in the fifth century of our era, we have preferred to use the BCE (Before Common Era)/CE system. The Greece we are seeking to explore and understand here was – in Christian terms – resolutely polytheistic and pagan, so that a Christian notation seems exceptionally inappropriate. (Unless specifically designated otherwise, all dates should be assumed to be BCE.)

THE ERA OF 'ANCIENT GREECE'

The rise of Christianity in the first two to three centuries CE serves as the cut-off point for our representation of the ancient Greeks. As a starting point we have taken the first certainly attested use by the Mycenaeans of a language that is unquestionably Greek – ancestral, that is, to the historical dialects first detectable in the eighth century BCE.

Within that broad span of some 1500 years it is, however, necessary to narrow the focus somewhat if we are to do anything like justice to the Greeks' prodigious achievements in many spheres. The survival pattern of the contemporary evidence makes it almost inevitable that we should focus on the 'classical' era of the fifth and fourth centuries BCE (*c*.500–300). This was the period of the fifth-century culture-heroes listed at the beginning, and of their fourth-century successors such as Aristotle, Eudoxus and Alexander the Great. It was their literature that the scholars working in the Museum and Library at Alexandria in the last three centuries BCE decided was worthy to be preserved, copied and transmitted to future generations through schooling and higher education. It was their literature on which the Greek-speaking rhetoricians and writers living under the Roman empire in the first and second centuries CE founded the intellectual movement that came to be known as the Second Sophistic (see Glossary). Even writers of the calibre of Plutarch (c.CE 46–120) felt that they stood in the shadow of their great predecessors, but it was their political freedom and its creatively inspiriting effects that they envied above all.

ATHENS AND BEYOND

The cultural epicentre of fifth- and fourth-century high classicism was of course Athens. It was to Athens that many of the most gifted Greeks born and raised elsewhere in the Greek world were drawn as if by magnetic attraction. They included Herodotus from Halicarnassus in Asia Minor; Aristotle from Stagira in northern Greece; Diogenes the Cynic from Sinope on the Black Sea; Zeno (possibly of mixed Greek and Phoenician parentage) from Cypriot Citium, and Aspasia from east Greek Miletus – to name but five.

Nevertheless, Athens was by no means the whole of Greece, and in this book we hope both to set Athenian achievement within its wider Greek matrix, and to bring out the peculiarities and distinctions of the many, heterogeneous, far-flung reaches of Hellenism. Examples of this heterogeneity include the Athenian democratic political and cultural model; the aristocratic Pythagorean philosophical-political experiments of southern Italy; the rather un-Hellenic predilection for tyranny displayed by the Greeks of Sicily; the extremely un- or even anti-Athenian cultural and political forms of Sparta, and the

Like Aristotle, Diogenes was originally from the northern Greek diaspora, coming from Sinope on the southern shore of the Black Sea. But he attained fame, or rather notoriety, chiefly in Athens, where his followers founded the consciously antinomian Cynic school of thought and behaviour. Diogenes' own words and actions were reportedly as unorthodox as they could possibly be – he is said to have masturbated in public, and to have ordered Alexander the Great to move away from the storage jar that served as his bed and bedroom as he was blocking Diogenes' light.

musical, military and political inventiveness of Thebes (home city of Pindar and Epaminondas) significantly different from both Sparta and Athens. Then there are the artistic and religious peculiarities of Crete; the brilliant local lyrical poetry of the Lesbians Alcaeus and Sappho; and the rival medical centres of Cos and Cnidus. These are also essential parts of ancient Greece and not to be lost in the long shadow cast by Athens.

High culture, like almost all aspects of public life in ancient Greece, was typically a masculine preserve, but Sappho of Lesbos (shown here in a modern sculpture) who flourished around 600 was one of the greatest of all exceptions to that rule. Her personal poetry, composed in local dialect and metre, achieved an astonishingly wide currency over many centuries and remains to this day an object of intense critical study and equally intense enthusiasm. Plato reckoned her to be the tenth Muse – one of his less controversial judgements. Even the Spartans, at any rate in the high Roman imperial era, came to appreciate her charms.

NON-STANDARD APPROACHES

Without neglecting the more traditional (since Homer!) 'from the top down' approach, in this book we have also sought to represent the anti-Olympian, 'worm's-eye' view from the bottom up: the view of the free poor, foreigners, women, or slaves – or what view or views might plausibly be attributed to them. For in taking this approach we hope to restore a voice to the voiceless or silenced and to place Greek democracy, theatre, philosophy, medicine, architecture, sculpture and so on in a fresh and truer historical perspective. Particular attention is paid throughout to the Greek legacy: that is, not so much what the Greeks had potentially to bequeath to subsequent civilizations, but rather what those civilizations chose to inherit from them and what they – including us – have made of their inheritance.

It is hard and not entirely desirable to escape entirely from the 'kings-and-battles' approach to ancient Greece. Greek cities were in many cases forged on the anvil of war, and the development of Greek civilization and culture was crucially affected, both positively and adversely, by particular wars, most notably the Persian (490, 480–79) and Peloponnesian (431–404). Nevertheless, although war-making – together with such political developments as the introduction of democracy at Athens in 508/7 – can help to provide a narrative story line, in this book the social implications and consequences of Greek warfare by land and sea are given as much emphasis as the purely technical details of strategy and tactics. For instance, it was war that served to delimit a peculiarly masculine space of endeavour and achievement and so to fix an essential element in Greek notions of gender and sexuality.

Warfare, too, was the inspiration of much of the greatest Greek literature, from Homer to Thucydides and beyond. It is also the subject of much Greek visual art. The sanctuary of Delphi, for instance, littered with artworks and monuments to piety, was also to a significant extent a gigantic war memorial, rather dismally – to our way of thinking – commemorating not only victories of Greeks over non-Greeks but also the outcomes of what Herodotus feelingly called 'discord within the [Greek] tribe'.

Rather than treating literature, visual art and philosophy simply as disembodied paradigms of aesthetic and intellectual excellence, this volume also seeks to set them in their social and political contexts of performance and reception. Likewise, democracy will be treated not so much as a formal system of constitutional prescriptions but rather as the living embodiment of the rule of the (poorer) majority of Greek citizens.

Most Greeks were poor and had to work for a living full time. Few were rich and members of a leisure class. But without some modicum of widely available and shared leisure there would have been no Greek civilization or culture for us to study or enjoy. That vital leisure time was importantly procured by the labour of the oppressed, above all by dependant peasants or foreign-born slaves working in fields or manufactories. Manufactories – not factories: this was a resolutely pre-industrial

Like Aristotle and Diogenes, Zeno was a non-Athenian who left behind him a band of followers constituting a philosophical school with its headquarters in Athens. But Zeno, who came from Cyprus, may have been of partly non-Greek descent, and he established his school in the very heart of Athens, the Agora. 'Stoics' took their name from the Stoa Poikile, or the Painted Stoa, constructed in the fifth century and decorated with patriotic murals depicting Athenian mythical and historical victories.

world of relatively low technological development. The environment in its physical sense will therefore be given priority treatment, with special attention being devoted to the dialectic of human–nature interaction.

'Dialectic' is an English word of impeccable Hellenic ancestry. So too is the etymologically related term 'dialogue', which it is hoped this book will serve to – and here I make a bow to our Latin linguistic heritage – provoke and promote.

A fictitious dialogue, one borrowed from the opening book of Herodotus' *History*, illustrates many of the themes of this book. At a dramatic date set somewhere in the first half of the sixth century BCE, Solon of Athens, traditionally reckoned among the wisest of Greeks, went on his travels, and while in Asia Minor he encountered the proverbially wealthy oriental ruler, King Croesus of Lydia. On being asked by Croesus who he thought was the happiest and most blessed of all humankind, Solon gave a long, complex and, to Croesus, wholly unexpected and unwelcome reply that included the following thought:

> Of course, it is impossible for one who is human to have all the good things together, just as there is no one country that is sufficient of itself to provide all good things for itself. But whoso possesses most of them, continuously, and then ends his life gracefully, he, my lord, may justly win the name you seek – at least in my judgement. But one must always look to the end of everything. For to many the god has shown a glimpse of blessedness only to extirpate them in the end.

That rather sobering message spoke to a strain of pessimism in Greek thinking which stressed the ephemerality of humankind's nature and achievements, but it is one on which we too perhaps might profitably ponder.

'Croesus and Solon' (*c.*1610) by Hendrick van Steenwyck the Younger (1580–*c.*1650). Solon is the first Greek political figure to be known to us in any depth, partly because some of his own political poetry survives. Appointed public arbitrator to resolve an economic and political crisis in his native Athens, he produced a set of reforms whose authority was still appealed to centuries later. Outside Athens he achieved the status of one of the Seven Sages of ancient Greece, first listed as such in Plato's dialogue *Protagoras*.

The World of Greece

PART I

History and Tradition

HISTORY?

History is yet another of those English words which have a Greek etymology. Its original root meaning was 'enquiry', a sense preserved in, for example, 'natural history'. Thereafter it came to mean a narrative story about the past, and it was in that sense that Cicero famously dubbed Herodotus 'the father of history'. But Herodotus' immediate successor and rival Thucydides (with whom, ironically, he is joined for ever in the Naples bust, or herm) avoided the word entirely and referred to his own activity as an 'account', as if he were drawing up an entirely objective, almost documentary record.

The ancient manuscripts of Herodotus' *Histories* call him alternatively 'Herodotus of Halicarnassus' or 'Herodotus of Thurii'. Halicarnassus, modern Bodrum in western Turkey, is where he was born, probably in the 480s, and Thurii in South Italy is where, following his exile from his native city, he took up citizenship some time after the foundation of the city in the mid-440s. Between Halicarnassus and Thurii, in more than one sense, was Athens, where Herodotus found both intellectual inspiration and a ready audience for a work that he delivered orally before having it reduced to written form probably in the 420s. All such 'portraits' are more or less free inventions. *(Right and opposite)* The Naples bust, or double-herm, in which Herodotus and Thucydides were joined back to back, from near Tivoli, now in the Naples Museum.

Throughout antiquity the word 'history' retained the controversial tinge of its intellectually radical origins. By using the term in his opening sentence, Herodotus meant to announce that he was heir to a tradition of non-mythical, non-religious, 'scientific' enquiry into how things really were – a tradition that had begun with Thales of Miletus in the sixth century. Herodotus' intention was not merely to retail a traditional account of the Greek past, but rather to examine the evidential basis for any account of the past. In this way he sought to explain why 'the Greeks and the barbarians [non-Greeks of the Persian empire] came to fight one another'.

Thucydides opted for a significantly different subject: a war among Greeks rather than one between Greeks and non-Greeks. However, he continued and, indeed, reinforced Herodotus' critical attitude to evidence. He explicitly stressed the difficulty of getting the facts of the past right, both because of the fallibility of human memory and because of the prejudice of informants who had a stake in one version

Thucydides too, like Herodotus, may have come from mixed Greek and non-Greek stock. His father's name, Olorus, is Thracian and royal, and Thucydides, as he tells us himself, retained hereditary mining rights in the silver-rich area of Mount Pangaeum in Chalcidice. Like Herodotus again, Thucydides spent a crucial time of his adult life as a political exile. But whereas Herodotus was exiled for attempting to overthrow a pro-Persian tyrant, Thucydides was given his marching orders in 424 for a vital military failure when acting as general (really, admiral) in the north Aegean area.

of past events rather than another. He too was primarily interested in causation, aiming to explain both why the Athenians and the Spartans and their allies had come to fight each other and why, after a uniquely long and savage conflict, lasting on and off for an entire human generation, the Spartan side had eventually won. Unfortunately, his work as preserved breaks off in mid-sentence, well short of its chronological goal, whereas that of Herodotus happily survives complete.

Our modern notion of history as a critical, disinterested enquiry into the significant facts of the past and a rational, objective explanation of them is thus a legacy of Herodotus and Thucydides, mediated by the Renaissance (for the Florentine Guicciardini, Thucydides was the model historian) and European Enlightenment (Herodotus was an especial favourite of Gibbon; see p. 11). But where the dominant strain of modern historiography parts company from its ancient Greek parent is in the nature of its preferred sources of evidence.

In the nineteenth century, when the study of History became a specialist subject at university – equipped with the necessary apparatus of departments, institutes, learned journals and so forth – it projected itself as a 'scientific' discipline, every bit as intellectually respectable in its arts or humanities framework as the 'hard' science disciplines of physics, biology and chemistry. The basis of this claim lay in History's professed method of treating evidence: the ideal sources of historical research and writing were deemed to be contemporary, documentary records of proven accuracy and authenticity, from which the truth of the past could be more or less straightforwardly read off. It was thought that perhaps the evidence available to historians might not enable them to formulate laws of human behaviour with the same degree of objective certainty as scientists such as Newton or Einstein formulated the laws of nature, but the best efforts of the most scrupulous historians (checking and rechecking the documentary facts and interpreting them in accordance with the canons of objectivity and rationality) should at least produce a sufficiently true and accurate account of the past to satisfy the discipline's claim to scientific method and status.

Of course, things are not so simple. History, written history as opposed to what actually happened in the past, is also always a story, and no two story-tellers will ever tell exactly the same tale, or tell it in exactly the same way. Written history is always more or less a branch of rhetoric; a species of persuasive literature. It is also inevitably selective. No historian has ever been able to reproduce in words the whole of any past human event, process or institution. Not only would that be physically impossible, it would also be meaningless; as meaningless as describing every object in a room without specifying that room's purpose or function within the wider context of the building as a whole.

History, in short, can never be scientific in an equivalent sense to that in which physicists can state that by identifying the sixth quark they have accounted descriptively for the entire known material composition of our universe. For obvious reasons, history cannot be scientific in the sense of discovering the laws of motion of past human societies; or wholly explaining any singular event or set of human events affecting any one society in the past. That is the case no matter how comprehensively historians assemble, nor how scrupulously they interpret, the available data.

As for Herodotus and Thucydides (and indeed all their successors in the writing of history before the Christian historians of the fourth century), their knowledge and understanding of the past were inevitably even more precarious and subjective because their primary sources were not, by and large, official or unofficial written documents, but contemporary oral testimonies. The Greeks did indeed invent an alphabetic script (see p. x), and applied it to the transcription of laws and other public documents. The earliest such document known to us is a law from Dreros on Crete, datable to the second half of the seventh century. However, Greek culture in an age before the invention of movable type and the mass distribution of printed texts was fundamentally oral – their word for to read, for instance, meant to 'recognize again', that is to recognize in script words that one had first of all heard. One of their words for 'reader' was, literally, 'hearer' – most Greeks heard rather than read their literature or other written texts. In general, their point of closest contact with written words would be through hearing them read aloud. In this pre-print culture, oral testimony remained the principal way in which would-be enquirers into the facts and significance of the past obtained their raw materials.

Panyassis, the last in the tradition of epic poets in the Homeric style, was a relative, possibly an uncle, of Herodotus. His name-ending, -assis, is non-Greek and attests some close connection, possibly by marriage, with the Carians living in or near his native city of Halicarnassus.

HERODOTUS

The text of Herodotus' *Histories* has, of course, come down to us only because it was written down by or for the author, disseminated at his instance, and then considered worthy of being copied by others; the copies thereafter survived somehow in royal, imperial, papal or monastic libraries until the West's discovery of printing in the fifteenth century. But as both its literary form and internal evidence show, the *Histories* was conceived and received as an oral discourse. Structurally it consists of *logoi* or 'tales' of varying length and complexity, the construction and language of which were designed to be instantly understood by an audience far better attuned than we to such a social rather than individual experience of story-telling. As such, the *Histories* is Homeric in a formal sense, as well as being superficially similar in subject-matter: it describes a great war between Greeks and non-Greeks. It is probably not irrelevant that a relative of Herodotus, Panyassis, was a noted composer of epic poetry, possibly the last in the line of original oral composers stemming from Homer himself (if indeed there was a single real Homer).

Several Greek cities laid claim to being the birthplace of Homer; all of them gave his poetry a hearth and home, since he was for all Greeks simply 'the poet'. When 'conquered Greece took her fierce conqueror captive' (in Horace's phrase), Homer moved house easily from Greece to Rome, and this famous relief, known as 'The Apotheosis of Homer', was found on the Appian Way. It was made by a Greek sculptor, Archelaus of Priene, in c.200 BCE. On the bottom row Homer is depicted seated, with representations of the *Iliad* and the *Odyssey* as his children kneeling on either side. Behind him are *Chronos* ('Time'), a winged male figure whose head recalls that of Ptolemy IV of Egypt (221–203), and *Oecumene* (the inhabited world), who crowns the poet with a wreath symbolizing immortality; in front of him are *Muthos* ('Myth'), a youth, and *Historia* ('History'), a female figure.

Herodotus drew also on a mass of oral traditions other than epic poetry, mainly prose traditions – though written prose was a relatively late Greek achievement, not attested before the second half of the sixth century. For example, he knew versions of the moralizing fables later associated with the supposed slave Aesop, whom Herodotus indeed mentions as if he were a historical character no less authentic than, say, Xerxes, Great King of Persia.

Aesop

The collection of tales known as *Aesop's Fables* is the result of editorial work during the Roman period of ancient Greek history. No doubt some are traditional, possibly even ancient, but none can certainly be attributed to Aesop – if indeed there ever was such a real person – and the animal fable has much earlier roots in the Near East. The earliest known version of Aesop's life story, preserved by Herodotus, credits him with being a non-Greek slave from Thrace (roughly Bulgaria today) who came into the possession of Iadmon, a Greek from the island of Samos, in roughly the early sixth century. Credulity is stretched a little too hard though when we are told by Herodotus that Iadmon also owned the famous prostitute Rhodopis (Tennyson's Rhodope) who plied her trade at the international Egyptian port of Naucratis until she was bought into freedom by a love-smitten client called Charaxus – who just happened to be the brother of Sappho. Small world.

But even if there was no real slave Aesop who single-handedly invented or collated his fables, there may be a germ of truth in the tradition that associated them with slaves. The message of most is that the naturally or culturally weak need not always be exploited by the naturally or culturally strong. Using wit and cunning the weak can at least reduce their suffering to a tolerable level or even in favourable circumstances turn the tables on their oppressors. Such a message would have been welcome to the thousands of slaves in the Greek world, at any rate to the Greeks among them and those non-Greeks who could understand Greek well enough.

Consistent with the fables' ideological tendency to identify with the underdog is the representation of Aesop as a member of another severely disadvantaged social group, the disabled; here on this red-figure drinking goblet now in the Vatican Museums he is shown as a cripple with grossly enlarged head, engaged in animated conversation with one of his best known subjects, a fox.

The Aesopian fables are the best known but not by any means the only examples of popular as opposed to high literature that we have access to from ancient Greece. Folk-tales, folk traditions, folk wisdom, proverbs, and fables have come down to us in various forms, as for example the fable of the hawk and the nightingale – a warning to the powerful – in Hesiod's early (c.700) didactic poem *The Works and Days*. On the other hand, for such fables, and especially for a collection of them like Aesop's, to be preserved in literary form they had to achieve currency above as well as below stairs, and, in so far as they were not simply a literary, philosophical or pedagogical exercise, it was to the poor and humble free population to whom they are likely to have made the greatest appeal.

The human figure with the hypertrophied head depicted on the interior of this Attic red-figure drinking-cup of the fifth century must surely be meant to represent Aesop. Sitting opposite him, as if engaged in animated conversation, is one of Aesop's favourite characters, the fox, who features as the hero – or rather antihero – of fables like 'The Fox and the Raven'.

THUCYDIDES

Thucydides too took as his subject a great war – he thought a greater war even than Homer's – but his style alone is sufficient to mark the dramatic change that had come over Greek intellectual culture, most markedly at Athens, within the space of just a generation or so. For whereas Herodotus' style is Homeric, that of Thucydides is forensic and sophistic; a style characterized by the development of *rhetoric* both formally in the law-courts and Assembly, and informally in philosophical disputations and debates. It is a style that begs to be read and re-read rather than simply heard. Whereas Herodotus had modestly and not quite accurately claimed that his task was merely 'to say the things which are said', to retail the current stories and traditions, Thucydides loftily proclaimed that his work was not a prize competition designed for the immediate applause of an audience, but rather a possession for all time, an eternal object to be appreciated fully only outside the context of a live recitation.

All the same, Thucydides, no less than Herodotus, was dependent essentially on oral testimony for his primary sources of evidence. Indeed, it was precisely because he was so dependent that he chose to restrict himself severely to contemporary history – a history of only those times which he had himself been of an age to remember and understand, or of which he could learn from similar, first-hand (and more or less trustworthy) witnesses. Nor was that his only self-imposed restriction. Whereas Herodotus had ranged freely across both space and time, covering non-Greek as well as Greek affairs, and showing a special interest in social and religious customs, Thucydides was exclusively a historian of political power, chiefly as expressed in clashes between Greek states in war. But if his vision was comparatively narrow, it was also correspondingly deep. His insights into the horrible condition of civil war, or relations between a great power and a small community, have rarely been matched since.

XENOPHON

The best known of Thucydides' immediate successors and continuators is another Athenian who spent large amounts of his adult life in exile: Xenophon. He too concentrated in his historical work on contemporary events, though he appraised his sources with far less critical rigour than either Thucydides or Herodotus, and he placed such research as he did conduct in the service of a personalized, moralizing, and partisan (anti-democratic, pro-Spartan) version of his life and times. With his misnamed *Hellenica* ('Greek History', but in fact it deals largely with those Peloponnesian affairs of which Xenophon was personally cognizant), Xenophon was but one of four historians who attempted to pick up the stylus where Thucydides had perforce set it down. If his work survives, that is not because of its historical acumen but chiefly because later literary critics – anticipating generations of modern school teachers – rightly admired Xenophon's limpid Attic (Athenian) prose.

It is unfortunate from one point of view that his critical success led to the non-survival of his rivals. One of them at least was a historian of a quality comparable to that of Thucydides. Luckily, the dry sands of Egypt have preserved on papyrus some substantial fragments of his impressive work. But his identity is not certain, and he is thus known to science as 'The Oxyrhynchus Historian', after the Fayum findspot of the fragmentary remains.

Xenophon, on the other hand, did not by any means restrict himself to writing chronological narrative history. He also wrote a historical travelogue, several technical handbooks, and philosophical memoirs of his teacher Socrates. Perhaps most interesting of all, he wrote a sort of historical novel, or at any rate a heavily fictionalized history, centring on the exploits of the founder of the Persian empire, Cyrus II the Great (reigned 559–530). Actually, as Xenophon was composing *The Education of Cyrus* in the mid-fourth century, the real Persian empire was entering its final decline, soon to be opposed and then superseded by the Macedonian empire of Philip II and his son Alexander.

Xenophon's biographical interest in the founder of an empire was echoed by another Thucydidean continuator and pro-Spartan political exile, Theopompus of Chios. He too wrote a *Hellenica*, which covered the years from 411 to 394. But far more original was his *Philippic Histories*, the first work of (contemporary) general history to be written around the career of a single individual, Philip of Macedon (reigned 359–336).

THEOPOMPUS OF CHIOS

By repute, Theopompus was a former pupil of the rhetorical school established at Athens in the 390s by Isocrates, a one-time orator and, subsequently, speech-writer and political pamphleteer. The establishment of his school, Athens' first institute for advanced study, anticipated Plato's Academy and Aristotle's Lyceum, and is further evidence of the professionalization and classification of Greek learning and knowledge inaugurated by the Sophists – pedagogic rivals, against whom Isocrates railed in a typically Greek competitive fashion. It is unclear what direct impact, if any, Isocrates' theories and his many pupils had on the practical conduct of public affairs. Their impact on the world of learning is far more certain, if impossible to quantify precisely. At any rate, another alleged pupil of Isocrates was the first to

(Opposite) Xenophon (born at Athens in the early 420s) grew to manhood during the increasingly embittered Peloponnesian War. His wealthy background and intellectual bent brought him into the orbit of Socrates, but Socratic circles were not conspicuously democratic in outlook, and as a member of Athens' cavalry Xenophon in 404–3 found himself engaged in doing the dirty work of the pro-Spartan oligarchic junta of the Thirty Tyrants led by Plato's relative Critias. Worse, mercenary service in Asia Minor led to his fighting on Sparta's side against Athens, for which he was exiled from the 390s until at least the 360s. During his exile he began the series of compositions – philosophical, technical, didactic, autobiographical – for which he is chiefly remembered.

write a 'universal' history; that is a history of the Greeks since soon after the Trojan War. Its author, Ephorus of Cyme, does not, for the most part, survive in his own right, but in quotations or paraphrases to be found in other extant authors – most notably the Sicilian Greek Diodorus, composer or rather compiler of a *Library of History* in the first century BCE. This curious title is probably a nod to that intellectual power-house of the Hellenistic age, the Library established at Alexandria in the early third century by Ptolemy I.

POLYBIUS

For all its many defects, Ephorus' history of Greece earns its place in any account of the story of Greek history-writing because of its influence on Polybius, the true successor of Thucydides among surviving historians. He wrote what he called 'pragmatic' or transactional history, that is an essentially political history of the most compelling events and processes of his own and the immediately preceding era. Born at Megalopolis (the 'Great City') in Peloponnesian Arcadia in about 200 BCE, Polybius could not fail to register the impact of the conquest and political transformation of his somewhat parochial Greek world by Rome. Indeed, that was a process in which he himself played no small part, and he wrote it up from a privileged, if also prejudiced, standpoint. Because Rome had in his view created one political universe, by means of the rapidly expanding empire which he had personally experienced, both on the periphery and at its core, he saw himself as a universal historian, achieving the truly universal Greek history to which his acknowledged predecessor Ephorus could merely aspire.

Polybius was the last of the great Greek historians, though history continued to be written in the Attic-derived version of the ancient Greek language right through to the sixth-century chronicle of the Palestinian Procopius. The latter is better known for his so-called *Secret History*, an often scandalous tale of the doings of the actress-turned-empress Theodora, which – like Herodotus' *Histories* – was much to Edward Gibbon's taste. But his general history of his times has a keen interest for the historian of Greek literary tradition. It includes for example an account of the plague of Constantinople in CE 540 that was modelled on Thucydides' famous description of the great plague of Athens – which in turn drew on Homeric precedent: the *Iliad* opens with a god-sent plague afflicting the Greek camp, owing to an act of gross impiety.

Historical accounts written in Greek continued as late as the histories of the seventh-century Egyptian Greek Theophylact Simocatta. But after Polybius, the historians judged most worthy of preservation by critics bilingual in both Greek and Latin were those who wrote in the latter not the former; above all Sallust, Livy and Tacitus. It was indicative of the evolving linguistic and cultural shift that when Ammianus, a native Greek speaker from Syrian Antioch, chose to continue the *Histories* of Tacitus he did so in Latin rather than Greek.

EDWARD GIBBON

No less eloquent of cultural change in its way is the linguistic expertise (or lack of it) of the writer who may justly be acclaimed the first modern historian of the ancient world. Edward Gibbon's education, both secondary and tertiary, was notoriously deficient. Nevertheless, he was typical of the cultivated literati of the eighteenth century in having very little ancient Greek – for all his expressed love of its musicality and rational euphony. Nor did he have a sufficient knowledge of any of the other ancient languages on which a historian today would be required to base an adequate account of the history of Byzantium between the fourth and the fifteenth centuries, leading up to its terminal clash with Islam. Gibbon was, however, a most accomplished Latinist – fortunately, since Latin was the language of a significant number of his more recent 'authorities' as well as his primary sources. He was also, in a sense, the last of the Renaissance humanists, as well as a child of his own Enlightenment times.

As far as the modern vernacular languages were concerned, he was almost a native speaker and reader of French. This gave him direct access to the pioneering sociological approaches to history of Montesquieu and Voltaire, who sought to explain the course of human history in terms of climatic, political, social and other broadly environmental factors rather than by individual traits of character or divine pre-ordination. But the German language remained foreign to him, and hence so also did the very latest in historical method, the development of *Quellenforschung* or source-enquiry and *Quellenkritik*, source-criticism.

Although Gibbon yielded to none in his critical unmasking of lies, prejudice or cant, he failed to see that a piece of evidence weakened in force and authority as it passed through successive hands and grew more remote from the fountainhead (the 'source' in the French sense of spring). Against that deficiency, however, may be set his early appreciation of the value of what are sometimes called the auxiliary disciplines of epigraphy and archaeology.

Actually, epigraphy – the study of public and private, formal and informal inscriptions – can not only supplement but also correct literary accounts that, however primary they may seem to us, were nevertheless secondary and derivative in their own day. For instance, the primary evidence of the lists inscribed on marble pillars and set up on the Athenian Acropolis to record the amounts of tribute paid by Athens' subordinate allies serves significantly to modify Thucydides' account of the Athenian fifth-century empire.

Our word, *museum*, comes ultimately from the shrine of the Muses (*Mouseion*) at Alexandria which formed the centre of an institute for advanced literary studies founded by the first Ptolemy. A separate, but associated, institution was Alexandria's famous Library, also founded and patronized by Ptolemy I (*opposite*). Leading scholars and writers from various parts of the Hellenistic Greek world were attracted to this intellectual mecca, men such as the polymath Eratosthenes of Cyrene in north Africa (nicknamed 'Beta', because for all his encyclopaedic learning across many different fields he was rated no higher than number 2 in any one). Between them they established the canon of texts of which but a tiny sample has survived the vicissitudes of transmission to our own day.

Archaeology, moreover, arguably does not and should not be forced to tell the same sort of story as event-centred political history. This is especially true of the newer kinds of archaeology which involve intensive regional field-survey (see p. 21) rather than, or in addition to, conventional excavation of a necessarily more limited area. Survey can reveal a great deal of useful information, for example, on such fundamental economic issues as changing land-use and demographic patterns. In any case, a chiefly literary-based history containing some appreciation of epigraphy and archaeology, such as that of Gibbon, is likely to be superior to one without.

COMPARATIVE HISTORY

One of the most fruitful developments within history-writing during the twentieth century has been the development of comparative history. Here the general historian of classical Greece is in the enviable position of being compelled to consider well over a thousand separate, often very diverse communities located all round the Mediterranean and Black Sea and occupying different environmental and historical niches. Of course, there is the problem of uneven distribution of evidence in time and space to be accommodated. But the scope for comparing and contrasting, for instance, Athens and Sparta, and thereby bringing out the more sharply the characteristics peculiar to each, is almost limitless.

Then there is comparison between Greece and the world or worlds outside, most obviously in the first instance with the Bronze Age kingdoms of the Middle East, then with the city-states of Phoenicia and Etruria, and finally with both conquering and preserving Rome. Greeks had significant contact with all of these, peaceful or martial, and were the beneficiaries of economic or cultural exchange.

Of course, comparative history was nothing strange to Gibbon. But there is one historical method developed since his day that would surely have attracted him: the use of visual images as a way to understand the society that produced them. This has special application to the ancient Greeks, whose culture was very image-conscious, indeed almost image-ridden. For despite the relative simplicity of the Greek alphabet, most Greeks would probably not have been functionally literate. At any rate, with the possible exception of citizens of a developed democracy like Athens, they would not regularly have been called upon to read or write in order to function effectively as participating members of a citizen community. Images, by contrast, whether on painted pottery or on temple facades, in the home or the public square, would have been common currency, and modern scholars of ancient Greek culture and mentality have shown how profitably they too can be 'read'. This book also is filled with images, which are supposed to tell their own stories rather than merely provide background colour to tales told solely in words.

In short, if today like dwarves on the shoulders of giants we may see further than Gibbon into the ancient Greek past, this is probably thanks to our enlarged vision of what a study of history should properly incorporate.

Environment

CHAPTER 2

Susan E. Alcock

Among his many learned works, Aristotle composed a *Meteorology*, in which he wrote:

> In the time of the Trojan wars, the Argive land was marshy and could support only a small population, whereas the land of Mycenae was in good condition (and for this reason Mycenae was the superior). But now the opposite is the case ... the land of Mycenae has become ... dry and barren, while the Argive land...has now become fruitful. Now the same process that has taken place in this small district must be supposed to be going on over whole countries and on a large scale ...

Twenty-two centuries later, in the first volume of his *History of Greece*, Ernst Curtius took a more philosophical approach:

> Thus the special advantages of the land of Greece consist in the measure of its natural properties ... Earth and water, hill and plain, drought and damp, the snow storms of Thrace and the heat of a tropical sun – all the contrasts, all the forms of the life of nature, combine in the greatest variety of ways to awaken and move the mind of man. But as these contrasts all dissolve into a higher harmony, which embraces the entire coast and island-country of the Archipelago, so man was led to complete the measure of harmony between the contrasts which animate conscious life, between enjoyment and labour, between the sensual and the spiritual, between thought and feeling ...

These two very different quotations – one from the famous Greek philosopher of the fourth century BCE, the other from a nineteenth-century German historian – demonstrate that the impact of the environment on the evolution of Greek society has long been a theme for discussion. More than for most countries, the climate and topography of the southern Balkan peninsula had been considered responsible for many of its specific historical developments; from the rise and fall of political and military powers (as Aristotle suggests), and the encouragement of Greek philosophical thinking (as Curtius supposes), to the general notion that warm weather inspires gregarious and argumentative behaviour – literally providing a climate in which democracy could flourish.

In the late twentieth century, this rather naive type of environmental determinism is no longer accepted. Yet it cannot be denied that the climate and environment of Greece did have a profound, if subtle, effect upon the country's inhabitants, their economic and social organization, and their way of life.

GEOGRAPHY AND CLIMATE

The heartland of classical Greece (which covers approximately the same territory as the modern nation-state of Greece) is a peninsula, divided roughly into two sections

The irregular topography of
Greece can be traced to the
dramatic tectonic history of
the eastern Mediterranean,
where collisions between
micro-continents continue to
result in volcanic activity and
the uplift or subsidence of
certain zones. Seismic activity
is common today, and prayers
to Poseidon 'Earthshaker'
and 'Earth-holder' attest to
the same scourge in the past.
The mountains created by this
geological violence form the
most prominent features of
the Greek landscape today.
As geological barriers, they
divided region from region,
encouraging (though not
'causing') the emergence of a
political mosaic of relatively
small, but independent, city-
states. Mountains channelled
routes of trade, communication
and invasion. Passages through
mountainous terrain became
highly charged strategic and
symbolic locations, such as
the pass at Thermopylae in
northern Greece, a narrow
point caught between the
mountains and the sea. Several
battles were fought to repulse
invaders here, of which the
most celebrated was a suicidal
stand – by a small band of outnumbered Spartans and their
allies – against the Persian
invasion in 480 BCE.

connected by a very narrow isthmus. It also included associated islands in the
Aegean Sea. Thanks to significant tectonic activity in the eastern Mediterranean, the
landscape is marked by numerous mountain systems. As a result, there are few large
open plains in Greece, and those are to be found more in the north of the country.
The dissected and divided character of much of Greece meant significant barriers to
swift and easy communication around the country.

The country's climate is officially described as 'Mediterranean', meaning that it
experiences hot and dry summers, coolish and wet winters. Even across Greece's
relatively small area, however, some climatic differences emerge – notably in the
distribution of rainfall. Owing to the mountainous topography of the peninsula, its
east side receives considerably less rain than the west side, leading to much local
variation in the landscape's physical appearance and agricultural potential. For
example, in the Aegean Sea to the east lies the Cycladic island of Ceos with its relatively arid landscape. (Traces of agricultural terracing on its hills, however,
demonstrate that at one point it was intensively farmed.) By contrast, the western
edge of the Peloponnese, such as Messenia (see p. 17), is a wetter, greener, and
appreciably more fertile zone.

In geographical terms, of course, classical Greece encompassed more than just the southern Balkan peninsula. Numerous Greek cities, including such famous places as Ephesus or Miletus, lined the western coast of present-day Turkey. Population movement in the archaic period (eighth to sixth centuries BCE) resulted in Greek colonies being established in lands as far afield as southern Italy and Sicily (known as *Magna Graecia*, or 'Great Greece'), North Africa and the Black Sea region. The Greeks surrounded the Mediterranean, living – to repeat Plato's evocative term – 'like ants or frogs around a pond' (*Phaedo*). While each of these regions had its own particular topography and environmental constraints (Sicily and the Black Sea region, for example, being agriculturally richer than Greece itself), most Greeks lived in broadly similar environments, with all the advantages – and disadvantages – that entailed.

Mosaic of satellite images showing the eastern part of the Mediterranean Sea. The colours of the frame have been exaggerated to emphasise surface cover: pale and mid-green for grassland and deciduous forest, dark green for coniferous forest, and pale brown for arid scrub. The yellow in the bottom of the frame shows part of the desert of North Africa. In the centre of the frame are the islands of the Aegean Sea. To the left of these is Greece, to the right is Turkey. The dark green curve at top centre shows the Carpathian Mountains. The Nile Delta (green) is at bottom right. The image data were gathered by NOAA weather satellites.

View of the Cycladic island of Ceos, looking north-west towards the shores of Attica. The modern coastal village seen here lies at the foot of the acropolis of the ancient city of Coressus. Traces of agricultural terracing are visible on many of the island's hillslopes.

How was the classical Greek landscape viewed by its inhabitants? How did individuals and communities interact and cope with their environment? And, finally, to what extent were Greek society and economy in the classical age in fact shaped by their physical surroundings? And to what extent did *they* shape *it*?

THE ANCIENT VIEW OF THE ENVIRONMENT

Strange as it might seem to those who sell calendars or postcards to tourists today, the stunning beauties of Greece's natural landscape were not a subject for celebration in ancient literature or art. While it is difficult for us to recover the perceptions of those who lived in this setting, it seems clear that they 'saw' a very different landscape from modern visitors. One essential difference was their recognition and worship of gods in the countryside.

Deities were venerated everywhere in the landscape: on mountain tops, in caves, at springs, in cultivated fields, on hillsides, in groves of trees, in piles of stones (see Chapter 12). In some cases, but by no means all, temples or altars were erected in these locations.

The Argive Heraeum, for example, was a sanctuary to the goddess Hera dedicated by the people of Argos. Hera's temple was situated on a hillside with a commanding view over the plain of Argos. Processions from the city (visible in the distance) to this sanctuary established symbolic Argive control over this rich agricultural plain.

View of Messenia, in the south-western Peloponnese. The Aegaleon mountain range lies in the distance. Olive production is an important part of the economy in this part of modern Greece.

Myths and legends revolved around specific topographical elements of the landscape as well; thus, an oddly-shaped mountain top was explained as a place where Pegasus, the winged horse of the hero Bellerophon, stamped his hoof. Among the most famous of mountains, of course, was the home of the gods themselves, Mount Olympus.

Probably the most famous natural feature of Greece is the high, shelf-like limestone outcrop which forms the Athenian Acropolis, or 'high city'. The Acropolis not only served as a fortified citadel and as the home for numerous religious buildings, notably the temple to Athena Parthenos (the Parthenon), but it became the site of

The Argive Heraeum, with the city of Argos in the distance across the Argive plain. This photograph was probably taken around the time of the temple's excavation in the 1890s.

'Dream of Arcadia' (1838), by the American painter Thomas Cole (1801–48), is a romanticized nineteenth-century version of the Greek landscape. The presence of a distant temple, however, is an accurate reflection of the religious significance with which the Greeks invested the countryside. When the home of the gods was assigned a physical location, it was placed on the highest mountain in the Greek peninsula, Mount Olympus in northern Greece, thus giving the name 'Olympian gods' to the traditional Greek pantheon. In objective terms, Mount Olympus is not one of the world's largest mountains (at 9573 feet, it is about one-third the height of Mount Everest) – but in the imaginations of the Greeks it was an immense presence, from which the gods looked down on mortals.

Photograph of the limestone plateau of the Athenian Acropolis, taken in the mid-nineteenth century by William Stillman. The Parthenon is clearly visible on top. The standing columns to the right are the ruins of an enormous temple to Zeus, the Olympieum, completed by the Roman emperor Hadrian.

important mythic events in the Athenian past, such as the contest between Athena and Poseidon for possession of the city itself. If asked to explain what was important about their physical setting, the Greeks of the classical period would no doubt have stressed its religious and mythic significance, rather than its natural beauties.

THE SILENT LANDSCAPE

What they would *not* have stressed – possibly not even mentioned – are more practical, productive uses of their physical environment; activities as basic as farming or herding. This seems an odd silence given their absolute dependence upon the land for subsistence and survival. Comparative research on pre-industrial populations has convincingly demonstrated that as much as 80 per cent of any such population would have been actively involved in the cultivation or production of food. Yet ancient sources say remarkably little about rural activities. This paradox of the Greek city (how the Greeks appear to ignore what was most essential to their survival) has been explained largely as a bias on the part of those male, urban-based, élite individuals whose writings survive. Such individuals either took a dim view of the perceived lack of urbanity in the countryside (*agroikos* means both 'dwelling in the country' and 'boorish') or they took life in the countryside for granted – and thus thought it not worth commenting upon.

This imbalance endured for a very long time in later scholarship, where respect for Greek artistic, literary, philosophical and political achievements tended to obscure the fact that, like everyone else, the Greeks had to eat. In recent years, however, historians and archaeologists have begun to take a greater interest in the practicalities of life in the ancient world. Because of the shortage of literary testimony on such matters, alternative techniques have been employed to find out about life in the Greek countryside. This has become an interdisciplinary effort in the Mediterranean world, involving historians, archaeologists, geologists, palynologists (pollen analysts), botanists, and anthropologists.

Archaeological work certainly could provide detailed evidence about the rural, humble behaviour ignored by the literary sources. Unfortunately, classical archaeology, like ancient history, was long influenced by that silence, and so only a very few 'ordinary' rural sites in Greece have been excavated to date. More encouraging are the results of archaeological surface survey, a fairly recent methodological innovation in Mediterranean archaeology. Rather than investigating a single particular site, as excavation does, survey operates at a regional level, searching for traces of human

A view of archaeological surface survey in action. A survey team, working near the Panhellenic sanctuary of Nemea in the north-eastern Peloponnese, here walks in parallel lines across the landscape, recording and collecting the remains of past human activity (broken pottery, roof-tiles) from the earth's surface. When mapped and analysed, such finds can provide significant information about trends in settlement and land-use patterns over time.

A team of palynologists examines a deep soil core taken in a marshy location near the Panhellenic sanctuary of Nemea in the north-eastern Peloponnese. Pollen samples have been recovered from this core, testifying to changes over time in the variety of plant life (wild and cultivated) in this region.

settlement or other activities over much larger areas, often many square kilometres in extent. In survey, teams of individuals walk systematically across the present-day countryside, observing, recording and collecting artifacts from the ground's surface. Broken pottery, known for its durability, is the most common find, but chipped stone tools, roof-tiles, agricultural processing equipment such as millstones, and even religious votives can be found in the modern landscape. When these finds are studied and mapped, a picture can be built up of where, at different periods in the past, people lived and worked in the countryside.

In interpreting their finds, archaeologists realized it would be naive to imagine that the present-day landscape they surveyed was identical to that of millennia ago. The co-operation of geologists, especially those who study landscape change, was therefore necessary. Past episodes of erosion and soil deposition, in many cases related to human activity such as field clearance or ploughing, can be identified by geological examination. Other scientists too became involved in reconstructing the human impact upon the ancient environment. Although Greece is a relatively dry country, some permanently wet areas (such as springs or marshes) have been found and explored by palynologists. From deep cores driven into such locations, preserved pollen can reveal changing plant communities through time.

A shift from a predominance of oak pollen to olive pollen, for example, has been observed in the palynological record for Greece, and is clearly attributable to human intervention through the clearing of oak forests for olive cultivation. Modern-day vegetation too has been studied by botanists interested in the environmental effects of human exploitation, not least the damage done by herding and grazing animals. Cultural anthropologists working in present-day Greece are also contributing to our understanding of its past. Although it would be dangerous to draw too many direct parallels between the modern and ancient world, research into Greek village life today can shed light on the organization of ancient communities. Studies of traditional farming practices can help us imaginatively reconstruct the life of the ancient farmer.

CLASSICAL LANDSCAPE WITH FIGURES

Most families in classical times would probably have lived in the urban centre of their home polis. It is clear that agricultural 'commuting' was a common phenomenon, with men leaving the city to travel to their fields by day and returning by night. Farmers deliberately organized their holdings to maximize efficiency, so that the most labour-intensive crops (vegetables, fruit) were planted closest to their residence, and those requiring the least care (olives, cereals) the furthest away. Such tactics are still standard practice in many parts of Greece today. Urban residence, in the past as in the present, was preferred for many reasons, not least for proximity to political activity, entertainment, and support networks in times of need.

Before the advent of archaeological surface survey, this nucleated pattern of living was assumed to be the rule. One of survey's greatest surprises was the discovery of a scattering of very small classical sites in the countryside, characterized by a mixture of fine table-ware, coarse cooking-ware, roof-tiles and agricultural equipment such as grindstones or millstones. These tiny sites, which have been found in almost all parts of Greece surveyed so far, have been interpreted as the

Photograph taken on Crete in 1974 showing the continuity of traditional farming practices in Greece. A threshing sledge with sharp flint teeth on its underside is drawn over the harvested grain; the pressure of the sledge, and of the animals' hooves, helps to separate the wheat from the chaff.

Vines and viticulture

It is difficult to exaggerate the centrality of viticulture and the vine in Greek life. A constant element in every farmer's year would have been the care of his grapes: planting, digging, pruning, gathering, treading, pressing. Wine (mixed with water) was an accepted staple in everyone's diet, including slaves and children. Numerous religious festivals, such as the Athenian Anthesteria and Dionysia, revolved around the production and consumption of wine. And wine drinking was perceived as more or less co-terminous with the bounds of the civilized world.

Everyone drank wine: but not everyone drank the same stuff. Various grades were produced, the first press of the grapes yielding the best quality drink. As with olive-oil,

subsequent pressings were thought to produce a less desirable product, and the last lees were deemed fit only for the poor and slaves.

While viticulture was practised everywhere, some places clearly specialized in wine production and export. One was the island of Thasos in the northern Aegean Sea. Laws regulating the wine trade have been found there dating to classical times; failure to obey in some cases resulted in fines payable to the city's gods. Archaeology, especially abundant evidence for the manufacture of amphorae (large storage jars used for trade and export), also testifies to the importance of the vine in the Thasian economy.

Table showing the cycle of farming activities throughout the ancient Greek agricultural year. Time and labour for other activities, such as construction, were available chiefly in the 'slower' periods of the cycle, as demonstrated by records of building expenditure from the sanctuary of Demeter, the goddess of agricultural fertility, and her daughter Persephone at Eleusis.

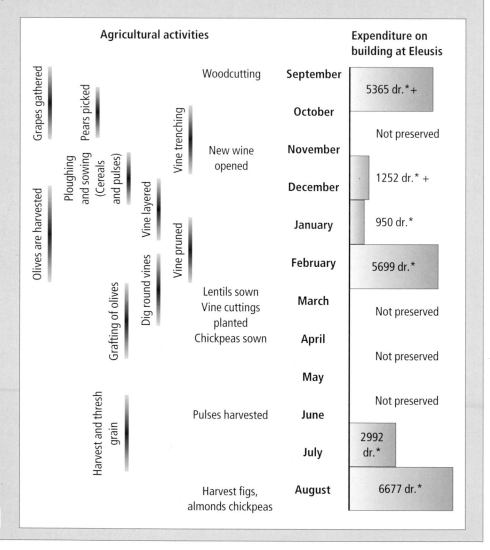

Agricultural activities

Expenditure on building at Eleusis

Activities	Month	Expenditure
Woodcutting	September	5365 dr.*+
	October	Not preserved
New wine opened	November	
	December	1252 dr.* +
	January	950 dr.*
	February	5699 dr.*
Lentils sown / Vine cuttings planted / Chickpeas sown	March	Not preserved
	April	Not preserved
	May	
Pulses harvested	June	Not preserved
	July	2992 dr.*
Harvest figs, almonds chickpeas	August	6677 dr.*

Grapes gathered · Pears picked · Olives are harvested · Ploughing and sowing (Cereals and pulses) · Vine layered · Vine trenching · Vine pruned · Dig round vines · Grafting of olives · Harvest and thresh grain

*dr. = drachmae

remains of farmhouses or seasonal shelters. Living on the land, rather than commuting back and forth, allowed more time to be put into cultivation; the resulting higher crop yields must, for these individuals, have compensated for losing the advantages of urban residence. Whether such rural structures were occupied year-round, or only when the agricultural workload was particularly intense (for example, at harvest times), they argue for a much 'busier', more populated landscape than had previously been imagined.

What crops were being cultivated, either at these small farmsteads or from a distance by urban dwellers? The staple foodstuffs of the ancient Mediterranean are often called the 'Mediterranean triad': olives, cereals and vines.

From the Bronze Age to the present day, this dietary package has provided the lion's share of the daily calorific intake of Mediterranean peoples. Other crops, notably legumes such as chick peas and beans which replenished soil fertility, were also regularly grown. Almost all farmers would have cultivated a mixture of these crops, sometimes side by side, in the hope of ensuring, as far as possible, the self-sufficiency of their household. That household would have worked through the

Photograph taken in the 1970s of a flock of transhumant goats being moved by shepherds to upland summer pastures.

cyclical calendar of the agricultural year, presented in poetic form by the early seventh-century poet Hesiod in his *Works and Days*, with different tasks appropriate to different seasons: 'At the time when the Pleiades, the daughters of Atlas, are rising, begin your harvest, and plough again when they are setting... '.

Hesiod also stressed the importance of animal husbandry in the farmer's life: 'First of all, get yourself an ox for ploughing ...' (*Works and Days*). Oxen provided traction power for ploughing and transportation, but – with their need for considerable food and water – they were not a poor man's animal. Horses, the symbol of Greek aristocracy, fell into the same expensive and restricted category. Most farms however, even the poorest, would have kept some sheep, goats, chickens, pigs – even bees. In some instances these animals were used for their meat, being consumed after sacrifice, a central element in Greek religious ritual. Equally often, however, animals provided secondary products for their owners, such as honey and wax, milk, wool, and manure for soil fertilization. Many animals were probably kept quite close to the home in order to fertilize the small vegetable gardens and other intensively cultivated crops located by houses. This pattern of animal husbandry, the most common in classical Greece, stressed a highly symbiotic relationship between agricultural and animal resources. Other types of pastoral activity also existed in the classical landscape, however, including long-distance transhumance – in which larger herds were moved by shepherds, on a seasonal basis, from one grazing ground to another, usually from mountain pastures to lower elevations and back again. According to the playwright Sophocles, the baby Oedipus, who had been exposed to die on Mount Cithaeron in Boeotia, was discovered and saved by a shepherd herding in upland summer pastures. Mountainous zones, and other wild territory, also provided space for the pursuit of wild animals. For the Greeks, the sport of hunting was a symbolically charged practice; on another level game also added a welcome savoury element to the diet.

Apart from arable land and maritime resources, the region's complex geological history generated scattered deposits of valuable natural resources, notably gold, silver, iron, lead, and marble. Such resources began to be exploited in prehistoric times, and quarrying and mining were carried on intensively throughout the classical period and beyond. Popular marble sources included the fine white marbles of Mount Pentelicum in Attica, and those of the Cycladic island of Paros; these raw materials were used in many of the masterpieces of Greek art and architecture so celebrated today.

Mines and mining

Since mining methods in Greece remained relatively unchanged from antiquity until the introduction of explosives in the nineteenth century, it can be difficult to identify and analyse the workings of specifically *ancient* mines. This is not so, however, in the case of the silver and lead mines at Laurium, located at the very southern tip of Attica. These mines, the most renowned source of precious metals in classical times, supplied Athens with an unrivalled financial base for civic and military activities. Wealthy Athenians would lease concessions to work the ore deposits, making their individual fortunes as well as boosting the Athenian economy at large.

At the other end of the social spectrum, of course, were those who dug the shafts and tunnels, worked at the washing tables, and piled up the slag heaps at Laurium. Almost all miners would have been slaves. Estimates of their numbers vary, but there may have been as many as 30,000 at work at the height of exploitation. Of the more than 20,000 Athenian slaves who deserted to the Spartan side during the Peloponnesian War, many are supposed to have been mine-workers. Such desertion would not be surprising: mine slaves were generally agreed to be the lowest of the low, working and dying in often appalling conditions.

Later, in the fourth century, control of metals would guarantee political and military prominence to another rising power: in this case, the gold resources of northern Greece. The mines of Mount Pangaeum are said to have produced an annual revenue of 1000 talents for Philip II of Macedon – a vast sum that encouraged his expansionist dreams, and those of his son, Alexander the Great.

Gold and silver were the most intensely desired, and most intensely exploited, metals of the ancient world. The most frequently employed and most commonly found, of course, was something much less valuable: iron. Iron ore deposits are distributed quite widely throughout Greece, and they were exploited to make such day-to-day necessities as agricultural implements and household tools, as well as military equipment and weapons.

If these various forms of human activity – dwelling, farming, herding, bee-keeping, fishing, salt-making, quarrying, mining – are combined with the religious practices already acknowledged, then the classical landscape emerges as a very full and busy environment. But just how stable and secure were the lives of the people living in it?

THE PRECARIOUS COUNTRYSIDE

Several time bombs – of both natural and human origin – threatened the stability of Greek economic and social life. The most ominous environmental factor was the weather. A characteristic of the Mediterranean climate is that precipitation levels vary unpredictably from year to year. Particular types of plants require a certain amount of rain to flourish (for example, barley needs about 200 millimetres a year,

The resources of the sea

Nowhere in Greece, nor in the lands colonized by the Greeks, was very far from the sea. While agriculture and animal husbandry served as the crucial sources of food production in the ancient world, maritime resources were also exploited in a variety of ways. Eating fish or shellfish, fishing and fish marketing are all mentioned by ancient authors and depicted in vase painting scenes. Archaeologists have found more mundane signs of such activity, such as fishhooks, fishbones and mollusc shells. Despite the coastal orientation of many Greek communities, the importance of this evidence should not be exaggerated: the Mediterranean is not a particularly abundant fishing ground and, without modern means of storage, transportation of fish any great distance was problematic (although runners did apparently carry fish from the coast inland, in the process training at least one Olympic victor). Fish always remained a supplementary part of the diet, if a tasty one – even in small quantities fish could give relish to an otherwise bland meal more often than not based on cereals and legumes.

Apart from foodstuffs, resources of the sea included sponges, and molluscs which produced a famous, colour-fast purple dye. Salt pans, where seawater could be trapped and allowed to evaporate in the summer sun, also dotted portions of the Greek coastline. Many of these resources were very localized in distribution and, together with traffic in fish and shellfish, the exchange of such products fuelled trade and contact among Greek communities. Much of this trade would itself have been by sea, and ports and harbour facilities developed to accommodate dealing in these and other commodities. Ships and harbours also played a part, of course, in forms of less co-operative interaction – such as piracy and naval warfare – as well. In the long run, proximity to the sea was less important for contributing particular products to the Greek diet and lifestyle, than for providing access to seaborne commerce and communication, both among Greeks themselves and with other, more distant parts of the Mediterranean world.

A collection of fishhooks, discovered in excavations at the classical city of Halieis in the Southern Argolid.

Golden stalk of grain, found in a grave at Syracuse, a Greek colony founded on the island of Sicily.

wheat 300 millimetres, and legumes 400 millimetres). Failure of one or more crop could occur frequently, but at unpredictable intervals. In a serious drought, several successive harvests, across a range of crops, could be inadequate. To complicate matters further, rainfall could vary dramatically over very small distances:

> Sometimes it happens that drought or rain affects a great area of country at the same time, but sometimes the effect is only local. For often the country in general receives due rainfall for the season or even more, but in one part of the country is drought. And occasionally the opposite is true: when all the country around has but moderate rainfall or even a drought, one particular part receives boundless supply of rain.
>
> (Aristotle *Meteorology*)

If climatic unpredictability helped make life in the countryside a precarious endeavour, human actions also created crisis. Warfare could disrupt the farming cycle or, more distressingly, involve the deliberate destruction of crops and agricultural facilities. It should be noted, however, that the traditional hoplite (infantry) encounters of the classical period seem to have been organized so as to minimize such disruption. Major outbreaks of hostility, such as the Peloponnesian War between Athens and Sparta, did none the less have a profound impact upon the Athenian subsistence base as the population of Attica moved into the city, leaving the Spartans to devastate their fields and farmhouses. It is unlikely that ancient armies had the time or technology to destroy completely the sturdy olives and vines of their enemies' holdings, so agricultural recovery from such ravages may have been quicker than has sometimes been thought. Consequences for local populations, however, including psychological effects, must still have been very severe. Worst of all would be the times when natural and human factors combined, for example if a period of drought coincided with an outbreak of warfare. Both were sufficiently endemic to Greek society that such coincidences could easily occur.

These factors, either separately or in conjunction, lead to the inescapable conclusion that food shortage must have been a periodic, but persistent, occurrence in Greek society. Depending on the particular forces at work, these episodes would have ranged in scale and in severity, sometimes affecting families, sometimes communities, sometimes entire regions of Greece. At the most extreme end of the spectrum, far less frequent than food shortage but far more deadly, was the possibility of famine, one of the biblical Four Horsemen of the Apocalypse. The human consequences of these incidents varied, too, from temporary belt-tightening to perceptible malnutrition to actual death by starvation. Few literary sources comment on what must have been endemic food shortages, although some harrowing descriptions of famine conditions, usually the result of warfare, do survive. Religious responses to crisis – the consultation of oracles, the intensification of worship at certain shrines, or the introduction of new gods or cults – also sometimes emerge in our sources. More mundanely, palaeopathologists (people who study health and disease in extinct populations) have begun to study ancient diets through skeletal remains. Although little conclusive work has so far been done with Greek data, traces of malnutrition (in bone and teeth development) show it must have been a recurrent problem in the classical world.

What all this leaves us with is the picture of a grim environment, dealing out a hard and precarious life for its inhabitants. This is a very long way from the more traditional view of Greek society that focuses on its monuments and cultural achievements. What the monuments and cultural achievements remind us of, however, is that individuals and communities must have found ways to cope with threats, both to their personal safety and to the stability of their society. Coping mechanisms could be as basic and unremarkable as storing away surplus foods 'against a rainy day', finding various ways to preserve foodstuffs, planting a range of crops (some more resilient to climatic variability than others), and cultivating fields scattered over a wide area in order to average out the risk of low rainfall or other disasters. While a household's goal was to be self-sufficient, it was accepted that outside help would periodically be necessary to survive. This led to the formation of social alliances designed to serve in times of need. They took the form either of reciprocal links between men of equal status; or patronage relationships between individuals of greater wealth and power and the 'clients' they would protect. Hesiod's advice to farmers covers these issues: 'Take good measure from your neighbour, then pay him back fairly with the same measure, or better yet, if you can manage it; so, when you need him some other time, you will find him steadfast' (*Works and Days*). Related to these social bonds was the classical preference for urban, nucleated residence. The decision to live within an immediate support network, rather than choosing a more isolated life in the countryside, now emerges as – in part – a survival strategy. All these mechanisms were – and in traditional Mediterranean societies still are – basic insurance against the unpredictable Greek environment.

When these mechanisms failed, however, or the crisis was so widespread that help could not be sought from one's neighbour or one's patron, more serious steps had to be taken. Responses varied, depending on the severity and duration of the crisis. First steps included the cultivation of less desirable, but tougher crops (such as millet). Foraging for 'famine foods' was another alternative. Nuts and berries were always a background element in the Greek diet, but in hungry times, people would seek out and eat whatever they could find. The Greek doctor, Galen, writing in the second century CE, reports the escalation in such behaviour:

> Countryfolk habitually eat the fruit of the cornel tree and blackberries and acorns, and the fruit of the arbutus, and rather less those of the other trees and shrubs. But when famine grips our land, and there are plenty of acorns and medlars, they store them in pits and consume them instead of food from cereals throughout the winter and in early spring ...
>
> (*On the Wholesome and Unwholesome Properties of Foodstuffs*)

This map illustrates the wide distribution of communities which received grain donations from Cyrene in the fourth century BCE. Two individuals – Olympias and Cleopatra, the mother and sister of Alexander the Great – were also given substantial amounts of grain (indeed more than most cities) at this time. Such gifts clearly bolstered the reputation and served the political objectives of Cyrene.

Working for wealthier individuals or selling livestock would probably be the next steps (food prices would of course be rising steadily as the shortage persisted) before moving to what would be truly drastic measures, such as selling land or even emigrating permanently. Some of these strategies took much longer to bounce back from than others; some indeed meant that the life of the individuals involved would never be the same again.

These particular coping mechanisms worked more at the level of the family, but the community at large also took steps to protect itself. As neighbours could exchange aid in times of need, so cities established alliances and relationships with other communities, relying on the likelihood that adverse weather conditions would strike some regions and spare others. Athens, the city for which we have the most evidence, took active political and military steps to expand and protect its grain

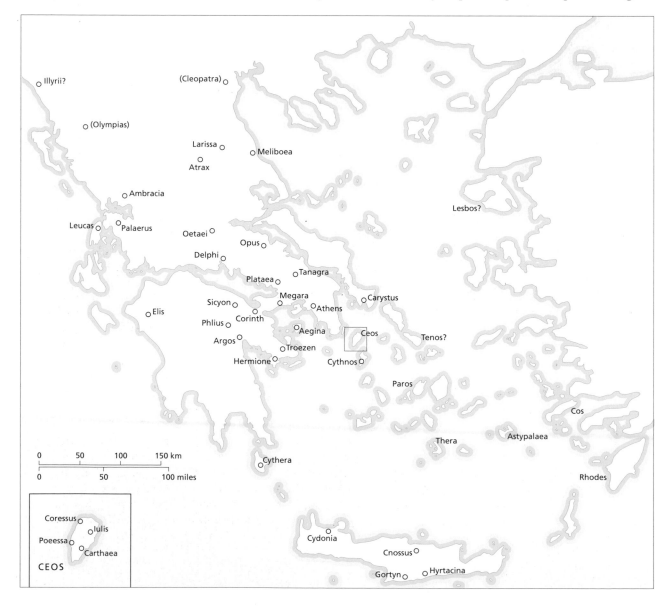

The myth of Arcadia

Arcadia, the region lying at the centre of the Greek Peloponnese, is a rugged area surrounded by high mountains; its ancient inhabitants lived, worked and occasionally suffered under the various climatic and environmental constraints endemic throughout the Greek world. Literary Arcadia, on the other hand, is an idyllic, abundant landscape, a place of shepherds and rustic maidens, of poetry and music, where love is the dominant concern of its dwellers.

This myth of Arcadia coloured European impressions of what Greece, the land considered the fountainhead of Western civilization, should look like. Authors and painters, steeped in classical myth and history, envisaged glorious deeds and mythic episodes taking place in a suitably beautiful and verdant landscape – a landscape modelled very much on their own northern, more temperate climes. As Europeans began to tour Greece in ever-increasing numbers throughout the eighteenth and nineteenth century, what they saw must have come as something of a shock. As the noted botanist, Oliver Rackham, observed: 'The French or English visitor ... expects to see heroes spearing the boar in noble forests and nymphs swimming in crystal fountains; finding instead the tangled prickly-oaks and trickling springs of the real Greece, he infers that the land has gone to the bad since classical times'. Even when confronted with the realities of the situation, artists continued to represent what they preferred to imagine.

The assumption of major environmental degradation since ancient times is tempting, for it allows us to romanticize classical Greece without having to accept its harsher, grimmer face. There is, however, no real reason to believe that such a catastrophic decline has occurred, or that the rural landscape of ancient Greece was significantly different from what we see today. 'Arcadia' remains an imaginary country.

'Hylas and the Nymphs' (1896), by the Victorian painter J. W. Waterhouse (1849–1917), is an excellent example of romantic idealization of the Greek countryside. In the mythic account of the voyage of the Argonauts, Hylas was Heracles' page. During this voyage, he went to fetch water from a spring. The spring's nymphs fell in love with his beauty and seized him, pulling him in to the water. Waterhouse depicts this encounter, but places it in a setting more appropriate to temperate Europe than the ancient Mediterranean.

supply; this concern in part fuelled its imperial interests in the fifth century BCE. Other cities also fostered trade in foodstuffs between individual citizens, encouraging the development of overseas contacts and discouraging insularity.

As a final resort, cities would 'export' hungry mouths. While the phenomenon of Greek colonization cannot be considered solely as a response to food shortage and hunger, in some instances such factors were clearly involved. According to Herodotus, a seven-year drought, which withered all but one tree on the island of Thera (modern Santorini), was responsible for the seventh-century BCE foundation of the colony at Cyrene in North Africa.

Finally, as gifts of grain made by this same Cyrene in the fourth century demonstrate, food could become a pawn in international diplomacy and power politics. Such donations were perceived as a way both to impress and to score political points. The prestige of having food when others did not was much appreciated in the ancient world, be it at the level of the individual, the family, or the city.

THE INFLUENCE OF THE ENVIRONMENT

What these various survival strategies reveal is how the pressures of the environment shaped and encouraged certain aspects of Greek society. Many characteristic features – urban residence, networks of exchange and patronage among individuals, inter-city alliances, overseas contacts and trade, colonization – can be related, although not exclusively, to a fear of food shortage, of famine, of hunger.

The influence of its natural setting upon Greek social and economic life continues to this very day, although there has been a very decisive and (given the attitudes of the ancient Greeks themselves) a very paradoxical shift in what is considered most important about that landscape. Since the European 'rediscovery' of Greece in the eighteenth and nineteenth century, it has been the country's physical beauties – its glorious vistas, punctuated by romantic ruins – that have dominated our imagination.

Early travellers sketched and painted this landscape, largely ignoring the country's contemporary residents in their eagerness to concentrate upon natural wonders, such as the volcano at Santorini (then Thera), or places important in history or myth, such as the mountain pass at Thermopylae. In the later twentieth century, sun, fun, and scenery have drawn tourists in huge numbers to Greece, making tourism the chief industry of the modern country. This leads to a very different view of the advantages and disadvantages of a Mediterranean climate.

(Opposite) In the foreground lie the ruins of the fourth century BCE theatre at Megalopolis in Arcadia, the largest theatre in the Greek world; in the background stands a modern power station.

Travellers and tourists aside, it is worth remembering that until very recently many Greek farmers and farming communities, despite improvements in agricultural technology, have continued to confront the same environmental constraints, continued to face the same periodic crop failures, and continued to cope by the same means as their ancient predecessors. That situation, however, is now rapidly changing. New political and economic forces (such as the European Union) are radically

transforming the appearance of the Greek countryside and the decisions taken by its inhabitants. As a result, traditional methods of farming and traditional survival strategies are becoming – for the first time in the human occupation of the Mediterranean – increasingly obsolete. These changes, so positive in reducing the perilous quality of life in the region, certainly exact a price in terms of urban development, tourism, industry, and pollution. What is more imperilled now is not the people but the environment itself.

Peoples: Who were the Greeks?

'OBJECTIVE' CRITERIA?

'Who were the Greeks?' is a question that could be answered in several different ways, depending on context and approach. In the nineteenth and first half of the twentieth centuries, the definition might well have been racial – or even racist. For example, size and shape of cranium might have been supposed to yield an objective classification of the Greek racial type. This could then have been related histori-cally, in accordance with theories of evolution or migration, to the physical characteristics of other Mediterranean or European 'races'. Such a means of classi-fication is understandably discredited today. Not only does it lack a properly scientific basis, but in the recent past it has been used as a tool of genocide. Race is a term and a concept best avoided.

Another supposedly objective approach is by way of language group. One of the most useful philological theories ever formulated has been that of an original Indo-European language: the ultimate common ancestor of a widely dispersed family of actually attested historical languages, including Greek. However, the main diffi-culty with applying this to the origins of a people is the assumed equation of language with race. Partly this is because it is so difficult to individuate a people unambiguously by any criteria, let alone just a linguistic one. Partly it is because before a language is attested by extant written texts, the evidence for its use is nec-essarily inferential, and in a text-free, pre-historic environment the only directly relevant evidence is provided by archaeology. The spade may be incapable of lying, but then it cannot speak. The mute data of archaeology have to be made to utter, and once more this involves inference and interpretation.

A third approach to the identification of the Greek people is neither physiologi-cal nor philological, but cultural; that is, to go back to the surviving Greek texts themselves to see who the Greeks thought they were. Here at least you might think we would be on more solid ground. Actually, we find ourselves plunged into a morass of myth and legend, coloured retrospectively to suit the speaker's, writer's or audience's particular circumstances; often with a view to providing what the anthro-pologist Bronislaw Malinowski called a 'charter' that would justify present social and political arrangements in terms of some alleged original condition or status.

LITERARY SOURCES

Our earliest literary sources, Homer and Hesiod, were among other things prime purveyors of such sanctifying mythological charters. Hesiod's *Theogony*, indeed, purported to relate the Greeks to the origins of the universe. Homer, singing mainly about Greek aristocrats, operated with a genealogical model to account for the present distribution of people and power in his Greek world.

Plato, writing at a time when the intellectual concept of mythology (and, indeed, the word) had been invented, commented slyly on this eternal Greek propensity to mythopoiesis, or myth-making: 'Since we don't know the truth about the ancients, may it not be useful to approximate falsity to truth as closely as possible?' (*Republic*).

Far be it from us to try to pass off falsehoods as likely-seeming truths ... Given the interpretative difficulties, maybe it is as well to confine ourselves to the relatively few certainties (or, at least, probabilities) we have. For instance, we know when the Greek language is first attested, roughly who wrote it and in what script and media, when the different historical dialects became established, and what they signified culturally. We know how the various dialects were spread through what became the extended Greek world (see p. 39). We know that the Greek language and other non-linguistic aspects of their culture by which they defined themselves were affected by contact with non-Greek peoples. And we know how the Greeks in turn influenced their Mediterranean and Black Sea neighbours.

The civilization of Bronze Age Crete, dubbed 'Minoan' by Arthur Evans after legendary king Minos, entered a palatial phase around 2000 BCE. Settlements remained unfortified, which presumably eased the task of conquest by Mycenaeans from the Greek mainland in about 1500. But the Minoans were by no means entirely pacific, and within the palace compounds they practised dangerously athletic sports like the bull-leaping depicted on this fresco from Cnossus.

LINEAR B

For the purposes of this book the Greek language is first attested by the use of the Linear B script (a modern term) in the latter half of the second millennium BCE. Two of the sites which have produced examples of the tablets bearing this script, Cnossus and Chania, are palaces on the southern island of Crete; the tablets were made of clay that was baked hard in the fires that destroyed the palaces. Crete is also the home of the Linear A script, but although Linear A is the ancestor of the Linear B syllabary, it does not transcribe Greek and its language is yet to be satisfactorily deciphered.

Clearly the Linear B script was first adapted, rather clumsily, to write Greek on Crete before it was used in comparable palatial settings on the Greek mainland (Mycenae, Tiryns, Pylos, Thebes). But what precisely the relationship was between the Linear A-using Cretan population, who have left us a host of marvellously delicate and vivacious artifacts, and the inventors of Linear B, is uncertain. Conquest of Crete (which Sir Arthur Evans, excavator and restorer of Cnossus, named

Seemingly out of nowhere, the rulers of Mycenae suddenly, around 1600, took to burying themselves in elaborate graves stuffed with accumulated treasures of the most disparate origins. Two presumably royal grave-circles have been excavated, of which Circle A, consisting of six deeply dug and several times re-used shaft graves, is the later. Shaft Grave V (as Heinrich Schliemann labelled it) contained among much else a male corpse whose face was covered with this exquisite gold death-mask. So moved was the excitable Schliemann that he proclaimed he had 'gazed upon the face of Agamemnon'.

Minoan after Homer's legendary king Minos) by Greek mainlanders known today as Mycenaeans (following Homer's location of the Greek high king Agamemnon at Mycenae 'rich in gold') is only one possibility.

However, the contexts and contents of the Linear B tablets make it unambiguously clear that this was a restricted, administrative script, not one for general use. Its chief function was to record economic transactions for the political benefit of the palaces' rulers – the real-life equivalents of Agamemnon and the other Greek kings whose exploits are recorded, or invented, in Homer's epics.

Apart from being scratched on clay tablets, which were designed for temporary not permanent storage, Linear B symbols were also scratched or painted, again presumably for economic purposes, on pottery vessels which have been found at a somewhat wider range of sites. There is no evidence, indeed, that the version of Greek employed for Linear B notation was, if spoken at all, spoken widely outside the few known find spots. Possibly Linear B Greek was simply a sort of special jargon known only to the scribal initiates. At any rate, specialists today differ in their explanations of the relationship between this early or proto-Greek, not attested after 1150 BCE at the latest, and the Greek attested from the eighth century onwards – one of the distinguishing features of which is that it comprises several quite clearly separate regional dialects.

However these dialects had come to be so separated from each other, the process had been completed by about 800 and may have occurred substantially during the period between the end of the Mycenaean civilization in about 1150 and the beginning of the eighth century. This was a period of general cultural impoverishment which is often referred to as the Greek Dark Age, although spots of illumination are becoming increasingly visible. This may well have been also the formative period of the Homeric epics, since sagas of this general heroic type have in many cultures pre-supposed, if not been inspired by, the ruin of an earlier, perceptibly more successful civilization.

Dialect map of Greece (*below*), showing the distribution of dialects in the Aegean heart-land attained by *c.* 800 BCE.

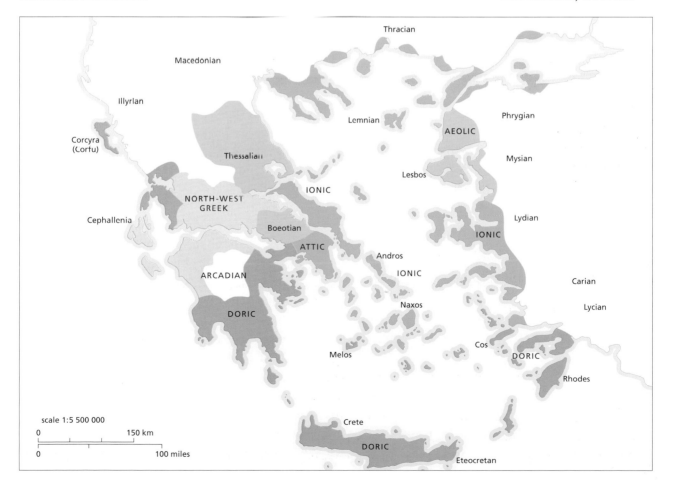

IONIC GREEK

The language of Homeric poetry, however, was what the Germans call a *Kunst-sprache*, an artificial literary amalgam never spoken outside the context of an epic recital. But we know enough of contemporary Greek dialectology to be able to state categorically that Homer's Greek was compounded chiefly of words and forms from the Ionic dialect group, together with some elements of the Aeolic dialect and a few traces of the historical dialect that would appear to be most nearly akin to that spoken in the Mycenaean period, Arcado-Cypriot.

Each of these three classificatory names tells its own tale. Ionia is that area of what is now the western coast of Turkey in which were located the cities sharing in religious worship at the Panionium or 'All-Ionian' cult centre devoted to Poseidon. Prominent among these cities were Miletus and Ephesus. Since it was Greeks from this area who spoke the Ionic dialect of Greek with which non-Greek oriental powers and peoples such as Assyria and the Jews most regularly came into contact, 'Ionians' became the standard oriental term for Greeks. (The Greeks' own term for themselves was – and is – *Hellenes*, whereas our word is derived from the Romans' label, *Graeci*.)

AEOLIC GREEK

To the north of Ionia, in the north-west of Anatolia, lay Aeolis, home of the Aeolic dialect. It was in this region that Greeks in the eighth century resettled the likeliest site of Homer's Troy, a site which they anyhow cheerfully named Ilion (one of Homer's alternative names for Troy) in commemoration of their ancestors' great national victory.

ARCADO-CYPRIOT GREEK

Thirdly, 'Arcado-Cypriot' is so named because the historical dialect of Greek spoken on Cyprus shows distinct linguistic kinship with the dialect spoken in land-locked Arcadia in the central Peloponnese. The most likely explanation for this is to suppose that it was mainland Greeks speaking an Arcadian, or proto-Arcadian dialect, who emigrated to Cyprus – as the archaeological evidence shows to have happened during the twelfth and eleventh centuries. In the eighth century BCE some wealthy descendants of those settlers at Cypriot Salamis had themselves lavishly buried in what they clearly intended to be considered 'Homeric' fashion.

To account further for the distinction between the Arcadian dialect, on the one hand, and Ionic and Aeolic on the other (despite their common features), the likeliest theory is that Arcadian, spoken in a self-enclosed and relatively inaccessible upland area of inland Peloponnese, more closely preserved the common Mycenaean ancestor, whereas the latter two developed separately during the Dark Age.

THE MIGRATION THEORY

These arguments do not by any means exhaust explanations of the historical dialect map of Greece, for two reasons.

Salamis on Cyprus was a Greek foundation subject to heavy Phoenician influence. In about 700 one of its rulers had himself buried in 'Homeric' style, in a chamber entered by a passageway containing his chariots and sacrificed horses and flanked by large numbers of vases. The chamber itself contained, besides his cremated remains, a great many fancy goods, including his throne to which this elaborately decorated ivory open work plaque was attached. The style is Phoenician, heavily influenced by Egypt – the sphinx is depicted wearing the double crown of Upper and Lower Egypt.

First, Ionic and Aeolic were not confined to the western Asia Minor area where, in all probability, the Homeric poems achieved their monumental consummation after generations of oral transmission of smaller lays. Ionic, or a sub-group of it, was spoken also in Attica, the territory of Athens, and in the islands strung out across the Aegean between Attica and Ionia. Aeolic, or a sub-group of it, was spoken also in Boeotia and Thessaly and in the Aegean islands between that part of the Greek mainland and Aeolis. Again, as with Arcado-Cypriot, migration of Greek speakers from the two areas would seem to account most easily for this pattern of dialect distribution, except that the migrations will have occurred rather later in the Dark Ages and even as late as the eighth century. That was also the century in which contact between Greeks and Phoenicians, attested in other media too, led to the invention of a Greek alphabetic script. The Cypriot Greeks, however, persisted with a syllabary rather than an alphabet.

Schliemann, Mycenae and Homer

The ancient Greeks, being an unusually inventive and inordinately competitive people, were devotees of the game of 'first discoverers'. They compiled lists – rival lists, of course – of the first discoverers of everything, from pottery to pederasty. Had Heinrich Schliemann been born an ancient Greek, as he fervently wished he had been, he would surely have found his way onto someone's list as the 'first discoverer' of Aegean Bronze Age archaeology. Making his fortune in trade, and heir to the Germans' Romantic identification with ancient Greece, Schliemann discovered a way of putting his money where his soul was by conducting hugely expensive and enormously destructive excavations at sites to which he had been led by his reading of Homer. His aim, to put it only a little unfairly, was to prove that his beloved Homer was a historian as well as an epic poet.

Hence his excavation of Hissarlik in northwest Turkey, almost certainly the site of Homer's Troy – although as current excavations are showing, Schliemann failed to take note of anything like the full extent of the late Bronze Age city (besides notoriously misdating Priam's Troy by about a millennium). Hence, too, his further digs at Mycenae, Tiryns and Orchomenus (the supposed Treasury of Minyas) – with Cnossus escaping his attentions only because the Turks, their fingers burned at Troy, would not grant permission for him to dig there.

Two Homeric palaces, however, remained not only undug but unidentified until well into the present century: Menelaus' Sparta and old Nestor's Pylos. In fact, Menelaus' palace has yet to be certainly identified – if there ever was a palace, or indeed a Menelaus. But of the location of the real original of Nestor's Pylos there has been no doubt since 1939, when on the very brink of the Second World War the American archaeologist, Carl Blegen, struck gold – or rather the palace's archive room. Soon after the War, and thanks to work done on the Pylos tablets, their 'Linear B' script (as Arthur Evans had dubbed it on the basis of his finds at Cnossus) was deciphered as transcribing an early form of the Greek language. The rest, as they say, is history – 'Greek' history, that is, which could now be traced back in some sense at least to about 1200 BCE.

Heinrich Schliemann (1822–90) made a fortune in trade, in (among other articles) furs. Here we see him, the very model of a bourgeois entrepreneur, suitably attired in a fur-trimmed coat over evening dress. From the age of forty-six he devoted himself to unearthing the historical fact behind heroic, especially Homeric, legend.

But Linear B was a syllabary, not an alphabetic script like those devised already during the thirteenth century in the Levant by peoples with whom the late Bronze Age or Mycenaean Greeks were in contact. And it was a clumsy syllabary too, inefficient for writing Greek, as its eventual decipherers Michael Ventris and John Chadwick found to their cost. So when the script disappeared during the Dark Age of the twelfth to ninth centuries, along with the palace bureaucracies and economies that it had served, that was not necessarily a cultural disaster. And when the Greeks rediscovered writing during the eighth century, through renewed contact with those same alphabet-using Levantine peoples, it was an alphabetic not syllabic script that they borrowed and modified. One of the functions to which the new medium of communication was instantly put was the transcription of metrical verse – some scholars indeed believe that this may have been one of the main reasons why the Greeks adopted alphabetic writing in the first place.

One of the nicest of the early surviving examples of written verse was scratched on a pottery drinking cup of the last quarter of the eighth century excavated on the island of Ischia in the bay of Naples. The cup itself has a history. Made on Rhodes, it was brought to Ischia on a trading vessel that had perhaps been built on the island of Euboea. The settlement on Ischia had certainly been founded by Euboean Greeks only a generation or so before our Rhodian cup was transported there and eventually buried as a grave-good.

It is the message, however, rather than the medium that tells us most about the cultural world of these adventurous and much-travelled early Greeks. The three lines of verse, according to one possible reading, go something like this:

Nestor's highly potable cup am I:
Whoever drinks this cupful, straight
upon him
Desire for fair-crowned Aphrodite
will seize.

The first of the three lines is in the trochaic metre, but the second two are hexameters: the metre of Homer. And although 'Nestor' could conceivably be the real name of the cup's owner, it is clearly also a humorous allusion to *the* cup of Nestor – as described in the eleventh book of the *Iliad*. Already, by about 720 BCE, therefore, a Greek colonial at the outermost western fringe of the expanding Greek world was in this small way self-consciously asserting his Greekness through the great epic tradition that linked the Greeks of the eighth century to their forebears of half a millennium or more before.

Linear B tablet, thirteenth-century BCE, from Pylos. This accidentally baked clay tablet shows a list of goods in Mycenaean script, represented by ideograms and number symbols.

Cyprus in the fifth century BCE was occupied, as it had been for centuries, by both Greek speakers and Semitic speakers of Phoenician origin, who were usually hostile to each other. Unlike the Greeks of the Aegean heartland, the Cypriot Greeks tended still to be organized in king-doms, and it is from the kingdom of Idalium **that this bronze 'tablet' of (probably) the 470s comes. On the back of it, in thirty-one lines of script (syllabic not alphabetic), is recorded a con**tract between King Stasicyprus and the city of Idalium, on the one hand, and Onasilus, a doctor, and his brothers, on the other. The contract's context is a siege, probably the one conducted around 480 by neighbouring Phoenician Citium and its Persian backers. Provided onasilus and his brothers tended the casualties without a fee, they were guaranteed, under oath, rich rewards in either cash or land. To ensure that both sides kept to their oaths the tablet was hung up in the Temple of Athena for the goddess to oversee. By 450, however, Idalium had succumbed to the control of Citium.

(*Opposite*) Conjectural recon-struction of migration routes followed by different groups of Greek-speakers, which pro-duced eventually the historical distribution of the four main dialects: Ionic, Aeolic, Arcado-Cypriot and Doric.

Second, Ionic, Aeolic and Arcado-Cypriot leave dialectally unaccounted for the swathe of the Greek mainland running down the west coast from historic Epirus to the north shore of the Corinthian gulf and embracing the non-Arcadian remainder of the Peloponnese peninsula. This area dialectologists distribute between two main groups of West Greek speakers, those of the North-West group, on one hand, and the Doric-speakers (or Dorians), on the other. The latter were confined to the Peloponnese and its northerly extension, the Isthmus of Corinth.

A confirmation of the migration theory could perhaps be inferred from the fact that Doric-speakers occupy a linguistic band stretching across the southern Aegean, from the Peloponnese to the south-west corner of Asia Minor and adjacent islands such as Rhodes. Indeed, the simplest version of the theory would relate all the migrations to each other and suggest that it was the arrival from the north of Doric-speakers in central Greece and the Peloponnese which prompted the migra-tion of Ionic- and Aeolic-speakers to Asia Minor.

That, however, despite – or because of – the apparent support it receives from later Greek myth-history, may be just a little too simple. We do not in fact know exactly when and where the four main dialect-groups were formed, nor precisely what relationship the dialect-differentiation bore to the other ways in which the many small and scattered Greek communities identified themselves culturally in this confusingly fluid period. Many historians, for example, would deny the reality of any 'Dorian invasion' of southern Greece from the north, and some philologists detect traces of proto-Doric dialect already present in Linear B Greek.

What we do know is that dialect was not in itself the be-all and end-all of identity, then or ever. Dorians and Ionians, although they were differentiated by some mutually exclusive religious and other cultural practices – the Ionian Apaturia nd the Dorian Carneia religious festivals, for instance – were nevertheless united

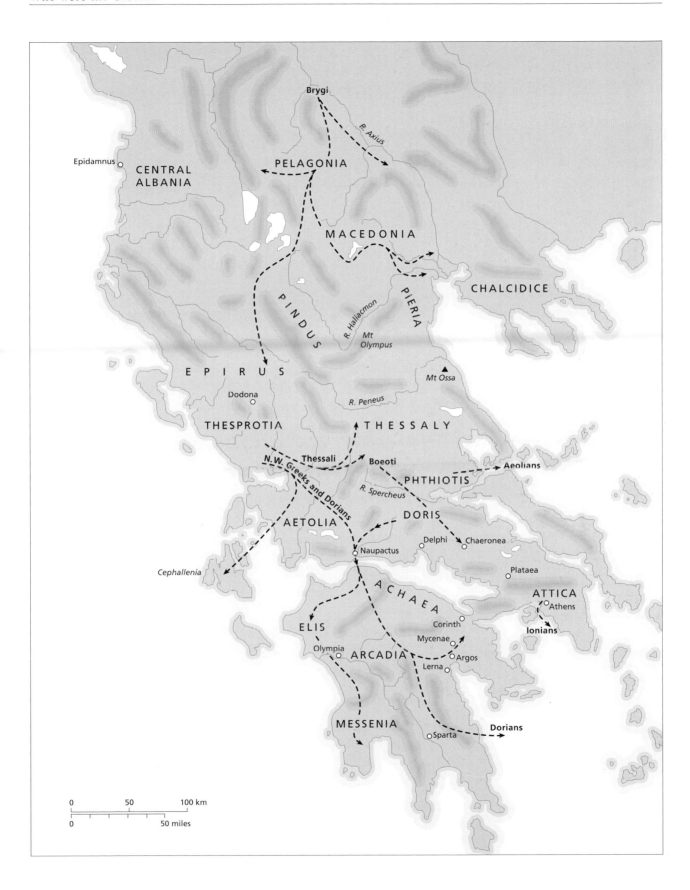

Brygi

R. Axius

PELAGONIA

Epidamnus

CENTRAL
ALBANIA

MACEDONIA

CHALCIDICE

PINDUS

R. Haliacmon

PIERIA

Mt
Olympus

Mt Ossa

EPIRUS

Dodona

R. Peneus

THESPROTIA

THESSALY

Thessali

Boeoti

Aeolians

N.W. Greeks and Dorians

PHTHIOTIS

R. Spercheus

AETOLIA

DORIS

Delphi

Chaeronea

Naupactus

Plataea

Cephallenia

ACHAEA

ATTICA

Athens

ELIS

Corinth

Ionians

Olympia

Mycenae

ARCADIA

Argos

Lerna

MESSENIA

Sparta

Dorians

0   50   100 km

0   50 miles

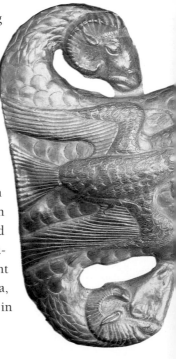

(Above) Towards the end of the sixth century one or perhaps two immigrant Greek artists from East Greece decorated a series of fine water-jars for their Etruscan patrons in Caere. This scene illustrates the myth of the Greek culture-hero Heracles' adventures at the would-be murderous hands of the Egyptian king Busiris. While Heracles is shown heroically nude, in good Greek style, the effeminate and panic-stricken orientals are elaborately clothed. The painter has cheekily reversed the official Egyptian iconography of the Pharaoh who tramples on his defeated enemies.

culturally by far more than divided them. Doric-speaking Spartans and Ionic-speaking Athenians were perfectly able to understand each other – Aristophanic jokes suggesting otherwise were just that. Dialect, moreover, should not be confused with ethnicity, let alone race. Greeks were Greeks, whether they spoke Theban Aeolic, Siphnian Ionic, Rhodian Doric, or Phigaleian Arcado-Cypriot.

'THE COLONIZATION MOVEMENT'

There were two further Greek population movements with dialectal and other cultural implications. First, between about 750 and 550 BCE there occurred what is often referred to in modern writing as 'the colonization movement'. Actually, both 'the' and 'colonization' are misleading. Ancient Greeks were always moving around the Mediterranean area, founding or joining new permanent settlements – not just in

(Left) *(Left)* Non-Greek Thracians picked up the Greek alphabet from the Greeks who lived along the north shore of the Aegean. Here a silver libation vessel has been inscribed 'KOTYOS', presumably the genitive of the male personal name Kotys, before being interred in a grave datable around 360 BCE.

the eighth to sixth centuries BCE. 'Colonization' is misleading because most of the new Greek foundations of the eighth to sixth centuries began as independent political communities, neither outposts of empire nor dependencies of their metropolitan founders. However, in all fairness it must be added that it was this extended population movement and no other which resulted in the spatial definition of 'Hellas' as stretching from the Straits of Gibraltar to the eastern end of the Black Sea. Megara's foundation of Byzantium had perhaps the longest-lasting historical consequences, but it had also founded rather earlier a Sicilian Megara, which soon became a city of some consequence too.

What caused this mass movement of Greeks was some combination of 'push' and 'pull' factors, varying in individual cases. The attractions of Etruscan metals (felt

(Below) This handsome object, a gold fish, was found in 1882 at Vettersfelde (now Witaskowo in west Poland); made about 500 BCE, it is usually classified as 'Scytho-Greek', that is as made either by a Greek craftsman influenced by Scythian ideas or, more likely, by a native Scythian in contact with Greek influences transmitted by the immigrants who had been making their way into the northern Black Sea area from the mid-seventh century on.

also by their Phoenician rivals as traders and patrons), or of the profits to be made in Levantine or Egyptian entrepôts, weighed most with some. For others it was the pressure of economic or political disaster at home. The evidence rarely allows us to be sure of the balance of decisive factors in the case of any individual settlement. Archaeology does, however, reveal a remarkably complex pattern of cultural interchange, especially between Greeks and non-Greeks. Sometimes it is not clear

Greece and Egypt

A wooden panel painting from the shrine of Isis at Saqqara, depicting a thoroughly familiar Egyptian scene of men leading cattle, but executed in a purely Ionian, East Greek style of about 500 BCE. By then both Egypt and Ionia were no longer politically independent, being alike subjects of the mighty Persian empire. But common political dependence was perfectly compatible with continued artistic interchange.

Ancient Greek civilization and culture were crucially influenced at different times by contact with the orient, specifically with Egypt, Cyprus and elsewhere in the Middle East. Greeks and Egyptians had had cultural and commercial interconnections as early as the third millennium BCE. One modern school of thought goes so far as to credit prehistoric Egypt with having been the immediate source of the Greeks' religious pantheon. More soberly, interconnections between Greece and Egypt ceased during the Dark Age and did not actively resume until the late eighth century. In the following century they became sufficiently intense for Greeks, especially from the islands and Anatolia, to institute a permanent

settlement in the Delta at a place known to the Greeks at Naucratis. This was primarily a trading post, a port of exchange of Egyptian goods and produce for Greek artifacts. One tangible result of this commerce is the wooden statuette (see p. 254) of a woman found on Samos and preserved thanks to the exceptional, waterlogged conditions of the shrine of Hera: perhaps she was thought to represent a goddess and so to be a suitable present for Hera.

But even if the Greeks of the early historic era did not derive the idea and identity of their pantheon from Egypt, they certainly did borrow from the Egyptians their characteristic manner of representing gods and other male

whether an item was made by a Greek or a native craftsman; in other cases non-Greeks adopted Greek letter-forms and other Greek cultural trappings without being considered any the less 'barbarian' by their Greek neighbours.

As for the literary evidence, what this emphasizes is the sentimental, allegedly genetic, nature of the ties between a 'colony' and its 'mother-city'. In genuinely colonial societies (Canada, the United States,

figures in hard stone sculpture. This granite statue *(far right)* of a man in a loincloth from Karnak belongs to the early seventh century, but the block-like way of presenting the standing male figure already had a very long local tradition. Stylistically fixed forms of art, preserved over centuries and even millennia, were in fact an Egyptian hallmark – presumably because it was felt unwise or impossible to improve on something so aesthetically pleasing. The Greeks felt differently, and, conscious or unconscious, a definite movement away from the stylization of their Egyptian masters towards an increasingly naturalistic depiction of the human figure is observable in Greek sculpture during the sixth century. Also characteristically Greek is the heroic nudity of the male (but not the female) figure.

(Right) **Kouros** (*c.*610–600 BCE), **marble, height nearly 2 metres. This example of the** *Kouros* **('Youth') type was made for display in a rural Athenian cemetery. The Greek sculptor's ultimate Egyptian model is exemplified by the sculpture** *(far right)* **of Vizier Bakenrenef, in green schist, made during the reign of Psamtik (in Greek Psammetichus) I (664–609 BCE).**

The tomb of Philip

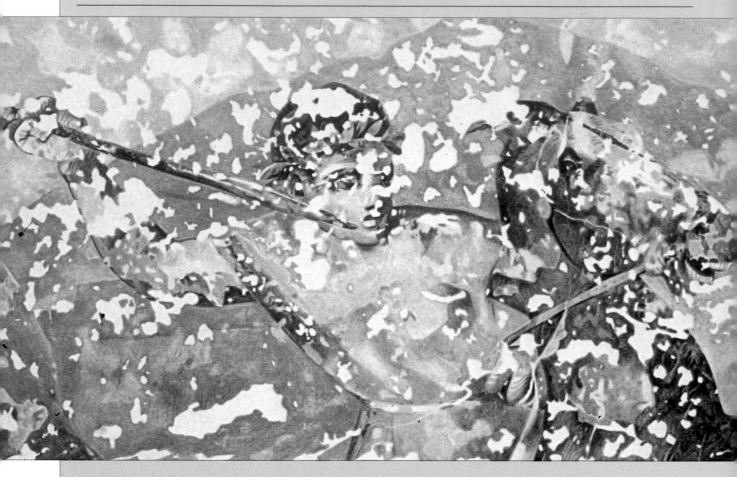

Macedon, eponymous ancestor of the historical Macedonians, is mentioned in a fragmentary poem of Hesiod in the usual Greek mythological style. But since the northern Macedonians lived on the very fringes of the Greek world, and since their language (although probably a dialect of Greek) was not always readily comprehensible to other Greeks, King Alexander I had to get his claim to Greekness formally validated by the authorities in charge of the Panhellenic (all-Greek and only-Greek) Olympic Games before he could compete in them in the early fifth century.

Not all Greeks, however, were equally convinced of the validity of the claim, and perhaps it was to counter this suspicion of un-Greekness that Alexander's royal successors spent a lot of time and effort in promoting their genuine Hellenism. Euripides, for example, was invited by Archelaus to his new royal court at Pella, where he died, and athletic games were instituted at Dium on Macedon's southern border to serve as a sort of northern Olympics.

But the full extent of the Macedonian kings' Hellenic self-promotion became apparent only within the past couple of decades through the discovery and excavation of a number of impressively built and lavishly equipped royal tombs at ancient Aegae (modern Verghina). Of these, the most magnificent by far is the one confidently ascribed to King Philip II, who died – or rather was assassinated – at Aegae in 336.

The fresco (detail *above*) that adorned the exterior of the tomb above its Doric-style facade was a continuous frieze illustrating a favourite royal pastime, hunting, which was performed on horseback in a society in which horses retained a crucial military as well as symbolic significance. Among the riders, portraits of Philip himself, and of his son and successor Alexander the Great, have been recognized.

Within the tomb's main chamber the deceased was buried in a golden casket (*bottom right*) bearing on its lid the sunburst motif that was the 'logo' of the Macedonian royal dynasty. A second golden casket was placed in the tomb's antechamber, and in this was found an unusually well preserved cloth of purple and gold (*right*) used to wrap the burnt bones of a woman.

'When they were all gathered together in one place, first they extinguished the pyre with gleaming wine ... and then gathered the white bones and put them in a golden box, wrapping them in soft purple cloths ...' – not an eyewitness account of the burial of Philip and his consort, but part of Homer's description of the burial of Hector at the very end of the *Iliad*. How better to assert one's Greekness than by maintaining, apparently, the royal burial customs of the great age of the Greek heroes as described by the national bard?

Within the elaborate burial chamber at Verghina, known as the Tomb of Philip, Greek excavators found a set of fourteen small ivory heads which they plausibly took to represent members of the Macedonian royal house. Philip's may be distinguished by the loss of one eye, caused by an arrow-head that pierced his skull during the siege of Greek Methone in 354. A head (*below*) was reconstructed in wax by forensic scientist Richard Neave from the remains of the skull (which showed damage to the eye socket) found in the main chamber of the tomb mound.

Australia, for example), one thing that a settler family does not easily forget is its roots in the old country. Such roots, in the Greek case, were kept regularly watered by religion; both through two-way participation in festivals common to mother- and daughter-city, and by participation in such Panhellenic or all-Greek festivals as the Olympic and Pythian Games, which acquired sharper definition and careful organization in the course of the sixth century.

Not that this prevented Greeks fighting each other. Corinth and its daughter Corcyra (modern Corfu, traditionally founded 734) were reputedly the first colonial pair to come to blows, within a couple of generations of the latter's foundation. Nor did it prevent Greeks from siding with non-Greeks against their fellow-Greeks. A particularly awkward case was Sicily, where the Greek settlers found themselves having to contend not only with each other and with native Sicels but also with Phoenician colonists from Carthage, whose African mother-city showed an alarming propensity to intervene militarily on the island in defence of its commercial interests.

Nevertheless, by about 500 the new enlarged 'colonial' Greek world had acquired the rudiments of a genuine sense of Hellenic identity. This was just in time for a few heroic Greek cities to resist the Persian onslaught from the east, precisely as 'Hellenes'.

PHILIP OF MACEDON — AND HELLAS

Almost 150 years after Great King Xerxes' unsuccessful attempt on mainland Greece, the military boot was on the other foot. Philip II, at the head of a Greece that he had newly conquered, prepared to invade the Persian empire in the name of a crusade of revenge for Xerxes' sacrilegious destruction of Greek shrines. Philip was assassinated before he could effect his grand design personally, but his son Alexander fully earned his tag 'the Great' in a campaign of conquest lasting a decade – and still incomplete at the moment of his untimely death in 323.

Before the recent spectacular archaeological discoveries at Verghina and elsewhere in Macedonia, the extent of Philip's Greekness and the genuineness of his commitment to the fostering and expansion of Hellenism were seriously in doubt. But whatever his or his son's true motivation was, there is no doubt as to the outcome of Alexander's conquering achievements. In the third century and later, Greek was being spoken as far east as Afghanistan and Pakistan, and Greek religion and culture had penetrated the Indian subcontinent. Nearer to home, Egypt and the Middle East were, with the exception only of some parts of

Palestine, firmly in Greek or hellenizing hands. This was the cultural world that captivated its eventual political conqueror, Rome, which in turn ensured that the Western heritage would be ultimately Greek (see Epilogue).

INTERMEZZO

Paul Cartledge

Historical Outline c.1500–146 BCE

The opening date of 1500 BCE is largely a convenient round figure. It does not mark any reliably attested Greek event, but falls towards the beginning of the era known archaeologically as the Late Bronze Age – or as the Mycenaean period, in deference

The massive enceinte wall encircling six fabulously rich Late Bronze Age shaft-graves was constructed in about 1300, as part of Mycenae's rebuilt defence system. But the graves themselves are some 300 years older. They contain multiple burials, both male and female, presumably all belonging to a single family or dynasty. Like Homer's epithet for the city as a whole, they are 'rich in gold', though gold is but one of the precious materials from which the vast store of grave-goods was made. It was a gold death-mask depicting an impressively moustachioed male that prompted Schliemann to tele-graph the King of Greece that he had 'gazed upon the face of Agamemnon' (see p. 38) – though actually if there was a Homeric Agamemnon, he would have lived in the thirteenth not the sixteenth century BCE.

(*Opposite top*) This outstretched skeleton of a woman bedecked with gold jewellery and other ornaments was entombed beneath a large purpose-built burial structure at Lefkandi on the island of Euboea not later than 950 BCE. Under the same structure was buried her husband, whose cremated remains were placed, together with his cloak, in a lavishly decorated bronze *krater* or wine-mixing vessel probably made on Cyprus. Beside the urn were his iron sword, his spear and a whetstone, marks of his warrior status.

(*Opposite bottom*) Lefkandi Centaur. This terracotta figurine, partly wheel-made, was crafted around 900 BCE. It has been called the first masterpiece of Greek sculpture. Elephantine ears, the hint of a smile, a deliberate gash to its left knee – the figure is instinct with vigorous individuality. Undoubtedly it alludes to some myth, but which one we cannot say for certain; one possibility is that it is meant to depict wise Chiron, tutor of the young Achilles.

to Homer's picture of a loosely united Greece presided over by the lord of Mycenae 'rich in gold'. The terminal date of 146 BCE does, however, mark a specific event: the last unavailing attempt by large numbers of mainland Greeks to prevent their political subjugation by Rome.

Within this span of thirteen to fourteen centuries (see Chronology) the emphasis in Part II will fall on the period between c.500 and 300 BCE (see p. xiv).

MYCENAE

In the seventeenth and sixteenth centuries BCE (these dates for Greece are derived by cross-reference to Egyptian regnal chronology, which is fixed ultimately by astronomical calculations) something rather remarkable occurred in the Peloponnese, for reasons that are ill-understood. At Mycenae a new dynasty or dynasties arose which had a, for us, fortunate taste for lavish burial.

Two intercutting grave circles found there enclosed extraordinarily rich shaftgraves. In about 1300 the later of these (confusingly labelled Circle A) was incorporated reverently into the new circuit of Mycenae's city-wall. Not surprisingly, their amateur excavator and devotee of Homer, Heinrich Schliemann (see p. 42), succumbed instantly to the temptation to link these shaft-grave rulers with Greek legend – or rather to transform legend into history by identifying an especially handsome gold grave-mask as that of Homer's Agamemnon (see p. 38).

Actually, though, if prehistoric Greece ever was united in a loose, personalized confederation and equipped to fight a Homeric-style Trojan War, that would have been in the thirteenth century, hundreds of years after the burial of Schliemann's 'Agamemnon'. And there are now not a few sceptical historians who – in defiance of continuing archaeological efforts (inspired to some extent still by the desire to authenticate Homer) – incline to believe that the Trojan War, or at any rate Homer's Trojan War, may be nothing but a looking-glass fiction; a mirror in which later, wishfully thinking Greeks could see reflected (and distorted) an ideal image of their glorious past. The truth will never be known for sure. The likeliest site of Homer's Troy has yet to yield anything like proof of a large-scale Greek attack at the relevant period. In any case, archaeology alone could never prove (or disprove) the role of the fabulously beautiful Helen in motivating this supposedly ten-years' war.

THE GREEK DARK AGE

All the same, archaeology has shown conclusively that, in the thirteenth century, mainland Greece (from Thessaly southwards) and the adjacent Aegean area across to the west Turkish coast were as prosperous and densely settled as they had ever been – or were to be again for another 500 years or more. However, in 1200 or thereabouts something went catastrophically wrong. The palatial sites suffered serious destructions. At Mycenae this happened more than once. Some were annihilated, as in the case of Pylos in south-west Greece. With the palaces went the centralized, redistributive economies of which the Linear B documents are the surviving evidence

(see p.37). Artistic, economic and political interconnections between different regions of Greece, once so strong, now diminished or disappeared altogether.

Fast forward a hundred years or so to the eleventh century BCE and we see a totally different picture from that of *c*.1200. There are far fewer inhabited sites, with much smaller populations, and vastly less wealth of material possessions, whether used in life or deposited in graves after death. The Linear B script has disappeared and not been replaced by any other writing system. In short, we find ourselves in a Dark Age.

Darkness is of course to some extent in the eye of the beholder, and it may be that future finds will modify the picture somewhat, but generally the situation seems to have been bleak, and life poor, solitary and short, if not necessarily brutish. There were, however, a few exceptions, notably Cyprus, to which Mycenaeans emigrated (or fled?) in the twelfth and eleventh centuries, using a descendant of the Linear B script. And some areas recovered earlier and more strongly than others. There was obvious light in the darkness at Lefkandi on the island of Euboea, for example, in the form of metal-working and overseas contacts well before the end of the tenth century. Also, in Attica and Crete, some form of continuous occupation was sustained throughout the Dark Age. On the other hand, in Laconia, formerly home to a significant Mycenaean culture and the seat of Homer's Menelaus, darkness remained the order of the day.

MIGRATIONS

Greek myth-historical tradition had it that after the Trojan War there was a disturbed period of palace revolutions and wanderings of peoples within and outside Greece, first eastwards then to the south and south-east. So far this accords with the archaeological picture. But one of those alleged wanderings, the migration of

Sparta, situated in Homer's 'hollow Lacedaemon', rose to prominence only after the Bronze Age (when the main settlement hereabouts had been located further to the east). The rich alluvium of the perennially watered Eurotas river valley ensured an abundance of crops. Mountains to east and west provided natural protection, and for long the Spartans disdained to build a city-wall. The site of Sparta was first extensively excavated in the first decades of the twentieth century by archaeologists from the British School at Athens. Rather to their surprise, the Sparta they uncovered was not always the cultural desert portrayed by the written sources. Exploration and excavation continue actively to this day.

Dorians from northern or central Greece into the Peloponnese, is thus far unproven archaeologically. The site of Sparta, for example, where lived the most powerful Dorian community of the historical period, cannot be shown to have been occupied from after *c.*1200 to much before 800. If there was a Dorian immigration here, it has either left no recoverable trace, or it occurred much later than myth-history claimed. The latter is much the more plausible of these two hypotheses, not least because the historical Spartans' claim that they were not invading newcomers but simply returning to reclaim the land from which their leaders had been expelled before the Trojan War is so palpably a charter myth.

The Spartans were by no means the only Greeks of the Dark Age to be staking a claim to their holdings in the language of myth. The succession of bards who sang the lays that eventually became the written Homeric epics were doing the same for their Greek audiences in Asia Minor during the eleventh to eighth

centuries. Once regular connections between the mainland and Asia Minor were resumed in the ninth century, Homeric and other epic poetry played a vital part in affirming a common Greek cultural identity, as did the new or remodelled religious shrines of Olympia, Delphi and Delos that attracted pilgrims from many different Greek communities.

The Greeks who, from the middle of the eighth century, set out in the opposite direction to make new homes for themselves in the west also took with them their bardic traditions. One of the most eloquent Greek artifacts to make the long journey from Rhodes to Ischia in the bay of Naples before 700 is a drinking-cup (see p. 43). It is, in itself, fairly undistinguished, but its owner had it stylishly incised with Homeric-style hexameter verses written in the Euboean script.

THE RISE OF THE POLIS

Coinciding with, and maybe because of, this Greek 'colonization' movement came the rise of the *polis*, or citizen-state. For the first time Greeks could refer to themselves as Athenians or Spartans or whatever, identifying themselves as citizens not of a country but of rudimentary political communities. Or rather some Greeks could: as always, women were allowed no direct part in the political process, despite the importance of their reproductive and religious roles. It was these fledgling communities which enabled the emigration of large numbers of Greek settlers round almost all the Mediterranean and the Black Sea in the course of the next centuries. In some cases indeed, as for example on Thera in the later seventh century, emigration was enforced on unwilling citizens to meet an economic crisis. Not all Greek communities, however, participated equally in this movement of overseas migration. In fact, two of the most important, Athens and Sparta, did so hardly at all.

Athens
During the Dark Age, so later Athenian tradition liked to boast, Athens had played a key role in the movement of people from mainland Greece to western Asia Minor in the eleventh to ninth centuries. Whatever its genuine role may then have been, Athens did not significantly colonize overseas in the eighth or seventh centuries.

What seems to have happened is that from the later eighth century Attica, its surrounding territory, began to fill up with its overspill. There was at first no need felt for Athenians also to migrate abroad to relieve this situation. Only later, towards the end of the sixth century, for reasons probably to do mainly with domestic politics rather than economic necessity, did Athens found official settlements abroad in the approaches to the Black Sea.

Sparta
Sparta in the late eighth century did send, or at any rate recognize, one overseas settlement as an official Spartan foundation, Taras (modern Taranto) in South Italy. Later traditions suggested this outcrop was the result of extreme political

unrest at home, but modern scholars have tied it rather to the Spartans' chief pre-occupation at this time – their war of conquest and expropriation against their Messenian neighbours on the far side of the Taygetus mountain range in south-west Peloponnese.

The original motivation of that war is unclear, but its outcome left the Spartans in possession of a huge city-territory (some 3000 square miles, about twice as large as that of the next biggest in the Greek world, Syracuse), and of a large number of unfree Greek labourers called helots working the land for them under duress. In the seventh century, Sparta was the most powerful and perhaps already the most odd of Greek cities. At any rate, Sparta (see chapters 5, 7 and 8) was later famous or notorious for its austere social regimen, peculiar sexual practices, dominantly military mores, and all-encompassing political and economic arrangements, all supposedly prescribed at one go by an amazingly far-sighted law-giver, Lycurgus (see p. 82). More probably, they were the result of a fairly long process rather than a one-off enactment.

HOPLITE WARFARE

Something Sparta shared with all the other most important cities of early Greece was the adoption of *hoplite* military equipment and fighting formation (see p. 168). By 600 BCE at the latest, hoplite phalanx warfare between massed ranks of heavily armed infantrymen had become the norm in mainland Greece. Battles took place on and over the farmland on which each city depended for its independent existence.

Some of the richest citizens continued to fight as cavalrymen, or at least had themselves transported to the battlefield on horseback. At the other end of the social spectrum the poorest fought as light-armed support troops on land, or crewed the warships of maritime cities. But the hoplite, standing his ground in solidarity with his fellow-phalangites, became the dominant figure of the era, both politically and socially as well as militarily. Indeed he remained so even after the rise of Athenian democracy in the fifth century, the power base of which was actually the fleet.

TYRANNY

Somehow this hoplite revolution of the seventh century was connected to the rise of tyranny that affected or afflicted a significant number of the more prominent cities. *Tyrant* may have been a loan-word from the Orient, possibly Lydia, but the phenomenon itself did not require external inspiration. At first in Argos or Corinth, then Sicyon, Megara, Mytilene, Miletus and elsewhere, sole rulers came to power either in defiance of or just in despite of the existing rules of government. Being usurpers, although they all seem to have emerged out of the previously ruling aristocratic élites, they required force of arms as well as persuasive personal charm to keep themselves in power. This force was provided, not without reward, by the hoplites, or by the critical majority of them.

Underneath the Sacred Way at Delphi just before the Second World War French archaeologists uncovered the remains of a shrine dating to around the middle of the sixth century BCE. The shrine had apparently been destroyed in a fire and its remains ceremonially buried below the paving stones of the pathway leading up to the temple of Delphi's patron god, Apollo. Among the finds were a life-size silver bull, with horns and genitalia of gold, and three life-size chryselephantine statues, made of gold and ivory over a wooden core. It is thought that they represented Apollo (right), his twin sister Artemis and their mother Leto. The style of the modelling has suggested that they were created by Ionian craftsmen working on commission for the fabulously wealthy King Croesus of Lydia.

Sparta somehow managed to avoid the threat of tyranny, probably because of the paramount political necessity of maintaining a united front among the citizens against the helots, and probably because all Spartan citizens – not just the top 30–40 per cent of citizen males that was usual in other cities – were hoplites.

Athens managed only to postpone tyranny, but the way it did so was crucial to its later emergence as the first Greek democracy. The first attempt at tyranny in Athens, by an aristocrat and Olympic victor called Cylon in c.632, provoked a concerted local resistance, partly because he presented himself with foreign military support from his father-in-law, Theagenes, the tyrant of Megara. Cylon was unceremoniously, indeed sacrilegiously, put to death, slaughtered with his supporters at the altar where they had taken sanctuary. But his attempt does seem to have prompted the ruling Athenian aristocracy to draw up, or at any rate to publish for the first time, some formal set of laws in about 620. This rudimentary law-code, of which we know only the provisions regarding homicide, was attributed to a man with the sinister name of Draco ('snake'), but despite our word 'draconian' not all the punishments were actually written in blood.

A mere twenty years later, though, the domestic conditions that had elsewhere fostered tyranny seem to have arisen in Athens. However, Solon, a moderately wealthy aristocrat who many feared and some hoped would play the tyrant, chose to assume the role of law-giver instead, arbitrating between the rich and powerful few and the poor and dispossessed majority of Athenian citizens. His reforms of 594 were both economic and political, and they had far-reaching effects on the distribution and exercise of political power, and on the definition of Athenian citizenship.

His reforms did not go uncontested. From about 560 Athens did at last experience a tyranny, or rather three tyrannies held by the same man, Pisistratus. The third of these, established in about 545, finally proved stable and durable. Remarkably, Pisistratus chose to retain the political reforms of Solon, while at the same time extending economic prosperity and fostering a sense of 'national' Athenian pride and unity. Between 545 and 510 Pisistratus and his sons transformed the physical and symbolic shape of Athens, preparing the way – as of course no one could have guessed – for democracy.

TROUBLE FROM THE EAST

Meanwhile, away to the East a cloud was looming: the rise of the Achaemenid Persian empire under Cyrus the Great (559–30). By about the time that Pisistratus was establishing himself firmly at Athens, Cyrus had extended his sway as far west as Ionia, the Greek territory of the Aegean littoral in Asia Minor. In the process he had absorbed, among much else, Mesopotamia and the gold-laden Lydian kingdom of the philhellenic Croesus.

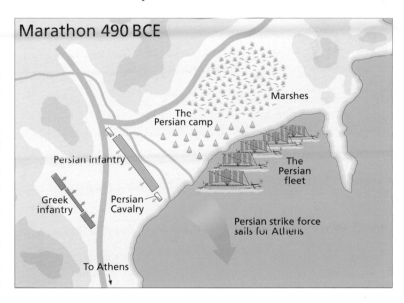

In east Greece a prodigious intellectual revolution, pioneered by Thales of Miletus (*c*.600), was well underway by the mid-sixth century (see p. 291). An outlook was taking hold among the boldest intellects of Ionia that with hindsight might be called scientific, in that it sought to explain the cosmos in natural not religious terms with the aid of human reason and (some) empirical investigation. Thales was later accorded the status of one of the Seven Sages of early Greece – most of these were

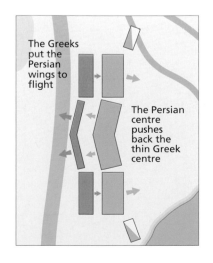

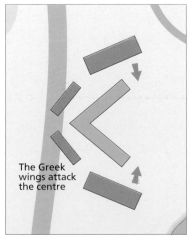

(Previous page) The Battle of Marathon, in 490 BCE, has etched itself into not only Athenian and ancient Greek, but all Western memory, as a triumph of civilization over barbarism, of David over Goliath. The truth is hard to discover beneath the overlay of triumphalist myth. To punish Athens for supporting a Greek rebellion in western Asia Minor, Great King Darius I of Persia sent a fleet and an army under the command of a Mede, Datis, and one of his own brothers, Artaphernes. Forewarned, the Athenians dispatched an army to their eastern coastline, around Marathon, opposite the island of Euboea, where the Persians had already destroyed the city of Eretria. Thus blocked from approaching Athens by road, the Persians planned to send their main strike force by sea to attack Athens itself, but decided first to engage the Athenians – and their allies from Plataea – at Marathon to prevent them from returning to defend their city. Miltiades, the inspirational Athenian general, was credited with devising the winning tactics. Keeping their centre thin and their wings deep, the Athenians and Plataeans advanced to within bowshot and then charged, despite their heavy arms and armour. The Persian wings gave way, whereupon the Greek wings turned in on the Persian centre and crushed it. Reportedly some 6000 were killed on the Persian side, as against only 192 Athenians, who after their death were regarded – and worshipped – as heroes.

practical men, however, not ivory-tower intellectuals. They were as likely to devise ways of damming huge rivers or predicting eclipses as to investigate the ultimate matter of the universe.

Another Ionian sage, Xenophanes of Colophon, whose long life spanned the sixth and fifth centuries, is even credited with a Darwin-like interest in fossils. Like Pythagoras of Samos, he chose to emigrate from Ionia to southern Italy, partly to escape the engulfing Persian tide of conquest. Here he is in reflective and retrospective mood:

> So you should speak by the fire in the season of winter,
> lying on a soft couch, full of food,
> drinking sweet wine, chewing chickpeas:
> 'who are you, from where among men,
> how many years do you have, sir?
> how old were you when the Mede came?'

The Greeks habitually confused the Persians with their kinsmen and neighbours the Medes, but they could not long remain confused about the altered geopolitical status quo. For 200 or more years they would have to reckon with the Persian empire in some shape or form. Some Greeks embraced it more or less voluntarily – they 'medized'. Others preferred a die-hard resistance, like the countrymen of Xenophanes and Pythagoras who launched the ultimately futile Ionian revolt at the start of the fifth century. Some swung from acceptance to resistance, like Polycrates the tyrant of Samos in the second half of the sixth century.

His capture and crucifixion by the local Persian satrap (viceroy) in about 522 coincided with a period of widespread instability, including outright revolt, in the Persian empire – though not in its Greek areas. That period of uncertainty was firmly ended by the empire's second founder, Darius I, who ruled from *c.*521 to 486 and succeeded in enlarging his domain at its north-western extremity. It was against him that the Ionian and other east Greeks, together with some Phoenicians of Cyprus, revolted unsuccessfully in the 490s. It was he who, in 490, to punish the Athenians for supporting their Ionian kinsmen, launched a naval expedition across the Aegean only to have it met and defeated at Marathon. This famous Greek victory provoked an inevitable Persian response, though by the time it came, in the form of a massive amphibious expedition of conquest and presumably annexation, Darius himself was dead and had been succeeded by his son Xerxes (486–465).

THE ATHENIAN EMPIRE

Xerxes in the end proved no more successful than his father. The pioneering *Histories* of Herodotus, who was born a subject of Persia in Halicarnassus, takes as its theme the heroic Greek resistance to his invasion of 480–479 and gives it a theological colouring. Anticipating Herodotus, Aeschylus, a combatant, had based our earliest surviving tragic drama, the *Persians* (472), around the mainly Athenian

In 480 and again in 479 the Persian invaders under Great King Xerxes sacked the city of Athens, not sparing even the sacred site of the Acropolis Remarkably, the invaders were repulsed, thanks not least to the inspired naval strategy of the Athenian commander Themistocles. It was he too who masterminded the rebuilding of Athens' city walls in 479/8, but the job was done in haste, and almost any stones lying to hand, worked and unworked, were thrown in. These included even gravestones, such as this one depicting in relief a boxer with a splendidly formed cauliflower ear. Gravestones like this were expensive, and perhaps our boxer was a successful competitor in the Olympic and other games.

naval victory over Xerxes at Salamis (480). But crucial though that success was, responsibility for decisive victory belonged chiefly to the land-lubberly Spartans. It was their Peloponnesian League alliance that formed the basis of the hastily thrown together Hellenic coalition (comprising only some thirty cities), and their hoplite prowess on the field of Plataea (479) that sealed the Persians' fate. But precisely because Sparta was a land-based power, it failed to capitalize on the victory. Athens seized the opportunity. By now it had easily the largest Greek *trireme* navy – built with silver from the local mines of Laurium and bursting with confidence from its feats at Salamis and Mycale (479). After restoring domestic security by rebuilding the city walls destroyed by Xerxes' troops, Athens was in a position to form a naval alliance now known as the Delian League (after the island of Delos where the oaths of alliance were exchanged in 478/7, and where the League's treasury and other common resources were at first based).

The Delian League became an Athenian empire, some would say sooner rather than later, but at any rate well before the Athenians reached some sort of accommodation with Persia in mid-century (Peace of Callias) and turned their attention to fighting Sparta instead (First Peloponnesian War). Like Persia, Athens grew fat on the profits of empire, but quite unlike Persia ploughed them into a rich tilth of political democratization. The reforms of Ephialtes and Pericles in the late 460s and 450s confirmed and rewarded the shift of military and political influence from the Athenian hoplites to the *thetes*, the lowest of Athens' four property-classes, who rowed the trireme warships. The Acropolis

Somewhere in the Oxus river valley, in ancient Bactria (modern Tadjikistan), a heterogeneous hoard of gold and silver objects was unearthed by chance in 1877. A majority date to the fifth or fourth centuries, when Bactria was part of the Achaemenid Persian empire, and were probably made in local workshops. But Greek influence seems present in the un-Persian nudity of this fifth-century silver statuette of a youth with pierced ears and gilt Persian-style head-dress.

The limestone temple of Apollo the Helper at Bassae in Arcadia was built in about 420 BCE. It may commemorate deliverance from a bout of plague; alternatively, it may have been paid for by mercenaries on their successful return from lucrative fighting abroad, possibly for Persian paymasters. Naturally poor, Arcadia was a prime supplier of mercenary soldiers. The temple's supposed architect, the Athenian Ictinus ('the kite'), was also credited with co-designing the Parthenon. Distinctive features include the earliest known 'Corinthian' column capital and an interior frieze, depicting Heracles in struggle with the Amazons and (as here) Centaurs with Lapiths. The Lapith women are clinging on to an Archaic-style statue of a goddess, perhaps Apollo's sister Artemis.

building-programme, of which the Parthenon was the jewel in the crown, physically represented Athens' proud belief that thanks to the divine favour of their patron, Athena, the city stood four-square for freedom in opposition both to Persian oriental despotism and to the narrower, oligarchic regimes favoured in Greece by Sparta. The second half of the fifth century, however, saw the debilitating and ultimately (for Athens) disastrous clash in arms of these two antithetical Greek powers.

THE PELOPONNESIAN WAR

Thucydides, hoping to trump not only his immediate predecessor and rival, Herodotus, but also Homer, announced that the war he was going to write up had been the greatest war in all Hellenic history. Certainly what we know as the Peloponnesian War of 431 to 404 did produce an enormous disturbance, not only in the Aegean Greek world but as far west as Sicily.

At first the two sides could achieve only a stalemate, but the calamitous failure of Athens' attempt to conquer Syracuse and Sicily (415–413) swung the balance sharply in Sparta's favour, especially as Athenian naval weakness in the Aegean allowed the Persians once more to intervene in Greek affairs, this time with cash aid to Sparta. In their desperation the Athenians were even forced to strike a gold coinage. After surviving one vicious episode of civil war and oligarchic counter-revolution, together with the loss of almost all the empire, Athens at last was brought to final submission by naval blockade and starvation in 404. The Spartans at once overthrew the democracy in Athens and replaced it with a puppet junta of convinced oligarchs. So bloodily did they rule, however, that they acquired the tag

of the 'Thirty Tyrants' and prompted even Sparta to tolerate the return of democracy to Athens in 403. The restored democracy conducted itself with sufficient prudence to last for eighty more years, before another foreign power, Macedon, put an end to it for good.

SPARTAN ASCENDANCY

The fourth century, indeed, was the heyday of Greek democracy. Cities like Chios and Thebes, which had been firmly if moderately oligarchic hitherto, now adopted some version of democratic government. Sparta, however, retained its peculiar system of government at home, and for the most part continued its traditional policy of supporting and promoting oligarchy outside. Until 371 Sparta succeeded in remaining the most powerful state in the mainland and Aegean Greek areas. But Sparta was not used, or suited, to practising aggressive imperialism outside its territorial borders, and found itself faced eventually with a fatal combination of over-reach abroad and extreme social and political tension at home.

In 386 Sparta was temporarily compelled to draw back from all military involvement overseas, including any serious anti-Persian aggression, and to acquiesce in a Peace imposed by the Persian King, Artaxerxes II. This in effect restored the political status quo obtaining in Asia before 480, when the Persian empire extended to the Aegean sea. In Greece, however, Sparta under King Agesilaus II vigorously and cynically exploited the clause of the Peace that prescribed autonomy for all Greek cities great or small by putting an end to all multi-state organizations and alliances – apart from its own Peloponnesian League. Sparta went so far indeed as to break up the confederacy of Chalcidian cities headed by Olynthus in northern Greece, and to impose a Spartan garrison on Thebes. It thereby restored and extended the position gained through the defeat of Athens in 404, but also by its blatant imperialism provoked an equal, opposite and – for once – conjoint reaction from Thebes and Athens. In 378 they combined to re-found the naval alliance of 478, but this time against Sparta not Persia. In 371 at Leuctra in Boeotia Sparta suffered its first major defeat in hoplite battle for 200 years.

This crippling blow exposed the rottenness at the core of the Spartan achievement. Within half a dozen years Sparta not only had been deprived of Messenia, and so of its most fertile farmland and more than half its servile helot workforce, but had also been obliged to accept the demise of the Peloponnesian League. Moreover, the newly founded cities of Messene (369) and Megalopolis (c.368), both sponsored by Thebes under the inspired leadership of the philosophic general Epaminondas, ensured that those losses would be permanent. Sparta now found its easiest access to Messenia

Several sources stress that a Greek city was more than just its walls, and one city – Sparta – did without city walls throughout the period of its greatest power and glory. But for the new city of Messene, created in 369 following the liberation of helots from a centuries-long servitude, they were the showiest possible demonstration of statehood and a constant provocation to the Messenians' old oppressors, the Spartans. The fortifications extend for some five miles along the tops and spurs of Mount Ithome, a stupendous engineering achievement.

through Arcadia blocked, and in Messene it was faced with a city whose identity and self-image were predicated upon irredentist hostility to the former oppressor.

In desperation Sparta turned even to its former deadly enemy Athens, which shared a deep-seated suspicion of Thebes. However, the two were unable to defeat Thebes at the second major battle to be fought at Arcadian Mantinea within sixty years (418, 362). Victory, however, brought Thebes no lasting advantage. Indeed, the squabbling and internecine fighting that had gone on between the main powers of Greece over the past two generations had left them exhausted and opened the field of potential Greek hegemony to new, northern Greek and Macedonian claimants.

PHILIP II OF MACEDON

Jason, tyrant of Pherae in Thessaly, inspired perhaps by the prowess of Dionysius, tyrant of Syracuse, the most powerful Greek of his day, had briefly threatened in the 370s to become a major force in the Greek mainland. His assassination in 370 had paved the way for the Thebans' almost equally brief moment of glory during the 360s. It was, however, Philip of Macedon, who knew Thebes from the inside at the height of its power, and who appreciated the strategic significance of Jason's unification of neighbouring Thessaly, who was successfully to apply this knowledge and understanding to the conquest and domination of a forcibly unified mainland Greece.

Having secured his throne by dint of bribery and diplomacy no less than by military prowess, Philip had next to unite his fissiparous Macedonian kingdom in the face of both Greek and non-Greek challengers. He thereafter advanced by degrees southwards, destroying Athens' ally Phocis in central Greece in 346 and thus seizing the initiative for future conquest. Decisive victory followed in 338, at Chaeronea in Boeotia, over a Greek coalition hastily put together by Athens and Thebes.

By then, and perhaps long since, Philip saw the control of Greece as a means, not an end in itself. His over-riding objective was to extend his sway to the east so as to encompass at least the western reaches of the Persian empire, the weakness of which had been conspicuously exposed by the prolonged revolt of Egypt (404–343) and the emergence of semi-independent or openly rebellious satraps.

In 338/7 Philip arranged for the establishment of what is now called the League of Corinth, an innovative combination of military alliance and permanent governmental council with himself elected as its first *hegemon* or leader. This united most of the important cities of the Greek mainland, with the notable and deliberate exception of Sparta (whose exclusion and enmity would help to cement the allies'

Though traditionally labelled 'Mausolus' this huge (almost 10-feet high) marble statue probably depicts an ancestor of the Carian ruler (377–353) who gave his name to the mausoleum. It was found at the site of the original Mausoleum, the tomb-monument erected by his sister-widow Artemisia at Halicarnassus in Caria (now Bodrum in western Turkey). Facial features and hairstyle are meant to indicate that this is the figure of a non-Greek, but the carving was done by a Greek sculptor for a strongly hellenizing dynasty which ruled a mixed population of Greeks and Carians on behalf of the Persian Great King.

loyalty to Philip). The League's first act (Philip was ever an adept exploiter of religious propaganda) was to declare a holy war on the Achaemenid empire, ostensibly in revenge for the sacrileges perpetrated by Xerxes' troops in destroying Greek holy places such as the Athenian Acropolis in 480–479. His most loyal general, Parmenion, was dispatched in 336 to establish a bridgehead in north-west Asia Minor, but before Philip himself could assume the command in person he was assassinated as he celebrated his daughter's wedding at Macedon's ceremonial capital of Aegae. If, as is widely believed, the 'Tomb of Philip' recently discovered and excavated at Verghina (see pp. 50–1) is indeed Philip's tomb, then his son and successor, Alexander the Great, clearly spared no expense in laying his father to rest, advertising through the extraordinary quantity, range and richness of burial goods the extent of Philip's conquests.

ALEXANDER THE GREAT

Alexander in 336 was only twenty, and his throne was insecure. Prominent Greek cities of the League of Corinth understandably thought they would get away with throwing off their Macedonian allegiance. They were very wrong. In 335 Alexander not only commanded an expedition northwards as far as the Danube, quelling non-Greek resistance, but he also led an army south immediately afterwards to Boeotia, covering some 300 miles in well under two weeks. Here, following the grim example of his father who had annihilated Olynthus in 348, Alexander authorized the total destruction of Thebes – apart from its religious shrines and the house that had belonged to the master lyric poet Pindar. The message was unambiguous: you resist Macedon at your peril.

In 334 Alexander felt secure enough in Greece to embark for Asia to complete his father's mission. His eleven years of phenomenally arduous and equally phenomenally successful campaigning took him as far east as the Punjab and left him notionally master not only of the Aegean Greek world but of all the old Achaemenid empire of Cyrus and Darius as well. Indeed, within half a dozen years he had become, outwardly at least, almost as much an oriental despot as a Macedonian Greek king. But he was never to return to Pella, the seat of Macedon's administrative capital. Rumour had it that at the time of his early death at Babylon in 323 he was planning even more grandiose exploits of conquest, further south and west.

ALEXANDER'S LEGACY

Alexander's meteorically brief reign ushered in what has been known since the early nineteenth century as the Hellenistic age (conventionally 323–30 BCE). The Hellenization of the Middle East (i.e. the adoption by non-Greeks of Greek cultural forms such as the theatre and the *gymnasium*) was probably not Alexander's chief objective. Rather his foundation of Greek cities in key strategic locations was a means to easier political control of his empire and a way of accommodating large numbers of time-expired veterans, especially mercenaries. Yet this Hellenization is his lasting legacy. Native languages such as Egyptian and Syriac did not disappear, but Greek became the *lingua franca* of culture and political administration throughout the Hellenistic world, the bulk of which was split soon after Alexander's death into three and then four territorial, dynastic monarchies: Antigonid Macedon, Ptolemaic Egypt, Seleucid Asia, and finally Attalid Pergamum.

The other principal legacy of Alexander, indirectly, was the survival of Greek literature – or rather a selected literary canon – belonging to the fourth century and earlier. This was achieved mainly through the establishment by the first Ptolemy of the Museum and Library at Alexandria – Alexander's most famous eponymous city foundation. Scholars working there (reportedly enjoying the benefit of Aristotle's library acquired from the Lyceum, his institute for advanced study in Athens) undertook to establish the most authentic possible texts of all the brightest and best Greek poets and other *littérateurs* from Homer and Hesiod onwards. But the

A feminine and feline Dionysus takes a ride on a leopard-like creature conventionally labelled a panther. The medium is pebble mosaic, set here in the floor of a large colonnaded house at Pella in about 300 BCE. Dionysus is garlanded and carries a magic wand – to charm some new conquest, no doubt.

Hellenistic era was by no means merely imitative in intellectual terms. *Stoicism*, for example, arose as a new philosophical creed appropriate to the needs of a more cosmopolitan and perhaps more unsettling age. *Epicureanism* too achieved a very wide following. New art-forms and new modes of artistic expression, largely patronized by the new Hellenistic court societies, convey an impression of bustling energy and fruitful endeavour.

Politically, however, the picture is less inspiring. The Hellenistic monarchies could be said to represent a new state-form, though they have clear antecedents in the tyranny of Dionysius of Syracuse or the satrapy of Maussollos (Mausolus) of Caria. But they developed and flourished at the expense of the old-style Greek polis (the citizen-state premissed on external freedom and open internal debate) and especially at the expense of democracy. The crushing of the Greek uprising led by Athens against Macedon immediately after Alexander's death was followed by the instant suppression of democracy in Athens. This anti-democratic tendency spread throughout the Hellenistic Greek world. The upper-classes of the Greek cities, new and old, proved only too happy to collaborate with their Macedonian Greek suzerains in stamping out a system that to them seemed little better than the dictatorship of the proletariat.

The city of Rhodes was a partial exception to this rule for a considerable time. Like classical Athens, Hellenistic Rhodes based its democracy firmly on sea-power, and it remained a power to be reckoned with down into the second century BCE. Another much more surprising example of popular revolution occurred in land-locked Sparta in the third century. This, though, was revolution of a socio-economic rather than political kind since its leaders were themselves kings or perhaps more

Acrocorinth, literally 'the top of Corinth', is the great natural guardian of the gateway to the Peloponnese. It was at the nearby Isthmus that in 481 the loyalist Greeks met to plan their resistance to the invading Persian horde. The Corinthians of course made every effort to keep it in their hands but in 338 it fell to conquering Macedon, not for the last time, and the Macedonian garrison stationed here served as one of the 'fetters' with which the subjugated Greeks were bound – until their independence was formally and hollowly declared by Rome in 196 BCE.

accurately tyrants, most notably Agis IV and Cleomenes III. For the most part, how-ever, democracy of the old type was doomed to remain but a name and a shadow, at most an ill-conceived aspiration. The Hellenistic world was one made safe for monarchy and oligarchy.

THE ROMANS

Such a world accorded perfectly with the world-view of the Romans, the people responsible for delivering democracy's – and indeed Greek independence's – ultimate *coup de grâce*.

The Romans first became seriously involved with Greek affairs towards the end of the third century, when Agelaus of Naupactus famously warned his fellow-Greeks of the 'cloud rising in the West'. That was in fact the starting date of Rome's rise to domination, not only of Greece, but of the entire Mediterranean world and a good deal else besides. Rome's initial rise was recorded in the second century by the philo-Roman Greek Polybius of Megalopolis, who demanded to know how anyone could fail to be interested in the history of such a cosmic event. That was of course espe-cially true of those mainland Greeks who, like him, had personally lived through the topsy-turvy period from Rome's announcement of its commitment to Greek inde-pendence made in 196 at Corinth – a symbolically apt location, since this was where in 481 the Greek loyalists had sworn to resist Persia – to Rome's destruction of the last major Greek resistance to Roman rule, also at Corinth, in 146.

The victorious Roman commander, Mummius, then took a leaf out of the Mace-donian pattern-book and had Corinth razed to the ground as a deterrent to future resistance. At the same time, he made elaborate arrangements to have shipped back to Rome some of Corinth's principal artistic treasures. That seemingly paradoxical combination of destruction and preservation may stand as a perfect emblem of Rome's twofold historical function – as both the destroyer of the Greek political legacy and the preserver of Hellenism in its cultural forms.

Hellenism indeed continued to develop and mutate under Roman tutelage. Sparta, for example, long since deprived of political or military significance, became a sort of ancient theme park drawing visitors from far and wide to witness its allegedly archaic but actually reinvented social rituals, like the notoriously brutal flogging of youths before an altar of Artemis. Athens on the other hand became a university town, where leading Romans would come to get themselves a higher education in philosophy and rhetoric.

So great in fact was the attractive power of Greek culture that peoples hitherto proudly or even militantly resistant such as the Jews embraced certain aspects of Hel-lenism under Rome's aegis. It is thanks to this process, for example, that the Christian New Testament was written in Greek, by Greek-speaking ex-Jewish Christians wish-ing to spread their gospel to 'Hellenes' or non-Jewish, non-Christian Greek-speakers. That is perhaps Hellenism's most widespread legacy to the modern world, but not by any means its only one (see Epilogue).

The Life of Greece

PART II

Rich and Poor

ARISTOTLE THE CLASS-ANALYST?

Aristotle, the most systematic and fair-minded of Greek philosophers, was in the habit of beginning all his varied lectures with surveys of the prevailing *phenomena*. These surveys incorporated the main facts and/or the most substantial opinions (in his view) generally held. Unlike his teacher, Plato, he was never happy espousing a theory radically at variance with these 'common sense' or consensus views – hence his opposition to, for example, Plato's Theory of Forms (see p. 305). So, while his own thoughts on political theory and practice were being developed in the series of lectures which have survived for us as his *Politics*, he was also directing a major research programme, under which he and his pupils published *Politeiai*, studies of the historical development and current structures of 158 Greek and some non-Greek city- or citizen-states (see Chapter 6). The only surviving example, on papyrus of such a *Politeia*, the *Constitution of the Athenians*, was rescued from the sands of Egypt and first published in 1891.

The project which produced *Politeiai* was run from the Lyceum, the school which Aristotle founded on his return to Athens in *c*.335 BCE after a period at the Macedonian court as tutor of the young Alexander the Great, followed by travels in the Aegean and Asia Minor. It displays four important characteristics.

First, the programme was almost totally Hellenocentric. It saw the Greek *polis* as the characteristic and 'natural' political form for human beings. In other words, a small political community, with a defined agricultural territory and a civic centre, which also comprised and organized smaller social groups such as households, villages, and kinship or other associations.

Second, this focus on the polis devalued those larger groupings of communities which tended to be called not *poleis* but *ethnê*; whereas the polis, in theory at least, was a politically autonomous body, the different communities linked in an *ethnos* surrendered some powers to a common assembly. In fact, however, many such *ethnê* (such as the Thessalian and Aetolian states) were covered in the Aristotelian programme. Even more striking is the neglect in his work of the kingdom of Macedon, though he knew it well. He was writing his lectures on *Politics* just after Philip II of Macedon had compelled, by a mixture of diplomacy, threats and warfare, most mainland Greek poleis to join the 'League of Corinth', under Macedonian leadership (338/7), and while Aristotle's own former pupil Alexander the Great was transforming the whole of the East by his conquest of the Persian empire (see pp. 163 and 189).

Third, this programme emphasises diversity as well as similarity. The poleis, whatever their geographical interrelationships, started with individual economic, religious and cultural patterns. They continued to develop their separate identities and underwent their individual political changes. Sometimes, however, especially in the archaic period, poleis followed comparable patterns of development, as a result of a complex process of voluntary mutual influence (this process is often called 'peer polity interaction'). At other times political changes came about rather as a result of deliberate pressure applied by more powerful states, such as Athens, Sparta and Thebes, as they sought to dominate neighbouring states and force them to adopt similar political systems to their own, such as democracy or oligarchy. These developments and changes in the poleis' constitutions were often the result of intense economic and political conflict, and not infrequently involved violence. This tendency in Greek politics is brought out clearly by a fourth characteristic of Aristotle's work, the constant concern to analyse the causes of what he calls *stasis* and to encourage states to learn how to avoid it. This term stasis, which is central to Thucydides' history as well as to Aristotle's analysis of Greek politics, originally meant in ancient Greek a political position or opinion; but it came quickly to denote rather a competing political faction, or the condition in a city of dangerous unrest and conflict or even outright civil war.

How, then, did Aristotle analyse the political structures of the poleis? What for him were the causes of change and instability? And how might stasis be avoided? Central to his idea of the city-state was the idea of 'full membership', of citizenship. This he usually defined in terms of participation in the decision-making processes: voting in assemblies, acting as jurors and holding political offices (*archai*). But citizenship also meant enjoying the protection afforded by citizen status (see Chapter 5). Of course, these 'honours' were everywhere restricted to free adult males who were able to demonstrate membership by descent (see p. 149).

Aristotle recognized various distinctions between citizens – for example by occupation. Of course, a citizen could have more than one occupation. For example a soldier could also be a farmer – there were no standing, professional armies (though mercenaries were increasingly employed from the latter part of the fifth century onwards).

He also argued that in some societies a tripartite distinction between the rich, the poor and a strong, moderating group of 'middling people' lies behind a state's sound government and stability. But, as he went on to claim, in most states the middling group was too small to be a significant factor. For him, the most important distinction, from which arose the most conflict, lay between the few rich and the many poor, the propertied and the rest. Aristotle saw an inevitable connection between the dominance of either group and the type of constitution established: oligarchy by the rich, and democracy by the poor. In practice the rich are always few in number and the poor many (Aristotle often explicitly referred to the rich as 'the Few', and the poor as 'the Many', 'the Majority' or 'the Mass'). However, he rather oddly insisted that even if the rich were the ruling majority, the state should still be classified as an oligarchy, as they would tend to arrange affairs in the interests of the wealthy.

Aristotle has been claimed as a forerunner of Marx because of his emphasis on economic class as the main determinant of political behaviour for most individuals

Archaic justice

Contemporary archaic poetry reflects the political changes between c.700 and 550 BCE. Extracts from Hesiod, the didactic poet of c.700 BCE, show that in agrarian Boeotian villages at this time, peasants were excluded from the decision-making processes. These were firmly in the hands of the *basileis*, the local aristocrats. Only the relatively wealthy peasants, who chiefly derived their money from working their farms, would have had the time or means to get favourable judgements from the basileis (legal action was then, as now, time-consuming and expensive). But these farmers could be encouraged to criticize the nobles' justice in the following way, invoking standards of fairness backed by the gods. In this extract Hesiod is addressing his brother Perses, who has allegedly taken more than his proper share of the inheritance from their father, and given gifts to the ruling nobles to give a judgement in his favour.

Perses, you should store up this advice in your mind,
  and not let the Strife that delights in trouble keep
  back your spirit from work,
while you gaze at men's disputes, as a listener to the
  agora speeches.
Little business has he with disputes and agoras
who does not have a year's supply of ripe wealth laid up,
which the earth produces, the grain of Demeter.
When you have an excess of that you may promote
  disputes and trouble
over the possessions of others; you will have no second
  chance
to do that. Let us settle our dispute here and now
  with straight judgements, which are the best things
  from Zeus.
We had already divided our inheritance, but you kept
  stealing
the greater share and carrying it off, greatly increasing
  the glory of the rulers [basileis]
devourers of presents, who are willing to give this
  judgement.

  (*Works and Days* 27–39)

But you should remember always my instruction,
and work, Perses of godly stock, so that hunger
may hate you, and respected fair-crowned Demeter
may befriend you, and fill your barn with substance.
Hunger is a fit companion for a man who does no work.
Gods and men are properly angry with him, the man
  who lives

without working, whose temperament resembles the
  blunt-tailed drones,
who waste the work of the bees, eating it up
without working; let it be your concern to arrange your
  tasks in due order,
so that your barns are full of rich substance.
It is from work that men become rich in flocks
  and wealthy,
and hard-working men are dearer to the immortal gods.
There is no disgrace in work, but idleness is a disgrace.
If you work, soon the idle man will envy you
as you get rich; worth and glory go with wealth.
Whatever your personal fate, work is the best for you,
if you turn your foolish mind away from the possessions
  of others,
and train your mind to the work that brings livelihood, as
  I command you.
Shame is not good at taking care of the needy man,
shame which both greatly harms and helps men,
shame, after all, goes with poverty, and confidence
  with wealth.
Wealth should not be taken by force, god-given wealth is
  much better.
For if a man takes hold of great wealth with hands
  and force,
or if he steals it by use of his tongue, as very often
happens, when hope of profit deceives the minds
of men, and shamelessness drives out shame,
the gods easily make him nothing, but diminish
  the household
of such a man, and his wealth accompanies him only a
  short time.

  (*Works and Days 298–326*)

The poems of Solon, the Athenian legislator of the early sixth century, put forward several new ideas. Firstly, that wealth was more readily acquirable, and by a variety of means (many unjust). Secondly, that widespread injustice and *hubris* damaged the cohesion of the whole community, but the introduction of new, fairer laws might bring good order (*eunomia*). Thirdly, that some participation by all citizens (in the general assembly, and the new 'law-court') also brought fairness and harmony, and was a suitable 'honour' for them.

In these extracts from a poem which is now often given the title *Eunomia* or 'Good Order', and was apparently directed to the Athenian citizens and designed to alert them to Athens' economic and political crisis, Solon fixes the blame above all on the nobles (the leaders), and highlights the need for change through new laws (poem 4).

> This city of ours will never be destroyed by the
> > apportioning of Zeus, or through the wills of the
> > blessed immortal gods;
> such is she, the great-hearted guardian, of the powerful
> > father,
> > Pallas Athena, who holds her hands out over us.
> The citizens themselves, through their foolish acts, are
> > willing
> > to destroy the great city, yielding to their desire
> > for wealth,
> and the leaders of the people have unjust minds, for
> > whom soon
> > there will be many griefs to suffer as a result of their
> > great *hubris*.
> For they do not know how to control their excess, nor to
> > order well
> > their present good cheer in the peace of the feast
> ...
> > and they grow rich, prompted by their unjust acts,
> ...
> > and sparing neither sacred possessions nor public ones
> they steal in violent seizure, one from one source one
> > from another,
> > and do not observe the solemn foundations of Justice.

The poems of the Megarian Theognis (late seventh, or mid-sixth century) present the picture of the poet as a rather grumpy aristocrat reacting adversely both to new wealth and to wider participation by non-nobles in government, as well as their marrying into the older aristocratic families. They often take the form of moral advice offered to a younger 'boyfriend', called Cyrnus or Polypaides.

> Cyrnus, the polis is still the polis, but the people are
> > different,
> > who before knew nothing of the processes of justice
> > or of laws,
> but they wore out old goatskins on their sides,
> > and outside the city, like deer, they lived on the land.
> And now they are the 'good men', Polypaides; those who
> > were good before
> > are now the lowly men. Who can endure such a sight?
> They deceive each other, while laughing at each
> > other's ills,
> > not able to know the minds of the bad or the good.

> ...
> For rams, and donkeys, Cyrnus, and for horses,
> > we seek out good stock, and one wishes to breed
> from good beasts; but the noble man does not mind a
> > bad woman
> > daughter of a bad man, if much wealth is given
> > to him,
> nor does a woman refuse to be the wife of a bad man,
> > if he is rich, but wants the wealthy man, not the good.
> It's wealth that they honour; good marries from bad stock,
> > and bad from good; wealth has mixed up
> > the bloodlines.
> Do not be surprised, Polypaides, that the race of
> > the citizens
> > is fading away; for good is being mixed with bad.

Later Greeks would have had no idea what early poets like Homer and Hesiod looked like, but traditions of how to represent them on statues or painting none the less grew up. This is a mosaic representing Hesiod as a dignified old man with a long pointed beard. It was found in Trier in Germany, and dates from the fourth century CE.

and groups. But one should notice also that Aristotle's understanding of what each side most resents when the other side is in power includes at least three separable elements: economic exploitation (whether by squeezing the lands of the poor or by imposing heavy tax burdens on the rich); exclusion from political offices or from participation in assemblies and law-courts (significantly, the term often used for political offices or power is *timai*, 'honours', implying extra prestige and honour derived from power-sharing as well as from the actual exercise of power); and various forms of direct assault on the individual's personal status or honour (*timê*). Such serious assaults were often strongly condemned as *hubris* (insolence or arrogance), and might take the form of physical violence, sexual assaults on one's dependants, or formal deprivation of citizen status. So Aristotle's analysis of what is involved in what we might call class conflict centred on issues of honour and status as well as economic exploitation and power.

MONEY MAKETH THE MAN?

It is not possible to give anything like a precise account of the origins of class divisions as the city-state developed in the archaic period. Greek traditions tended to assume that everywhere in the post-heroic age (what we call the Dark Age) a loose form of monarchy gave way to aristocracies of birth. From the mid-seventh century further changes become more clearly visible, often involving a brief period of tyranny and leading either to reformulated oligarchies based on wealth rather than birth, or to moves towards more egalitarian regimes.

From the early archaic period, material remains found in graves or at sanctuaries clearly suggest élite displays of prestige goods, for example the dedications of metal tripod cauldrons and figurines found at Olympia and Delphi. There were also varied types of élite burials in Attica when, at different times, high status seems designated by, for example, the burial of large numbers of weapons, or by the deposition of a very large, elaborately decorated geometric-style pot as a grave marker.

Most, of course, would have had no such memorial. But we should be cautious in assuming from this either an unchallenged dominance of a fixed élite of a few families in any one place, or uniform practices from one city to another. Excavation evidence for burial rituals, for example, suggests considerable diversity from place to place. The exclusiveness with which élite status was marked also apparently varied. As the sense of belonging to an identifiable community began to take shape, and polis territory became more defined – with sacred, public and private lands and buildings clearly delineated – the claim of the richest families to a monopoly of power and decision-making seems, from our earliest literary texts, to be under challenge. These texts (and later accounts whose details are all too often doubtful) also display the moral and political ambivalence and contentiousness of wealth and power. Archaic poetry from Hesiod onwards enables us to chart the growing claims of the poor members of communities to protection from exploitation and a share in participation.

Many less rich Greeks were commemorated after death by plain grave slabs or stones, perhaps with the mere name inscribed. In many cases the name of the deceased came early to be added on the stone, once the habit of writing was reintroduced to Greece in the eighth century BCE. Here is a drawn example of a rough gravestone for a woman called Eteocleia, from the island of Thera, inscribed in the second half of the seventh century BCE. The name is written from right to left and turned through ninety degrees.

One commonly repeated pattern in the seventh and sixth centuries BCE was the seizure of power by a tyrant (see p. 61), establishing a form of monarchy which rarely lasted as many as three generations (for example Cypselus and Periander in Corinth, Theagenes in Megara, or Cleisthenes in Sicyon). In general, the tyrants' bids for power were made possible because many of the effective fighters in the community (by now organized in hoplite phalanxes) chose either to support them in the hope of better economic conditions or more honours, or at least refused to support the status quo. Either way, the tyrants broke the exclusive rights of the nobles, and often worked to advance the prestige and civic splendour of their cities. However, they only seldom, if ever, actually improved economic conditions or political participation for most citizens. Individually, often marginal nobles themselves, they naturally behaved as super-aristocrats, displaying their wealth in dedications at Panhellenic sanctuaries and at their own lavish courts.

Aristocrats in the archaic period displayed their power visibly at their funerals. This Attic Geometric vase of. *c.*740 BCE is in itself a grand prestige item marking the grave. The dead man lies on a four-legged bier covered with a chequered cloth and placed on a horse-drawn cart. Men wearing swords attend, along with many mourning women. Later, regulations restricting display at aristocratic funerals were introduced in many Greek cities.

THE SPARTAN ROUTE TO CONSENSUS: UNIFORMITY?

The radically different political and economic developments of what became by *c.*480 the two most powerful mainland Greek states, Athens and Sparta, led to their adoption of very different strategies for the creation of cohesion and co-operation between rich and poor citizens. In fact, the classical Spartan state was created not so much, as their tradition proudly asserted, by a single set of reforms proposed by a combination of their law-giver/hero Lycurgus and the oracle at Delphi, as by a slow process of change, from the early seventh to the early fifth centuries. The starting point was the conquest and reduction to helot (or community-slave) status of the very large Greek populations of Laconia and Messenia. This gave the full Spartan citizens (the Spartiates) extensive territory as a basis for agricultural wealth, and freed them from the necessity of direct labour on the land. But equally it imposed on them the burden of constant supervision of a resentful, and not infrequently insurgent, serf population much larger than themselves (and the numerical disproportion was to increase radically from the mid-fifth century). In

This Spartan cup is one of a series showing an elegant young horseman attended by a winged human figure carrying wreaths and surrounded by marsh birds. Perhaps the youth is an idealized Spartan warrior at the start of his career. The water birds may suggest the shrine of Artemis Orthia at Sparta, set in low-lying marshes by the river Eurotas, at which manhood ceremonies took place. Rider Painter (*c.* 550–540 BCE)

Dynastic dedication and display

Lavish and extravagant display was character-istic of the early Greek tyrants. Soon after taking power, Cypselus, the first tyrant of Corinth, claimed he had had the support of Apollo's oracle at Delphi. So he established there the first state treasury, to hold his many grateful dedications to the god and demon-strate the new (illegitimate) regime's piety and wealth. But the most spectacular account we have of self-display on a heroic scale is the search by Cleisthenes, the most powerful of the tyrannical dynasty at Sicyon, to find a suit-able husband for his daughter Agariste. This happened some time around 580 and was related by Herodotus. Following a proclama-tion at Olympia, where the tyrant had added to his fame by winning the chariot race, suit-ors converged from all over Greece for the year-long selection process. They were re-quired to display their athletic prowess in Cleisthenes' purpose-built race-track and wrestling ground. In the words of Herodotus, the suitors were tested for their 'brave manli-ness, temperament, education and manners; he [Cleisthenes] took the younger ones each day to the gymnasia, but the greatest test of all was at the dinner table'. Herodotus' anec-dote had an Athenian agenda, specifically concerned with the rise of the family of the Alcmaeonids. It was told in order to explain how, of the two Athenian suitors, it was not the 'front-runner', Hippocleides, 'the wealthi-est and best-looking man in Athens', but the Alcmaeonid Megacles who was selected.

Hippocleides unfortunately blew his chances, when at the final and decisive ban-quet, following the sacrifice of 100 oxen, he got excessively drunk, and 'climbing on a table, danced first Laconian, then Attic, dances, then third, standing on his head on the table, beat time with his legs'. Cleisthenes could not stom-ach such a son-in-law, and burst out 'Hippo-cleides, you have danced away your marriage', but the dancer only replied 'Hippocleides doesn't care'. Since Hippocleides would not have been wearing underwear, the recent suggestion that we have here also a pun (*orcheisthai*, 'to dance' / *orcheis*, 'testicles') along the lines of 'you have ballsed up your marriage' seems extremely plausible. Hip-pocleides might then be seen to be imitating, disastrously, the vulgar dances usually per-formed by lower class jesters – the Spartan helots, Athenian serfs or similar down-trodden groups elsewhere who were forced thus to humiliate themselves for scraps from the nobles' tables.

Greek tyrants of the archaic period were particularly anxious to achieve legiti-macy for their rule and proclaim their wealth and achievements by paying for buildings, and dedicating statues and spoils, at major sanctuaries, above all the Panhellenic shrines such as Olympia and Delphi. Few of the most valuable dedica-tions have survived as most of the wealth was to be plundered and melted down in classical and later times. This fine gold bowl, how-ever, was found at Olympia, and its inscription indicates that it was dedicated by 'the Cypselids, from the spoils of Heracleia': probably not the Cypselid tyrants from Corinth, but a junior branch ruling in north-west Greece in the region of Ambracia.

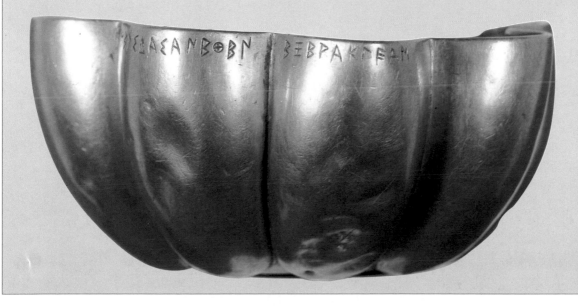

the mid-seventh century there was a major revolt by the Messenian helots, and at much the same time, it appears, serious political and economic tensions between rich and poor Spartiates emerged that may have been related to the introduction at about this time of a hoplite army, which gave an greater military importance to a greater number of Spartan soldiers. The tensions were resolved by the granting of greater powers to the Spartan assembly, and by redistribution of the Messenian lands; henceforth Spartiates began to call themselves the 'Peers' (*Homoioi*), and each received a (minimal) land allotment to be worked by the helots. Over the next two centuries, the Spartans developed a largely homogeneous and somewhat militaristic common life style, based above all on a rigorous and uniform educational system of physical, military and musical training and competitions, and reinforced by homosexual pair-bonding between young men and youths. This training was maintained by constant collective dining in common messes (called *syssitia*, *syskania* or *phiditia*) and admission to these messes (as life-members) was a condition of citizenship. Staple mess fare was an unpleasant if sustaining 'black broth', and entertainment and conversation focused on military or hunting exploits, or homosexual friendships.

Thucydides claimed that the Spartans were the first to dress simply, and that in Sparta the rich had life styles as much as possible like those of ordinary people. However, the extent of this homogeneity, described by many of our fourth-century and later sources on Sparta (especially in Plutarch's *Life of Lycurgus*), is no doubt exaggerated. It probably forms a nostalgic reflection of concerns to contrast Sparta with other states (above all with Athens); and (after the defeat at Leuctra in 371 and its effects) to explain Sparta's demographic and political demise in terms of a moral decline from her former standards of austerity. In fact there were, from the outset, clear divisions between richer Spartiates, who also tended to be more dominant politically, above all by being elected when old to the powerful Council of twenty-eight 'Elders' (*Gerousia*), and those with smaller estates and less disposable produce. In order to minimize the disruptive effects of these divisions, richer mess members, more able to compete in games, to ride and to hunt, were supposed (in theory) to introduce better quality meats or bread to enliven the basic fare: see the idealizing account of the messes in Xenophon's *Spartan Constitution*, of which this extract gives the flavour:

> He (*Lycurgus*) laid down fixed amounts of cereal foods for them so that there should be neither too much nor too little. Many extra items besides these calculations are provided from the hunts; the rich on occasions also make other contributions of wheat bread. As a result the table is never bare of foods until they leave the mess tents, nor is there great expense. He also imposed a break on unnecessary drinking, which weakens bodies and causes minds to slip up, and ordained that each man should drink when thirsty, believing that that was the least harmful and pleasantest form of drinking.

Probably there were always rich Spartiates who did not observe these norms and enjoyed, privately, a more extravagant life style; but the frequency of such deviance from the rules of uniformity, and its resulting social tensions, seems to have increased from the time of the Peloponnesian War and the subsequent Spartan hegemony of 404–371 BCE, when leading Spartans found irresistible the opportunities for wealth, luxury and exercise of power provided by their commands of armies and their positions of influence throughout Greece. So the Spartan strategy for harmony, through uniformity, restraint and the equalization of competitions and enjoyments, lost some of its force during the fourth century and later, even while the myths of good order (*eunomia*) and citizen uniformity were being created.

As the leader of a major alliance of mostly Peloponnesian states, Sparta tended to favour regimes broadly classifiable as oligarchies, that is regimes where important forms of political participation and office-holding were restricted to those with more than a stated level of property. Some of these managed to preserve stable governments for long periods of time during the sixth and fifth centuries. Corinth, Megara and Chios were significant examples. In this way (by mechanisms obscure to us) they may have avoided extremes of exploitation of the poorer members of the community. However, almost all such states came to experience serious bouts of stasis, civil wars and changes of regimes during the turbulent periods of major conflicts and upheavals that affected most Greek states from the beginning of the great Peloponnesian War (431–404 BCE).

ATHENIAN ROUTES TO CONSENSUS: INCENTIVES, FREEDOM, DIVERSITY, AND CONTROL

Alternative, more egalitarian, and more complex routes to consensus were pioneered by Athens, and some attempts were made to export aspects of her political system as well, especially during the period of her fifth-century Aegean empire. The patterns of relationships between the (changing) rich élites and the poorer majority underwent some alterations from the sixth to the fourth centuries in Athens. Usable written evidence begins with Solon's poems and the (much later) historical accounts of his legislative activity. These suggest a major social crisis. Solon was appointed as a special law-giver to solve the multiple, and dangerous, conflicts between the traditional nobles, men who had recently become rich and were disgruntled by their exclusion from power and influence, and many of the poorer farmers. Some of the latter were destitute and in danger of being sold into slavery, some perhaps resented long term share-cropping arrangements with richer landowners, which may have been made some generations earlier when the hillier hinterground of Attica was brought into cultivation. Conceivably, too, some better-off peasants, also serving as hoplites in the (as yet undistinguished) army, felt their military service to the state entitled them to greater political participation. No doubt the sub-hoplite poor resented the conspicuous luxuries and arrogance of the rich; their aggressive ostentation at their funerals, and their extravagant private

(*Following pages*) **From the beggar Iros in Homer's *Odyssey* to the 'flatterers' and 'parasites' of fifth- and fourth-century Attic comedy, lower-class people might be compelled, or choose, to entertain the guests at elite drinking-parties (*symposia*), with comic dances, athletic turns, or jokes. This drinking-cup is one of a series of Attic black-figure cups of the early sixth-century (the so-called 'Siana cups'), where padded figures seem to entertain reclining banqueters with coarse dances. They may well illustrate this custom, and come from the time of the reforms of Solon, when Athens experienced considerable economic and social discontents. Alternatively, they may represent more formalized entertainments offered at rather more public banquets.**

This elaborate marble statue (a *korê*) of a young girl, bedecked with floral headdress, earrings and necklace, was found in 1972 buried with the statue of the young man (a *kouros*), at Merenda in Attica: they had been made about 550 BCE to act as fine grave-markers over the graves. The base of the korê had been long known, and the verse epitaph identifies the dead maiden as Phrasicleia, and shows clearly how the death of a young girl was conceived:

The monument of Phrasicleia: I shall be called a maiden [*korê*] for ever having been allotted this title by the gods instead of marriage.

drinking-parties (*symposia*) and feasts, at which some of the poor may have had to dance – as 'uninvited guests' or hangers-on – in comically undignified ways for the entertainment of their betters.

Solon sought to offer protection to all citizens and their dependants. To prevent their economic exploitation he abolished debt-slavery and the share-cropping arrangements, and cancelled debts. Through his inheritance laws he also tried to maintain economic and political stability by making it less likely that smaller households would become extinguished. He legislated against dishonouring or violent acts with, for example, his law against hubris, and he restrained display, conspicuous mourning and extravagant deposits at funerals.

More generally, Solon divided citizens into four classes based on agricultural wealth: these were the *pentakosiomedimnoi* ('500-bushel men') and the *hippeis* (cavalry) – two categories of the rich; the *zeugitai* (the middling citizens, those who served as hoplites in the army); and the *thetes* (the poor). He assigned political offices hierarchically between them, encouraging all citizens to share in the final decisions, on matters of public policy through attendance at a popular assembly, on legal cases through the new popular law-court, the *Heliaea*. But the most important overall effect of this definition of the rights and duties of citizenship was probably to identify the citizen much more firmly as a full member of the community, and to equip him with a set of privileges, rights, honours and duties. This also served to sharpen the contrast between citizens and the other groups living in Athens. Immigrants, for example, did not qualify as Athenians by residence. But the most important distinction was between free and slave. A consequence of the Solonian land reforms, and perhaps also a reason for the surprising acceptance of them by many of the old rich, was an increase in the importation of chattel slaves from non-Greek-speaking lands – above all from the vast areas north and south of the Black Sea.

Solon's reforms did not immediately create political stability. Factional feuding between aristocratic families and their local supporters, with perhaps some more class-based struggles between rich and poor, led to the establishment *c*.546 of a tyranny, under Pisistratus and his sons, which lasted until 510. This was remembered later as a relatively benign tyranny, under which most of the new Solonian laws were permitted to operate and take root. When the tyranny was ended, and aristocratic conflict resumed with renewed intensity, one of the leaders, Cleisthenes of the Alcmaeonid family, won popular support for a further series of remarkable reforms. These instituted new, more democratic structures, offering fresh opportunities for all citizens to participate in detail in their own political affairs – giving a sharper focus to the notion of citizenship. It became much harder for immigrants to be awarded Athenian citizenship, however long they remained living in Attica. Such newcomers, now officially designated *metics*, had rather to be registered as living in the *deme* (or parish) of their Athenian sponsor, and (from the second half of the fifth century) had to pay a poll-tax of twelve drachmae a year for men, six for women (not a very large sum, but of considerable ideological significance). Metics could become Athenian citizens only by special vote of the Assembly, as a reward for exceptional services, though they might be granted lesser privileges. None the less, foreigners flocked to enjoy the economic and other benefits of Athenian fifth-century expansion, and at the mid-point of the century a further tightening of citizenship rules took place. Athenian citizens henceforth had to have an Athenian mother as well as an Athenian father, and a major consequence must have been that Athenian boys ceased marrying foreign girls, whether (for the aristocratic élite) daughters of élite families in other states, linked by ties of hospitality and alliance (*xenia* or 'guest-friendship'); or (for all) the daughters of metics.

During the sixth century aristocratic Athenian families were able to demonstrate piety, wealth and power by placing impressive monuments on their graves, especially when boys died young in war, or daughters before marriage (for example the Anavyssus *kouros* and the Phrasicleia *korê*). But at the time of Cleisthenes and a little later increased restraints and pressures were placed on the élite to spend their wealth more on the community and less on personal display. A law prohibited grave memorials involving 'more work than ten men can do in three days' – and lavish monuments dried up almost completely, until they made an appearance again in the last quarter

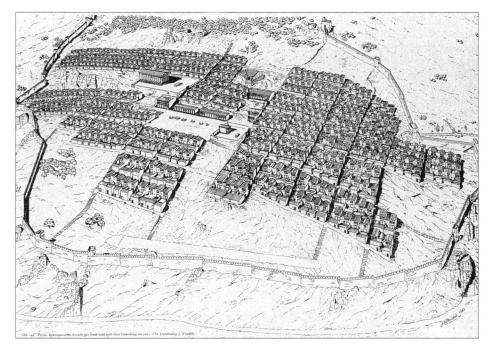

Abb. 144 Priene: Rekonstruierte Ansicht der Stadt bald nach ihrer Gründung um 350 v. Chr. (Zeichnung J. Wendel)

Priene, a small Ionian city near the mouth of the river Maeander in Asia Minor, needed to be completely rebuilt on a new site in the second half of the fourth century BCE, probably because the earlier city was badly affected by the silting up of the river. The rebuilding was carried out in accordance with the principles of egalitarian town planning which the Greeks associated with the fifth century planner Hippodamus of Miletus, whose work has been identified at the Piraeus, Miletus and Rhodes, though the basic ideas were clearly older. The main elements which can be seen at Priene are clearly defined open areas for the city-centre (*agora*), and the main civic buildings such as the major sanctuaries and the theatre, a strict grid plan for the streets, and basic blocks of roughly similar housing (eight houses to a block, running north–south). Each house has a courtyard in the middle, a living room, a 'best room' used for entertaining visitors or for *symposia*, and bedrooms upstairs.

Manufacturing goods became an important source of wealth as the Athenian economy developed, and made considerable use of slave-labour. This fine Attic red-figure vase by the Foundry Painter, from the early fifth century, shows work in a foundry, making bronze statues: perhaps the naked workers with hats and coarse features are slaves, those with loin cloths perhaps free workers. Those lounging with sticks may be clients.

of the fifth century. (There are signs of similar restraint developing, and then retreating, in other cities.) However, as an immediate result of that legislation, Athenians regularly used plain columnar grave markers, and the war-dead were annually commemorated with a public ceremony, a collective, altar-like stone tomb, and a patriotic funeral speech delivered by a leading statesman; Thucydides' history describes the institution of the public funeral, and gives us his version of Pericles' speech, delivered at the end of the first year of the Peloponnesian War in 430 BCE.

The houses and clothes of the Athenian élite do not seem to have been extravagantly luxurious, though houses are said in contemporary rhetoric to have become slightly more so in the fourth century (a picture supported to some extent by the archaeological record). However, many cities in Greece, including the harbour-town of Attica, the Piraeus, developed standard patterns of town-planning, with a firm street-grid and equal blocks of strictly egalitarian housing.

The rich of Athens were not prevented from spending their surplus on luxurious food, fine gold- and silver ware, and lavish drinking-parties (see p. 86–7 and p. 212). But they were put under very strong pressure to conform to a more egalitarian and democratic ideology by minimizing such extravagance, and by spending time and money more lavishly and conspicuously for the benefit of all citizens, above all through the *liturgy* system (also developed from the time of Cleisthenes onwards). Through this, rich men financed and contributed to the running of many state festivals, and sponsored and commanded Athens' warships (*triremes*) – the foundation of her military success. The inducements to contribute in this way were not only fear

(Previous page) **Overseas trade, both in staples such as cereals, to ameliorate years of bad harvests at home, and in other foods and drinks, metals and many types of luxury goods, was of considerable economic significance for the Greek cities. As this sixth-century Attic black-figure vase shows, merchant-ships, round-bellied and essentially driven by sail, were totally different in shape and performance from the faster, slimmed-down, rowed warships (*triremes*); here a merchant ship is about to be rammed, perhaps by a pirate warship.**

of adverse gossip and hostility, but more positively and importantly a conditional promise of the community's gratitude, shown in 'honour' or 'political office' (both expressed by the Greek term *timê*). This took the forms of greater political prestige, better chances of election to office, and success in the law-courts – now mostly controlled by the Athenian poor citizens as jurors.

Sources of wealth became more various from the early fifth century on, as Athenian political power, her empire, and her economy developed. As elsewhere in Greece, however, land remained the most significant source of wealth, economically and ideologically. Most Athenians owned some land. When, around 400 BCE, it was proposed, unsuccessfully, that citizenship be removed from all those who owned no land at all, it seems that all but about 5000 Athenians were land-owners to some degree. Ownership of land and buildings was restricted to citizens (who were also, of course, all males), which further distinguished them from metics. Down to the mid-fifth century, all members of the political élite were substantial land-owners, and many were members of families influential for generations, such as the Alcmaeonids, to which Cleisthenes belonged. Pericles' father married into this family: he married, in fact, a girl whose name (Agariste) proclaimed her descent from the daughter of Cleisthenes the tyrant of Sicyon (see p. 83). Such men may reasonably be called aristocrats. But new rich men were appearing, whose primary wealth often came from slave-made manufactured goods (weapons, clothes, lamps et cetera). Initially, it seems, many of the old-rich, and indeed many of the more conservative ordinary peasant citizens, were appalled by the successful new-rich when they went into politics and reached the top during the 420s: this emerges most clearly from the constant and evidently acceptable attacks, in Aristophanes' popular comedies of the period, directed against arrivistes such as Cleon with his tanning business. Here is a sample of the abuse, from *Knights* of 424, in which Cleon is satirized by Demosthenes (a general opposed to Cleon) as a barbarian slave (Paphlagon), who is also a tanner, and a foul-mouthed, aggressive and corrupt politician, flattering the people (*Demos*), who are personified as a foolish old man:

> I'll tell you now. We have a master,
> a countryman in spirit, a bean-chewer, quick to anger,
> Demos of the Pnyx, a bad-tempered little old man,
> rather deaf. At last month's market-day
> he bought a slave, a tanner, Paphlagon,
> an utter criminal, a complete slanderer.
> This slave learnt the habits of his old master,
> did this hide-making splutterer, fell at his feet
> and started fawning, toadying, flattering and cheating
> him with end off-cuts of leather.

Cleon, and some others of this class, seem to have responded by adopting an aggressively populist and anti-rich political programme.

Other new sources of wealth, and signs of the successfully expanding economy of fifth-century Athens included the renting out of houses, especially to metics. Also, many traditional land-owners, owners of scattered farms, leased them out for cash crops. Significant too was an increase in the lending out of money at interest, for example to merchant-shipping. Of great economic value to state and individuals were the rich silver mines of the Laurium region of south-east Attica. Interestingly, wealth derived from mining seemed poised between the respectability of land-owning and the bad odour of manufacturing. Nicias, the politician who owned the largest number of mining slaves that we hear of (1000), managed to avoid all preju-diced jokes about his new wealth; perhaps the fact that this wealth came from beneath the ground made it easier to assimilate it to the more respectable wealth derived from agriculture.

By the fourth century, many traditional families have died out, and mixed sources of wealth have become standard: hence the prejudice against these forms of 'new money' is manifestly less in evidence. Most of the estates for which we have detailed accounts (see p. 96) consisted of mixed holdings. A few of the wealthy individuals we know about owned little or even no land at all. The propertied classes comprised those rich enough to have to contribute regularly to liturgies (perhaps between 1000–1200 citizens) and those liable for the *eisphora* – a prop-erty tax levied for military purposes on the richer inhabitants of Athens, including the metics (another 1000–4000 people). But all of them had to be able to produce serious amounts of ready cash for these levies at relatively short notice. They must have done so in part by strategically raising cash crops for urban markets in Athens and the Piraeus areas. In that way they maintained their élite positions in the com-munity, politically and socially. But high-level participation in politics was a precarious thing; it might lead to death, exile or financial ruin. Or the rich might suffer sudden economic losses, as in the case, for example, of failed harvests (see Chapter 2). Unsurprisingly, there was a fairly swift turnover of personnel at the top of Athenian society.

At the lower ends of the scale, most of the 25,000–30,000 ordinary citizens undoubtedly remained small farmers, and may perhaps be classified as 'peasants' – though the extent of their economic and political freedom distinguished them from peasants in most other places and periods. And they were not culturally invisible – the standard leading character in many of Aristophanes' plays (for example Dicaeopolis in the *Acharnians*) is a hoplite farmer. Much, too, in the rhetoric of public discourse (such as the funeral speeches) and of public art (such as the Parthenon sculptures) presented the ideal citizen as a hoplite. Some texts (see p. 94) suggest that, as a result of the undoubted havoc and disruption of the Peloponnesian War, poverty was seriously increased among these farmers; and many scholars have suggested that the class of poor farmers went into steep decline. But no good evi-dence supports this view, and the very stability and economic conservatism of the fourth-century democratic regime speak loudly against it. In fact, as recent, rather

Poverty's self-defence

Pittakos was an aristocrat active in the politics of Mytilene, on the island of Lesbos, *c.*600 BCE, at the same time as the poets Alcaeus and Sappho. He held power as an elected leader for ten years, and passed several new laws designed to increase social harmony and restrain the excesses of the aristocrats, including a measure imposing double penalties for offences committed when drunk. Alcaeus hated him and accused him of being (among other things) low-born, dirty, flat-footed and fat. This (much later) terra-cotta statuette from Pompeii, in a Hellenistic 'realist' style, combines elements of the physical description taken from Alcaeus' poems with the supposed capacity for 'deep thought' of the law-giver, like Solon, one of the Seven Wise men of the Greek archaic Age.

In Aristophanes' last play, *Wealth* (388 BCE), the fantasy of the plot assumes that the god Wealth, blind (hence the unjust are rich and the just are poor), is cured, and society is transformed. But in a formal debate the goddess Poverty appears to put the case against the comic hero Chremylus and his friend, and argues that if everyone becomes rich, no-one will have any incentive to work. Against her, Chremylus responds that poverty is miserable anyway, but Poverty replies with an important distinction between respectable, hard-working and honest poverty, and beggary. This distinction has much truth but, hardly surprisingly, fails in this context to persuade the newly enriched Athenian peasant. Here is an extract from the debate (lines 510–571).

POVERTY: If Wealth were to see
again, and distribute himself
equally among all,
no-one among men would
attend to any craft or skill,
no-one; if both of these were
destroyed by you, who
would be willing
to do metalwork, or
build ships, make
clothes or craft
wheels,
or do cobbling,
make bricks, launder
clothes or do the
tanning,
or break up
earth's clods
with the plough
and harvest the
fruit of Demeter,
if it is open to
you to live idly
and forget all of
that?

CHREMYLUS: You're talking rubbish. Everything
you've just mentioned to us
the slaves will work to produce.
POVERTY: Where will you get slaves from?
CHREMYLUS: We'll buy them with our money,
of course.
POVERTY: Well, first, who will be selling them,
if he too has got money?
CHREMYLUS: Oh, some merchant will come
from Thessaly, keen to make a profit, land
of insatiable slave dealers.
POVERTY: But first of all there won't be a single
slave dealer about, according to the argument you're making. What rich man would
wish to take risks with his own life to do
that sort of thing?
So you'll be compelled to plough yourself
and dig and do all the other hard jobs,
and you'll have a much more painful life
than you do now.
CHREMYLUS: May that threat rebound on your
head.
POVERTY: You won't have a bed you can lie on
– there won't be any – nor any carpets –
for who is going to want to weave if he's
got gold?
Nor, when you lead the bride out, will you
be able to perfume her with droplets,
nor adorn her with the expense of richly
decorated dyed clothes.
And what is the advantage in being rich, if
one lacks all these things?
But with me you'll easily have all you need;
for I sit like a slave-mistress, putting pressure on the craftsman to seek a means of
earning a living, through need and poverty.
CHREMYLUS: What good can you ever provide,
but blisters from bath-house stoves,
and starving little children, and a rabble of
old women?
I can't tell you the number of lice and mos-
quitoes and fleas,
so many there are, that buzz around our
heads and irritate us,
waking us up and saying 'You're hungry, so
up you get'.

We have to wear rags, not a decent cloak; instead of a bed, a rush-strewn pallet full of bugs, which wake us up if we're asleep. A rotten rush mat instead of a carpet; instead of a pillow, a dirty great stone by the head. To eat, instead of loaves of bread, shoots of mallow; instead of barley cake, weedy radish leaves; instead of a chair, the top of a broken wine jar, instead of a kneading trough, a rib of a storage cask, also smashed; do I not demonstrate all the many good things you are responsible for giving to all mankind?

POVERTY: You have not described my life, but you've hammered at the life of the beggars.

CHREMYLUS: But do we not say that Poverty is Beggary's sister?

POVERTY: You may, if you also say that Thrasybulus is the same as the tyrant Dionysius. But this is not the experience of the life I represent, by Zeus, nor will it ever be, It is the life of the beggar, which you're describing, which is to live possessing nothing, to live in poverty is to live thriftily, holding hard to your work, having nothing in excess, but not going short in anything either.

CHREMYLUS: What a blessed life here, by Demeter, you have described when a man lives in thrift, works hard, and leaves not enough for a funeral.

POVERTY: You're trying to poke fun and make comedy, and have no care to be serious, not realizing that I provide better men than does Wealth both in mind and in appearance. Wealth's men are the gouty,

the pot-bellies, thick-calved, and the disgustingly fat, mine are lean, and wasp-shaped, and a terror to their enemies.

CHREMYLUS: It's hunger no doubt that makes the men you provide so wasp-shaped.

POVERTY: I pass on now to talk of self-control, and I shall show you that order and decency live with me, but Wealth's possession is *hubris*.

CHREMYLUS: Yes, it's very orderly and decent to steal and dig through house-walls.

BLEPSIDEMUS: Well yes, if they have to stay hidden, then how can they not be decent?

POVERTY: Well look at the political speakers in the cities, how whenever they are poor, they are just in their dealings with the people and the city, but when they get rich, from the state's funds, they become unjust straight away, and conspire against the masses and make war on the people.

CHREMYLUS: Well, that at least is no lie.

Aristophanes' plays, it is now clear, were performed not only in Athens and Attica, but also in some Greek cities in South Italy, and for some decades after his death. The evidence is provided by vases like this one, a red-figure mixing-bowl from Tarentum of *c*.370 BCE, which is certainly to be interpreted as showing a scene from Aristophanes' *Women Celebrating the Thesmophoria*. The man in drag is Euripides' relative who in that play has infiltrated the women's festival to plead for Euripides, has had his male identity discovered. He has then, in parody of a Euripides' play, the *Telephos*, seized a wineskin (instead of the baby Orestes in the Euripides' play) as a hostage and is threatening to 'kill' it at the altar (hence the wineskin has baby bootees). The humour of the scene depends on the comic male assumption that all women, rich and poor, were devoted to wine, and spent much of the time at their own festivals getting drunk.

speculative, calculations have suggested, perhaps something like 8–10 per cent – the propertied rich – owned something like one-third of the available farming land (usually in several different holdings), whereas most hoplites and a few of the poorer citizens classified on Solon's system as thetes would have had small farms, perhaps as little as 6 hectares or less. Many of the thetes, however, would have operated primarily as hired agricultural labourers or worked in the city in manufacturing or in retail trade. Other citizens would be engaged in overseas trading, alongside and in competition with a larger number of non-citizens.

Though by necessity used to hard work and scrimping, the majority of citizens recognized the distinction between acceptable poverty and destitution or beggary (see p. 94). They enjoyed the relatively small amounts of economic redistribution through the liturgy and taxation systems for which they themselves had voted as assembly members. For example, in the mid-fourth century a special theatre-audience fund was created. It was intended (for ideological reasons as a symbol of the democracy) to enable all citizens to attend the City Dionysia festival more easily. The City Dionysia was one of the two great festivals designed to unite the whole city

Two Athenian estates

Here are two inventories of estates of rich men, preserved as part of legal speeches. Both show some diversity of assets and holdings, as well as money invested in workshops, or lent out in various forms of interest-bearing loans. There also appear to be some large sums lying idle or available on deposit in banks.

In the first, Demosthenes, the great orator and politician is describing the property left by his father in c.375 BCE when he himself was about nine. It was administered, and much of it misappropriated, by the relatives left as Demosthenes' guardians. When he came of age he had a prolonged legal battle to recover even a small proportion of it. This initial statement of the estate comes from the first of a series of speeches in prosecution of one of his guardians, Aphobos.

This very substantial estate is most unusual in that it contains no landed property at all. It seems that his father, also called Demosthenes, had tried hard to keep the extent of his wealth secret. One reason may have been that his father-in-law Gylon had been condemned to pay a heavy fine as a result of military failure in the Black Sea region during the Peloponnesian War, and hence Demosthenes wished to avoid any question of being liable for Gylon's debts owed to the state; another might be to avoid paying liturgies.

My father, members of the jury, left two workshops each operating a sizeable craft-business: thirty-two or thirty-three knife-makers, each worth mostly 5 or 6 minas, and

none less than 3 minas – from which my father derived income of 30 minas a year; and twenty bed-makers, given as security on a loan worth 40 minas, bringing an income of 12 minas. In money he left up to a talent, out on loan at 12 per cent, bringing in as interest more than 70 minas a year. This was the productive capital he left, as my opponents will admit, amounting in total value to 4 talents 5000 drachmae – and the annual profit to 5000 drachmae. Besides, he left ivory and iron, which the workers used; and wood for the beds, worth about 80 minas; oak-gall dye and copper, bought for 70 minas; a house worth 3000 drachmae; furniture and drinking cups, gold jewellery and clothes, these two items the possessions of my mother – worth in all 10,000 drachmae; and 80 minas in cash in the house. In addition to all of this which he left in the house there were 70 minas in a maritime loan, lent out to Xuthus; 2400 drachmae on deposit in Pasion's bank; 600 in Pylades' bank; 1600 on loan to Demomelês son of Demon [Demosthenes' cousin], and about a talent loaned out without interest in amounts of 200 or 300 drachmae. The total of these amounts is more than 8 talents and 50 minas. You will find if you investigate it that the total of everything is about 14 talents.

Demosthenes 27, *Against Aphobus* 9–11 (364 BCE)

The second passage comes from a case in which Aeschines (himself about to be prosecuted by Demosthenes for alleged

and celebrate its civic identity (the other being the Panathenaea); by means of the productions of the great tragedies and comedies the festival also played its part in scrutinizing and questioning different aspects of the city's political and social principles and practices (see Chapter 9).

Even more important for the stability of the system was probably the fact that the poorer citizens did have some control over the behaviour of the élite, in their capacity as jurors in the popular law-courts (see p. 152). However, how far the respectable poor resented the greater prestige attributed to hoplites and other more powerful groups is unclear. After all, they had also contributed, as sailors, to Athens' military success, and their contributions were, from 480 onwards, markedly more important militarily than those of the hoplites or the cavalry because of the maritime nature of Athens' empire (see p. 178). The emphasis in public discourse and art on hoplite virtues may have caused some bitterness in the many whose contributions were apparently not lauded in the same way as were the discipline, courage and community values of the ideal hoplite citizen – not because they weren't courageous or disciplined, but because they were not hoplites. But perhaps also a good many of

misconduct on a peace embassy to Philip of Macedon) managed to have Demosthenes' political ally Timarchus disenfranchized, by persuading the jury that as a youth he had lived off older men and had consumed, through luxury and debauchery, his own property.

The relevant law, referred to as the 'scrutiny of orators', exemplifies the control of the people over the élite. It was directed at maintaining higher moral standards for the politically active citizens than for ordinary ones, and operated a sanction against maltreatment of parents, avoidance of military service, selling oneself sexually, dissipating one's inherited estate, and generally failing to act as a proper man and citizen. The sanction – in the form of a prosecution from a political opponent or personal enemy – could operate only when the citizen who had allegedly committed one of these offences chose to exercise active citizenship, by speaking in the assembly, bringing a prosecution in the law-courts, or standing for a public office. It seems to have been used very rarely.

The estate of Timarchus' father is a good example of a mixed collection of assets among the liturgical class (the people liable for payment of the liturgy).

His father left Timarchus a property from which another man would even have been able to perform liturgies, but which he was unable to preserve even for himself: there was a house behind the Acropolis, a marginal piece of land

[eschatia] at Sphettus, another piece of land [chorion] at Alopece, and besides some slaves set up working in the shoemaking trade, nine or ten, each one of whom brought in a fixed payment [apophora] of 2 obols a day, while the manager of the workshop brought in a fixed payment of 3 obols; there was in addition to these a woman skilled in flax-working who took her fine products to the market, and a man skilled at embroidery; and there were men who owed him money; and some furniture ... . The house in the city he sold to Nausicrates the comic poet, and afterwards Cleaenetus the chorus-master bought it from Nausicrates for 20 minas. The marginal plot Mnesitheus of Myrrhinous bought from him, a large place, but Timarchus had allowed it to run terribly wild. The piece of land at Alopece, which was 11 or 12 stades from the city wall, his mother supplicated and begged him to let alone, as I have heard, and not to sell; let him leave that, if nothing else, for her to be buried in. He did not keep off even that land, but sold that too for 2000 drachmae. The slave-women and slave-men he has not kept, but has sold them all. His father lent money out, which Timarchus has collected in and has spent; for this, I shall produce as a witness Metagenes of Sphettus, who owed him more than thirty minas, and paid to Timarchus what was still owing on his father's death, namely 7 minas.

(Aeschines, *Against Timarchus* – 346/5 BCE)

them managed to identify themselves, in reality or in aspiration, with these values of the ideal hoplite.

In any case, we must remember that adult male citizens constituted only around 15 per cent of the total population of Attica, numbering perhaps 30,000 out of 200,000. They must all naturally have felt superior to the rest of the population, and, albeit in different ways, all must have exercised some power over non-citizens: the women and children in their families, the metic families and the slaves. Of course, not all Athenians were able to afford their own slaves, and the extent of slave-owning, especially on small farms, is greatly disputed (see p. 201). But all could think of themselves as potential slave-owners, and many poorish farmers or shop-keepers perhaps bought and sold slaves at different times, according to their individual circumstances. In this way slavery proved exceptionally useful in staving off the potential dissatisfaction of poorer citizens. Athenians saw all slaves essen-

The Greek tendency to label all foreigners as 'barbarians' and especially those who belonged to the Persian empire as cowardly, effeminate, and suited to be slaves, was vastly increased by their great victories over the Persian forces during the wars of 480–450 BCE. On this wine jug of the mid-fifth century BCE, a near-naked man is advancing aggressively and holding his phallus. The words on the jug, 'I am Eurymedon', are probably to be read as coming from the youth, who may thus identify himself as the symbol of the Athenian alliance's victory over the Persians at the river of that name in c.469 BCE. The man in oriental costume making an apparently submissive gesture is certainly (and appropriately) saying 'I stand bent over'. In this political interpretation (though others have been proposed) the Greek victory over the Persians is expressed as sexual aggression inflicted on a weak and submissive enemy.

tially as barbarians, taken by right of conquest from peoples whose inferiority to the Greeks had been demonstrated by their defeat in many wars, above all in the great victories over the Persians from 490 to 450.

Rather fewer Athenians than could own slaves were in a position to sponsor a metic, or lease a farm or business to a metic. All, however, would encounter this disenfranchised class on a daily basis and were able to enjoy a feeling of legal and social superiority. Of course, many metics had accumulated substantial wealth as manufacturers, traders, bankers and so on. Some, like Protagoras or Aristotle, were among the leading intellectual figures of their day. None the less, ordinary Athenian citizens were conscious, on the one hand, of the radical differences between themselves and the rich political élite; and, on the other, of the links that made them part of a coherent and superior group. They were members of the citizen body, a 'male club' united by its attendant privileges and distinction.

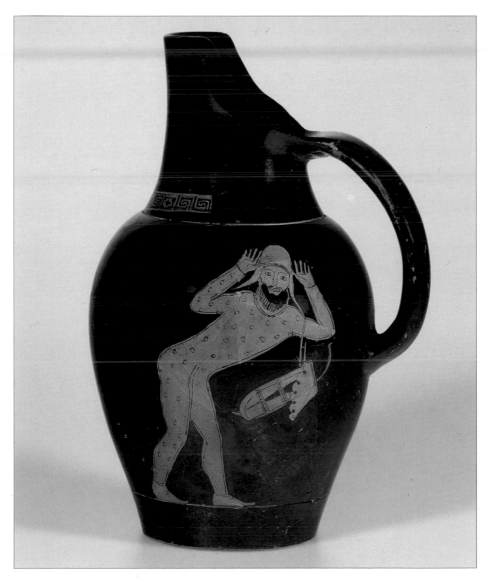

CHAPTER 5

Marilyn A. Katz

Women, Children and Men

In both the ancient Greek popular imagination and our own, Greek women spent their time indoors working wool and occupied with other household tasks, like the figures on this vase. The woman seated on the left, with a wool-basket beside her chair, is examining a slave girl's spinning. The woman seated on the right is twisting loose wool around her knee, with her leg propped on a special foot-support. (For this work, women sometimes covered their knees with a special ceramic implement of the type depicted opposite.) Another woman is spinning yarn onto a spindle, which she holds over a wool-basket. The seated woman to her left is drawing out a thick strand of wool, and a dancing woman with castanets in her right hand entertains the group as they work. Pyxis. School of Douris (Hiketes group). 460 BCE.

The polis is often characterized as a 'male club', since women were excluded from political rights in the ancient city-state. Men constituted the citizen assembly which made decisions affecting the community as a whole; men were the jurymen in the courts; and all of the polis' several hundred public officials were men. Furthermore, from the perspective of social ideals, the spaces of the polis were segregated: the public realm belonged to men, whereas women were consigned to the private domain of the home.

This picture, however, is not an entirely accurate one. In the first place, the men who possessed citizen rights were themselves a minority of the population of all city-states, including the most famous one, Athens. And our sources for the lives of ancient Greek women and children are predominantly Athenian. Athens, to be sure, was not a typical polis, but neither was it unique in the world of the ancient Greeks: many others shared the broad outlines of Athens' political history, constitutional arrangements, and social structure.

The inhabitants of Athens included, besides its male citizens, a large number of male and female slaves, a population of male and female resident aliens, or *metics*, roughly equal in number to citizens, and the wives and children of citizen men. Citizens' wives shared in citizen status, but this entitled them principally to bear sons who would become citizens or daughters who would become the wives of citizens.

Secondly, there were other areas of civic and communal life in the ancient polis besides the political one, and women, non-citizens, and even slaves played important parts in many of them: the religious and economic spheres, for example, as well as the various aspects of community in the demes or villages. And finally, the social ideal which consigned men to the public, and women to the private realm, was no more than that: an ideal. It figures very prominently in much of Greek art and literature, but when we examine more closely some of the details of ancient Greek social and cultural practices, the reality looks quite different.

THE POLIS AS A SACRIFICIAL COMMUNITY

The polis has also been described as a sacrificial community, since religion permeated every aspect of its activities and since the offering to the gods of animal or vegetable sacrifice constituted the core of religious observance in ancient Greece (see Chapter 12). Furthermore, in Athens festival celebrations of one kind or another were held on about half of the days of a given year; thirty-five or so of these were major festivals, and many of them lasted for several days. Pride of place in the city's ritual observances was assigned most frequently to citizens and their sons, but some festivals were restricted to citizen women and others gave them important

Ideology

Aristotle reports that among Pythagorean philosophers, who were organized as religious societies in the southern and Greek parts of Italy, one group taught that there was not one principle underlying the sensible universe, but ten, and that these were organized in contrasting pairs: Limit and Unlimited, Odd and Even, One and Plurality, Right and Left, Male and Female, Rest and Motion, Straight and Crooked, Light and Darkness, Good and Evil, Square and Oblong (Aristotle, *Metaphysics*).

The ideological space of the polis was structured through the principles of polarity and analogy, and the opposition between male and female was one of its governing categories. The set of ten Pythagorean oppositions listed above articulates this contrast starkly, and a saying attributed by a late author to Thales of Miletus (585 BCE), traditionally the first of the Greek philosophers, elaborates an analogous but considerably less abstract set of contrasts. Thales was reportedly thankful to Fortune on three accounts: 'that I was born a human and not a beast, a man and not a woman, a Greek and not a barbarian'.

The opposition between civilized and monstrous, Greek and barbarian, however, was not always represented as analogous to that between male and female. For example, the distinction in the Parthenon sculptures between the warrior-goddess Athena and the warrior-women Amazons suggests a contrast instead between the goddess who acknowledges submission to the male and the mythical females who refuse it.

Translated to the human sphere and to the domestic realm, a version of this same ideology found expression on even humble artistic media. For example, one side of the knee-guard illustrated here, which was used by women in working wool, represents Amazons arming in preparation for battle. The other side of the vase, however, depicts proper Athenian wives working wool in the women's quarters of the home: embodiments in their own way of Athena who, as Athena *Erganê* ('Worker'), was also the patron of their domestic skills. Attributed to the Diosphos Painter, c. 450 BCE.

The Panathenaea celebrated Athena's birthday, and her famous birth fully armed from the head of Zeus was a popular subject on black-figured vases. This amphora (a vase used for transporting and storing wine) depicts the scene described in the *Homeric Hymn* to *Athena*: 'Zeus himself bore her from his august head, and she was clad in warlike armour, golden and shining. All the gods looked on and were awe-struck as she sprang forth, brandishing a sharply pointed spear, from the immortal head of aegis-bearing Zeus'. Here, the company of admiring gods is restricted to Hermes on the left, Apollo, who is playing his lyre, and Ares, who is fully armed on the right. Before Zeus stands the white-armed birth-goddess Eileithyia, raising her arms in the gesture associated with midwives. Amphora. Group E Painter. Around 540 BCE.

roles. Metics and their families participated in some major polis celebrations; and in other festivals even slaves had a role to play.

The Panathenaea, which celebrated the birthday of Athena, the city's tutelary deity, in the first month of the festival year (corresponding roughly with July), was notably inclusive: among the celebrants were citizen men along with their sons, daughters, and wives; metics and their families; freed slaves and non-Greeks; and, during the period of the Athenian empire, representatives of the allied city-states. At the same time, however, distinctions of status among these groups were clearly marked.

The Panathenaic sacrificial procession, for example, was headed by various groups of maidens bearing different sets of ritual objects. Girls from noble families, however, preceded those from the ordinary citizen class; old men marched separately from those of military age; religious officials along with priests and priestesses made up their own contingent; metic sons processed separately from metic daughters, and so on. Similar protocols obtained for other festival occasions, and especially in those in which a *pompê* or ritual procession was part of the celebration.

Cutting across the overall inclusivity of the Panathenaea and its preliminary festivals, then, were the same distinctions of age, class, gender, and status which

One of the privileges reserved to Athenian maidens was that of being named a *kanêphoros* ('basket-carrier') in religious processions, such as that of the Panathenaea. The chorus of women in Aristophanes' *Lysistrata*, for example, speaking with one voice, claims among its distinctions and services to the city that 'once, when I was a beautiful maiden, I was a *kanêphoros* and wore a necklace of dried figs' (associated with fertility).

On this vase, a young girl of (probably) noble birth holds in her left arm a ritual basket (*kanoun*) while, with her right hand, she pours wine on a flaming altar. Behind her, an incense burner is depicted on a pedestal. The basket typically held the instruments used in blood sacrifice, and at the conclusion of the procession and after libations, the maiden handed over the *kanoun* to a male priest who carried out the sacrifice. Girls and women were prohibited from participating in blood sacrifice, but they had a role to play in the ritual activities leading up to and following the sacrifice proper.

The scene is painted on the inside surface of a *kylix*, a broad, flat drinking vessel mostly associated with *symposia* (see p. 119). Macron. Early fifth-century BCE.

operated in other areas of civic life. Girls and women of citizen status enjoyed a variety of privileges in the ritual sphere, and in all likelihood they derived some measure of civic pride from these perquisites of status, and felt themselves to be, as they were, a distinct and distinguished social group.

Specific ritual roles for girls in the polis were more elaborated, in fact, than those for boys. Girls performed a number of ritual functions, like weaving the *peplos* ('robe') for Athena or washing the cult-statue, grinding the corn for ritual cakes offered to Athena or Demeter, serving Artemis as acolytes in her sanctuary at Brauron, or carrying special ritual olive-branches as they processed to the temple of Apollo Delphinios in the harbour, where they offered propitiatory prayers to the god. Participation in many of these cult-functions was restricted either to a few girls or to those of aristocratic birth, but it is likely that the distinctions conferred upon these few were meant to stand symbolically for the ritual importance to the city of its young girls as a group.

Young boys must have participated in cult most often by accompanying their fathers, where they learned the protocols they would later be expected to observe. It was not until they were *ephebes* (young men in military training) that the male children of the polis had a regularly assigned and honoured role in most of the city's major festivals. But there were also some festivals in which they participated as children. At the Anthesteria, for example, boys engaged in some kind of ritual involving swings and also shared in festivities on the day of the drinking-rite (see p. 323); and at the Pyanopsia and Thargelia, both festivals of Apollo, boys carried round branches of olive-trees decorated with wool and hung with fruits, while they sang and asked for treats.

Both boys and girls participated in choral song and dance on ritual occasions. *Pannychides* ('all-night festivals'), for example, were especially associated with the participation of girls and women, and were prominent in the worship of Dionysus and Demeter. Choruses of men and boys competed separately for prizes at the Thargelia. And boys and men took part in the athletic and musical contests which were part of major festivals like the Panathenaea.

Citizen women figure especially in religious observances connected with Demeter and Kore, goddesses whose beneficence protected the city's crops of grain. The most prominent of these rituals, the Thesmophoria, was an exclusively women's festival, celebrated throughout Greece at both the city-state and local levels, but open only to citizen wives. The festival at Athens extended across three days in late October: on the first, the women set out from their homes and assembled together in an encampment, on the second, they fasted, and on the third day they feasted and celebrated. In the course of the festival the composted remains of offerings which the women had sacrificed earlier were retrieved and later mixed with the seed-grain.

Interpretation of the meaning of the Thesmophoria for women usually focuses on its function as a holiday from the routines of domestic life and as an affirmation of women's association with fertility both agricultural and human. But the seasonal rhythms of the Haloa (a women's festival in honour of Demeter and Dionysus celebrated in January), Skira (a threshing festival celebrated in July), and Thesmophoria intersected with that of various agricultural tasks performed by men. Thus, in this cycle of festivals, not only did women constitute themselves as a distinct social and political group, they also took responsibility for ensuring, through their rituals, the success and prosperity of men's more practical agricultural work.

Metics participated in the Panathenaic procession, and were similarly honoured with ritual roles in the processions of the Greater Dionysia. In others, like the Hephaestia, they were assigned a portion of the sacrificial offerings. Metics were probably excluded, however, from a share in the sacrifice at the Panathenaea and other major polis festivals. Nevertheless, especially in the Piraeus district of Athens, metics might be authorized by the polis to establish cults in honour of their own divinities: Egyptian metics had a cult of Isis there; Thracians one of Bendis; and Cypriots their own sanctuary of Astarte (Aphrodite).

Slaves had a recognized part in some city celebrations like the Anthesteria. And initiation into the Eleusinian Mysteries was open to all Greeks, including slaves. The Kronia was a holiday especially for slaves on which state business was suspended, and slaves dined together with their masters in a raucous and unrestrained atmosphere. They drank wine and ate newly harvested fruits and grains, in recollection perhaps of the golden age of Kronos (Zeus' father), when the earth produced her fruits spontaneously and there was no need for labour.

(Opposite) On the second or third day of the Anthesteria Festival, boys and girls participated in a swinging ritual. The ritual involved swinging over fumes from a vessel on the ground, but its purpose and meaning are unclear. It was connected in some way with Erigone, the daughter of Icarius, legendary Athenian inventor of the process of making wine. Icarius tested his discovery upon some shepherds, who became intoxicated and killed him in a drunken frenzy; when Erigone discovered his body she hanged herself. Here, a mythological version of the ritual is depicted on a *skyphos*, or wine cup, with a satyr pushing a nymph named Antheia ('Blossom') on a swing. There is no vessel beneath the swing, but it does appear on other vases associated with the same ritual. Penelope Painter. Mid-fifth century BCE.

The whole population of the city shared in celebrating the Diasia, a festival of Zeus *Meilichios* ('the kindly one' – the god in his underworld manifestation) where, following more solemn observances, families and friends feasted in an atmosphere of gaiety. And there were doubtless many ritual occasions on which women, metics, and slaves participated informally. The prosecutor in a fourth-century law case, at any rate, explains that a woman caught in adultery was prohibited from attending any of the public sacrifices, to which, he adds, even metic and slave women were permitted entry, either to view the spectacle or to offer prayer. The implication seems clear that even when the city's politically marginalized groups did not have an official role to perform, their presence as spectators was taken for granted, except at those festivals where they were specifically prohibited. And when present, they were free to offer private devotions either on their own behalf or that of the city.

THE BODY OF EVIDENCE

In Lucian's *Dialogue on Love* (second century CE), a misogynist debates the merits of women with a lover of women; the lover of women defends them so well that the misogynist claims about his opponent: 'If the assembly and law-courts were open to women, and if they could participate in public affairs, they would elect you general or vote you a bronze statue'. But these venues were not in fact open to women, as the misogynist goes on to point out, reminding his interlocutor that 'men characteristically speak on behalf of women'.

And this, indeed, is what we find them doing in many of the cases which were argued in the law-courts of Athens located in the north-east and southern sections of the Agora, and at other sites around the city. For example, a woman in a fifth-century case who is accused of having murdered her husband is prosecuted for the crime by her stepson and defended by her son, even though she herself was still living. We have only the prosecutor's side of the story, and it is notable that he does not hesitate to appeal to mythological precedent in characterizing his stepmother as a Clytemnestra, or to borrow loosely from the arguments of Aeschylus' famous trilogy the *Oresteia* in claiming that a son's duty consists more in avenging a father than in defending a mother.

In other, less sensational cases, however, a woman's testimony, given privately before family members, is introduced into the arguments and often carries considerable weight. And women could give evidence under oath, by a special procedure which required them to swear before arbitrators in the Delphinion, a sanctuary of Apollo. But women of citizen status did not ever appear in court as litigants, and indeed a certain discretion is observed in the practice of not even mentioning a woman by name unless she is an individual of low repute – or the litigant wishes so to represent her.

Women, in any case, would not have had the opportunity to commit most of the crimes we hear about: assault, damage to property, treason, and other such offences required access to the public sphere or to the realm of politics. And matters involving

(*Opposite*) **In Hesiod's epic poem, *Theogony*, which recounted the coming-into-being of the world and the births of the gods, Kronos was the son of Sky (Ouranos) and Earth (Gaia), and one of the Titans, the first and older generation of the gods. In order to forestall his overthrow by a son, Kronos swallowed his children as they issued from the womb of his consort, Rhea. But when Zeus was born, Rhea deceived Kronos by hiding Zeus away and offering Kronos a stone wrapped in swaddling clothes, the scene which is depicted on this vase. In the *Theogony*, Kronos swallows the stone and is later forced to disgorge it by Zeus when he grows up. But in this representation, Kronos responds to the presentation of his baby more like a human father, with amazed surprise.**

From a different mythological perspective, the one represented by Hesiod in another epic poem, *Works and Days*, the era of Kronos was the Greek 'golden age,' a time when men 'lived like gods, free from toils and pain', when old age did not exist, and when 'the grain-giving earth brought forth her fruits spontaneously'. Since there was no need for agricultural labour, slavery was also unknown in this mythological era, and the participation of slaves in the annual Kronia religious festival recreated this time of freedom within the constraints of everyday realities. Pelike. Attributed to the Nausikaa Painter. Around 450 BCE.

Upon his return from the Trojan War, Agamemnon, the leader of the Greek expedition, was murdered by his wife Clytemnestra and her lover Aegisthus, who was also Agamemnon's cousin and the usurper of his throne. The crime and its aftermath – the retaliatory murder of Clytemnestra by her son Orestes and his subsequent trial and acquittal – were the subject of Aeschylus' famous trilogy of plays, the *Oresteia*. This vase assigns principal responsibility for the crime to Aegisthus, who strikes down the helpless king, shrouded in a transparent robe, while Clytemnestra, wielding an axe, follows behind him. (The female figure on the right with unbound hair is probably Agamemnon's daughter, Electra.)

On the reverse of this vase, Orestes slays the adulterous Aegisthus, a feat for which he was traditionally celebrated. His murder of his mother, however, was more problematic. In the *Oresteia*, Orestes calls upon Athena to liberate him from pursuit by his mother's furies. In response, Athena establishes the principle of jury-trial by selecting a court of citizens to hear the case (the Areopagus court), setting forth 'laws for all time to come' and specifying its procedures. The vote results in a tie, which Athena breaks in Orestes' favour, proclaiming herself, much like the prosecutor in Antiphon's oration, 'on the side of the husband, lord of the house'. Calyx krater. Dokimasia Painter. About 460 BCE.

family law would have been handled by a woman's guardian: her husband, father, son, or other adult male relative. But, given the prominence of women in matters involving religion, it is not surprising that we know of cases where women were prosecuted (and acquitted) for impiety.

When petty offences were at issue, a woman of citizen status might well employ the procedure which a bread-seller uses against Philocleon in Aristophanes' *Wasps*, when she hauled him before a polis official on the charge of 'damage to goods'. Such remedies, when the sum at stake was below a certain amount, were available to all, and there must have been many legal cases which were settled outside the courts by polis officials or privately, through arbitrators.

A woman whose status was open to question, however, might have been called upon to appear in court in person, as seems possible in the case of Neaera, who was prosecuted as a foreigner on a charge of illegitimately assuming citizen rights. And according to an account which is probably apocryphal, the orator Hyperides defended the courtesan Phryne on a charge of impiety by resorting, when the force of his arguments failed, to having Phryne brought into the courtroom and her breasts bared, in order to convince the jury to acquit her.

Children, like women, were represented in court by their fathers or guardians. The orator Antiphon, for example, composed a model speech in which a boy was accused of accidentally killing another with a throw of the javelin, and the hypothetical case was argued out by the boys' fathers. For it was not until a young man had reached his majority (the age of eighteen) that he could bring an action at law or defend himself against one; and it was not until he reached the age of thirty that he was eligible to serve as a juryman in the law-courts. But if the complaints of several orators are any guide, a few boys (and girls) will have had experience of the

Men's deliberations in the law-courts were expected to be guided by the laws of the polis or, when none of these applied specifically, by the principle of justice (*dikê*). *Dikê* was herself a divinity, born from Zeus' second wife, Themis, along with the *Horai* ('Seasons'), *Eunomia* ('Lawfulness'), and *Eirênê* ('Peace'), goddesses who, according to Hesiod's *Theogony*, 'watch over the works of mortal men.' Thus, the presence of female divinities was invoked in many areas of Greek society from which women themselves were barred. On this vase, *Dikê* is shown triumphantly subduing *Adikia* or Injustice. *Dikê* is reserved and composed: her hair is bound up in a knot; the drapery of her chiton falls in ordered folds and is restrained by a girdle. *Adikia*, with her flailing arms, large and grotesque facial features, gaping mouth, loose hair and chiton, and tattooed arms and legs is disordered and monstrous. Attic red-figure neck-amphora. 520 BCE.

(*Opposite*) **Women were exempted from the duties of the male citizen, as well as excluded from his privileges. Military service was the most important and dangerous of a citizen's obligations to the polis, and scenes of the warrior's departure for battle are common on many vases. In such scenes, like the one depicted here, family members left behind commonly surround the departing warrior, and the hoplite's wife holds the ritual implements for marking the transition. After pouring wine into a shallow bowl, she will spill some on the ground as a libation to the gods, and then the warrior, his wife, and his aged father will share the rest, in a last gesture of family unity. Stamnos. Achilles Painter. 450 BCE.**

law-courts from an early age. For it was apparently not uncommon for a man to bring his small children into the court, group them around himself, and weep and beseech the jurymen for pity – something which Socrates, in a famous passage of the *Apology*, specifically refuses to do, even though, as he says, 'I too have relatives ... and three sons, two of them not yet grown'. Socrates explains that he does not think that it is right for a man of his age and with his reputation to do such a thing.

Metics had direct access to the Athenian courts, and a special legal official (the *polemarch*) supervised cases in which a metic was the plaintiff or defendant. An accused metic, however, had to post bail, as a citizen did not, and it appears that the sanction for the murder of a metic by a citizen was lighter than that for killing a citizen. Metics were obliged to have a citizen sponsor (*prostatês*), and to pay a residency-tax (*metoikion*); they were thus also uniquely liable to prosecution in these areas, and to enslavement if convicted.

In one such case, the metic woman Zobia was accused of failing to pay her tax. And in this case, it is notable that Zobia was represented in court by her sponsor. For male metics represented themselves, but it was apparently preferable for female metics, like women of citizen status, to be represented by men.

No such distinctions of gender obtained in the case of slaves, who, whether male or female, were treated mostly as property under Athenian law. They could be bought, sold, beaten (by their masters but not by others), and legal action for offences against slaves had to be brought by their masters. The killer of a slave, however, was prosecuted for murder, and this may have been the case even when the slave's master had committed the crime.

When testimony in lawsuits was required from them, slaves quite literally provided the body of evidence: their information was invalid unless it had been procured through torture, which was carried out publicly in the Agora using the whip or the rack. Of the slave-woman who actually (and unknowingly) administered the poison in the case of the allegedly murderous wife (see p. 107), for example, the plaintiff reports simply: 'she was tortured and handed over to the executioner'.

THE BODY POLITIC

Public slaves (*dêmosioi douloi*) were the property of the polis, and they formed something of an élite: one corps of them, for example, was used in the fifth century as a police force to keep order in assembly meetings. Thus, if an unpopular speaker did not sit down of his own accord, his voice drowned out by shouts and clamours, then the officials would order the police to drag him down from the platform or even eject him from the meeting.

Slaves, of course, were not citizens. But there was no absolute barrier *in theory* to a (male) slave's becoming a citizen. If freed, he became a metic, and might thereupon be granted citizenship. The slave Pasion, for example, after having been emancipated, assumed management of the bank belonging to his former owners and was later granted citizenship as a result of his services to the city. Pasion's case

(*Opposite*) Up until the end of the sixth century, the citizen assembly met in the Agora, to which it also returned for meetings on extraordinary occasions in the fifth century (ostracism, for example, see p. 149). But thereafter, the *ekklēsia* was convened on a hill to the south-west of the Agora – hence 'Demos of the Pnyx' in Aristophanes' *Knights* (see p. 92). In the fourth century, the hill was fortified with the embankment visible in this photograph by William Stillman, and in the valley just visible in the lower left (south-west of the Areopagus) there were shrines interspersed with private houses. Perhaps it was in one of these that Praxagora, the leading character of the *Ecclesiazusae*, was supposed to have lodged and overheard assembly debates.

was certainly an unusual one, but it demonstrates the point that there was no 'constitutional' barrier, as it were, to the full enfranchizement of either former slaves or metics in the Athenian polis.

In 338 BCE, in fact, after Athens' disastrous defeat at Chaeronea (see pp. 69 and 187), a proposal was brought forward and carried through in the assembly to free all slaves and enfranchise all metics so that they could participate in the defence of the city. Unfortunately, we do not know whether this programme was ever implemented, and scholars have argued that the decree must have been annulled when it became clear that Philip was prepared to conclude a peace.

Under normal circumstances, metics, like all non-citizens, were precluded from access to the assembly and from holding public office. But they might be called before the assembly to offer information or might wish to address the *dêmos* (the 'people' of Athens as a political body) on their own behalf. In such cases, metics and other foreigners (*xenoi*) who were non-residents had first to present a formal petition that they be allowed to address either the council or the assembly, and a citizen had to propose any motion which concerned them. A group of metics from Olynthus, for example, in the mid-fourth century, sought relief from the *metoikion* ('metic-tax'), and were granted access to the assembly in a formula which appears in several fourth-century inscriptions: '[on the matter] concerning which the Olynthians were decreed to have the right to make supplication [i.e. present a petition] in the *dêmos* [assembly]'.

Metics, like other *xenoi*, might be honoured, either individually or as a group, with grants of citizenship or, more usually, with various of its privileges: the right to own land, for example; or, as in the case of the Olynthians, exemption from the *metoikion*.

Women in the Assembly

The city of Athens was named in honour of its tutelary deity, Athena, but Greek mythology elaborated two different aetiologies of the contest between Athena and Poseidon which resulted in the goddess' victory: in both Athena was credited with the city's first olive-tree, and Poseidon with a spring or lake. In the account of Apollodorus, a second-century BCE mythographer, Zeus entrusted the decision between the two divinities to a jury of the twelve gods, who found in favour of Athena, since Cecrops, Athens' first legendary king, bore witness that she had been the first to plant the olive tree.

Varro, however, the great first-century BCE Roman scholar, gave a different account of how the ultimate decision was reached, and this was preserved by Saint Augustine in his *City of God*:

> Cecrops called an assembly of all the citizens, male and female, to vote on the question; for at that time and in that part of the world the custom was that women as well as

men should take part in deliberations on matters of state. Now when the matter was put before the multitude, the men voted for Neptune [Poseidon], the women for Minerva [Athena]; and, as it happened, the women outnumbered the men by one; and so the victory went to Minerva.

> Then Neptune was furious, and devastated the Athenian territory by floods of sea-water … . To appease his wrath … the women suffered a threefold punishment: they were never to have the vote again; their children were never to take their mother's name; and no one was ever to call them 'Athenian women'.

Augustine, in commenting on this myth, does not hesitate to express his disapproval of Athena's failure to come to the defence of her champions: 'Minerva could at least have ensured them the right to be called "Athenian women", and to be rewarded by bearing the name of the goddess to whom their votes had brought victory over the male divinity'.

But most metics, doubtless, possessed none of the political rights which citizens enjoyed as a matter of course, and this group would have included even such well-known and wealthy men as the philosopher Aristotle and the orator Lysias.

Once an Athenian boy had reached the age of majority and had passed his scrutiny (the examination of his qualifications for citizenship), his first duty as a new citizen was army service, and thereafter his first privilege was participation in the citizen assembly. He was not eligible to hold public office, however, or aerve as juror until he had reached the age of thirty.

By the mid-second century CE Athens had been a subordinate city of the Roman empire for three centuries. Its leading cultural role had been preserved under the new political regime – the new library of Pantaenus as well as the ancient Odeum (Odeion) bore witness to that. But, architecturally, Rome's dominance was firmly stamped on the civic centre. A Roman basilica (administrative structure) abutted on the Panathenaic Way. Roman stoas (porticoes) now joined those of classical (Zeus Eleutherius) and Hellenistic (Attalus) date. But most significant of all was the hiving off of the Agora's commercial function into a new, purpose-built market separated from the civic sphere (now greatly reduced in importance, since Athens had lost its autonomy).

Thus, of all the resident groups in Athens who were normally excluded from political rights (slaves, metics, other foreigners, children and women), only for women was there an absolute barrier against ever achieving them. To be sure, in the mythological tradition, women had once possessed the vote: in the days of Cecrops, the first king of Attica, they used it to elect Athena over Poseidon as the city's tutelary deity, and were punished with disenfranchizement (see p. 112).

And in Aristophanes' *Ecclesiazusae* ('Women in the Assembly') women take over the polis and vote through a programme abolishing private property and the family, but not, significantly, slavery. For even in this comic fantasy, where the city will be dominated by what, from a male point of view, were women's chief interests – food and sex – socio-economic reality intrudes: labour will, after all, be required to produce the food and wine for the banqueters' feasts (see also p. 94).

There was, however, one time during the year when the women of citizen status did, as it were, take over the assembly: on the occasion of the Thesmophoria (see p. 105). During their three-day celebration of this festival, the women set up an encampment on the Pnyx, the normal site for meetings of the citizen assembly. On the second day of the festival, when the women were fasting, the council and law-courts were not in session, and if meetings of the assembly were required, they were held elsewhere.

Furthermore, women, like men, elected their own officials for this festival, availing themselves for the purpose of procedures normally restricted to the political sphere. And it is notable that when, in Aristophanes' *Thesmophoriazusae* ('Women

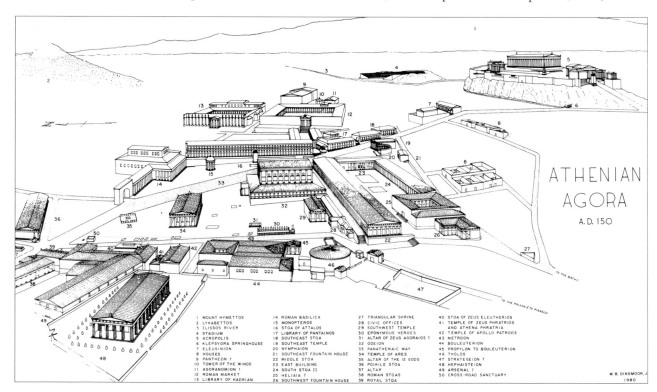

ATHENIAN AGORA
A.D. 150

1	MOUNT HYMETTOS	14	ROMAN BASILICA	27	TRIANGULAR SHRINE	40	STOA OF ZEUS ELEUTHERIOS
2	LYKABETTOS	15	MONOPTEROS	28	SOUTHWEST TEMPLE	41	TEMPLE OF ZEUS PHRATRIOS
3	ILISSOS RIVER	16	STOA OF ATTALOS	29	SOUTHWEST TEMPLE		AND ATHENA PHRATRIA
4	STADIUM	17	LIBRARY OF PANTAINOS	30	EPONYMOUS HEROES	42	TEMPLE OF APOLLO PATROOS
5	ACROPOLIS	18	SOUTHEAST STOA	31	ALTAR OF ZEUS AGORAIOS ?	43	METROON
6	KLEPSYDRA SPRINGHOUSE	19	SOUTHEAST TEMPLE	32	ODEION	44	BOULEUTERION
7	ELEUSINION	20	NYMPHAION	33	PANATHENAIC WAY	45	PROPYLON TO BOULEUTERION
8	HOUSES	21	SOUTHEAST FOUNTAIN HOUSE	34	TEMPLE OF ARES	46	THOLOS
9	PANTHEON ?	22	MIDDLE STOA	35	ALTAR OF THE 12 GODS	47	STRATEGEION ?
10	TOWER OF THE WINDS	23	EAST BUILDING	36	POIKILE STOA	48	HEPHAISTEION
11	AGORANOMION ?	24	SOUTH STOA II	37	ALTAR	49	ARSENAL ?
12	ROMAN MARKET	25	HELIAIA ?	38	ROMAN STOAS	50	CROSS-ROAD SANCTUARY
13	LIBRARY OF HADRIAN	26	SOUTHWEST FOUNTAIN HOUSE	39	ROYAL STOA		

W. B. DINSMOOR, J
1980

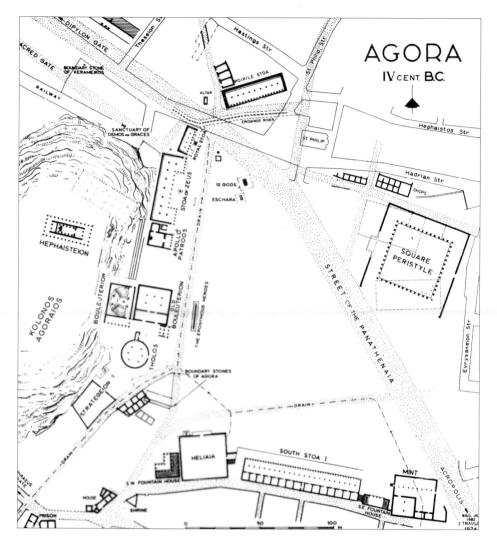

Celebrating the Thesmophoria'), the women hold a mock assembly, they are perfectly familiar with the assembly's ritual and political protocols, and with speakers' rhetorical techniques. In the more fantastic world of the *Ecclesiazusae*, by contrast, the leading female character's knowledge of proper protocol requires explanation: she had acquired it, she says, when she and her husband lived on the slopes on the Pnyx.

Only in mythology or comic fantasy, then, did women ever have access to the citizen assembly. Even when the citizen body required a woman's information – a priestess' oracular response, for example – it was brought before the assembly by her male relative.

TRADING PLACES

In Athens, as in many ancient Greek cities, 'it [was] regarded as inappropriate for a young person to be seen abroad before the market [*agora*] is full [mid-morning] or after dark, or for a woman to keep a shop or do any other market business', as

The Agora, Athens' main gathering place, flourished in the fourth century as both a political (including religious) and a commercial centre. Traversed by the city's major processional way, the route taken by the annual Panathenaic procession, and flanked by political, legal and religious structures, it stood not so much in the shadow of the Acropolis as in a complementary and almost equal relationship with it. To enter the Agora was to enter space that was in some sense sacred, and certain classes of convicted criminals were therefore formally barred. On the other hand, it was not a space reserved only for adult male citizens. What the plan cannot show is the mass (and mess) of temporary booths and stalls of hawkers and peddlers selling a whole range of articles from trinkets and gewgaws to staple necessities. And the sellers and customers included citizen women, and foreigners and slaves of both sexes, the latter not always there of their own volition (slaves both bought and were themselves bought). Strict regulations were supposed to ensure fair and peaceful trading, but fighting as well as faking was not unknown. Aristophanes in his *Knights* comedy of 424 gives to the Sausage-Seller character the speaking name of 'Agoracritus', meaning (so the Sausage-Seller himself claims) 'reared on disputes in the Agora'. Rarely can a name alone have conveyed so much precise information.

Constraint of trade

As *Katouchios* ('Constrainer'), the god Hermes was called upon in curse-tablets to ratify imprecations against male and female shopkeepers together with their shops and their manufacturing skills. Curse-tablets are thin lead sheets inscribed with maledictions, and often divinities associated with the underworld are invoked to ensure that the curse is efficacious. Most curse-tablets, like the one cited below, date from a late period, but there are earlier examples which are similar in form. Imprecations might be directed against competitors in the areas of love, sports, or the law-courts, as well as commerce.

Typically, in the tablets concerned with commerce, a shopkeeper is 'bound' together with his wife, male and female associates, and along with their workshops, skills, and profits. Perhaps these retailers had cheated their customers: a character in Aristophanes' *Plutus*, for example, complains that 'the (female) tavern-keeper in my neighbourhood is always short-changing me in the drinks'. And Plato, in the *Laws*, says that disparagement and abuse are commonly heaped upon 'the whole class of shopkeepers and traders' since they are always trying to maximize their profits.

But it is more likely that these *katadesmoi* ('binding spells') reflect the spirited and agonistic context of commercial competition. In one set of Attic tablets from the third century CE, a group of men and women is cursed either separately or together with a number of (presumably) their neighbours and/or associates. Their occupations are not indicated, but the imprecator presumably represents a rival group of entrepreneurs who are seeking the aid of the god of commerce and other deities in order to gain an advantage in the market over their chief competitors:

I bind Ophilion (m.) and Ophilime (f.) and Olympos (m.) and Pistias (m.) and Magadis (f.) and Protos (m.) and Kados (m.), Thoukleides (m.) and Melana (f.) and Komos (m.) and Bakkhis (f.) and Kittos (m.), and these men's and women's expectations [of livelihood] (*elpidas*) from both gods and heroes, and all their [manufacturing] skills (*ergasias*), by Hermes Katoukhios and by Hekate and by Earth and by all the gods and by the Mother of the Gods.

Menander Rhetor, a late author, reports. This, clearly, was the social ideal. And there are some instances of conformity to it: for example, the Athenian Euthydemus, in one of Xenophon's Socratic dialogues, did not enter the Agora because of his age, and instead sat conversing in a saddler's shop near it. And from other sources it is clear that, in well-to-do households, either men or slaves – rather than respectable women – did the shopping.

The Agora was the city's central public space: the core of its political, judicial, economic, and cultural life. Within its perimeter in the classical period were located the council-house, the offices of many of the public officials, several courtrooms, many religious shrines and, especially, the city's marketplace, where goods and services were traded (see pp. 114–15). And before the Pnyx was constructed, the assembly had also met in the Agora.

Ideally, women were absent from this arena of public business and commerce, and young men did not appear in it until after noon. But here we have one of our clearest examples of a discrepancy between social ideals and social practice. For, as Aristotle remarks, it is impossible to prevent 'the wives of the poor' from going about.

Who were these women? And how many of them were there? Recent calculations have estimated that about 4 per cent. of Athenian citizens were well-to-do, and that of these, the really wealthy represented only about 1 per cent. The majority of Athenians, then, were 'poor,' although only a small percentage of these – something like 1 per cent – were really impoverished.

The Aristotelian category of 'wives of the poor', then, will have comprised the majority of women of citizen status. And so it is not surprising that we hear of many women working in or around the Agora, although it is usually hard to tell if these are citizen, metic, or slave women. Some of them engaged in petty trade, selling foodstuffs (like the bread-seller mentioned above), or items like perfumes and garlands; others were tavern-keepers or woolworkers.

Women workers and traders are found exclusively at the low end of the economic scale, and are entirely absent from those occupations in which the real money, as it were, was to be made: crafts, manufacture, money-lending, slave-farming, business, and the like (see Chapter 4). The occupations in which women are prominent, indeed, overlap significantly with those attested for female slaves in emancipation-tablets (woolworking, retail trade, wet-nursing). And it is revealing that, in one oration by Demosthenes, the fact that a citizen's mother had been reduced by poverty to selling garlands and wet-nursing raises questions about her citizen status.

It is clear that male and female citizens, metics, and slaves often worked alongside one another in the many craft shops located in and around the Agora. And the building accounts for the Erechtheum indicate that, at the end of the fifth century BCE, about a quarter of the (male) workers were slaves, about a quarter citizens, and the rest metics: all skilled workmen were paid at the same rate, one drachma a day. (Women, by comparison, were prohibited by law from transacting business in amounts over one medimnus – a unit of weight equivalent to between three and five drachmae.)

From the curse-tablets, it appears that the men and women who worked together in the Agora shops formed a lively society, both competing and co-operating with their neighbours. And it is notable that, in Aristophanes, vulgar shouting and abuse were associated with female retailers. In the *Frogs*, for example, the god Dionysus reminds the competing poets Aeschylus and Euripides that it is 'not fitting for them to berate one another like bread-sellers'. If, as Pericles suggests in the famous funeral oration attributed to him by Thucydides, the best woman was she of whom the least was heard and said, it is evident that the women of the Agora did not aspire to membership in this élite.

There was one potentially lucrative area of commerce largely under female control – the traffic in women. To be sure, no woman of citizen status would have engaged in sex for money unless, like one in a fragment of the comic poet Antiphanes

The woman selling perfumes to a slave-girl in this shop dispenses her goods in an alabastron, or small perfume vase; a lekythos (vase for olive-oil) hangs on the wall, and a pelike or storage jar used for water, wine, or oil, sits on the floor – the same type of vase on which the scene is depicted. (On the other side of the vase, not shown here, the slave-girl brings the alabastron home to her mistress, seated indoors with her wool-basket on the floor beside her.)

Women retailers trafficked commonly in perfumes, which were used, not only by women, but also by men at symposia and in *palaestrae* (wrestling-schools). It was reportedly disreputable for a man to be a perfume-seller, but this was clearly not the case when large-scale dealings were at issue, since there are disputes in the orators over loans and debts incurred when men undertook to establish perfumeries. The discrepancy illustrates the larger point that women often sold as retailers the same items that might form the basis of a more profitable, full-scale business establishment for men. Around 460 BCE.

who became a courtesan, she was *both* poor *and* 'bereft of guardian and relatives'. Thus, courtesans (*hetairai* or 'female companions') were generally metics; and prostitutes (*pornai* or 'women for sale') were mostly slaves who worked from brothels run by a woman or, more commonly, man, who paid a tax on his (i.e. their) earnings to the polis.

Ordinary prostitutes commanded a price of only a drachma or less, but courtesans charged whatever the market could bear, and this might have been as much as a mina (100 drachmae) for the services of a legendary Athenian courtesan like Phryne (see p. 108). And when Socrates visited the courtesan Theodote, he observed that both she and her mother were finely dressed, that her many maids were well outfitted, and that her house was lavishly furnished.

In unusual circumstances, as noted above, slaves or former slaves might become quite wealthy. A larger number, besides working in manufacture, trade, and banking, might belong to the category of slaves described as 'living apart': those who lived and worked independently, and who rendered periodic payments to their masters. Most slaves who laboured in the 'public domain' – in or around the Agora – were skilled workers. But if we might think of these as a privileged group, they did not, apparently, so regard themselves. Of the allegedly more than 20,000 who escaped from the city and its environs in the last phase of the Peloponnesian War, a large number were skilled workers (whether mining slaves, artisans, craftsmen, or skilled agricultural workers is unclear).

This symposium scene is represented on a *kylix*, the most popular kind of drinking-cup, which appears commonly in symposium scenes, and on which, as in this case, symposiastic orgies were often depicted. The garland worn by the bearded man was one of the most common items sold by female retailers, and it was used both in religious rituals and on celebratory occasions.

The sexual activities represented should serve to disabuse us of any romanticized notions about the lives and wealth of prostitutes and courtesans. Neaera, for example, who reportedly began life as a slave prostitute, eventually bought her freedom, with funds amounting to 20 minas (2000 drachmae) raised from her earnings and from an Athenian named Phrynion. But when Phrynion brought her to Athens, he allegedly used her much like the women on this vase:

'He treated her without decency or restraint, taking her everywhere with him to dinners where there was drinking and making her a partner in his revels; and he had intercourse with her openly whenever and wherever he wished, making his privilege a display to the onlookers'.

The famous courtesans about whose learning, beauty, and skills we hear much in our sources certainly constituted a minority. Most prostitutes and hetaerae would have been subjected to the kinds of humiliations that Phrynion felt free to inflict upon Neaera. Pedieus Painter. Late sixth-century BCE.

Most metics and their wives, like the men and women of most citizen families, were persons of modest means. When honours were voted in 401/400 BCE to metics who helped overthrow the tyranny of the Thirty (see pp. 66–7), the occupations listed for them in the decree are lowly ones: farmer, cook, carpenter, muleteer, builder, gardener, ass-driver, oil merchant, nut-seller, baker, fuller, hired servant, statuette-maker.

Just as in the case of citizens, however, a minority of metics were wealthy and prestigious. In the opening of the *Republic*, for example, Socrates (an Athenian citizen) walks down to the Piraeus to visit his friend Cephalus, originally from Syracuse, who owned a shield-factory employing over 100 slaves. (The orator Lysias was Cephalus' son.) Another metic, Cephisodorus, whose property was confiscated and sold upon his conviction for sacrilege, also lived in the Piraeus and owned male and female slaves worth some 2500 drachmae (the rough equivalent of seven years' pay for a skilled workman).

Socrates converses in the *Republic* with Cephalus and his sons as social equals, and this pattern appears elsewhere. Cutting across the line dividing metic from citizen was another social barrier separating rich from poor (see Chapter 4). Upper-class metics, their lack of political rights aside, lived in a manner not materially different from that of their citizen counterparts, and espoused the same set of social ideals. Similarly, the wives and daughters of such metics would doubtless have adopted for themselves, as a way of signalling their social status, the rules of decorum to which upper-class women of citizen status conformed as a matter of custom.

ATHENS ON DISPLAY

Women appear prominently in ancient Greek drama. Tragedy featured many of the famous heroines of the Greek tradition in leading roles, and an interest in women dominates many comedies, like those of Aristophanes. But the conventions of the dramatic stage also marked it as distinct from ordinary social life. For example, male actors portrayed female characters; all actors wore masks; and most of the plots were derived from the Greeks' mythological traditions (see Chapter 9).

The dramatic stage was thus a realm of the imagination, where dramatists could explore the tensions, ambiguities, and contradictions of the present-day polis and its ideals within the plot-context of mythological paradigms. In these plays, social, political, and religious issues were sometimes played out as family dramas, and tragic polarities often found expression in the language of sexual conflict. In Aeschylus' *Oresteia*, for example, the issue of homicide pitted wife against husband and son against mother. In Sophocles' *Antigone*, the heroine's disobedience of a ruler's edict brings her into conflict with Creon, her uncle and guardian. And Pentheus' opposition to the advent of the god Dionysus, in Euripides' *Bacchae*, results in his tragic murder by his mother (see p.333).

Family conflict figures in Aristophanic comedy, too: a father tries to bring his spendthrift son under control in the *Clouds*; a son attempts to restrain his father's craze for jury-service in the *Wasps*. And the plots of several comedies were organized around a battle between the sexes: the *Thesmophoriazusae*, in which women seek revenge on Euripides for his unflattering portrayals of their sex; the *Lysistrata*, in which women take over the Acropolis and stage a sex-strike to bring an end to war; and the *Ecclesiazusae*, where women appropriate the male realm of the assembly.

Today, we encounter these tragedies and comedies principally as texts. These, however, are no more than 'scripts' for a set of performances which, in antiquity, were presented as only one part of a major polis festival, held in the spring in honour of the god Dionysus.

The earliest form of the festival, indeed, was not focused on drama. Rather, it was centred, like the Panathenaea in honour of Athena, around a great procession (*pompê*) leading, on this occasion, to the shrine of Dionysus at the foot of the south-east slope of the Acropolis. Citizens, metics, slaves, and women all took part, and, as in the Panathenaic *pompê*, each group marched separately and had different functions to perform. Metics wore purple robes and carried offering-trays; citizen men brought wine-skins; and an aristocratic maiden bearing a golden basket of first-fruits headed the procession. Along the way there was dancing and singing, and at the end of the day there was a great feast. In 333 BCE this required the sacrificial slaughter of at least 100 bulls.

By the early fifth century, dramatic performances had been added to the festival. These were presented in an area just north of the god's shrine which had probably first been used for the performance of choral dances in honour of Dionysus. The space was gradually enlarged, and eventually embankments of seats were constructed out of stone on the slope of the Acropolis.

The City Dionysia, as it was called, still began with a day of procession, feasting, and general celebration. Afterwards, plays were presented on three or four separate days, and tickets of admission were required for entry. Before the plays began, however, a set of rituals established a context of civic, political, and military pride: the ten generals poured libations; the tribute from the cities of the Athenian empire was carried onto the stage and displayed; the orphans of the war dead who had been raised at public expense were invested with hoplite armour on coming of age; benefactors of the city were publicly honoured; and, finally, the names of slaves being emancipated were proclaimed.

Foreigners, metics, representatives of the allied states and other city-states were present for this exhibition of civic unity, and for the dramatic performances which followed them. Were women there too? In the *Thesmophoriazusae* they are familiar with Euripidean tragedy. Did they watch these dramas themselves or only read them or hear about them from their husbands? We don't know for sure; the evidence is contradictory and the question has been debated inconclusively for over two hundred years.

(Opposite) A bearded image of Dionysus, crowned with ivy, appears to watch passively beside his altar as women celebrate him in ritual dance to the rhythm piped by a flute-player. Flat sacred cakes swirl about his head, and an ivy-wreathed stamnos (wine-mixing vase) stands on the ground under the handle. As in Euripides' *Bacchae*, the barefooted maenads' hair flows freely, and one of them carries the thyrsus, a wand wreathed in ivy. In a section of the vase not visible here, another woman in maenadic garb dances holding both a thyrsus and a young fawn.

The ritual on this vase and others like it may depict Dionysiac worship at the Lenaea or at the Anthesteria, where a group of women performed secret rituals for Dionysus on behalf of the polis. Neither celebration had anything in common with the wild orgies of the *Bacchae*, but women employed maenadic ritual equipment like the thyrsus and crowns of ivy in polis festivals. The figure of the maenad was a familiar one in both art and literature, and appears as early as the *Iliad*: Andromache, hearing from within her room the cries of lamentation over Hector, drops her shuttle and races forth wildly to the walls of Troy 'like a maenad'. Macron. Early fifth century BCE.

On the one hand it seems unlikely that women were the only group excluded from a part of the Dionysia which was open to all Greeks, and at which, in fact, attendance by foreigners was not only encouraged, but required (in the case of the allies during the period of the empire). And it seems clear that lower-class women – those who hawked their wares (and themselves) – to the general public of men, were present; perhaps they slipped in after the performances had begun and when entry was free. Aristotle's associate Theophrastus, in a collection of character-sketches, includes the type of a miser who, with his children, gains entrance to the performances in this manner.

On the other hand, the ritual setting of the theatrical presentations highlighted the military and political aspects of Athenian civic identity, and these were the preserve of the city's men. In addition, the choral and dramatic performances of the festival were an occasion for competition among playwrights and *chorêgoi*, and a panel of ten judges, one from each tribe, determined the award of prizes. This political dimension of the Great Dionysia was also evident in the assembly connected with the celebration: it was convened just afterwards to scrutinize the conduct of the officials responsible for the festival, and was open, of course, only to citizen men.

Women of citizen status, then, may not have been present in the theatre audience, even if, on the stage, female characters were featured prominently. And women may have been excluded also from the dramatic presentations at the Lenaea, a mid-winter Dionysian festival at which tragedies and comedies were enacted. For these, in contrast with the City Dionysia, metics could serve as *chorêgoi*.

Only wealthy metics, to be sure, would have undertaken such liturgies. But everyone, including women, would have participated in the *pompê* which opened this festival, like others. And if the so-called 'Lenaea vases' are any guide, women also celebrated by dancing as maenads around an idol of the god.

DEMOGRAPHICS

At the Lenaea festival of 425 BCE, five years after the beginning of the Peloponnesian War, Aristophanes presented his *Acharnians*, whose protagonist Dicaeopolis, a peasant farmer, 'hates the city and loves [his] deme'. Dicaeopolis exemplifies well the discontent which most Athenians felt, according to Thucydides, when the Spartan invasion of 431 forced evacuation of the countryside: 'they were deeply distressed at abandoning their homes ... and their hereditary holy shrines, at having to change their way of life and at leaving what each regarded as no less than his own native city'.

An Athenian's sense of civic identity was both local and 'national': all citizens belonged to one of the 139 demes or 'villages', of which Athens was composed, and of which the largest was Acharnae. Within the city walls of Athens itself there were five demes, and another ten or fifteen were located in the immediately surrounding suburbs. Some demes were quite small: that of Halimous, located just south of the port of Phaleron, was composed of only about seventy or eighty citizens in the mid-

fourth century. A great many Athenians, however, lived in one of the villages of the Attic countryside, like Dicaeopolis, and most, like him, would have felt strong attachments to their homes, farms, and the variety of local political, religious, and other forms of association which flourished in the demes.

Both citizens and metics were registered in demes, and a citizen's deme-membership was hereditary. An Athenian citizen was identified by his patronymic and deme: for example, 'Socrates the son of Sophroniscus of the deme of Alopece'. A metic belonged to his (or her) deme of residence: 'Sosias living in Alopece'. A woman of citizen status, by contrast, belonged to a deme through her husband or father: 'Alcimache daughter of Callimachus of Anagyrous'.

The deme was something like a miniature polis, sharing several of its most notable institutions: an assembly and public officials, for example. The deme assembly's business differed from that of the polis assembly only in that matters of foreign policy did not come before it, and in that registration of citizens on the citizenship

Wedding celebrations were one of the many forms of festivity that families shared with other members of their deme or phratry. As on many occasions, doubtless, this was one in which men and women celebrated together, although in separate groups.

A wedding-procession is depicted on the body of this vase. It took place by torchlight, and brought the bride from her father's to her husband's home. The bride's mother leads the procession, holding torches in her hands; in the view shown here, the bride and groom ride in a mule-drawn cart together with the groomsman, and the bride grasps her veil in the gesture called *anakalypteria* ('unveiling'), which was the focus of a wedding ceremony of the same name. In the same hand, the bride holds the crown or *stephanê*, which she had worn beneath her veil before the *anakalypteria*. The groom's mother stands in the doorway of the couple's new home, holding a torch in one hand and raising the other in a gesture of greeting. Another mule-cart follows (its front section just visible on the left), with four men seated in it, and other men and women walk alongside – all of them, presumably, wedding-guests.

Lekythos. Amasis Painter. Mid sixth-century BCE.

lists did. Otherwise the deme assembly and its chief official, the demarch, debated and passed decrees having to do with finances, the bestowal of honours, the management of public property, the appointment of officials, and the administration of cults and festivals.

In the *Acharnians*, Dicaeopolis concludes a private peace with a Spartan emissary and thereupon proceeds to celebrate, with his daughter, wife, and two slaves, the rural or Country Dionysia. The Country Dionysia, focused on wine, feasting, song, and phallic processions, were part of the city's ritual calendar but were celebrated in the demes. And in the larger demes dramatic performances and contests were part of the festival, just as they were in the City Dionysia.

Some deme festivals were celebrated as local variants of polis festivals, on days preceding or following polis celebrations. But a significant number of other deme festivals were exclusively regional – those honouring local heroes or agrarian deities, for example, like Icarius, the eponymous hero of the deme Icarion.

Women of citizen status were active participants in deme life, and especially in its most prominent aspect, religion. A number of priestesses appear in deme-decrees, and we hear of women being selected by their peers ('the wives of the demesmen') to serve as officials (*archousai*) in charge of supervising the celebration of the Thesmophoria along with the priestess of the cult. On this and other such occasions, as an inscription specifies, 'the women assemble in the traditional way'.

This Thesmophoria may have been either a local or a polis rite; the festival, like a number of others connected with Demeter and Persephone, was celebrated at both levels. And women were also taken into account in other deme festivals: in the local observance of the Dionysia in the rural deme Erchia, for example, a decree specifies that two goats, one sacrificed to Dionysus, and the other to Semele, are to be handed over to 'the women', and that the priestess is to receive the hides.

Metics were deme-residents also. Most lived in the demes of Athens or the immediately surrounding suburban area, and metics were especially concentrated in the harbour-deme of Piraeus; but some metics were also scattered about the country-side. Metics might share in the religious life of the deme, and in one of the urban demes they were allotted by decree a share in the sacrifices to the deme's tribal hero. But metics could not hold office as deme officials or priests, and a speaker in an oration of Demosthenes imagines the outrage that the citizens would have felt if a metic or foreigner had tried to do either. Dinarchus, an Athenian orator and a metic from Corinth himself, wrote a speech for the prosecution of a metic from Piraeus who had bought his way into deme-registration and hence citizenship in Halimous.

Metics were wholly excluded from membership in phratries, social and cultic 'fraternities' to which all citizens belonged, and which were especially concerned with matters of legitimacy, descent, and inheritance. Membership in a phratry, of which there were at least thirty, was hereditary, like that in demes, and although phratries had meeting-places, owned shrines and agricultural land, their most important activities were carried out in the context of religious celebrations. Most of these activities had to do with the principal events in a citizen's life cycle (birth, coming-of-age, betrothal and marriage), but a man's *phrateres* ('brothers') also functioned as the extra-familial group of first recourse, to whom he would turn if he found himself in legal or financial difficulty.

A citizen's son was introduced to his phratry twice, in infancy and at adolescence, at the annual celebration of the Apatouria, a three-day phratry festival in honour of Zeus, Athena, and Hephaestus, held in the same month as the

In the Hellenistic period (323–30 BCE), the gymnasium was the quintessentially 'Greek' institution. In the cities of the classical period, however, it was just one of many features of most *poleis*. The gymnasium and the *palaestra* ('wrestling-school') were both training-grounds and social centres for young men, principally those from eighteen to twenty years old, and their typical denizens were citizen youths and men of the upper classes.

Gymnasia housed exercise-rooms and equipment, baths, sanctuaries of gods (especially Heracles), and libraries; gardens and parks might also form part of its grounds. In Athens, the three oldest and most famous gymnasia were the Academy, the Lyceum, and the Cynosarges: each of these also housed a philosophical school in the fourth century (of Plato, Aristotle, and Diogenes the Cynic, respectively), and several of Plato's dialogues are set in palaestrae.

Gymnasia and palaestrae were also sites for the pursuit of pederastic relationships. On one side of the exterior of this drinking-cup, for example, men and boys engage in courtship and love-making; sponges, strigils, and small oil-flasks establish that the setting is an athletic one. The larger and more active figures are the lovers (*erastai*); the smaller and more passive ones, the

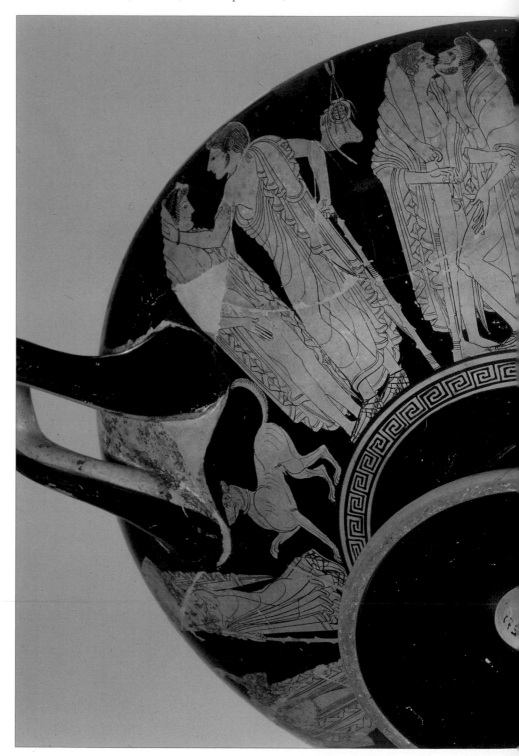

Thesmophoria. On both occasions sacrifice was offered, and an official scrutiny of the boy's qualifications for citizenship also took place. In an oration by Isaeus, for example, a speaker whose entitlement to inherit his maternal grandfather's estate

erōmenoi ('beloveds'). The protocols of pederastic relationships required modesty and reluctance of the younger partners, whose favours were usually solicited through courtship gifts. Such love-relationships, requiring both leisure time and wealth, were thus limited to the upper classes, like those to whom the boys here clearly belong. Wreaths, fillets, and elaborate hair-styles mark them out as belonging to the class of beautiful young men from wealthy and prominent families of the type that Socrates admires in the palaestra in Plato's *Charmides*.

On the other side of the same vase, three young men court women with somewhat more reticence. The women are elaborately dressed and coiffed, and are almost certainly not hetaerae. It is difficult to hypothesize a context for the scene, and for similar ones on other vases, especially if we assume the seclusion of all upper-class women. But the juxtaposition of the two types of courtship illustrates the well-known principle of Greek erotic life that desire was not defined by love-object (which might be male or female), but by erotic aim: active, associated with older men, or passive, associated with boys and women. Peithinos. Around 510 BCE.

is in question asserts that, when his father introduced him to his phratry-members shortly after his birth, none of them raised any objections to his (the speaker's) enrolment, 'although many phratry-members were present and they always examine such matters rigorously'.

Girls may have been introduced to their fathers' phratries also, but a woman's qualifications for citizen status were more usually scrutinized through inquiries about a boy's mother and his father's wife. Bridegrooms did, however, normally celebrate a wedding-feast, the *gamêlia*, with their phratry-members, and in one oration this is taken as evidence that the bride in question was of citizen birth.

As in the demes, women of citizen status seem to have taken part in the phratry's religious life. In one inscription, the wives and daughters of a phratry sub-group participated in the sacrifice and were allotted sacrificial portions. We know nothing of priestesses in connection with phratries, but priests are attested in only one set of decrees, and other officials like phratriarchs (the phratry equivalent of the

Spartan women, men and children

Spartan society in our ancient sources, which are almost exclusively non-Spartan, was notoriously militaristic and regimented. A strict system of age-grades (the *agôgê* or 'upbringing'), dating traditionally from the time of the legendary lawgiver Lycurgus, separated boys of seven to seventeen (*paides*, 'boys'), who learned dancing and singing, from those of eighteen to nineteen (*paidiskoi*, 'older boys'), whose training encompassed survival techniques, and those of twenty to twenty-nine (*hêbôntes*, 'youths'), who underwent rigorous military indoctrination. Spartan young adults (*hêbôntes*) were full citizens and were expected or required to marry.

From the earliest period of the *agôgê*, Spartan boys lived in barracks, separately from their families, and as adults all citizen men belonged to *syskania* or 'messes', small groups meeting and dining communally and housed in individual 'men's houses'. Institutionalized pederasty, beginning for boys at about age thirteen, was a well-known feature of Spartan communal life, and Spartan *syskania* are sometimes compared inexactly with Athenian symposia.

The Lacedaemonian *perioikoi* ('dwellers-round'), who constituted the free population of Laconia and Messenia living outside Sparta, were obliged to provide military service, but were excluded from the privileges of citizenship, which encompassed membership in the assembly and the right to stand for election to the five-member civil magistracy, the *ephorate*. Since Spartan citizens were prohibited from engaging in mercantile

demarch, see p. 124) appear only rarely. So the absence of information about phratry priestesses may not indicate that they did not exist.

At the local level of polis organization, then, there were a variety of official and unofficial associations. The most significant was the deme, which was an administrative unit of the polis, but the phratry was also an important centre of social life for citizens. Alongside these associations, and sometimes within them, a number of other groups flourished: burial clubs, aristocratic religious organizations, trade societies, philosophical schools, and the like. Most were all-male and open to citizens only; but women played an important role in some, and others were organized by metics for their own benefit. Discrimination among slaves, by contrast, was unrelated to other forms of status-determination: occupation distinguished one group of slaves from another, and separated artisans from bankers, for example, agricultural workers from household slaves, or prostitutes and hetaeras from labourers and public slaves.

activities, the management of trade and manufacture was in the hands of the *perioikoi*.

The servile population of Sparta, the helots, was Greek and owned by the Spartan community as a whole, and the ephors declared war annually upon them. Helots supplied the bulk of the agricultural produce upon which the rest of the population depended and thus formed a permanent population of serfs; those of Messenia (the south-west region of the Peloponnese) engaged in periodic revolts.

A modified form of physical training for Spartan girls apparently focused on gymnastics and choral song and dance. Some of our sources indicate that institutionalized homoeroticism was also part of girls' upbringing, and we encounter explicitly erotic language in fragments of the *Partheneia* (choral 'Maiden-Songs') of the seventh-century Spartan poet Alcman. In one, for example, a girl (or choral group) sings of desire for Astymeloisa: '... and the desire that looses the limbs, but she looks glances more melting than sleep and death ... . If she [Astymeloisa] should come near and take me by the soft hand, at once I would become her suppliant'.

The goal of a Spartan woman's training was to make her a mother of warriors, according to Xenophon, who reports that Lycurgus 'instituted competitions in running and physical strength for women as for men, believing that if both parents are strong they produce more vigorous offspring'. Xenophon also says that Lycurgus thought woolworking and the sedentary life associated with it in other city-states was better left to slavewomen. But in Elis, another Peloponnesian polis, a group of 'sixteen women' was entrusted with the honour of weaving a peplos for the goddess Hera. It was presented to the goddess at the Heraea, the festival in honour of Hera analogous to the Athenian Panathenaea. These same women managed the games in honour of Hera, foot-races run by girls according to age-group, and supervised girls' choral dances in honour of the goddess. The victorious maidens in the foot-race were honoured with olive-crowns, a choice portion of the sacrificial offering, and the right to dedicate statues inscribed with their names.

The cup illustrated here celebrates victory of a different sort: one having to do with skill in woolworking. It was a prize won in a girls' carding contest, which required speed and dexterity in the disentangling and drawing out of woollen fibres (see p. 100). The mid-sixth-century cup comes from Tarentum, a Spartan colony in South Italy known for fine wool and weaving; it is a drinking-cup and is decorated with large eyes and battle scenes, including one in which a female captive is led away. Perhaps the conjunction of themes is meant to suggest the fate that might await women who did not support their warrior sons and husbands by confining themselves to conventional female pursuits.

Traditionally, however, Spartan women disdained weaving and sedentary occupations. Among the sayings attributed to Spartan women by Plutarch, for example, a Spartan woman responded to an Ionian woman who showed pride in her weaving by pointing to her four well-behaved sons and saying, 'These should be the occupation of a good and noble woman, and over these she should be exhilarated and proud.' (*Moralia*)

Eye-cup, Attic. Mid-sixth century.

HOMEBODIES

According to the social ideals elaborated in most of our ancient sources, the lives of most Athenian women were spent mostly at home and indoors. This ideal, however, will have encompassed only a minority of the women of Athens, whether of citizen or metic status. For most women, like most men, however, were not sufficiently well-to-do to live without working; those who resided in the country would

Ischomachus' wife, from Xenophon's *Oeconomicus*, like many upper-class women, knew how to sing and dance at religious festivals, and could probably also read and write. Among the tasks she is assigned in the household are those of counting and making, together with her husband, a written inventory of all the household utensils. And she must budget carefully, he tells her, so that 'provisions stored for a year are not used up in a month'.

The activities depicted on this vase and many like them dating from the mid-fifth century are rather less utilitarian. The *alabastron* (perfume flask) on the wall establishes that this is an indoor scene in the women's quarters. A woman sits reading aloud from a scroll on which rows of dots are arranged to suggest letters. Another stands before her, holding a chest in which papyrus scrolls were stored; the other two women are listening to the recitation with rapt attention.

The vase on which the scene is depicted is a *hydria* (water-jar), used by women for fetching water from the well in the courtyard or the communal fountain. Many *hydriai* show women gathered together and conversing amicably as they go about their household tasks. The scene on this vase and on others like it suggests that women of the upper classes, at any rate, got together for cultural activities as well.

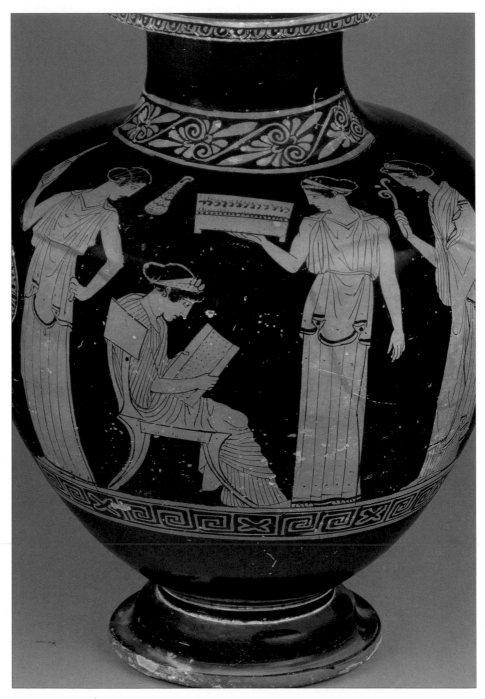

probably have shared in agricultural labour, and those living in town would have engaged in petty trade or kept shops with their husbands. Housekeeping, childcare, woolworking, and food preparation would not have occupied the majority of their working day.

And even the group of Athenian men and women who were somewhat better off spent a significant part of their time engaged in religious activities: either performing private devotions within and without the home or participating in the many festivals which were scattered throughout the ritual year. But many of our sources also afford us glimpses into the everyday family life of that group of prominent and well-to-do Athenians whose activities do accord roughly with a social ideal which claimed that 'man's job is in the fields, the agora, the affairs of the city; women's work is spinning wool, baking bread, keeping house'.

The religious life of Athenians was not confined to their participation in the plenitude of city or deme festivals. Families, we know, sacrificed together, and cult observances of various kinds were important family activities. In Xenophon's *Oeconomicus*, for example, Ischomachus' wife sacrificed and offered prayers along with her husband when they began their married life together. In this illustration, a woman carries offerings to the altar before the door of the house, which is represented on the left.

Women in the home might also initiate ritual action on their own. A character in Menander's *Dyscolus*, for example, complains that his superstitious mother travels around her district making sacrifices at various shrines. In another play a woman excavates a hole in the wall so that she can communicate with her illegitimate daughter who lives next door, and disguises the breach as a household shrine. Painter of London. 470 BCE.

The women represented on this vase are all given mythological names: from the left, Helen, Clytemnestra, an unidentified figure, Cassandra, Iphigenia, and Danae. But their activities are typical of those represented on many vases depicting the women's quarters. Helen is winding yarn into a basket; Clytemnestra holds out an *alabastron* (perfume-jar) to her, and there is a mirror on the wall between them; to the right of the column a woman extends a basket to Cassandra, who is adjusting her veil; and, standing in the open doorway, Iphigenia is wrapping a ribbon around her head as she looks toward Danae, who is walking towards her and removing a crown from a chest. The vase is a *pyxis*, a round and lidded jar used for holding women's cosmetics. In this view, the body of the vase has been 'unrolled' so as to show the whole view of a typical *gynaeceum* (women's quarters) scene. Around 460 BCE.

In Xenophon's *Oeconomicus*, for example, a treatise on estate-management, Socrates explains the fine points of the topic to his wealthy interlocutor by recounting his conversation with Ischomachus, a man who, he says, was regarded as a 'gentleman' by everyone, 'men and women, foreigners and citizens'. For Ischomachus, unlike others of his class, does not waste his wealth on hetaeras, boyfriends, gambling, or keeping bad company. Nor, on the other hand, is he a craftsman, whose occupation would leave him 'no leisure for friends and the affairs of the city'.

Rather, Ischomachus is a wealthy landowner, whose holdings include several parcels of land worked by slaves under the direction of a foreman, whose work he supervises himself. Ischomachus' daily routine includes riding into town early in the morning, taking care of business there, and then walking back home while his slave leads the horse back to the farm. Then Ischomachus returns to the farm, rides out to the fields, inspects the slaves' work, and practises military manoeuvres for exercise. He walks back into town in time to arrive home for the mid-day meal.

Like most men, Ischomachus had married at thirty, and took as his wife a young girl of fourteen. The marriage was arranged between the groom and the girl's parents, and both parties had been concerned to find the best possible partner for the purposes of household management and the begetting of children.

The young bride had spent her early years under strict supervision 'so that she might see, hear, and speak as little as possible', and it thus falls to Ischomachus to train his new wife in her household duties. She, like he, was already schooled in modesty and self-control (*sophrosynê*), and both of them, he claims, possess equally capacities for memory and management in the general sense (*epimeleia*). Otherwise, the woman is designed by nature (*physis*) for indoor work (childcare, breadmaking,

(Bottom) Breadmaking was women's work within the home, and the task was important to the daily functioning of the household, since the everyday Greek diet consisted of bread and various things eaten with it: cheese, vegetables, and especially fish (see p. 27). (Meat was consumed mostly on festival occasions.)

The process of breadmaking was an onerous one. The meal (from wheat or barley) had first to be ground into flour, then mixed with liquid, kneaded, shaped and, finally, baked. In wealthier homes, household slaves would have performed much of this labour: Ischomachus' wife supervises the baker in their home, but her husband also suggests to her that mixing flour and kneading dough are good exercise. These and other kitchen tasks are represented often by terracotta figurines, like the one shown here: the woman is kneading dough or rolling out her cakes.

By the end of the fifth century city-residents might have purchased their daily bread. For by then there were bread-markets in Athens, and some of the most talented bakers were known by name. Xenophon reports, for example, that a man named Cyrebus 'feeds his whole family well and lives in abundance' from breadmaking. Late-sixth-century Boeotian terracotta figurine.

Ischomachus advises his wife to teach her slaves weaving by standing before the loom herself in an authoritative manner. For she had already learned from her own mother how to weave, as well as how to allocate spinning tasks to the slavewomen. Spinning and weaving were, above all, the province of women, an activity which might be performed by slaves as gruelling household labour, by wives to exercise and display their artistic skills, or by heroines and goddesses. Penelope's weaving was proof both of her virtue and her wiliness; Athena was worshipped as *Erganē* ('Worker') in her function as patron of the women's craft; and the *Moirae* ('Fates') spun out the thread of life and cut it at life's end.

Woolworking is represented on vases from the archaic through the classical periods, and women are often and woolworking), and the man for outdoor activity (ploughing, sowing, planting, and herding).

The household, in Ischomachus' view, is ideally a partnership beneficial to both husband and wife: one to which she deposited her dowry, and he contributes his property and continued earnings. In order for the household to flourish, however, careful attention on both their parts is required. Ischomachus' wife will learn how to supervise the household slaves, guard the household provisions, budget expenditures carefully, and arrange for the household belongings to be stored neatly.

Ischomachus has the service of a foreman, and his wife will have a housekeeper to aid her in her tasks. She will spend her day walking about the house, supervising the servants' work, and inspecting whether everything is in its place. This, along with weaving, mixing flour, kneading dough, and folding clothes and linens, will provide her exercise, since the house is quite large and spacious.

Ischomachus' wife, he tells Socrates, is an admirable housewife, 'more than capable of managing everything indoors by herself'. He, for his part, is concerned to treat her well: for well-treated wives, he assures Socrates, become 'fellow-workers' in the task of improving their husbands' estates. Ischomachus thus regards marriage as a productive, reproductive, social, and sexual partnership: his wife supervises the household and keeps the household accounts; she learns from him that she is more sexually attractive if she does not wear make-up; she plays the part of the jury when he conducts mock trials at home; and she will assume responsibility for the nurture of the children that he hopes they will eventually have.

Ischomachus has friends with whom he associates, but he makes no mention of social life for his wife. And some tragic heroines complain that wives are forced to

stay at home alone. But in the plays of Aristophanes and Menander, in orations and on vase-paintings, women are frequently in one another's company. One speaker in an oration reports that before his opponents brought suit against him, his mother and theirs used to be fast friends: 'they used to visit one another – naturally, since they both lived in the country and since their husbands had been friends'. In another case, a speaker reports that he brought into the household his old nurse-maid – now a widowed freedwoman – to serve as company for his wife, and in the oration they sit together in the garden lunching.

Ischomachus' marriage is certainly a patriarchal one: his wife's authority in the home is delegated to her by him; and for all her contributions to the economic well-being of the household, he regards himself as responsible for the estate's income: 'property comes into the house', as he says, 'through the husband's exertions; but it is dispensed through the wife's housekeeping'. In other respects, however, including that of their mutual affection for one another, the marriage of Ischomachus and his wife resembles the ideal which Odysseus celebrates in the *Odyssey*:

> No finer, greater gift in the world than that...
> when man and woman possess their home, two minds,
> two hearts that work as one. Despair to their enemies,
> joy to all their friends. Their own best claim to glory.

It is a surprising irony that the Ischomachus and his wife of Xenophon's treatise were, in all likelihood, historical figures. He was born by 460 BCE and married Chrysilla in about 435. They had a daughter who married a wealthy man, and who then, after he died, married Callias, a rich Athenian nobleman and notorious prof-ligate. After less than a year of marriage, Callias brought Chrysilla into the house,

shown performing the many tasks involved together, as on the vase represented above. Here, five groups of women perform separate tasks associ-ated with woolworking: the two on the left fill a basket with yarn; the next two fold the finished cloths; one spins fine thread next to a woman combing wool into a basket; two others work together at a warp-weighted vertical loom; and the two on the right weigh out the balls of yarn.

Poor women also made a living for themselves through woolworking. In a set of inscriptions listing the occupa-tions of freed slaves, the women are identified principally as *talasiourgoi*, women who cleaned, carded, combed, and spun the wool into a mass that could be weighed out and sold. Transcript of lekythos. Amasis Painter. Around 560 BCE.

Eventually, Ischomachus hopes, he and his wife will have children, and then she will assume responsibility for their nurture, in accordance with the dictates of nature, since 'the god dispensed to the woman a greater share of love for newborn babies'. But they will 'deliberate together on how best to raise them', since Ischomachus expected to take a lively interest in his children, especially males, like the father on this vase.

A mother hands her baby boy to his nurse, as the father looks on, leaning on his walking stick. A loom identifies the setting as the women's quarters, and the wreath hanging on the wall is perhaps a memento from the couple's wedding in the not too distant past.

Girls usually remained at home until marriage, under the supervision of their mothers and female slaves. Boys, however, conventionally passed under the tutelage of men at the age of seven, and those from wealthier families went to school under the watchful eye of a *paidagogos*, who was a male slave. Adult children were expected to behave respectfully toward both of their parents, and to provide for their care and maintenance in old age. Failure to do so at Athens was punishable by law.

Hydria. Attributed to circle of Polygnotus 440–430 BCE.

and proceeded to live with both mother and daughter. The daughter, in despair, tried to kill herself, but was subsequently driven out of the house by her mother. Soon afterwards, Callias grew tired of Chrysilla, and threw her out, even though she was pregnant by him. When a son was born, Callias denied that it was his, but some time later he fell in love again with Chrysilla, 'the outlandish old hag of a woman', welcomed her back into his house and acknowledged the son as his own.

Ischomachus, for his part, does not appear to have fared much better. Having been one of the wealthiest men in Athens known to us, his fortune upon his death was valued at less than one-seventh of its worth during his lifetime. (His property may have fared badly during the Decelean War of 413–404 BCE.)

This is perhaps only the most striking example of the discrepancy between social ideals and lived reality in ancient Athens. Other, less flamboyant or scandalous ones appear, however, as soon as we take into account the part that all women played in the city's and demes' religious life, the participation of most women in the ongoing economic activities of the town and country, and the contributions of even upper-class women to the prosperity of the household, which was the foundation of Greek

(*Previous page*) On this vase, women gather in the women's quarters to adorn themselves. One *alabastron* (perfume vessel) hangs on the wall, and a slave woman holds another. The other slave woman (both are identifiable by their cropped hair) holds up a mirror.

Ischomachus advised his wife against sitting around the house either 'like a slave' or 'in a haughty manner', and against the use of make-up and other forms of feminine adornment. Gatherings of the kind represented on this vase, evidently, were not regarded as appropriate for a wife who was expected to keep herself busy with household tasks. And indeed, a well-known character-type from literature of the archaic through classical periods was the aristocratic woman who occupies herself with luxuries and shuns the drudgery of housework. Her opposites were the slovenly woman on the one hand, and the queen bee, on the other, to which Ischomachus compares his wife at length.

Bees were also associated with chastity, and in recommending against the use of make-up, Ischomachus assures his wife that he will find her natural beauty a greater sexual stimulant. An unadorned, simply clothed, and affectionate wife, he says, is more appealing than a slavewoman. Ischomachus thus acknowledges the double standard, even if he would prefer not to avail himself of its opportunities. Wedding Painter. 460 BCE.

social, political, and economic life. For if the polis of ancient Athens was from one perspective a 'male club', as is often claimed, then it is evident that it was also one in which many women enjoyed a kind of guest membership, and to which others, of the more prosperous classes, constituted an important and necessary 'women's auxiliary'.

Power and the State

THE POLIS

Consider first a famous passage in Thucydides' *History of the Peloponnesian War*. The year is 413 BCE, and the armada sent by the Athenians two years earlier to conquer all Sicily is on the verge of annihilation. Nicias, the Athenian reluctantly holding supreme command, seeks to encourage his disheartened Athenian and allied troops, marooned as they are far from home and all too aware of their likely and impending fates – instant butchery, or a more lingering death by starvation in the stone quarries of Syracuse, or the desperate humiliation of being sold into slavery. Nicias at this climactic moment chooses (and it doesn't matter for our purposes whether Nicias really did so choose, or Thucydides has put into his mouth the words he thought most appropriate for such a dire crisis) to remind his listeners that 'men are the polis'.

This definition has a twofold significance. The polis for the Greeks of Nicias' day, as it had been for the past three centuries or so, was not some such abstraction as our term 'state' may conjure up, but a living, breathing, human entity – a corporate body of citizens, that is Greeks who enjoyed certain agreed public and private privileges and responsibilities that set them apart as a strong political community. The polis, that is to say (and Thucydides' Nicias does say it), was not a matter of walls or ships, mere artifacts, but a spiritual community. Secondly, the word Nicias uses for 'men' (*andres*) means physically, socially and politically adult members of the male sex. The Greek polis was an exclusive group in terms of both gender and 'nationality'.

Another way in which it differed from states of either the medieval or the modern periods was spatially. Sometimes polis is translated by the clumsy periphrasis 'city-state'. The idea of this is to point out that we are not dealing here with national states of any great size but something more closely resembling Amalfi or Genoa in the Middle Ages. These were Italian cities that were also sovereign political communities. 'City-state' also captures the fact that at the heart of most Greek *poleis* was some sort of urban centre, usually focused on an agora or place of gathering (whether for commercial or more narrowly political purposes). But a polis almost always had a rural hinterland, which often constituted its principal economic basis. Moreover, ideally the relationship between core and periphery, city centre and countryside, was not antagonistic but rather the reverse – a relationship of symbiosis. No one English term could possibly do justice to all these many senses and connotations of polis. 'Citizen-state' is perhaps the best compromise, because it corresponds more closely than any other to the spirit as well as the substance of the Greek polis.

Precisely how, or why, the polis emerged as a state-form in Greece cannot be answered with certainty for lack of relevant contemporary documentation. In any case, the process was probably untidier than the blanket phrase 'the emergence of the polis' might suggest. Somewhat similar political units emerged roughly simultaneously, if not earlier, in other parts of the Iron Age Mediterranean – notably in Phoenicia and central Italy (Latium and Etruria). The operative period would seem to be the century or so from 750 to 650, which not coincidentally also saw the beginnings of a 'colonization' movement of economically and politically motivated emigration; this again was a process not confined to Greece, though in the Greeks' case it was more prolonged, extensive and culturally decisive. By 500 there were Greek political communities scattered from one end of the Mediterranean to the other, with some exceptions (the Levant, Egypt, the Phoenicio-Carthaginian sphere of north Africa), and round much of the Black Sea.

Looking back (in the second half of the fourth century) over hundreds of different Greek cities at various stages of their evolution, Aristotle, in the *Politics*, thought he could discern an underlying pattern to the broad sweep of their political and constitutional development. It was characteristically Greek, a combination of war, economy and politics:

Solon: forefather of Athenian democracy

Solon of Athens, one of the original Seven Sages of ancient Greece, was of *Eupatrid* – that is, aristocratic – birth but not extreme wealth. As such, he appeared to the embattled ruling aristocrats of Athens the ideal person to resolve the crisis that was afflicting the city in the years around 600, and he was appointed by them as official arbitrator in 594. The crisis arose from a potentially disastrous combination of two distinct but related pressures for radical change: economic and political.

Economically, the countryside of Attica, Athens' civic territory, was split into two main opposing camps: the large and greedily exploitative landlords and the mass of indebted farmers. Some of the latter were debt-bondsmen, having pledged their bodies as security against loans of food and seed that they could not possibly repay; others had actually been sold into slavery outside Attica. The grasping landlords were mostly Eupatrids, the old aristocratic ruling class; but not all – there were also wealthy non-Eupatrids, excluded from political power by an accident of birth, but capable of playing a new military role as cavalrymen or hoplites. Hence, in part, the political aspect of the crisis.

What the non-aristocratic rich were demanding was some share in governing commensurate with their economic and military status. The political demands of the poor masses were more modest. Once relieved of the immediate burden of their debts, they mainly required protection against any possible recurrence of their servitude. Some bolder spirits among the poor, however, wanted more – not only a cancellation of their debts but a redistribution of the land held by the propertied.

At that, however, the moderate Solon drew the line. To rich and poor, so he stated in self-justification, he would give no more – but also no less – privilege than he considered each group merited. Thus while making it clear that he thought responsibility for the crisis had lain chiefly with the rich, he was not so radical as to interfere with their landed property-rights. He did nevertheless cancel all existing debts and he outlawed for the future the contracting of loans on the security of the person.

Politically, he deprived the Eupatrids of their political monopoly, but he did not disband the old aristocratic council of the Areopagus (so called because it met originally on the Hill of Ares, the war-god) and he allowed power to remain firmly in the hands of the rich, thereby gratifying chiefly the wealthy non-aristocrats. The poor for their part gained some protection against illegal or unjust treatment by rich officials through being granted a right of appeal, probably to a new court known as the *Heliaea*. Since that word could mean 'assembly', it is possible that the Heliaea was the regular assembly of citizens meeting in a judicial capacity, each citizen having a vote to be counted. But probably only the wealthier Athenians were considered members for the purposes of the act.

Nevertheless, no matter how restricted Solon's laws were in terms of their social and political empowerment of ordinary poor Athenians, they did embody the notion of universal and equal applicability. They were not only written down but also publicly displayed on wooden pillars in what was perhaps a newly sited Agora or civic centre. They were also to prove a sound basis for future political developments of a specifically democratic nature,

After the kingships the earliest constitution among the Greeks was in fact composed of warriors, of the cavalry in the first place, because it was in them that strength and superiority in war were to be found... Then when states became larger and those with [hoplite] arms became stronger, the number of sharers in the constitution became larger... The constitutions of these early times were, understandably enough, oligarchical or royal.

His evidence for the widespread or universal existence of kingships in early Greece was partly the fossilized survival of the word *basileus* ('king') as a title for non-royal civic officials in the poleis of his own day, but mainly the poetry of Homer. Not only were the Greeks who fought at Troy all subjects of one or another king, but so strongly grounded was the monarchical principle that the lesser kings all agreed to serve under the one supreme royal commander, 'lord of men' Agamemnon of Mycenae 'rich in gold'. Indeed, in Book Two of the *Iliad* Homer has one of these lesser royals, Odysseus of Ithaca, beat and berate an uppity commoner, Thersites,

which is why Solon was often looked back to, anachronistically, as the founder of democracy at Athens.

Democracy, however, was not in fact introduced until the reforms of Cleisthenes and was significantly enlarged by those of Ephialtes and Pericles. The first key innovation of Cleisthenes was to redraw the political map of Attica, by making membership of a *deme* (village or ward) the basic criterion of Athenian citizenship and enfolding the demes into new artificially constructed tribes that united citizens from the major geographical subregions of Attica. These ten new tribes were the new basis of Athens' military organization, and each of them also selected fifty members for a new Council, the main function of which was to enable the Assembly of all citizens to act as Athens' principal decision-making body.

Ephialtes and Pericles concentrated rather on judicial reform. The Areopagus was now stripped of its most important political prerogatives and confined to being a court for trying certain religious offences. Its old powers were variously transferred to Cleisthenes' Council of 500, to the Assembly, and above all to their revamped version of Solon's Heliaea. This new People's court was a court of first instance, not only of appeal, and for the first time it became a practical possibility for volunteer prosecutors (envisaged perhaps already by Solon) to advance the cause of popular justice.

Jurors for the People's court were selected by lot, in the democratic manner – the lot randomized selection and gave ordinary poor Athenians the maximum chance, and encouragement, to serve. A further incentive was that those selected were

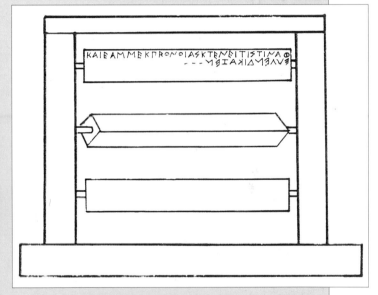

One possible reconstruction of Solon's new law-code, publicly displayed on wooden blocks (*kurbeis*) revolving on axles (*axones*) set in a frame.

paid a small but not insignificant per diem 'wage'. This was the first kind of political pay to be made available – later, remuneration was extended to service on the Council, also selected by lot, and even to attendance at the Assembly.

Of course, Athens was unusual for being the first democratic polis, but in its shift from aristocracy to oligarchy, its adoption of a published set of legally enforceable rules, and its commitment in principle to the rule of law it was moving in tandem with much of the more advanced Greek world.

reminding him forcefully and to universal acclaim that a multitude of rulers is a bad thing, that demagogy inevitably leads to bad decisions.

THE RISE OF THE ARISTOCRACY

Today we argue fiercely over whether the Homeric epics are in any sense historical and, if the poems may be so treated, to what period of the real Greek past their fictional pictures may most nearly apply. The commonest view would seem to be that if there was a real Homeric world of kings it was most likely to have been in, and not to have outlasted, the eighth century. By the time of Hesiod (c.700) we already have aristocracy rather than true monarchy. At any rate, there is general agreement that the earliest poleis were typically governed by aristocracies of 'best' (aristoi) men who earned or claimed that prerogative by virtue of their superior economic power, and by tracing their ancestry to some god or hero.

A passage from Plutarch's biography of Theseus, the Athenian founder-hero, may be inaccurate as a fact about Theseus, but it does neatly encapsulate the nature of early Greek aristocracy:

> To the noblemen Theseus assigned the care of religious rituals, the filling of the political offices, the teaching and the administration of the laws, and the interpretation of all sacred matters; and for the rest of the citizens he established as it were a balance of privilege, on the assumption that the noblemen would excel in dignity, the farmers in utility, and the craftsmen in numerical strength.

The stress here on religion and the aristocracy's exclusive religious control is to the point. The Greek city was a city of gods as well as men, and exclusive management of relations between the two gave the aristocrats an unrivalled lever on mundane power.

It was not long, however, before commoners mounted a challenge to aristocratic monopoly. Both Homer's invented character Thersites and the real Boeotian poet Hesiod in their different ways show this tendency. However, whereas Thersites and Hesiod merely complained, commoners in some cities, led crucially by dissident aristocrats, translated their grievances into effective action. Aristotle seems to have been right to suspect a military reason behind the change. Roughly speaking, what occurred was a shift or forcible transfer of power from narrow groups of aristocratic families to a wider socio-economic stratum of substantial landlords who exploited politically the purely military advantages provided by the new hoplite infantry phalanx that was being developed during the seventh century (see p.168). Best documented of all such oligarchic transformations is that ushered in at Athens by the reforms of Solon (see p.140).

Aristocracy was thereby for the most part replaced by oligarchy – though we must remember that Greek aristocrats, like their peers in other times and places, had a talent for clinging on to the last vestiges of their status long after their moment of glory as a ruling class had faded into a distant memory. The most conspicuous display of such talent was perhaps the *symposium* or private upper-class drinking-party, which became the forum and fulcrum of much high literary culture of the seventh and sixth centuries (and was still going strong in the fourth century, as Plato's and Xenophon's philosophical works entitled *Symposium* show).

Another such field of display for early Greek aristocrats was the civic religious festival with athletic or musical competitions as integral elements. The most famous of these were of course the Panhellenic athletics festivals, the Olympic, Pythian,

In shape and decoration this small *amphora* (wine-jar) imitates but does not precisely copy the amphoras awarded as prizes at the quadrennial Panathenaic Games. On the front face a helmeted and armed Athena strides out; here on the reverse a solo flute-player (*auletes*) plies his skill under the eye of two listeners, or judges.

Isthmian and Nemean Games, organized in an interlocking quadrennial cycle during the second quarter of the sixth century. But a large and ambitious city like Athens was quick to stage its own local attraction in the Panathenaic Games, which celebrated simultaneously both its divine patron, Athena, and the political unity (hence 'All-Athenian') of the unusually large and heterogeneous civic territory of Attica.

TYRANNY

Actually, unity then was more of an ideal than a reality. Within a decade of the Panathenaic Games' foundation, Athens had twice been subjected to attempted coups by a would-be tyrant called Pisistratus – himself, of course, a self-proclaimed aristocrat with a fictitious pedigree stretching back to a son of Homer's Nestor. Eventually Pisistratus did establish a stable tyranny at Athens, with wide international ramifications. He even founded a short-lived dynasty. But despite this, tyranny remained in Athenian and indeed all Greek eyes a *pis aller*, something not entirely Greek, a deviation from the norm of republican, civic self-rule.

A drunken or at any rate happy adult man, his hair bound in a wreath and wearing an expensive woven garment, reclines on his couch and sings 'O most beautiful of boys', fondling the while a hare that he has presumably already given as a love-token to his junior beloved. Here we are taken straight to the heart of an aristocratic *symposium* or drinking-party at Athens – but in the early fifth century, when this drinking-cup was made, the party was almost over for Athenians like these, politically speaking anyhow. Democracy had already arrived.

The second quarter of the sixth century threw up another tyrant with Athenian connections, but in this case acquired rather than inherited. Agariste, the daughter of Cleisthenes, tyrant of Peloponnesian Sicyon, was married to Megacles, an Athenian aristocrat (see p. 83). They had a son also called Cleisthenes, named in the usual way after his grandfather. In due course this Cleisthenes became in the words of Herodotus 'the founder of the (new) tribes and the democracy for the Athenians'.

Megacles, in order to cement (so he thought) a political alliance that would put an end to the complicated faction-fighting between groups representing different geographical areas as well as different socio-economic and political interests in Attica, married a daughter of his to Pisistratus. Initially, the marriage alliance was a success, and through it Pisistratus achieved, briefly, the second of his three tyrannies some time around the mid-550s. But it all too soon ended in tears, allegedly because Pisistratus refused to practise the sort of sexual intercourse that might lead to procreation (he already had two sons by an earlier marriage).

Forced into exile once more, this time for a decade, Pisistratus spent the time profitably marshalling economic, political and symbolic resources sufficient not only to defeat a coalition of his enemies in pitched battle but to secure his grip on power for a lengthy period thereafter (in the event almost twenty years). Religion, predictably, was a key part of his programme – not only did the Panathenaea receive his special attention but the performance of tragedy first came to prominence under his regime. He and his sons lavished resources also on public works of both a utilitarian and a spiritual character. One of the by-products of this expenditure was a great increase in the amount of silver coinage officially struck, always a symbol of civic pride in Greece. Another was the production of the first Athenian silver 'owls'. Less predictably, rather than simply ruling by dictatorial fiat Pisistratus chose to operate through the existing constitutional rules of Athens, that is those laid down at the beginning of the century by the moderately oligarchic reformer Solon. Of course, he was careful also to see to it that the top jobs were always held by the 'right' men, that is his men. No free and fair elections for Pisistratus. However, the upshot was that the middling layers of the Athenian citizen body, sandwiched between the old landed aristocracy and the mass of impoverished farmers and craftsmen, gained some experience of everyday politics in a way that would have been unthinkable under the ancien regime and impossible even under the reformed regime of Solon. By some, the era of Pisistratus was looked back upon as a golden age.

Yet, as Herodotus sagely observed in the preface to his *Histories*, it is an iron law of human history that prosperity is transient and that while the small may become great, the great will inexorably at some time become small. So it was with the Pisistratid tyranny, at first diminished by internal opposition and then overthrown by outside intervention. The opposition was activated most dramatically in about 514, when Hipparchus, one of Pisistratus' two sons, and brother of the reigning tyrant Hippias, was murdered. Harmodius and his older lover Aristogeiton were not in fact intending to strike a blow for civic liberty and equality, let alone democracy, when they murdered him for personal reasons. But that was how their action was later retrospectively conceived (in a fit of what we might call 'recovered memory'), and the bronze statues of the supposed 'Tyrannicides' were the first representations of purely mortal figures to be honoured in the Athenian Agora.

The goddess Athena was associated with the owl, and the Athenians took the owl as their national symbol. From the late sixth century onwards Athenian silver coins were adorned with almost comically endearing representations of the bird, behind which may be seen a spray of Athena's sacred plant, the olive.

Later on, the Tyrannicides statue group had to be replaced after the original was plundered by Great King Xerxes of Persia in 480 and taken back with him to Susa. By then, though, most ordinary Athenians had managed to forget the awkward interval of half a dozen years or so between the assassination in 514 and the reforms of Cleisthenes in 508/7. More importantly, they had also apparently forgotten the nasty bout of old-style faction-fighting that had flared up during the interval between Isagoras, an aristocrat of oligarchic if not tyrannical leanings, and Cleisthenes, an aristocrat who knew that he was against tyranny, especially if it was being sponsored (as was widely believed) by Athens' enemy Sparta, but probably did not know exactly what to put in its place, or what consequences calling on the support of the Athenian people in his faction-fight would eventually have.

Cleisthenes was a member of the aristocratic Alcmaeonid family to which Pericles would later belong through his mother. Between them, Cleisthenes and Pericles presided over first the introduction and then the radical development of the world's first citizen self-government of the people, by the people, and for the

people. The people in question were known as the *demos*, a term that could encompass the humblest tradesman no less than the grandest grandee, and their sovereign rule was a form of *kratos* (literally 'grasp', now the modern Greek term for 'state'): hence the word democracy.

DEMOCRACY

At first, though, the new regime ushered in by the reforms of Cleisthenes in 508/7 was not actually called democracy. A word meaning something more like equality of privileges under the law for all citizens (*isonomia*) was used instead – not least because it avoided the contentious overtones of demos, which, in addition to meaning the people in the sense of the citizen body as a whole, could also be interpreted in a class sense as referring only to the masses, the majority, the poor, the common people, the mob. Another formally class-neutral term expressing the basic idea of equality also made an early appearance on the developing Athenian democratic scene: *isegoria*. This literally meant equality of address for all citizens, and particularly the privilege of equal public speech in the Assembly. But actually it took considerable nerve and know-how, as well as powerful lungs and a dominating stage presence, to make an effective public speaker in the open air mass meetings

(Opposite) **The Athenian Harmodius and his partner Aristogeiton together assassinated Hipparchus in about 514 and were heroized thereafter as the Tyrannicides. The original statue group was removed to the Persian capital Susa by order of Xerxes in 480. What we see here is a Roman copy of its replacement, a Greek bronze original of about 475.**

One of only three representations of cobblers on Athenian painted pots, yet cobblers in the literary sources were often portrayed as the typical citizen small craftsmen. One, Simon, even engaged Socrates in dialogue, and it may be this Simon the cobbler whose house (and hobnails) have been excavated near the Athenian Agora.

that represented Athenian central government in action, so in practice throughout the history of the democracy most of the regular or professional public speakers were drawn from a small élite group.

The tribal structure

For the majority of Athenians, much if not most self-government meant not central but local government. It was one of the boldest and most brilliant strokes of

On this early fifth-century amphora a public speaker is depicted standing on a podium, with a mature man standing symbolically for his audience. The speaker keeps both arms within his cloak, to indicate his decorum and restraint – Cleon half a century later is supposed to have initiated the new, and indecorous, style of histrionic gesticulation.

Cleisthenes' regime to base the fledgling democracy on yet another sense of the protean word demos, namely demos as village or ward. Under his new dispensation there were some 140 such *demes* recognized throughout the 1000 or so square miles of Attica (roughly the size of Luxembourg). To became a citizen of Athens a man had to be registered by a citizen father or male guardian on the official roll of his local and ancestral deme. Demes were combined upwards in the decision-making hierarchy into thirty units divided equally into three geopolitical zones: the City, the Inland and the Coast. These thirty units in turn were distributed, one from each zone, to form ten *tribes*, each with a tribal hero as a focus both of loyalty and religious worship – hence Herodotus' description of Cleisthenes as the founder of 'the tribes and the democracy for the Athenians'. It was as tribesmen that citizens fought in the army or served on the Council of 500, the chief permanent organ of administration and managing committee for the primary Assembly (which now began to meet on the Pnyx hill, see Chapter 5).

The vote

Most Athenians would never once have ventured to speak at the meetings of the Assembly, which were held on an open hillside in almost all weathers (but rain might stop play) and involved several thousands of participants. More would have ventured to do so in the Council or in their deme assembly, perhaps. But in principle all would presumably have felt able to participate actively by voting. Aristotle eventually defined citizens as those who participated in rule (the holding of public office) and judgement (chiefly but not exclusively legal). The definition, he added, applied especially to citizens of a democracy, as opposed to an oligarchy dominated by the rich few, since democratic decisions were taken notionally through all the people deciding everything together in public by voting. In the Athenian Assembly most votes were taken by show of hands, which were then estimated rather than individually counted for purely practical reasons of time. But even that was an improvement on the Spartans' method of voting by shouting, where the stentorian-voiced carried disproportionate political weight. To satisfy the criterion of strict equality, however, votes, whether secret (as in the courts and occasionally in the Assembly) or open (as in the Council), had to be individually counted in accordance with the principle of one citizen one vote – regardless of wealth, birth, intelligence, beauty, or whatever.

One peculiarly democratic (though not uniquely Athenian) method of voting was known as *ostracism*, since the individual ballots cast were not stones (*psephoi*, whence our word psephology) or bronze tokens (as in the courts) but bits of broken pottery, potsherds (*ostraka*). Ostracism, as a form of reverse election, was a prime means of getting rid of serious rivals: the loser, namely the man who received the most votes (that is potsherds with his name on them), was obliged to retire into exile outside Attica for ten years, effectively killing his career for good. One ancient tradition attributes the invention of ostracism to Cleisthenes (which has prompted

the semi-humorous modern suggestion that the reason for Cleisthenes' abrupt and total disappearance from view after 507 was that he was hoist with his own potsherd). But although the system would not have been incompatible with the thrust of what we know of Cleisthenes' reform package, which was to give power to ordinary citizens, ostracism is not certainly known to have been used until twenty years later, in the early 480s. But once it was used, it was used with a vengeance.

In the 480s, when the foreign policy stakes were continuously rising with the growing threat of Persian revenge for the humiliation at Marathon in 490, the clear winner in the resulting domestic ostracism battles was Themistocles. It was his strategy and achievement at Salamis in 480 that were celebrated retrospectively by Aeschylus in our earliest surviving tragedy, the *Persians* of 472 (see Chapter 9). Shortly thereafter, however, he too was ostracized, and the leading role in Athenian politics passed to Cimon, son of Miltiades (the inspiration behind the Marathon triumph).

Military influences

Under Cimon, the Athenians developed their anti-Persian naval alliance (the Delian League) into a fledgling maritime empire, thereby helping to bring about a shift in the balance of military-political power from the wealthier hoplites to the poorer class of thetes, who powered the largely Athenian fleets put out by the alliance (see p. 178). Aristotle's model of political development, whereby constitutional change tended to follow military innovation, would lead us to expect that Athens' naval imperialism would have a significant constitutional impact, and such indeed occurred. In the late 460s Ephialtes with his junior adjutant Pericles persuaded a now radicalized Athenian Assembly to pass a package of reforms that effectively converted the moderate democracy of Cleisthenes into a full-blown government of the people. The Areopagus, once the supreme court of Athens but now an outmoded vestige of aristocratic privilege, was stripped of most of its remaining constitutional authority.

Democracy in danger

The reduced function of the Areopagus was alluded to and apparently commended in Aeschylus' *Oresteia* trilogy of 458. But by then Ephialtes himself had been assassinated, and the strong and persistent anti-democratic undercurrent in Athenian politics is reflected in the fact that almost all the surviving writers of history and philosophy at Athens were opponents of democracy on principle. The sorts of arguments the anti-democrats could muster are neatly displayed in the West's earliest surviving text of analytical political theory, the Persian Debate in Herodotus' *Histories*. What they boil down to is the contemptuous claim that the common people were not fit to rule Athens, since – being fickle, ignorant and stupid – they couldn't even rule themselves.

The lottery

Against them the pro-democrats argued a case based on the idea of citizen equality. Since each citizen was notionally equal and equally obliged to participate in making decisions affecting the common good, Athens' political institutions should be so designed as to allow the maximum of responsible participation. One of the principal methods used to achieve this desired outcome was the drawing of lots, by means of which appointment to offices was decided (except to the highest military and financial posts, where exceptional expertise or commitment were required). The lottery also determined appointment to the Council of 500 and the allocation of citizens to the popular jury-courts which, thanks to the reforms of Ephialtes and Pericles, were now as much an organ of democratic decision-making as the Assembly. (The Greeks did not recognize our modern principle of the separation of powers between the legislature and the judiciary.) Another key democratic innovation was the introduction of political pay: at first for service as jurors, then for service on the Council; for service in the army and fleet (but, on top of that, very

(Opposite top) The identification of the scene on this Athenian red-figure *cylix* of about 470 BCE is not absolutely certain, but it has plausibly been taken as representing the counting of votes in an ostracism. The bearded male figure at centre right holds a stylus and writing tablet, possibly to tally the votes, which are being brought in from left and right to be deposited in the *krater* (mixing-bowl) on the table.

(Opposite bottom) Themistocles used ostracism as a political weapon with exceptional assiduity and success in the 480s, but in about 470 the tables were finally turned and he found himself on the receiving end of the voters' rejection. His desperate opponents even resorted to preparing in advance batches of ostraca with his name scratched on them, possibly for use by illiterate or at any rate lazy voters; one hoard of 190 found in the Agora was written in only fourteen hands.

rich Athenians were obliged, as a public duty, to see to the equipment and maintenance of a *trireme* warship for a year); and finally – but not until the 390s – for attendance at the Assembly.

Jury-service and the legal system

Archaeological evidence complements the literary sources in aiding our understanding of how the Athenians' direct, participatory democracy actually worked. The remains have been found of a complicated allotment-machine used for selecting jurors and allocating them to a particular court. Every year 6000 Athenian citizens, typically rather older and rather poorer than average, were empanelled as potential jurors. From them were selected the number of jurors required on any of the 150–200 days per annum that courts were in session. To avoid bribery on the

Monarchy for ever?

In about 520 BCE, so Herodotus stoutly maintained, three noble Persian conspirators got together in Susa, the administrative capital of the young but already mighty Persian empire, for a discussion of political theory. They were conspiring against Gaumata, a usurper who had seized the throne after the death, in murky circumstances, of Cambyses (son of Cyrus the Great, the empire's founder). The leader of the conspiracy, and historically the eventual restorer of legitimate monarchical authority, was Darius. Darius was both a distant relative and brother-in-law of Cambyses (having married his sister, Atossa).

Darius, naturally, is the chief participant in Herodotus' account of the discussion, which is presented as a formal debate. He speaks last of the three and, with his arguments in favour of legitimate, constitutional monarchy, decisively wins. But he does not only speak positively for monarchy; he is obliged also to counter the arguments proposed by his two fellow-debaters for popular rule and élite government respectively.

First to speak is Otanes, who spends most of his time arguing against monarchy in its unambiguously bad form of tyranny:

> How could monarchy be a well-ordered thing when the monarch is able to do whatever he wants without accountability to anyone? ... Now the tyrant ought not to feel envy, having all the good things he wants, but he is really just the opposite in the way he treats his subjects ... The worst things he does are these: he will disrupt the traditional customs of our ancestors, rape our women, and murder indiscriminately.

Against these horrors Otanes urges *isonomia*, something like 'equality of respect and privilege under the laws', which he calls 'the fairest of names'. Three features in his view distinguish this system of majority rule above all others: 'people hold office by lot, they are accountable for their actions, and their deliberations are held in public'.

one hand, and to emphasize that jury-service was a public political act on the other, juries tended to be large by our standards – from 201 up to a massive 6000. The number (501) that tried and convicted Socrates for impiety in 399 was a normal sort of figure. Jurors who made it onto one of the annual panels of 6000 were given an identity tag (*pinakion*), a bronze strip with their official political name incised

Jurors selected by lot for service in the People's Court at Athens were provided with a bronze identity token (*pinakion*). This example from the fourth century bears the owner's name and patronymic (his father's name), and the name of the deme (Cephisia) in which his citizenship was registered. Some jurors were so attached to their tokens that they took them with them to the grave.

In other words, Otanes argues for democracy, but refrains from using that word, for a reason that becomes apparent in the next speech. For just as Otanes had conflated monarchy with tyranny, so Megabyzus conflates 'people' (*demos*) with 'idle mob' and 'unbridled masses'. So hostile is he to the common people that he is prepared to allow that even the tyrant is superior to them, in that he at any rate 'knows what he is doing'. His preference, however, is that the Persians should be governed by the 'best' (*aristoi*) men. Normally, 'best' was a coded way of referring to aristocrats, men of noble lineage, the wealthy few. But by 'best' Megabyzus rather unusually meant the most intelligent and best educated, a distinction the third and final speaker Darius chooses to ignore.

Agreeing with Megabyzus on the horrors of mob-rule, Darius however attacks what he (mis)understands to be his proposal in favour of oligarchy, the rule of the rich few.

Powerful private hatreds arise in an oligarchy when a large group of men vies for pre-eminence before the people ... From this comes civil strife, and from civil strife comes bloodshed, and after the bloodshed you end up with – a monarchy.

Provided of course that the monarch is 'the one best man', monarchy must therefore be 'far and away superior' to democracy and oligarchy for both pragmatic and principled reasons, as well as the fact that it was Persia's traditional mode of governance.

Herodotus did not share Darius' view of monarchy, at any rate so far as Greeks were concerned, and seems to have had some sympathy with Megabyzus' preference for an aristocracy of intellect. But his opinion of the new and purely Greek system of democracy cannot be certainly established. On the one hand, he praised to the skies Athenian *isegoria*, literally the equal

right of free public speech, but for its military rather than more narrowly political benefits. It was this, he thought, that had caused the Athenians to give of their very best in defence of their community, when under attack from Sparta and other Greek states, whereas under the yoke of the Pisistratid tyranny they had been no more than averagely good warriors. On the other hand, he shared the contempt of Megabyzus and Darius for the gullibility of the Athenian masses: it was an act of mass folly, he thought, to undertake a doomed campaign in Asia against Persia during the Ionian Revolt (499–494) that could lead only to the further oppression and enslavement of Greeks.

The political views of Thucydides are rather clearer. The best form of Athenian government that he was aware of was not democracy, even under the guidance of his hero Pericles, but the moderate oligarchy of the '5000' that ruled only for a few months in 411. Unlike Pericles, apparently, Thucydides seems to have shared the standard élite view of the masses as inherently stupid, ignorant, gullible and fickle, and hence unfit to govern. The signal merit of Pericles, as Thucydides represented him, was that he ruled the people and not – as he thought was typical of democracy – they him:

Pericles indeed by his rank, ability and known integrity was able to exercise an independent control over the masses – in short to lead them, instead of being led by them. As he never sought power by improper means, he was never obliged to flatter them but on the contrary enjoyed so high an estimation that he could afford to risk their anger by opposing them outright.

It would, however, be an exaggeration to regard Pericles as a sort of uncrowned king of Athens – Thucydides' own narrative reveals that the people retained the whip-hand even over him.

To measure the time allowed for speeches in the law-courts the Athenians used terracotta waterclocks (which they called a *clepsydra* or 'water-stealer'). The capacity of each clock was measured in terms of *choes* (jugs) or *amphoras* (jars). The one surviving example, of about 400 BCE, would have contained 2 *choes* or about 6.4 litres and taken about 6 minutes to run through.

on it. We can infer, in reverse, from Aristophanes' comedies *Wasps* (422) and *Birds* (414) just how seriously the Athenians took jury service. But perhaps an even more striking testimony to the status of being a juryman is that some Athenians were actually buried with their pinakion.

Voting in an Athenian jury-court was by secret ballot. Jurors were given two kinds of bronze ballot to cast, one for guilty, one for not guilty. They voted without prior consultation, partly because of the numbers of jurors involved, and there was no formal appeal from their verdict. If a 'guilty' verdict was returned, in certain cases the penalty was mandatory – for example, for treason, the death sentence; but in others, there was a further stage of debate and voting on the sentence. Thus in 399, after Socrates had been found guilty of impiety by a small majority of the 501 jurors,

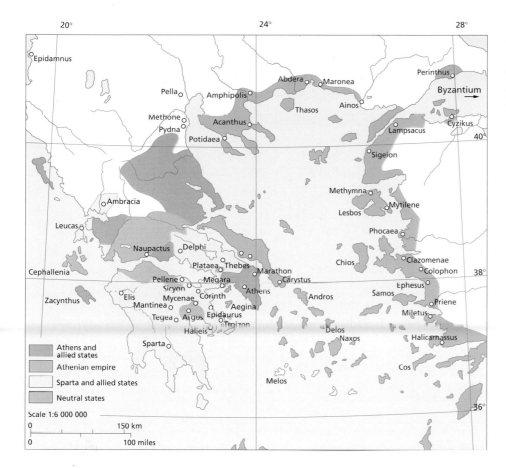

The Aegean Greek world at the time of the Peloponnesian War, divided into two main power blocs under, respectively, Athens and Sparta.

a larger majority of them voted for the death penalty, partly because they were irritated that Socrates had not proposed a sufficiently stiff penalty himself. Jurors were therefore also given wax tablets – a long line in the wax indicated a vote for the heavier sentence.

Another vital item of court equipment was the water clock that measured out the amount of time in amphoras (a unit of specified capacity) allocated to prosecutor and defendant, who each had to appear in person on their own behalf. The time allowed depended on the type of lawsuit and the nature of the alleged offence. A favourite rhetorical trick was to pretend a case was so strong that one didn't need all the time officially allowed and to cry imperiously 'throw out the water!'.

THE PELOPONNESIAN WAR

This newly revitalized and active Athenian democracy of some 30,000 or more citizens, duly registered in demes and by tribes, found itself unable to sit back. On average it was at war with some enemy, Greek and/or non-Greek, for three years in every four during the fifth and fourth centuries. It never enjoyed an unbroken period of peace that lasted as long as a decade. The most conspicuous, prolonged and historically decisive bout of warfare in which democratic Athens indulged – or became embroiled, depending on your viewpoint – was the Peloponnesian War (431–404).

Democracy hymned

Perhaps the greatest, and certainly the most influential, speech made in a modern democracy is Abraham Lincoln's Gettysburg address of 1863. Its ultimate model and inspiration was the Funeral Speech delivered by Pericles over the Athenian war dead in the early months of 430 BCE, at the close of the first season's campaigning in the Peloponnesian War. But whereas we have the very words of Lincoln's speech, what we have of Pericles' is a literary version or imitation, composed not by him but by Thucydides. Arguments continue to rage therefore over the relationship between the spoken original and the literary representation. Has Thucydides preserved anything like Pericles' own words in their original order and with their original emphasis? Or has he somehow reshaped them in accordance with his view of what Pericles probably said, or should have said, or (more worryingly) to fit in with Thucydides' own political outlook or artistic purposes?

We cannot say for sure. What we do know is that this was not the first occasion on which Pericles had been given the supreme honour of delivering this annual public address. At least once before he had stood up in the Cerameicus cemetery in the Potters' Quarter just outside the city's main Dipylon gate to speak to the grieving relatives of the dead men whose burnt bones were displayed before them in cypress-wood caskets prior to solemn state burial. The ceremony itself had probably been inaugurated in the 460s, shortly before the radical democratic reforms of Ephialtes. The connection between the ceremony and democratic government was a constant. It was up to the individual speaker to give the most uplifting portrayal he could of the connection between patriotic self-sacrifice and democratic citizenship. Pericles' hymn to democracy in Athens, as presented by Thucydides, could hardly have been bettered:

Bust of Pericles, a Roman copy after the fifth-century original by Cresilas. Malicious critics held that the helmet was included to hide Pericles' oddly shaped cranium. The inscription reads 'Pericles, son of Xanthippus, Athenian'.

Our constitution does not imitate the laws of neighbouring states. We are rather a model for others than imitators ourselves. Its administration favours the many instead of the few – that is why it is called a democracy. If we look to the laws, they afford equal justice to all in their private differences; if to social standing, advancement in public life falls to reputation for capacity. Class considerations are not allowed to interfere with merit, nor again does poverty bar the way: if a man is able to serve the state, he is not hindered by the obscurity of his condition...

Nor are these the only points in which our city is worthy of admiration. We cultivate refinement without extravagance and knowledge without effeminacy. Wealth we employ more for use than for show, and place the real disgrace of poverty not in owning up to the fact but in refusing to struggle against it. ... Unlike any other community, we Athenians regard him who takes no part in these civic duties not as unambitious but as useless. Even if we cannot originate policy, at all events we can judge it; and instead of looking on discussion as a stumbling-block in the way of action, we think it an indispensable preliminary to any wise action ... In short, I say that as a city we are the school of all Greece ...

My task is now finished ... and in word at least the requirements of the law have been satisfied. If it is a question of deeds, those who are here being interred have already received a part of their honours. For the rest, their male children will be educated at public expense until they reach adulthood. Thus does the state offer a valuable prize, the garland of victory in this race of valour, to reward both those who have fallen and their survivors. For where the rewards for merit are greatest, there are to be found the best citizens.

Carved marble relief, mid-fifth century BCE from Athens, known as the 'Mourning Athena'. The patron goddess of Athens is shown in military aspect wearing a helmet and leaning on a spear. She seems to be gazing down in sorrow on what may well be meant to represent an official state casualty list; from the mid-460s the Athenians also held an annual mourning ceremony for the war-dead of that season's campaigning at which a distinguished orator such as Pericles was chosen to pronounce a funeral oration over the warriors' ashes.

Democracy despised

Throughout the history of Athenian democracy there flowed a strong counter-current of oligarchic sentiment, theory and activity. The practising democratic politicians such as Pericles and Demosthenes did not seem to consider it necessary to write down their thoughts about democracy as a system, so almost all the surviving contemporary political theory and commentary is more or less anti-democratic. One such commentator was Xenophon, who favoured oligarchy – in this respect at least he was a worthy pupil of Socrates, for whom the majority was always wrong.

It was for this reason that the earliest surviving example of Athenian prose was subsequently claimed as a work of Xenophon. But in fact the so-called 'Athenian Constitution', a rabidly anti-democratic pamphlet on the Athenian democracy and empire of the fifth century, could not possibly have been his since it was most probably written in the mid-420s, when Xenophon was still a very small boy. It is conventionally attributed now to an author known as the Old Oligarch (though his age is as unknown as his identity). The real Xenophon's oligarchic political theory is to be found elsewhere, especially in the work of his entitled *Memoirs of Socrates*.

This is a collection of imaginary conversations in which Socrates talks with real Athenians about the practical and ethical underpinnings of contemporary Athenian politics. In one of these dialogues Xenophon gives his version of an imaginary dialogue within a dialogue. Supposedly, the original conversation had taken place in the 430s between the great Pericles and his ward, the teenage Alcibiades, who in a stroke of irony was to do more than anyone else to destroy his guardian's political legacy. The subject of their discussion was laws.

In his youth, Alcibiades was a great admirer of Socrates, whom he fought with and risked his life for at the Battle of Delium (repaying Socrates for saving him when he was wounded at Potidaea). Alcibiades' great personal courage and charisma, however, were flawed by extravagance and irresponsibility. He and Socrates soon parted ways and Alcibiades went on to embroil himself and Athens in diplomatic and political turmoil, which eventually resulted in his own disgrace and death, and contributed to the downfall of Socrates through their early association. The image of Alcibiades *opposite* is taken from a mosaic floor of the 4th century CE, found at Sparta.

Tell me, Pericles, can you explain to me what a law is?

Laws, Alcibiades, are what the mass of the citizens decree.

Do they think one ought to do good or evil?

Good, of course, my boy, not evil.

But if it's not the masses who come together and enact what is to be done, but – as happens under an oligarchy – a few, what do you call that?

Everything the sovereign power in the city decrees is called a 'law'.

What, even if a tyrant makes decrees for the citizens, is that a 'law' too?

Yes, whatever a tyrant as ruler enacts, that too is called a 'law'.

But when the stronger compels the weaker to do what he wants, not by persuasion but by force, is that not negation of law?

Well, yes, I suppose so.

Then whatever a tyrant compels the citizens to do by decree, without persuading them, is the negation of law?

Yes, I agree – and I take back my earlier statement that whatever a tyrant enacts without persuasion is law.

Suppose the Few make decrees, using force not persuasion – are we to call that coercion?

I should say that all forms of compulsion, whether by decree or otherwise, are a negation of law.

Alcibiades now has Pericles where he wants him, and can deliver the knockdown anti-democratic argument:

Then everything the *masses* decree, not persuading but compelling the owners of property [the few wealthiest citizens], would be coercion not 'law'?

Let me tell you, Alcibiades, I too was very clever at this sort of debating when I was your age.

'Ah, Pericles', said Alcibiades, who is given the last word, 'if only I had known you when you were in your prime!'

Dulce et decorum est pro patria mori ('sweet and fitting it is to die for the fatherland'): so wrote the Roman poet Horace in the midst of another extended passage of internecine war. Such a slogan was never needed more urgently than in 431 as a call to young Athenians to defend their maritime empire and the vigorous, participatory democracy which had thrived in the almost fifty years since the repulse of Xerxes and his barbarian hordes. Athenians found an eloquent spokesman of the noble and patriotic death in Pericles, who had been continuously elected to the top political office of General since 443. He was also easily the most authoritative democratic leader, despite (or even because of) his unimpeachable aristocratic lineage.

If Thucydides was right, then the worst enemy Athens had to face was neither Sparta nor Sparta's foreign ally Persia, but the Athenians themselves. It was their strategic mistakes and internal disunion rather than their enemies' skill or resources that most accounted for Athens' eventual, calamitous defeat. Thucydides' interpretation, however, arose largely from a political prejudice that led him to attribute Athenian mistakes to a fatal combination of the people's incompetence and the overweening personal ambition of Pericles' immeasurably inferior political successors. Actually, Thucydides' own narrative makes it doubtful whether the Athenians did depart quite so completely as he claimed from the strategy laid down by Pericles at the start of the war. On the other hand, his emphasis on internal political disagreement in Athens was not entirely misplaced.

In commenting brilliantly on the civil war between democrats and oligarchs that broke out on Corcyra in 427, Thucydides noted that such strife spread thereafter throughout the Greek world as the Peloponnesian War plunged into hitherto unplumbed depths of savagery. He accordingly gave a great deal of space and importance to the vicious and bloody outbreak at Athens in 411. Had he survived to complete his history, he would undoubtedly have done the same for the civil war that followed Athens' final defeat in the Hellespont (Dardanelles) in late 405. But the extreme oligarchs who successfully carried out the coups against the democracy in 411 and again, with Spartan aid, in 405/4 were following in the footsteps of earlier plotters, whose deeds he did record.

In 415, just as the great armada was due to set sail for the ill-fated Sicilian expedition, a graphic illustration of the close connection between politics and religion at Athens occurred. Overnight most of the *Herms*, or statues of the travellers' god Hermes in the form of rectangular pillars sporting erect phalli and topped with a representation of the god's head, were mutilated – the heads were smashed, the phalli lopped off.

Since the Herms served as divine protectors of private houses and public shrines, their destruction was a deliberately ill-omened act. It could only have been the result of careful conspiratorial planning – by anti-democrats among others. A long investigation resulted in the conviction and, in some cases, execution of fifty or so wealthy men, resident aliens as well as Athenians, whose property was confiscated and sold at public auction.

The most prominent fish to be caught in the dragnet was Alcibiades, accused not of Herm-smashing but of profaning the sacred Eleusinian Mysteries. A gilded aristocrat by birth and upbringing, who had been the ward of Pericles after his father's death, in politics Alcibiades was a complex figure of persuasive charm combined with unscrupulous personal ambition. He had been the prime mover of the Sicilian expedition, but was recalled after it had departed to face a capital charge of impiety. Instead, he absconded to the enemy, advising the Spartans that to him and men like him democracy as a system of government was nothing but an acknowledged lunacy. No wonder that clever oligarchic pamphleteers liked to pit him for propaganda purposes against his former guardian: the egotistical opportunist Alcibiades against the grave democrat Pericles.

For a second time, in 404, democracy was abrogated at Athens, this time through the direct intervention of Sparta. Simultaneously, the Athenians were stripped of the last vestiges of their Aegean empire — which the Spartans were quick to try to take over for themselves. The Athenians were placed under a narrow oligarchic government of thirty men, led by Plato's relative Critias. This regime so distinguished itself by its brutality that it was nicknamed the Thirty Tyrants, a nickname that has stuck. Sparta for a while propped it up, providing a garrison and supporting mercenary troops, but Critias unleashed such a reign of terror that Thebes, an ally of Sparta which had done exceptionally well out of the Peloponnesian War, began to show alarming sympathy for its Athenian enemy.

In an attempt to halt any further increase in the influence of Thebes in central Greece, Sparta stood aside as the Thirty were overthrown and even permitted the restoration of democracy at Athens, while taking care that it should remain powerless in foreign affairs. A general amnesty regarding political crimes committed before 403 was declared, for all except the survivors of the Thirty and their henchmen, and was – for the most part – observed, under the ever watchful eye of Sparta.

DEMOCRACY RESTORED

Thus it was that, in the last years of the fifth century and the early years of the fourth, the Athenians were preoccupied with setting their restored democracy in order and trying everything to prevent a recurrence of oligarchic rule. During this period the overhaul of the law-code that had been begun in 410 was brought to completion. The new code was inscribed in stone on walls within the Stoa where the city's most important religious official, the Basileus or 'king' Archon, had his office. It was to this official that in 399 Socrates was denounced by his three accusers, one of whom, Anytus, was among the most prominent post-war democratic leaders, for grave crimes of impiety and corruption of youth. It is a moot point whether Socrates was guilty as charged (we have chiefly the testimony of his supporters Plato and Xenophon to judge by). Aeschines, a leading orator of the mid-fourth century, no doubt correctly interpreted the popular perception of his

Demosthenes, hero of the democratic resistance to Macedon, was honoured posthumously with a statue that probably should not be regarded as a faithful portrait. The original of this Roman marble copy was fashioned in bronze by Polyeuctus and set up in the Athenian Agora in 280 BCE, over forty years after its subject's death (in 322).

(*Opposite*) In 336 the Athenians passed a law against tyranny. The *demos* (people) of Athens is represented in relief as a mature, bearded citizen being crowned by the personified goddess Democracy. The law forbids co-operation with those plotting an anti-democratic coup and calls for the acquittal of any citizen who is accused of murdering the would-be tyrant. Fear of a Macedon-imposed tyranny was very much on the public's mind at Athens in 336, with the memory of Philip's victory at Chaeronea still all too fresh.

fate when he said that the Athenians had condemned to death Socrates the Sophist (unorthodox intellectual) because he had been the teacher of the extreme oligarch Critias.

However, with the exception of the death of Socrates and a few other exemplary judicial executions that breached the general amnesty of 403 in spirit if not according to the letter, the restored democracy conducted itself with moderation and restraint.

It is a separate question whether the institutions as well as the spirit of the new democracy were less radical than those of its Periclean predecessor. Certainly there were changes. For example, after 403 the Assembly was no longer empowered to legislate – that power was transferred to a small body probably drawn from the annual panel of 6000 jurymen. But although, as intended, that prevented major decisions being taken on the spur of the moment under emotional duress, as had happened more than once in the fifth century, it is not clear that in principle the fourth-century system was any less democratic. It was still the Assembly that decided whether or not the legislative panel would sit, and the legislators were chosen at random by lot in order to be as representative as possible of the citizenry as a whole. Nevertheless, it is fair to say that in one sense the Athenians of the fourth century were more conservative, namely that in light of their bad experiences of oligarchic counter-revolution they were almost obsessively concerned to conserve the rule of the people against all internal and external threats.

MACEDONIAN HEGEMONY

One such threat came from Macedon from the late 350s onwards. Demosthenes, whose influence over Athenian politics was comparable to that of Pericles in his heyday, never lost a chance to impress on the Athenians the necessity to resist the expansion of Philip of Macedon at all costs. To no avail. At Chaeronea in Boeotia in 338 the Athenians and their Theban allies were decisively defeated by Philip's crack Macedonian and Greek troops. Willy-nilly, the Athenians were enrolled in 338/7 as subordinate members of Philip's alliance, known to us as the League of Corinth, through which he exercised hegemony over the Greek peninsula and by which he got himself appointed to lead a supposedly Panhellenic crusade of revenge against the Persian empire. To effect this, Philip required Athens' fleet, since he had none of his own, and that was one reason why Athens was treated rather more gently than some others of his defeated Greek opponents, especially the Thebans (who had a Macedonian garrison imposed on them).

In the event, however, Philip was assassinated at home before he could leave for Asia. His son Alexander, who succeeded to his father's role, achieved his stupendous conquests without making much use of the Athenians and their ships, treating their politically unreliable crews chiefly as hostages for their city's good behaviour. Otherwise Alexander like Philip for the most part left Athens alone. Yet it was only natural that the Athenians should fear the worst: an overthrow of their democratic system by Macedon – which, like Sparta in 404, was known to be no friend to democracy, having already promoted the imposition of pro-Macedonian tyrannies on its allies. This is the background to the passage in 337/6 of a law against tyranny. The text of this was inscribed on a surviving stone pillar, atop which Democracy, as the goddess Democratia, crowns Demos, the people of Athens personified as a middle-aged man.

No amount of laws, however, could be proof against the eventual destruction of democracy at Athens. It actually occurred at the hands of Antipater, after the death of Alexander in 323. That was not quite the end of democracy as such in ancient Greece. The city of Rhodes seems to have maintained a democratic tradition well into the next century. But succeeding Hellenistic kings and, later, Rome all actively promoted oligarchy and monarchy of various shades as instruments of imperial rule. By the second century of our era the Greek term *democratia* had become so devalued that the Roman empire itself could be hailed by a Greek rhetorician called Aelius Aristides as a 'perfect democracy – under one man'!

By the sixth century CE, in Byzantine Constantinople, this linguistic degeneration had gone even further, so that democratia could be used to mean an urban riot. In short, the powerful anti-democratic tradition with which Greek democrats had always had to contend won out triumphantly in the end. When, during the Renaissance and later, the Greek achievement was cited as a model and guide for contemporary political practice, conspicuous by its absence from that paradigm was the Athenian system of direct, participatory citizen democracy. We in the West may well call ourselves democrats today, but to an ancient Athenian what we call democracy would look uncommonly like elective oligarchy.

Democracy revised

The late eighteenth century witnessed two great political upheavals: the French and American revolutions. Each was preceded and accompanied by ferocious ideological debate, some of which was given written expression in letters, pamphlets and fictional literature as well as in formal treatises and visual representations. Since the eighteenth century was also the great age of neoclassicism, it was inevitable that participants in this debate should have looked back to classical antiquity for models to imitate or to avoid.

So it was that the issue of democracy was vigorously aired, and the choice between following Athens and following Rome sharply posed. Among the French revolutionaries there was a 'left-wing' grouping that advocated the sort of direct, participatory mass democracy practised in the Athens of Pericles and Demosthenes. After all, the main ideological slogans of democratic Athens had anticipated their own battle-cries of 'Liberté' and 'Egalité'. But these left-wingers were a small and ineffectual minority.

Among the American revolutionaries, who were no less dedicated to liberty and only slightly less to equality, the rejection of Greek democracy as a model was yet more forceful and thoroughgoing. This was partly because they were in general heir to the tradition of Western thought that (mis)represented democracy as a predominantly urban form of mob-rule. For them, a direct democracy like that of Athens bore therefore the stigma of violence, corruption, injustice and instability. But the American revolutionaries also rejected Greek democracy specifically because they saw themselves as the continuators of the anti-democratic Republican Romans – hence their choice of 'Capitol' (not 'Acropolis') and 'Senate', and George Washington's modelling himself on the famous Roman general Cincinnatus (who retired happily to private life as soon as the Republic's need for

him was in his view past). What particularly attracted America's founders about the Roman Republic was the soundness of its theory and practice regarding the sanctity of private, especially rural, property. Cicero, indeed, had even gone so far as to claim that the very purpose of the state was to preserve and protect it.

Here is an extract from Thomas Jefferson's *Notes on the State of Virginia*, in which the mutually dependent notions of the sturdy yeoman farmers and of the cankerous urban mob are given full rein, backed by liberal borrowings from the Scriptures:

> Those who labour in the earth are the chosen people of God, if ever he had a chosen people, whose breasts He has made His peculiar deposit for genuine and substantial virtue. He keeps alive that sacred fire, which otherwise might escape from the face of the earth. Corruption of morals in the mass of cultivators is a phenomenon of which no age nor nation has furnished an example. It is the mark set on those, who, not looking up to heaven and to their own soil and industry as does the husbandman, for their subsistence, depend for it on casualties and caprices of customers... The mobs of great cities add just so much to the support of pure government, as sores do to the strength of the human body. It is the manners and spirit of a people which preserve a republic in vigour. A degeneracy in these is a canker which soon eats to the heart of its laws and constitution.

Thomas Jefferson by James Sharples (*c.*1751–1811).

War and Peace

CHAPTER 7
Paul Cartledge

One way of expressing the concept of 'foreign policy' in ancient Greek was to say 'matters concerning peace and war' – with the proviso that in practice war, not peace, was the norm, however desirable peace might ideally seem to be. Another connection between politics and war is the one put forward by Aristotle. According to his model, a state's political structure corresponded to and facilitated the kind of fighting needed for its survival.

CAVALRY

Where Aristotle's model is at its weakest is in the assumption that once upon a time true cavalry warfare had predominated throughout the early Greek world. He had, perhaps, inferred this from Homer and the names of some historical aristocratic groups (for example the *Hippobotae* or 'Horse-rearers' of Chalcis in Euboea). Actually, the terrain of mainland Greece and the islands has always been for the most part quite unsuitable for cavalry. In the late sixth century, for example, ground in Attica had to be specially cleared by the Athenians to make it 'suitable for horses' (*hippasimos*), pending the arrival of allied cavalry from Thessaly – one of the handful of regions which were not so topographically unsuited to mounted warfare.

Elsewhere, in Asia Minor or South Italy, there might be other local exceptions, but in land campaigns the military significance of cavalry seems always to have been subordinated to various styles of infantry fighting. Chariots were therefore symbolic rather than functional vehicles; useful for making a grand impression at a funeral, for example, or on some other religious occasion – but not for practical warfare. On the other hand, the kudos of cavalry, especially in early Greece, can scarcely be exaggerated. Even in democratic Athens it never quite lost its cachet.

The reason for the social prestige of cavalry was quite simply a matter of wealth. Horses required extensive and well-watered pasture, rare in Greek lands, and their cost in fodder and other forms of upkeep was enormous. Only the privileged few could ever afford to keep a war-horse, let

(Opposite) Horse and rider were both cast solid, but separately. The find was made at Grumentum in Lucania, South Italy, but the group was perhaps made at Greek Metapontum. It dates to roughly the second quarter of the sixth century. The horse is a little angular and stiff but technically very competent; the rider wears a short tunic and a Corinthian-style helmet decorated with lotus buds and (originally) a transverse crest.

(Left) Like the Grumentum horseman, this huge bronze *krater* (mixing-bowl) was found in a non-Greek site. Possibly commissioned from a Spartan workshop, or alternatively from a Greek studio in South Italy, the krater ended up in the grave of a Celtic princess at Vix in central France. Around the neck there processes a series of well equipped chariots and hoplites, the figures bearing letters of the Greek alphabet scratched on their backs to aid the final assembly. The date of the burial is around 500, but the krater could have been made several years, even decades, earlier.

alone a race horse. Even on the land horses were rare. Oxen were preferred for traction and for transport in general. The famous story of the brothers Cleobis and Biton, who yoked themselves to their mother's cart to make sure she was able to get to the shrine of Hera some five miles from Argos to perform her function as a priestess, arose from the failure of the family's oxen – not their horses – to return from the fields on time. It is, however, conceivable that aristocrats in early Greece might have ridden to the battlefield on horseback before dismounting to fight on foot. Perhaps in this way they hoped, vainly, to preserve some status distinction in the face of the increasing importance of the foot-soldier.

INFANTRY AND THE RISE OF THE HOPLITE

The rise of the *hoplite* was nothing short of a military revolution. The hoplites were generally citizen land-owners, people who on average owned between about 5 and 10 acres of land and constituted about 30–40 per cent of the adult

Cavalry

The surviving literary and archaeological evidence for cavalrymen is curiously disproportionate to their military significance. Despite the kudos attaching to them, true cavalry (*Hippeis*, or 'Knights') typically played a subordinate military role in Athens and most other states. Their apparent prominence has more to do with the wealth that could afford to buy lasting memorials, and with political and artistic agendas. For example, in 424 when Aristophanes based a whole comedy (called *Knights*) on them, he did so for his own dramatic and political reasons: he wanted to juxtapose this honourable élite against the mass of poor citizens, the 'naval mob', for whom his main target, Cleon, claimed to speak.

Once, perhaps, cavalry had been more prominent on the battlefield, but the Persian Wars of 480–479 were fought and won by Greek hoplite soldiers and trireme sailors. Even so, the wealthy cavalry class were happy to commission pottery that figured them as a decisive part of the action. On this red-figure drinking-cup of the period, for example, we see a cavalry horse being attended by a black African groom – such an exotic servant would also have been a great status symbol in fifth-century Athens.

Almost a hundred years on, during the Corinthian War (395–386) against Sparta, Dexileos of Athens perished among a small Athenian cavalry force. The Athenian state took a particular pride in honouring its war dead, whatever their socio-economic status, and the wealthy relatives of an élite cavalryman like Dexileos naturally spared no expense in commissioning a magnificent *stele*, or grave marker, to be erected in the national cemetery of the Cerameicus.

The relatives of Dexileos had another reason for emphasizing their loyalty and patriotism. Just a decade before Dexileos' death, the aristocratic cavalry had all too willingly taken the side of the Thirty Tyrants, the anti-democratic junta imposed on Athens by Sparta as part of the peace-settlement of 404. So to make it quite clear that Dexileos could not possibly have been a member of that tainted set – as, for example, the historian Xenophon had been – his family took the unusual step of having Dexileos's birthdate included in the funerary epitaph, which reads as follows:

Dexileos son of Lysanius from Thoricus was born in the archonship of Teisandrus (414/13), died in the archonship of Euboulides (394/3) at Corinth, one of the five cavalrymen.

Who or what 'the five cavalrymen' were, we cannot say. But we do also have the official Athenian epitaph for the twenty-year-old Dexileos and ten other fellow-cavalrymen who shared his fate:

These cavalrymen died at Corinth: the tribal commander Antiphanes, Melesias, Onetorides, Lysitheus, Pandius, Nicomachus, Theangelus, Phanes, Democles, Dexileos, Endelus.

Rest In Peace.

The 'Chigi Vase'. The painter of this tiny frieze depicting hoplite phalanxes on the point of engagement worked in Corinth round about 640, but the vase was exported to Veii in Etruria. His is the earliest known wholly effective representation of the hoplite phalanx, though he has not always managed to get the number of feet quite right. All the hoplites wear Corinthian helmets, bell breastplates and greaves. The two interior handles of the hoplite shield are particularly clear, as are the blazons.

As hoplites neared the enemy in open formation (*above*), ranks closed and shields met to form a nearly solid wall of bronze and wood (*below*). Most phalanxes ranged from eight to sixteen men in depth. They resembled a series of rectangles, extending from a few hundred yards to a mile or two in length as armies grew in number to 10,000 or 30,000 warriors.

male citizen population of a city-state. These new-style infantrymen probably took their name from the *hoplon* (shield) which was the most distinctive feature of their equipment. Double-handled, round, and up to a metre in diameter, the hoplon was made basically of wood – though it might be faced and edged in bronze. It was heavy (about 20 pounds) and, except in the specific environment for which it was intended, more of an encumbrance than an asset. It was purpose-designed for close-order, hand-to-hand fighting.

A lone hoplite would have been a nonsense, even a contradiction in terms. He would have been a heavy-laden (his equipment weighing up to 75 pounds), slow-moving target. In the early days of hoplite warfare, perhaps, an infantryman did not necessarily fight as part of a rigid formation, but that was the direction in which infantry warfare inexorably tended – due in part to the nature of the shield, which protected at most only half of the bearer's body. The earliest surviving depictions of an organized hoplite *phalanx* in action date from around the middle of the seventh century, but successful phalanx fighting may already have been practised as early as the late eighth century in Argos under King Pheidon (his date is uncertain).

Armour

What the hoplite wore to battle was something akin to a uniform, though not every state adopted exactly the same elements, and there was probably some degree of variation tolerated within each force depending on the hoplites' individual means. Each warrior-landowner purchased his own armour and kept it at home until his military services were needed. Subject to its condition, equipment was handed down from father to son.

The most important single item, as described, was the shield. For the rest, starting at the top, there was the distinctive helmet, raised from a single sheet of bronze in a procedure demanding great technical skill. This provided good protection, but unfortunately it also reduced its wearer's vision and hearing to almost dangerous levels.

An impressively well-stocked warrior grave of the late eighth century (c.720) from Argos is important as a chronological marker of change. The helmet it contained is of a non- or pre-hoplite type, whereas the two-piece bronze breastplate confirms the pressing need felt for protection at close quarters. Illustrations of the new hoplite-type helmet, including a bronze figurine of a helmet-maker at work, belong to the last couple of decades of the eighth century. What soon became the characteristic combination of hoplite helmet and breastplate meant that a hoplite's two most vulnerable areas were his neck and abdomen.

The so-called 'Panoply Grave' at Argos, dated c.720, was stuffed with everything a fashionable warrior could require, including iron spits to cook his evening roast. The two-piece breastplate makes some attempt at anatomical accuracy but was presumably worn with a lining underneath for greater comfort. The helmet, on the other hand, was as much for magnificent show as for practical utility, since it offered little protection and a relatively easy hand-hold in the close-order style of fighting that the breastplate implies.

Most scenes on Spartan sixth-century painted pottery were of myth and legend, but occasionally verismo broke in, as here on this drinking-cup. Spartan hoplite warriors were noted physically for their long hair and, morally and mentally, for their extreme solidarity: both are well in evidence on this neatly painted artifact.

What they were vulnerable to was the hoplite's thrusting spear with its shaft of cornel wood 2–3 metres in length and long point of iron. Hence the need to keep in as close order as possible within a phalanx formation, normally some eight ranks deep, shield hard upon neighbour's shield. Hence too the moral as well as military imperative to stay in one's position in the ranks, 'in order' (*en taxei* – interestingly this is the modern Greek expression for 'okay'). No hoplites knew how to do this better than the Spartans.

The Spartan hoplite

Sparta, indeed, was the first and the quintessential hoplite state. Uniformity of equipment and behaviour suited a community of notional equals whose life style and indeed very existence were based on the repression of much larger numbers of unfree Greeks, the helots. Sparta, a city on constant military alert, not surprisingly brought hoplite phalanx warfare to a peak, employing religion, music and other aids to reinforce a discipline born of fear and necessity. Two battles stand out in the long history of Spartan hoplite supremacy: firstly, the Battle of the Champions (*c.*545); secondly, the Battle of Plataea (479).

The Battle of the Champions

This was a distinct oddity in hoplite terms. Both sides, Sparta and Argos, agreed at first to dispense with the usual hoplite-type attritional battle, based on sheer weight of numbers, in favour of an unusually ritualized combat between 300 élite troops on either side. This was to be a heroic contest, in other words, in which skill would play an exceptionally important role alongside bravery and discipline. The immediate outcome of the battle was that all but three of the 600 warriors had been killed – two Argives and one Spartan. But whereas the two Argive survivors rushed back home to announce what they imagined to be their victory (the battle was fought over disputed borderland much closer to Argos than to Sparta, and the expansionist Spartans were the aggressors), the lone Spartan remained on the battlefield *en taxei*, as the hoplite code demanded. He then claimed the victory in the accepted way, by erecting a battlefield trophy – fastening captured enemy weapons and armour to a stump of wood.

Unsurprisingly the Argives refused to accept that claim and the battle had to be refought, with each side now at full available strength. We are not told how many more men each side lost in the process – normally, it seems, a winning side could expect to lose some 5 per cent of their strength and the defeated side at least double that – but Sparta emerged the clear victor, with the disputed border territory firmly in its possession, where it remained for almost two centuries.

THE PERSIAN WARS

The Battle of Plataea was the decisive encounter of the Persian Wars of 480–479. Xerxes' enormous Persian-led invasion force of perhaps some 100,000 men had done well enough on land in 480. Those few who had dared to resist him, led by King Leonidas and his 300 Spartans, had come to grief at the pass of Thermopylae. Simonides' famous epitaph captured perfectly their laconic heroism:

> Take this news to the Lacedaemonians, friend,
> That here we lie, who followed their command.

Thereafter central Greece, including Attica and Athens itself, had quickly fallen prey to Xerxes' looting hordes.

Salamis and naval warfare

At sea, though, the advantage in 480 lay with the resisting Greeks. After an indecisive encounter off Euboea, the Athenians under Themistocles with their newly built fleet of triremes (see p. 178) had led the Greek resisters to a stunning victory at Salamis over Xerxes' fleet provided by his Phoenician and Greek subjects. After this disaster, Xerxes returned to Asia for good, but he left behind a land army under the command of Mardonius that he considered would be large and effective enough to complete the defeat of the remaining Greek loyalists and the occupation of the Peloponnese.

Plataea

Persian would-be hegemony was contested decisively in 479 at Plataea in Boeotia, a region that the Greeks knew as the 'dancing-ground of Ares' (the Greek war god) since it was the scene of so many crucial battles. The Greeks, perhaps numbering some 40,000 men, were commanded by the Spartan regent Pausanias. Sparta, with its league of mainly Peloponnesian allies and its unrivalled military reputation, was recognized as the senior Greek land power.

At first, it was by no means clear that the Greeks would have the measure of a very differently composed and (though exact numbers are not known) significantly larger army, but in the end the Persian forces under Mardonius were beaten essentially by the Spartan hoplites. Victory at Plataea was commemorated thereafter by all Greeks as a victory of liberation – but, Greeks being Greeks, the decisive role of Sparta was by no means always acknowledged.

Bow and arrow

One Athenian who did acknowledge it, however, was the great tragedian Aeschylus. He was a veteran of the famous victory over the Persians at Marathon in 490, as his epitaph proudly attests:

> Aeschylus son of Euphorion, Athenian, him this
> monument in wheat-bearing Gela hides in death.
> His glorious strength the grove of Marathon could tell,
> And the long-haired Mede too knows it full well.

Having lost their fleet at Salamis, the remaining Persian invaders in Thessaly, under Darius' nephew Mardonius, brought a force of 25,000 infantry and 5000 cavalry south to Plataea to continue the campaign by land. Mardonius' Greek allies, among them Thebes, supplied him with a further 13,000 infantry and 5000 cavalry. They were met at Plataea by a force of more than 40,000 hoplites and 70,000 light-armed troops. After a few days of manoeuvring and harassing supply lines, Mardonius eventually made an all-out assault. However, the ground gained by his cavalry could not be held by the foot-soldiers, who were overwhelmed by heavy Spartan infantry under Pausanias. Only 3000 of Mardonius' men survived the rout, and Mardonius himself was killed.

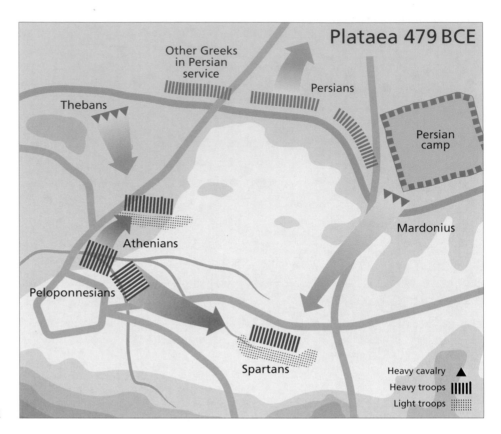

Aeschylus may also have fought at Salamis and Plataea. With the latter more particularly in mind, he described the Persian Wars in his tragedy of 472, *Persians*, as a victory of the Dorian (Spartan) spear over the Asian bow. Greeks, too, could be archers, and the prowess of Heracles and Odysseus was legendary (though Odysseus' was displayed indoors within his palace rather than on the battlefield, as he outshot and then slaughtered his wife Penelope's importunate suitors). But in everyday military life the bow was always regarded as an inferior, low-class weapon, not on a par with the hoplite's spear.

One reason for this was that archers depended on other types of soldier for cover. Another was that they were distance fighters – not regularly tried by eyeball-to-eyeball contact with the enemy, let alone the supreme test of hand-to-hand combat. From Homer onwards assertions of derision and contempt for the 'womanish' archer echo through the masculine and heroic war literature of the Greeks. There was a social reason for this contempt too: archers in Greece were usually by definition poor men, as cheap and expendable as their equipment.

Archers were not, of course, the only other kind of fighters besides cavalry and hoplites. The very poorest unskilled men could at least hurl stones if need be, though specialist slingers were also known, especially in Crete.

THE PELTAST

During the later fifth century a new type of light-armed fighter emerged to prominence from the northern end of the Greek peninsula, in non-Greek Thrace. Like the hoplite, the *peltast* was named for his shield (*pelta*), but this was lighter than the hoplon and usually made of wickerwork. It was during the Peloponnesian War and its successor the Corinthian War (395–386) that hoplites were first subjected to the peltasts' greater mobility, especially in hilly or mountainous terrain. Enemies of Sparta turned enthusiastically to peltasts as a means of disrupting Sparta's machine-like hoplite efficiency. In 390, most notably, the Spartans suffered a humiliating and

Hardly surprisingly, the scene of a Greek hoplite triumphing over a Persian adversary was popular in Athenian vase-painting in the years around 480. On this example from the Triptolemus Painter the helmeted but bare-armed Greek glares menacingly at his crouching Persian foe, who wears a leather cap and an elaborately patterned dress with sleeves and trousers in the oriental manner. A quiver or bowcase at his waist suggests that his sword, unlike the Greek's, is a weapon of last resort.

One of the most brilliant of Athens' sixth-century black-figure vase-painters, Exekias, placed Dionysus in a handsome warship to illustrate the myth in which the god of wine was captured by Etruscan pirates. But, partly because of the technical difficulty, and partly because Athens at the time (*c*.540) may have been rather backward in matters of naval warfare, the type of warship Exekias depicted was not a trireme, the very latest in nautical design. Normally, warships would be driven by oars (see p. 91), but for artistic effect Dionysus reclines under a billowing white sail set off against the deep coral-red background of the drinking-cup's interior.

crippling loss of most of a regiment of 600 men during the Corinthian War. This was inflicted at Lechaeum near Corinth by a crack force under the command of the Athenian Iphicrates, whose funds were being provided by Persia.

This defeat was catastrophic because it happened to Sparta on land. At sea the Spartans were only briefly a major force, between 413 and 394, during which period they won the Peloponnesian War in 404 (using non-Spartan sailors, of course, and Persian money) and decisively lost the battle of Cnidus in 394. The sea was far more the Athenians' element.

NAVAL WARFARE

The *trireme* (from the Latin form of the Greek word *triêrês*) was a three-banked, oared warship, probably first seen in either Egypt or Phoenicia in about 600 BCE. By 500 it had been adopted sporadically in Greece, but it did not become the regular ship of the line before the Persian Wars. The 'tri-' of trireme would seem to refer to the three banks of oars, two directly superimposed upon each other with the third occupying an outrigger.

Triremes have been aptly described as glorified racing eights; built for speed and manoeuvrability rather than strength. This meant that lightness of construction had to be combined with co-ordinated muscle-power and expert helmsmanship for maximum effectiveness in action. A trireme's crew numbered roughly 200 – comprising 170 oarsmen (drawn from the lower social classes), various officers, and a small complement of marines armed as hoplites. Storage space was virtually nil, so that a friendly, or at least neutral, supplies base in the area of offensive operations was a necessity. Relatively expensive to build, triremes were expensive above all to maintain in commission.

An experimental trireme named *Olympias* (after the mother of Alexander the Great) was recently reconstructed with considerable success and commissioned into the Greek navy. As yet, it has not achieved the speeds that the ancient literary sources indicate an ancient trireme did, so modifications continue to be introduced.

Labour – human muscle-power – was the principal fixed cost. Suppose a crew-man were paid half a drachma a day (as seems to have been normal in the period immediately before the Peloponnesian War), it would have cost half a talent simply to keep the crew of one trireme paid for a month. A small flotilla of ten ships would have cost on that basis five talents a month, or fifteen talents for a three-month campaigning season – far more than the average amount of cash being demanded in tribute from the members of Athens' naval empire. This burden was therefore borne by the Athenian imperial treasury out of revenues from the state-owned silver mines as well as from allied tribute.

So far as the maintenance of the ship's fabric was concerned, that financial burden the Athenians loaded onto the shoulders of exceptionally wealthy citizens on an annual basis. No other city than Athens could hope to build, let alone afford to keep in fighting trim, the navy of 300 triremes which Athens maintained for much of the fifth century. Yet in the end Athens lost the Peloponnesian War at sea, through a combination of self-inflicted disasters and massive Persian financial aid to landlubbing Sparta.

Helot rebellion and the fall of Pylos

Another of many military paradoxes in the Peloponnesian War contest between Athens and Sparta occurred in 425. Athenian naval power posed a threat to Sparta's home territory, especially to Messenia where most of the Spartans' local subject population of helots were concentrated. Seeking to exploit their advantage the Athenians sent a fleet round the Peloponnese, ostensibly en route to Corfu, or even further west to Sicily. But off Pylos on the south-west coast of Messenia the fleet was driven by strong winds to seek the safety of the shore, and there the Athenians dug in and built a fort, to which they succeeded in persuading many helots to desert. These rebel helots, armed by the Athenians, were then sent back into the nearby farming country and caused considerable destruction thanks both to their knowledge of the terrain and to the fact that they spoke the local dialect of Doric Greek.

Naturally, the Spartans could not long tolerate this hostile fortification in their own home territory (epiteichismos) and dispatched a force of hoplites to boost the resistance of loyal Messenian helots. But calamity was followed by disaster, as a section of this relief force of hoplites was ambushed and either killed or captured by the Athenians using principally light-armed troops – a victory of the Athenian bow over the Spartan spear, we might say. To the astonishment of many, not least of the Athenians, the surviving 292 members of the Spartan hoplite section did not fight to the death but surrendered, trying to save what face they could by claiming it was beneath them as true men to fight against the archers' 'spindles' – women's implements.

The survivors were transported back to Athens as hostages. There they remained for another four years, during which period their shields were displayed as trophies in the Agora. One of those shields found its way down a well, where it remained

The 'naval mob' strikes back

In classical Athens the navy was very much the junior service. There had been some sort of an Athenian navy since at least the seventh century, and in the sixth there may have been a fixed procedure for raising taxes in order to support a sea force – easily the costliest instrument of ancient warfare. Nevertheless, as late as the 490s Athens was still obliged to lease warships from Corinth, a pioneer and long-time leader in Greek naval architecture. It was only the chance of a lucky strike in the state-owned silver-mines during the 480s that enabled Athens to build for herself a huge, 200-strong fleet of the very latest three-banker triremes.

Under the inspired guidance of Themistocles this new and relatively untried fleet won a great victory over the Persians at Salamis off the Attic coast in 480, and thereafter the military and political fate of Athens was to hang principally on her performance at sea rather than on land. The heroic period of Athenian naval enterprise was the second and third quarters of the fifth century, during which fleets operated all round the eastern Mediterranean basin (as far east as Cyprus and as far south as the Nile delta) and even up into the Black Sea. Within the Aegean, the Athenians carved out and sustained a tributary maritime empire (see p. 155). It was during this epic period, in about 460, that some unknown Athenian proudly dedicated on the Acropolis a terracotta votive shield decorated in red-figure with a naval motif.

This naval-motif terracotta shield was perhaps a copy of the one worn by each of the ten or more hoplite marines that a trireme carried. However, important though the marine's role was, it was very much secondary to those of the helmsman (*kubernetes*) and the 170 rowers. The helmsman was a skilled man, and might be of high social class – Alcibiades in 406 was prepared to entrust an entire allied fleet to the command of his helmsman, though Antiochus in Alcibiades' absence then proceeded to lose the important battle of Notium. The rowers of an Athenian trireme, on the other hand, were lower class, indeed often very poor, even landless men. They included free foreigners and, indeed, slaves as well as Athenian citizens. Politically, however, it was the Athenian citizens among them that mattered. Their role in propelling the city's warships with such enormous success was what acquired for the 'naval mob' (as their upper-class detractors such as Thucydides liked to call them) more and more political power in the ever more radically democratic constitution (see Chapter 6).

Ideologically speaking, however, the hoplites continued to occupy the high ground. There was thought to be something not quite 'manly' in rowing a trireme, facing away from the unseen enemy at the moment of impact, and sometimes withdrawing tactically rather than steadily advancing to meet the foe head-on, as in a pitched hoplite encounter on land.

Not everyone thought this way however. Thucydides put these words into the mouth of Phormion, one of the great Athenian naval commanders, as part of a pre-battle oration to his sailors in the early years of the Peloponnesian War:

> As to the battle ... do you stay at your posts by your ships, and be sharp at catching the word of command, the more so as we and the enemy are observing one another from so short a distance. In action, consider order and silence all-important – qualities useful in war generally, and in naval warfare in particular. Behave in face of the enemy in a manner worthy of your past exploits. The issues you fight for are great – to destroy the naval hopes of the Peloponnesians or to make more imminent for the Athenians their fear of losing control of the sea.

Phormion's men went on to win a stunning victory in the Corinthian Gulf that summer of 429. But in the much longer run, the Athenians did indeed forfeit their control of the sea, as they lost the Peloponnesian War in another narrow strait at the other end of the Greek peninsula, at Aegospotami in the Hellespont (Dardanelles) in 405.

This fragment is from a votive shield made of terracotta and decorated in the red-figure technique; it was dedicated *c.*460 to Athena on the Athenian acropolis. An elegantly attired woman is shown holding in either hand an *aphlaston*, the stern ornament of a ship. The *aphlasta* are each decorated with a human face wearing oriental headgear. These are probably meant to be understood as spoils taken by Athenians from a Persian ship in the course of Athens' triumphant naval campaigns of *c.*475–450. The woman may indeed be Nike, goddess of Victory, to whom a new temple and altar were dedicated on the Athenian acropolis some time after 450. Most crew members on an Athenian trireme warship were rowers, but triremes also carried a small complement of hoplite marines, and it may be that this terracotta shield is a votive imitation of the real-life wood and bronze shield carried by one such marine.

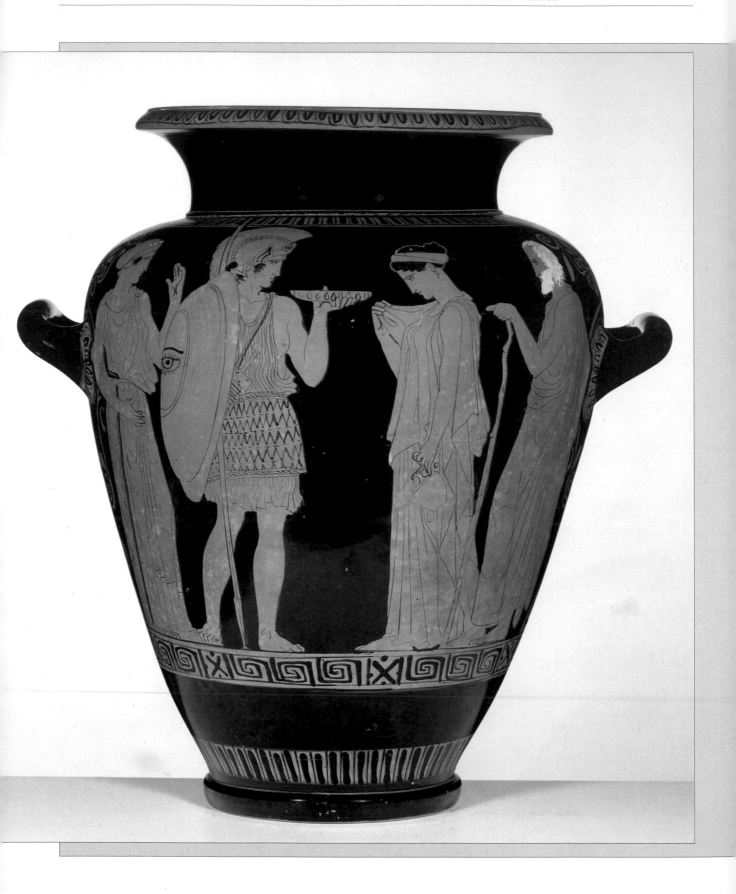

Engendering war

Greek warfare was a man's business and a men-only affair. Courage was gendered – the sort of martial pugnaciousness required to fight in Greek-style combat was equated with virility. However, women were not entirely excluded from the sphere of war-making. As countless pre-battle orations predictably repeated, it was for the sake of the city's women – among other things – that the men went to war. An emblematic image in this martial culture was that of the devoted wife bidding her warrior husband a fond farewell as he set off to battle on her and his city's behalf.

In Sparta the national mythology had it that mothers preferred their sons to win and die rather than suffer defeat and live – (come back) 'with your shield – or on it', was allegedly their parting command. It was even claimed that Spartan mothers of sons who died in battle openly rejoiced, whereas the mothers of survivors hung their heads for shame and avoided public spaces. In the somewhat gentler martial culture of Athens, a more even balance was struck between the public and the private, the personal and the collective, but we may be sure that here too a male citizen would consciously carry with him into battle the burden of his wife's expectations as well his desire to serve his city and acquire fame among his fellow-men.

One wife who threatened to subvert the whole Greek military-masculinist complex but perhaps ended up merely confirming it was Euripides' Medea. In a famous passage of his tragic drama named after her, Medea (played of course by a man) comes out of the marital home in Corinth to express to the chorus of Corinthian women her pain over her betrayal by Jason. She does so in explicitly gendered terms, culminating in a defiant comparison of battle with childbirth:

A man, when he is tired of being with those inside
goes out and relieves his heart of boredom,
or turns to some friend or contemporary.
But we women have to look to one person only.
They say we live a life secure from danger
living at home, while they brandish spears in battle.
They are wrong! I would rather stand three
times beside a shield than give birth once.

On one level, Medea was the wife from hell, a foreign woman and a sorceress from the other end of the known world (Colchis in modern Georgia) who deliberately murdered her own children to gain revenge on her husband. On another, she was an extreme embodiment of every Greek wife's predicament: a perpetual outsider liable to be cast aside by a husband in his search for pastures new. Even the radical Euripides, however, perhaps felt he could question the priority and centrality of the male battle experience only in this oblique way.

(*Left*) Medea the witch miraculously rejuvenates an old ram by pouring special potions into a boiling tripod cauldron. She promises the same results to the elderly Pelias, father of Jason, but with lethal results. Athenian red-figure *hydria* (water-jar) *c*.470.

(*Opposite*) Women were precisely the unmilitary half of the Greek population, but it was for them and with their unswerving support that the men were supposed to go out and fight. Before leaving home a religious ritual was performed to ensure that the gods would be on the right side. A libation of wine was poured from a *phiale* (shallow bowl) and prayers were offered. On this Athenian wine-jar of *c*.430 BCE (coincident with the outbreak of the Peloponnesian War) the hoplite husband is shown holding the bowl into which the wife has poured the libatory wine. She holds out her dress as if to veil her head in a gesture of modesty and devotion signifying wifely fidelity and loyalty. Behind the wife stands an old man beyond military age, with a white beard and leaning on a staff, probably representing the warrior's aged father.

sealed from about 300 BCE until the American excavations of the 1930s uncovered it. On close inspection the inscription could be seen to read '(The) Athenians [took this] from (the) Lacedaemonians from Pylos'.

SIEGE WARFARE AND WEAPON TECHNOLOGY

Another kind of warfare that became significant during and after the Peloponnesian War was the siege. However, before the use of powerful long-range missiles or seriously damaging battering rams, there was little any Greek siege force could do except use blockade tactics: surround the enemy, cut off their supplies and wait for starvation to take its toll.

Xanthus in Lycia in south-western Turkey came under strong Greek influence during the fifth century. This funerary monument of a ruler, c.400 BCE, known as the Nereid Monument, depicts a city under siege, by hoplites – probably before the technical developments in Sicily that began to shift the odds in favour of the besiegers.

Thus it took the Spartans two years to conclude their siege of Plataea, between 429 and 427, despite the use of complicated flame-throwers as an extra weapon. The Athenians proved no more successful with their ever more elaborate circumvallation at Syracuse between 415 and 413. It was not until the early fourth century that the siege tower and torsion catapult were effectively pioneered by Dionysius I tyrant of Syracuse. The next major technological advances were made in Macedon, under Philip. With his siege-train and superior weaponry, he managed to end most of his sieges in weeks rather than months or years – and failed altogether in only two cases. Alexander's seven-month siege of the Phoenician island-city of Tyre in 332 built spectacularly if precariously on the achievements of his father.

THE RISE OF THE MERCENARY

On the whole, however, it was not technical know-how so much as the more efficient deployment of manpower that was to prove decisive in the battles of the fourth century. For example, during the Peloponnesian conflict peltasts were commonly employed as mercenaries to supplement Greek hoplite forces, and this is one of the main reasons for their great impact on Greek warfare. The derring-do and apparent success of Xenophon and the 'Ten Thousand' mercenaries in Asia and the approaches to the Black Sea in the years on either side of 400 greatly encouraged the use of mercenaries by Greek states as well as foreign potentates. So common indeed did it become that the Athenian assembly increasingly preferred to vote money from the dwindling public reserves to pay mercenaries to fight on behalf of – and instead of – themselves. Hence Demosthenes' despairing, recurrent call to his fellow-citizens to 'serve in person'.

THE BATTLE OF CHAERONEA

Nevertheless, despite the development of siege-warfare and the increasing use of peltast mercenaries, what was perhaps *the* decisive battle of the fourth century was largely fought on the Greek side by hoplites. The background to the battle of Chaeronea in 338 was briefly as follows.

The rise of Macedon under Philip since 359 had forced Athens to acknowledge publicly its inferiority and weakness in the Peace of Philocrates (346), the terms of which the majority of Athenians

(Above) **This Thracian peltast, depicted on an Athenian red-figure drinking-cup of about 480 by a painter with Thracian connections (the Brygos Painter), wears Thracian boots and cap, and a wrap-around apron (*perizoma*). The top of the shield (*pelta*) was cut out to improve the wearer's vision.**

(Right) **Hoplites are depicted in action against Scythian archers on this elaborately decorated gold scabbard of the third quarter of the fourth century which was found in a non-Greek burial in the Crimea. The craftsman responsible was perhaps a local Scythian heavily influenced by Greek workmanship.**

could never stomach. In particular, they yearned to recover Amphipolis in Thrace, which they had themselves founded in 437 and then lost to Sparta in 424 – permanently, as it turned out.

In the autumn of 340 Philip's expansion eastwards towards the Black Sea, across Greek and non-Greek territories alike, signalled possible disaster for Athens. An entire Greek grain fleet of over 200 ships, bringing Crimean and Ukrainian wheat to the Aegean, and the bulk of it to the Piraeus, fell into his hands. Like the Spartans in 405/4 and 387/6, Philip now had a stranglehold on Athens. With

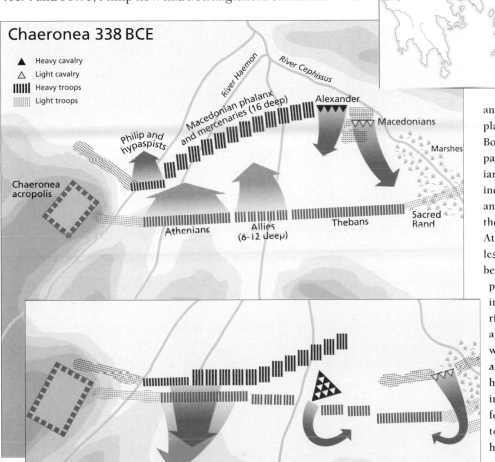

Chaeronea 338 BCE

▲ Heavy cavalry
△ Light cavalry
▥ Heavy troops
▦ Light troops

River Haemon
River Cephissus
Macedonian phalanx and mercenaries (16 deep)
Philip and hypaspists
Alexander
Macedonians
Marshes
Chaeronea acropolis
Athenians
Allies (8-12 deep)
Thebans
Sacred Band

Chaeronea

On 2 August, 338 BCE, Philip and his eighteen-year-old son Alexander, broke the Theban and Athenian phalanx on the plain of Chaeronea in northern Boeotia. The Greek defeat was partly due to clever Macedonian tactics, and partly to Greek indiscipline. Philip advanced and attacked the Athenians, then feigned a retreat. The Athenians pursued him heedlessly, leaving a great gap behind them. Alexander pushed through it, surrounding and cutting off the Theban right, and then Philip attacked the Athenians again, which caused consternation and panic. Demosthenes, who had belittled Philip as a limping, one-eyed monster 'so fond of danger ... that in order to make his empire greater, he has been wounded in every part of his body', fled the battle in shame.

Mercenaries

The word 'mercenary' has acquired a strongly pejorative sense in recent times, moving away from its original meaning of 'being for hire' towards 'being solely interested in personal gain'. In ancient Greek, mercenaries were either *xenoi*, foreigners, or yet more politely *epikouroi*, 'helpers'. It has even been suggested that Apollo Epikourios of Bassae in Arcadia (to whom was dedicated a famous late fifth-century temple designed by one of the architects of the Parthenon), owed his epithet to the support he gave to mercenaries. Arcadia, at any rate, was certainly one of the major suppliers of Greek mercenaries when the phenomenon of mercenary service first began to have a significant impact on Greek warfare in the fifth and fourth centuries.

The reason for this is straightforward enough. Most mercenaries were poor men, and rugged, upland Arcadia – the real Arcadia in the central Peloponnese, not the Arcadia of myth – was a notoriously impoverished region of Greece. Other reasons impelling men to look to mercenary soldiering for a livelihood might be political – for example, defeat in a civil war might entail a period of exile, and what better way to earn a crust as well as develop the skill and muscle required to effect one's return than to hire oneself out as mercenary? Or they might be more private – a means of living down personal disgrace.

All these reasons, not to mention the simple desire for adventure, probably motivated the individuals who came together in Asia Minor at the very end of the fifth century in the largest single band of Greek mercenaries yet raised. Known as the 'Ten Thousand', it had originally comprised some 13,000 men, of whom more than half were from Arcadia.

What caused this quite exceptional demand was a dynastic power-struggle between the reigning Great King of Persia, Artaxerxes II, and his younger brother, the pretender Cyrus. Cyrus had been appointed by their late father in 407

A comically unflattering third-century terracotta of a mercenary.

as generalissimo of all the Persian forces at the western end of the Persian empire. As such he had become embroiled in the Peloponnesian War on the Spartan side. In fact, it was the money that he channelled so lavishly to Lysander which decided the contest in Sparta's favour. In return, the Spartans did what they could to help Cyrus in his struggle to replace his brother on the Persian throne, encouraged by the fact that one of Cyrus' principal Greek mercenary recruiters and commanders was the Spartan Clearchus.

Among those who flocked to Cyrus's standard was the young Xenophon, then held in bad political odour at Athens for having supported the venomous regime of the Thirty Tyrants. It is thanks to Xenophon that in the *Anabasis* ('The March Up Country') we get a vivid insider's portrait of life as a mercenary in the Middle East and Asia Minor at the turn of the fifth and fourth centuries.

Not that his is an objective or wholly truthful portrait. Xenophon goes to suspiciously great lengths to distance himself from the materialistic motives of most of his fellow-mercenaries, and he glorifies his role as commander in extricating the Ten Thousand from Asia following the death of Cyrus in battle at Cunaxa near Babylon in 401. He cannot, however, entirely disguise just how much profit he made from the exercise, although he typically seeks to excuse his financial gain by stressing that he devoted it to pious ends.

Formally exiled from his native Athens for treason, he was given, thanks to his new patron, King Agesilaus of Sparta, a desirable estate not far from Olympia, where he lived the life of a grand country gentleman for the next couple of decades. Here is his third-person autobiographical account (from the *Anabasis*) of how he laundered some of his mercenary profits:

> He bought some land as an offering to the goddess Artemis ... and also used the sacred money for building an altar and sanctuary. Thenceforth he always dedicated a tithe of the season's produce in order to celebrate a sacrifice in the goddess's honour. All the inhabitants of Scillous and the surrounding area, men and women, would take part in the festival. Artemis provided those who joined in the feast with barley-flour, bread, wine, dried fruits, and a portion both of the domesticated animals sacrificed from the sacred herds and of the wild game... The temple is a small-scale reproduction of the great temple of Artemis at Ephesus, and the cult-statue is as close a likeness to the golden Ephesian original as an image made of cypress wood possibly could be.

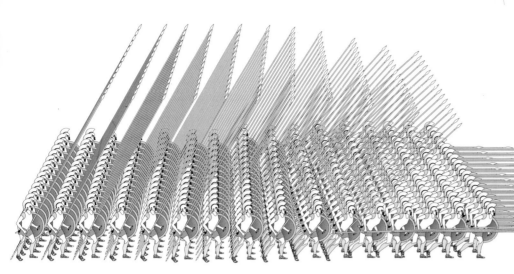

The Macedonian phalanx relied on unflinching discipline for its effect. The first five rows of pikes all reached targets in the initial collision, their wall of jostling spears harpooning attackers, and – like bristles – bouncing back the pressure of the enemy advance. Men in the middle and rear, too, kept busy, warding off arrows with raised pikes, stabbing the enemy wounded on the ground with their butt-spikes, pushing on with their shoulders the men ahead. Accidental casualties from a swarm of bobbing spear-butts in the faces of the men behind must have been severe. Exhaustion came in minutes, given the weight of the pike and the pressure of the pushing ranks. The carnage would have been horrific, so it was perhaps no wonder that sleek youth and elegant muscle were not wanted for this sort of fighting. Stout, war-wise, unsqueamish veterans with the nerve and experience not to flinch from the task would have been the driving force of a Macedonian phalanx.

no option but to fight him to the finish, Athens reluctantly allied itself with Thebes, its most powerful neighbour and old enemy, for the catastrophic conflict at Boeotian Chaeronea.

The then eighteen-year-old Alexander has been credited with playing a great part in the Macedonian victory as part of Philip's élite Companion Cavalry, but it was the awesome steadiness and drill of Philip's phalanx of pikemen that won the day.

The 5-metre long *sarissa* wielded by the front ranks made the Macedonian infantry resemble nothing so much as a metal-tipped porcupine. The pikemen were linked fluidly to the cavalry by the lighter-armed and more mobile élite bodyguard of Royal Shield-bearers so as to form a battle line at once supple, impenetrable and adaptable.

Under pressure from the unstoppable Macedonian phalanx, indiscipline in the left flank broke the Greek line and the Macedonian cavalry charged into the widening breach. The outcome thereafter was never in doubt. However, a unique force distinguished itself on the Greek side that day. Tradition had it that its members all died in their respective stations, *en taxei*, and were buried near if not under the lion monument that to this day marks the battle site. That force, founded in 378, was the so-called Sacred Band of 300 specially picked Theban hoplite warriors – reputedly a unit of 150 homosexual couples, who made war as well as love together, until they collectively made the ultimate sacrifice at Chaeronea.

ALEXANDER THE GREAT

Philip's military innovations were exploited by the armies successively commanded by his son Alexander as he marched restlessly first from one end of the Greek peninsula to the other, and then from one end of the Persian empire to the other between his accession in 336 and his death in 323.

After securing behind him a more or less peaceful Greece, Alexander embarked for Asia in 334. But the mainly Athenian ships in which he set off were destined to

be no more than transport vessels as Alexander put into practice his strategy of defeating the enemy's fleet from the land, that is by capturing its strategic naval bases – such as Tyre – by siege.

Three major and successful pitched battles, at the river Granicus (334), Issus (333) and Gaugamela (331), saw off the last reigning Persian monarch, Darius III, and it was these three battles that were later most celebrated.

Alexander's war of conquest ended only with his untimely death at Babylon. He had conducted guerrilla campaigns in what is now Afghanistan, fought his way across rivers and against elephants in the Punjab, and savagely progressed through a series of major and minor towns in north-west India before struggling back to Iran

(Opposite) Erected at the point where the slaughter of Greeks was most dense (many bones have been excavated underneath), the noble lion of Chaeronea (put together in recent times from many fragments) still keeps watch over the battlefield of Chaeronea in Boeotia where Macedon's hegemony was sealed.

Alexander

Alexander's father Philip II was said by a later biographer (Satyrus) to have fought his wars by marriages – in all, he notched up seven wives, several of them concurrently. A special position was occupied by his Greek wife Olympias, who gave birth to his heir apparent, Alexander, in 356. Already by the age of sixteen Alexander was considered mature enough to be left as regent in Macedon as Philip pursued his relentless path of conquest to the east. In 338 he distinguished himself at Chaeronea. In 336 he succeeded to the Macedonian throne as Alexander III.

Philip had been assassinated. The finger of suspicion pointed to Olympias, by then estranged. The truth of that can never be known, but there is no doubt that it was her son who most benefited from Philip's early demise. Alexander quickly revealed his

political and military mettle, including a ruthless streak that led him to endorse the destruction of Thebes in 335. From 334 to his death in 323 he was away from Macedon and Greece in Asia, for the most part on active campaign.

Apart from victory in the three major pitched battles, the most impressive aspect of his campaigning was his extended guerrilla war in what is now Afghanistan and northern Iran between 330 and 327. On the other hand, Alexander more than once seriously jeopardized his own and his troops' lives, and in 325 his hitherto unwaveringly loyal Macedonian troops finally rebelled and refused to go another step further east into what seemed to them to be the limitless unknown.

On his return to Iran in 324 he once again revealed his streak of ruthlessness and had executed several of the regional governors he had himself appointed. Exactly what future he had in mind for the governance of his hypertrophied Graeco-oriental empire can never be known. Further campaigning ensued, and at his death in Babylon in 323 there were rumours of yet more campaigns being planned against the Arabs among others.

Rumours also multiplied that his death was not due to natural causes. But disease, afflicting a body already seriously debilitated by hard drinking and even harder campaigning, still seems the likeliest cause.

The victories of Alexander the Great in Asia Minor, Palestine, Egypt, Persia and Bactria in 334–325 BCE, and the cities he founded, were instrumental in spreading the language and culture of the Greeks across the Near East as far as the lower Indus. Legendary for his military prowess, Alexander was also characterized by his great aspirations: to know, to discover, to conquer, to excel – even to be divine. In 332–331 he undertook a long, dangerous and militarily unnecessary march through the desert to the oracular shrine of Egyptian Ammon (equated with Greek Zeus) at the oasis of Siwah to be assured of his divine descent as a son of the god. This heroic coin portrait depicts him wearing the ram's horns of Ammon. He died of fever in Babylon in 323, aged nearly thirty-three.

along the north shore of the Persian Gulf. To maximize speed, Alexander pared down his baggage-train to a minimum: his toughened veterans, especially the hard core of Macedonians, were required not only to fight but also to be their own beasts of burden. Eventually, though, even they had had enough, and at Opis, near Babylon, in 324 they literally called a halt.

After his death Alexander's empire, so briefly held, quickly fell apart. His enduring legacy proved to be neither political nor military but cultural, evident in the string of Alexandrias (and other Greek cities) that he founded or inspired across the Middle East from Egypt (the original Alexandria, founded in 331) to Afghanistan (the furthest east was at Ai Khanum in ancient Sogdia).

Work and Leisure

CHAPTER 8

Nick Fisher

IDEAS OF WORK

Earlier chapters have explored complex connections between the environment, economic activities, military activity, politics and society. Here we take a closer look at the realities and the ideologies associated with work and status, and at typical forms of organized and collective leisure. Some leisure activities of the ancient *polis* were supported financially by the state and designed to enhance civic cohesion, both through religious ceremony and through intense competition. Others served private pleasures and, it can be argued, might either increase or lessen social tensions among the societies in the Greek cities. As in previous chapters, much of the surviving evidence concerns Athens, which was among the largest and most successful, but not the most typical, of the *poleis*.

The earliest Greek poems, Homer's *Iliad* and *Odyssey*, give the impression that the world of ordinary humans (as opposed to the worlds of the gods, or the mythical peoples of Odysseus' travels) was a domestic one in which men characteristically ate wheat and barley bread as staples; cooked, dressed their food and washed themselves with olive oil; and reared and worked with domestic animals. Some of the animals would end up being cooked and consumed after a sacrificial ritual to the gods, and washed down by wine and water – a libation of which had also been offered to the gods.

The portrait of agricultural scenes on Achilles' shield presented in book 18 of the *Iliad* is an idealized picture of a world mostly in harmony and peace, and was not intended to convey a standard view of the nature of agricultural work or of relations between rich and poor on the land. More realistic scenes appear in many Homeric similes (for example, ploughing, winnowing and threshing in the *Iliad*); and above all in the description of aged Laertes' careful development of a farmstead in *Odyssey*. Hesiod's poem *Works and Days*, composed at about the same time, gives much greater detail (see p.194).

Prominent in *Works and Days* are several related ideas. First, farming is the main work and it is done by men. Women are 'naturally' fitted to work inside the house, above all on textiles (see Chapter 5).

Second, work, and especially the basic extraction of crops from the earth, is hard and unyielding. It was seen in mythic terms as originating from a densely interlocking sequence of punishments and trials sent by Zeus, as the 'Golden Age' dissolved in separation and bitterness between gods and men. The central myth here, told both in Hesiod's *Works and Days* and also in his *Theogony*, concerns the punishment of Prometheus for successfully stealing fire from the gods and giving it to humankind: Zeus in retaliation created the first woman – Pandora – whose descendants, the 'race of women', were to be major causes of pain and troubles for

Farming: ideal and reality

He [Hephaestus] made on it an aristocrat's landed estate;
    there the hired workers
were reaping the corn, holding their sharp sickles in their
    hands.
The handfuls of cut corn fell to the ground in swathes and
    in thick numbers,
and the sheaf-binders tied up the sheaves with binding
    twine.
There were three sheaf-binders standing by; behind them
were boys picking up the cut sheaves, carrying them in
    their arms,
and bringing them to the binders continuously; the lord,
    among them in silence,
holding his sceptre, stood by the swathe glad in his heart.
Heralds a little way off under a tree prepared a feast,
and were making ready a great ox they had sacrificed; and
    the women
scattered abundant white barley on the dinner prepared
    for the workers.

This depiction taken from Homer's description in the *Iliad* of the
shield made by Hephaestus, god of fire, serves a narrative purpose. The ferocious hero, Achilles, would carry the new shield
into the sequence of final battles with the Trojans which were
to bring him glory and an early death – he was not in fact ever
to return to the world of peace – precisely the world which most
of the scenes on the shield display – as he had at times claimed
he would earlier in the poem. So these images of labourers
working happily under the benign gaze of a noble in charge of
his large estate, and all about to share in a feast, are probably
to be taken as representing an idealized picture of farming life,
designed to sharpen the tragic irony of the scene.

A more accurate idea of the rigours of rural life is probably
given in the description of Laertes and his slaves (in *Odyssey*
book 24) on a homestead farm developed probably on hilly and
marginal ground.

[Odysseus and his companions] went out of the city and
    came to Laertes'
farmstead, finely worked, which Laertes had built up
for himself, as he had laboured greatly on it.
On the farm was his house, and all around the house ran
    the outbuilding,
and in the building there they fed themselves, sat down,
    and slept,
the slave-workers under compulsion, who performed the
    work pleasing to him.

Odysseus (looking for Laertes)
went on in his quest towards the fruitful orchard.
There he did not find Dolius, as he entered the great
    orchard,
nor any of the slaves or of Dolius' sons; for they had gone
to collect rough stones for a terrace wall for the orchard,
and the old man had gone to show them the way.
Father Laertes he found in the well-constructed orchard,
weeding around a tree.

[Odysseus addresses his old, shabbily dressed father]
Old man, no lack of expertise holds you back from tending
your orchard; it is all well looked after, nor is there
    anything,
no plant, no fig tree, no vine, no olive tree,
no pear tree, no leek-bed which is untended in the garden.

The advice to independent small farmers in Hesiod's *Works
and Days* probably also conveys fairly accurately the beginnings
of a greater intensification of agriculture and the use by such
farmers of slave labour.

So when first the time for ploughing appears to
    mortal men,
then set yourselves hard to it, your slaves and you
    yourself, ploughing in wet and in dry through the time
    of the ploughing,
pressing on with the task early in the morning, so your
    fields may be full.
Plough in the spring; earth turned over also in the
    summer will not let you down.
Sow the fallow land when the soil is still
    getting light;
Fallow land is a defence against disaster, and a
    comfort for the children.
Pray to Zeus of the Earth and to holy Demeter,
so that Demeter's holy grain may ripen in
    good weight,
when first you begin the ploughing, when you take the
    end of the plough-handle
in your hand, and apply the stick to the back of the oxen,
as they pull the yoke-bar by the straps. Have a slave
keep a little behind with a mattock to make hard work
    for the birds
by hiding the seed. Good management is best
for mortal men, and bad management is worst.

Some aspects of life in the country in ancient Greece are illustrated in this sixth-century black-figure cup, which came from the Athenian pottery workshop managed by Nicosthenes. The layout may suggest the distinction between the cultivated land, where three ploughings and a sowing are portrayed, and the more distant uplands, where wild animals may be hunted.

men. Pandora herself exemplified women's malicious and deceitful nature by releasing into the world a host of other diseases and pests when she lifted the lid of a great storage-jar in which they had previously been confined. As a result of all these changes men now needed to live with and to marry women in order to produce heirs. Also, the food which nature had previously produced spontaneously and without men's labour, was hidden away in the earth, to be won only by back-breaking work. Moreover, relations between humans and the gods, once open and direct, had to be mediated through the ritual sacrificial killing, cooking and eating of animals, along with the accompanying wine-libations and prayers. Of course, these rituals also served to celebrate and sanctify the human consumption of both the products of the earth – food and wine – and the meat and milk of the very animals whose labour and manure helped to produce the crops.

Third, Hesiod's poem (*Works and Days*) plots agricultural activities through the seasons of the year, and gives suggestions too for collective leisure activities in the slacker periods, such as participating in religious festivals and contests, and in the shared feasts of friends; though he advises against spending too much time, even in winter, in idle conversations in the smithy and the club house (the *lesche*). This well reflects the way in which the developed religious and social calendars of the Greek city states were closely linked to the patterns of the agricultural year (see Chapter 2). However urbanized they became, all Greeks retained an acute awareness of their vital dependence on the gods' support for their city's agricultural production. There was a sense that the annual patterns of crop growth and harvest and the life-cycles of their animals all suggested a greater general order or a model for the more complex social patterns of human reproduction, birth, prosperity and death.

For the Greeks, then, hard work (*ponos*) was seen as an unwelcome necessity, imposed by Zeus. Many, like Hesiod and Solon, also argued that work, especially on the land, could lead to just and more lasting prosperity than more dubious methods of wealth-creation – excessive wealth and leisure carried the besetting dangers of exploitation, arrogance and luxury. But the view that work was in itself a good thing and brought moral benefits to the individual is found much less commonly than, for example, in Protestant Europe, or in the monastic tradition of *laborare est orare*, work is prayer.

LAND, AGRICULTURE AND LABOUR

Farming techniques

In all Greek states, land remained the economic asset that carried the greatest value and status in terms of political, social and symbolic power. Possession of disputed territory was at all times the commonest cause of the frequent small-scale wars between neighbouring cities. An example of the classical Greeks' awareness of this comes in Herodotus' narrative of the Ionians' revolt against the Persians c.500–494 BCE, where the Ionian leader Aristagoras, seeking support from mainland Greece, is made to urge Cleomenes the king of Sparta to 'put off the battles over small amounts

(Opposite) Fishing and fish consumption, while perhaps of fairly limited economic and dietary significance, were of very considerable social significance as a major source of variety and interest in cuisine. As prices of fresh fish varied considerably, and the ability to serve it often to one's guests was an important index of wealth, its price was often a sensitive political issue. Hence Athenian comedy, and other literature concerned with *symposia* and cooking, are remarkably full of references to types of fish and to gourmandizing fish-lovers. In this relatively rare representation of a fish-stall on a south Italian red-figure mixing-bowl, the white-haired fishmonger is cutting up a large fish for a bearded customer holding out his money.

of land, which is not good land, and short boundaries, against your rivals the Messenians, Arcadians and Argives, fighting against those who have nothing at all in the way of gold and silver that are worth fighting and dying for', and instead to seek the conquest of the whole of Asia (Herodotus, *Histories*).

The majority of Greeks in most states were actively engaged in agriculture, and most of them were primarily small farmers – who can be called 'peasants' provided that we remember that many enjoyed much greater freedom from dues to richer land-owners or from state taxes than most peasants elsewhere. They formed the

Oleiculture

The olive was and is fundamental to Mediterranean agricultural systems. Olives provided food, and olive-oil was used for cooking and flavouring, in oil lamps, was rubbed on the body by athletes about to train, to keep off the dust, and by athletes and others washing or bathing, as a form of soap (to be scraped off by a special tool called a *strigil*). The trees were well suited to the topography and climate of Attica, and a number of Solon's laws (c.590 BCE) were concerned to encourage and regulate their cultivation. Apparently he discouraged the export of other agricultural products than olive-oil, and legislated also to prevent farmers growing olive trees so close to the edges of their lands that the roots damaged their neighbours' land. The trees may take up to six years before producing a crop, and up to fifteen years before full maturity, but they can live for centuries; however, even mature trees crop well only every other year. Thus an olive grove represented a considerable long-term investment. The olive became a major symbol of the identity of Athens. One sign of this was that the prizes at the contests in the Panathenaic games were special 'Panathenaic amphorae', containing valuable amounts of olive-oil.

(Below) **Olive-harvesting, late in the agricultural year, was an especially labour-intensive and slow process, as is illustrated on this Attic black-figure amphora by the Antimenes Painter. It is not possible in this case to determine whether the labourers are intended to be seen as slave or free.**

(Right) **The Panathenaic *amphorae*, presented, filled with olive-oil, as prizes at the games, retained their standard, conservative form for centuries, and so remained black-figure after that style had generally given way to red-figure (see Chapter 10). They commonly displayed, as here, Athena herself on one side, supported by fighting cocks (the symbols of virile competitiveness) standing on columns, and on the other, scenes of athletic competition or training.**

basis of the hoplite citizen-armies of their states. This predominance of agriculture in the polis economy obtained even in the most economically highly developed cities such as Athens, Aegina or Corinth.

Much, perhaps most, of the available land, however, was owned by the propertied rich. On the one hand, there was relative stability of land tenure and independence of the peasant citizen – evident above all in democratic Athens, but also, perhaps to a lesser extent, in many other cities (including those of Athens' fifth-century allies where comparable democratic systems were encouraged). On the other hand, in many smaller states, subsistence farmers continued to risk falling into serious debt or the worse state of debt-bondage, where the indebted farmer pledges to provide crops or labour for the creditor more or less indefinitely. Increasingly, from the fourth century BCE onwards, these people could be induced to support either democratic politicians or would-be tyrants offering redistribution of land and cancellation of debts.

Our picture of ancient Greek farming techniques is becoming ever more complex (see Chapter 2). New evidence from, for example, archaeological field surveys, economic anthropology and palaeobotany suggests that much land was farmed intensively in a variety of ways designed to suit different circumstances. The different

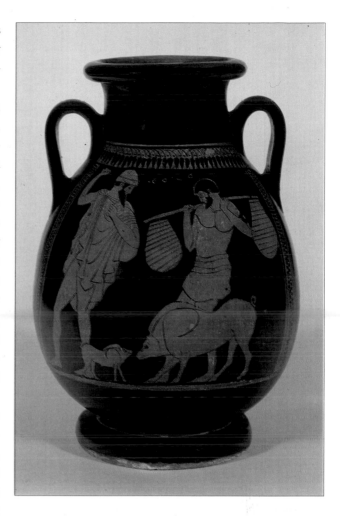

farming strategies applied included varied forms of fallowing; alternation of cereals and legumes; multi-cropping on the same fields; and owning a number of small farms in different parts of the territory. Thus farmers learnt cannily to spread their risks and maximized marketing success by raising as many different crops, vegetables and fruits as possible, while the three most important types of agricultural products remained the 'Mediterranean triad' of cereals, the olive and the vine. There is evidence too that farmers terraced hilly ground and made considerable use of small-scale symbiotic 'agro-pastoralism' by keeping grazing and working animals which were used to work and manure the land and also to provide food and in some cases leather.

The agricultural work force

Athens, and other major states such as Corinth or Chios, probably had large chattel slave populations (predominantly non-Greek) – although the only surviving ancient figures are totally incredible: 400,000 slaves in Attica, 470,000 slaves in Aegina, 460,000 slaves in Corinth, all of which imply impossibly high population

Pigs, mostly probably in small numbers, were an important part of animal husbandry on mixed farms, providing manure as well as meat. They were often used in sacrifices, especially, for example, to the goddess Demeter. Though they are not often portrayed on vases, here is an example on an Attic red-figure *pelike* of an adult and a young pig on the move with two farmers, perhaps being taken to be sold at market.

Cephisodorus – slave owner

In 415, shortly before the disastrous Sicilian expedition departed from Athens (see pp. 66 and 160), many prominent Athenians and metics were accused in a major political and religious scandal of profaning the Eleusinian Mysteries (an agrarian cult celebrating Demeter and Persephone) and of conspiring to mutilate many of the small Herms found outside Athenian houses. In the next few years the property of those found guilty was sold at auction by the appropriate Athenian magistrates, the 'sellers'.

A number of fragments of the inscriptions (the 'Attic *Stelae*') recording these sales have been discovered to the south-east of the Agora at Athens. These extracts record the sale prices in drachmae reached by some of the slaves belonging to Cephisodorus, a metic living in Piraeus (probably the same man also attested as a comic poet). He had at least sixteen slaves; others on these lists had at least seven or eight.

Property of Cephisodorus the metic [living in] Piraeus

(prices)	(description)
165	Thracian woman
135	Thracian woman
170	Thracian man
240	Syrian man
105	Carian man
161	Illyrian man
220	Thracian woman
115	Thracian man
144	Scythian man
125	Illyrian man
153	Colchian man
174	Carian boy
72	Carian child
301	Syrian man
151	Melitene man (probably in Cappadocia)
85	Lydian woman

Female slaves were often displayed on Athenian vases wearing ornamental tattoos on their necks, arms and legs, as here. These indicate their 'barbarian' origins, especially from Thrace. Tattooed or branded marks were also inflicted on runaway slaves (of either gender) as punishments and as permanent signs that they were not to be trusted.

densities for those states (in any case, no state ever had cause to hold a census of their slaves, whereas they did count those, such as citizens or metics, who were militarily useful). In some states permanent populations of subject Greeks were the major agricultural labour force, and they typically worked on relatively large and extensively farmed estates. The helots in Sparta, the *penestae* in Thessaly, or the *aphetairoi* in Crete are examples of these serf-type workers.

In other states large numbers of notionally free peasants could none the less be tied to larger land-owners by sharecropping or other arrangements of the type that Solon's reforms had removed from Athens (see Chapter 4). A number of wealthy citizens on some island states, such as Chios and Corfu (then Corcyra), appear to have operated large, slave-run estates, engaged in mixed farming and the export of quality wine.

The extent of agricultural slavery in Athens is not known for certain; direct evidence is in short supply. But it seems likely that much of the cultivable land was controlled by the propertied rich and managed in separate units. Sometimes these would be leased to tenants, but all would make some use of slave labour. It is also likely that many smaller, mixed farms were intensively managed by hoplites, with the help of one or a few slaves. (Hoplites are said to have been regularly accompanied on campaigns by their own slave attendant.) But managing the labour force had to take into account the strongly seasonal nature of many of the agricultural processes, especially viticulture and wine-making, and the olive cultivation for which Attica was particularly famous (see p. 198).

It remains unclear how many of the poorer independent Athenians, the *thetes*, the bottom class in Solon's four citizen divisions (see p. 88), had small farms and could afford a slave. This may well have varied considerably in times of greater or lesser prosperity. Slave prices too will have fluctuated widely – they are likely to have been attractively low after military success. Overall then, slavery or serfdom played a fundamental part in the most vital sector of the economy of most known states – not least Athens, the model of Greek democracy, and its leading rival and antithesis, Sparta.

MANUFACTURE AND EXCHANGE

The diversity of Greek produce and an awareness of goods available only from non-Greek communities led to complex patterns of exchange, despite the continuing ideological power of the self-sufficient household. Surplus agricultural products were exchanged for imported necessities such as metals. In years of poor harvests, staple cereals might be imported to Greek cities. But, increasingly, archaeological evidence suggests that a growing market for luxuries, delicacies or more specialized varieties of staple produce acted as an important stimulus for multiple trade links across the Mediterranean. Some of many examples of Greek imports, often from the east, include wheat from southern Russia (rather than home-grown barley); Phoenician or Chian wine (also in preference to the local product), and other foods, spices,

(Following page) **This black-figure vase well illustrates the complexity of exchanges of goods in the archaic period. It was made in Laconia c.560 BCE, but found, like so much of the surviving painted pottery of Greece, in Etruria. It represents King Arcesilas (named on the vase) of the Greek colony of Cyrene in Libya (probably Arcesilas II). The king is shown in exotic surroundings, seated on a stool under an awning, attended by a monkey, tame birds, a leopard and a crane, but he is engaged in supervising the weighing of a major crop of Cyrene, presumably for export (see p. 30) – though it is not clear whether the crop is wool, or the famous specialist product of Cyrene, *silphion*, a valuable plant (now extinct, perhaps related to *asafoetida*) with varied uses in cooking, medicine and as a contraceptive.**

medicines, perfumes or clothing. Pottery was also exported and imported in the form of plain containers; and fine painted pots (as well as the more valuable gold- and silverware) were used above all for display and for parties such as the *symposia*. Pottery tends to dominate our evidence because of its durability, but there is no reason to assume it was any more important a trade good than the rest.

Trade, money and banking

From the early sixth century, the introduction of coinage made exchanges easier in the Greek world, but the precise reasons for its gradual development remain obscure. The idea of replacing agreed weights of precious metals with standardized pieces of such metals (silver came to predominate), stamped with symbols on both sides, seems to have come from the Near-Eastern kingdom of the Lydians, border- ing Ionia. The various functions of coinage may have developed in stages. For tokens to function as money involves acceptance of the authority of whoever authenticated the symbols. The increasing power of civic government in the polis was apparently reflected in its coinage. There was a development from a variety of

symbols on the coins used within a city state (perhaps reflecting the several aristocratic families holding some sort of power) to lasting, easily identified symbols which represented the state: for example, Athena and the owl for Athens; the turtle for Aegina, and the silphion plant for Cyrene. Initially too, the purpose of creating these symbols may have been to facilitate payments from and to the state (such as land or harbour dues, or pay for mercenaries).

In time, though, an established coinage certainly benefited traders and enabled subsequent fifth-century developments such as the maritime loan, whereby richer men made high-interest loans to finance and gave some insurance to the operations of traders. It also gave rise to the profession of the money-changer or banker, as a means of facilitating exchange between the innumerable varieties of coinages used by the different states. The maintenance of an independent coinage remained a powerful symbol of virility for a polis; this was demonstrated for example by the resistance displayed by many of the members of the fifth-century Athenian empire when Athens attempted to 'rationalize' exchanges by imposing its own systems of money, weights and measures across the empire.

As well as changing money, bankers held deposits and lent out capital sums. The volume of trade grew rapidly and this was reinforced, as states introduced smaller denominations, by flourishing retail markets in the *agorai* (the religious, athletic and civic centres of towns and villages). A few lucky traders, such as Sostratus of Aegina and Colaeus of Samos, made huge profits. But most traders seem to have remained small-scale operators, typically owning only one ship, and were politically unimportant.

In Athens, and perhaps in many other cities as well, most traders were either *metics*, or non-resident foreigners, not citizens, and were therefore prevented from owning land or houses. Metics, including freedmen, could farm only as tenant farmers and had to rent their homes from citizens. This created a serious gulf between the economic worlds of land and trade, as metics, not owning land, could not borrow money on the security of land in order to develop other economic interests. In the worlds of trade and banking, slaves and freed slaves often worked in very close connection with their masters, and were frequently given positions of considerable responsibility and independence.

A special category for 'commercial cases' developed in Athens' legal system by the mid-fourth century BCE and was designed apparently to speed up these hearings. In such cases, foreigners were treated more on a par with citizens. They may also have been the only cases in which slaves, in the manner of free men, could give evidence not extracted under torture (see p. 110).

The small island of Aegina, in the gulf off Attica, began minting coins *c*.530 BCE, and this is among the earliest examples. Appropriately for an island which owed much of its prosperity to sea-trading, the standard symbol, as here on the obverse, was a turtle; it changed to a tortoise, probably when the island was conquered and forced to join the Athenian alliance in 457 BCE.

The Libyan city of Cyrene, settled by Greek colonists from Thera in the late seventh century BCE, became a prosperous city (see pp. 30 and 201), and was linked in a federal structure with other Greek foundations in the region. Its two proud symbols, displayed on its coins as here, were the main local deity, Ammon (see p. 191), identified by the Greek settlers as a version of Zeus, who had a famous oracle at Siwah in the desert, and the versatile crop silphion .

Transportation networks

Exchanges of agricultural produce, raw materials and manufactured goods necessitated new levels of transport infrastructure, both within and between individual states. In general, seaborne transport was markedly cheaper than movement by land – aided by the development of harbour constructions or haulage causeways. The most famous and important causeway was the paved *diolkos* with its grooved 'tramlines' for wheeled vehicles constructed across the isthmus at Corinth in *c*.600 BCE by the tyrant Periander, to enable ships and cargoes to be transferred from one gulf to the other. On land, networks of tracks, donkey paths and long-distance roads of great economic and military importance were put in place through the archaic and early classical periods – though roads in mountainous terrain were not always suited to wheeled transport. Hipparchus, one of the sons of Pisistratus who, by some accounts, shared the tyranny in Athens after their father's death (527–510 BCE), is said to have emphasized strikingly the integrative function of the internal road network being created: half way between the city and each of the *demes*, the villages in the countryside, he set up a *Herm* (a four-square 'statue' of Hermes, the god associated with travel and exchange). These featured only the face and the phallus (Hermes was also associated with fertility), and on the 'body' of the remaining stone were inscriptions telling passers-by which deme they were half-way towards or from, and conveying moral injunctions, such as 'Pass, thinking just thoughts'.

Quarrying and mining

Two natural resources and their resulting industries (quarrying and mining, found in certain poleis in abundance), certainly employed slave labour on a large scale. States generally used their local limestones for most building purposes, but certain high-quality marbles in limited supply came to be valued for use in the building of temples and for sculptures and inscriptions. The extraction and transportation of large numbers of roughed out statues or blocks of marble, from quarries such as those on the Aegean islands of Naxos, Paros, Chios or Thasos, or those in Attica at Pentelicum and Hymettus, was a sporadic economic activity. It provided variable income for owners (many of them probably metics) of slave stoneworkers, or farmers with wagons, oxen and slaves. At peak building times, such as the Athenian building programmes of the fifth and fourth centuries, such work could be substantial, and also involve the creation or repair of roads for the movement of the stone-carrying wagons.

Mining, above all of silver and gold, was most economically significant to the areas where it occurred – most notably the Laurium region of southern Attica, on Siphnos and in the Pangaeum region of Thrace (only fully exploited by the Macedonian kings from the mid-fourth century onwards). Profits could be very considerable for all but the slaves who worked, and in many cases died, in the mines.

This elegant cup by Epiktetos, an early master in red-figure, shows a young sculptor finishing off a wooden 'Herm', a characteristically Athenian stylized statuette of the god Hermes. These were placed at the gates of private houses and in sanctuaries, and used as markers in the road system. This example, like many such illustrations, shows a wooden Herm; stone Herms, like the ones targeted for 'mutilation' (see p. 160) in the famous scandal before the expedition to Sicily set sail in 415 BCE, may perhaps have been the sign of a better-off household. The painted inscription on this image reads 'Hipparchus [is] beautiful', and may refer to the son of Pisistratus. But it is also a typical pederastic acclamation which echoes the suggestive position of the ithyphallic adult Herm placed between the thighs of the beardless and garlanded youth.

At a shrine near the potters'
quarter in Corinth, many small
clay plaques were dedicated.
In this one, workers are quarrying the clay from the pits, and
refreshments are being lowered
in baskets.

A view looking over a square mine shaft towards the important deme site of Thorikos (the Thorikos theatre is just visible at the base of the hill) in the silver-mining region of Laurium. Mines in the region were probably worked as early as 1000 BCE and were operating at peak capacity in 483 to finance the Athenian fleet which went on to defeat the Persians at Salamis in 480. Athenian silver coinage was made from Laurium silver and circulated throughout the classical world, until competition from the gold and silver mines of Pangaeum in Macedonia during Roman times caused the Laurium region to decline. Eventually, at about the beginning of the Christian or Common Era, the silver vein at Laurium was exhausted and only the empty shafts remained.

(Inset) A mine shaft near Thorikos; rectangular, neatly cut into the hard rock. The holes would have supported ladders or something similar for ascent and descent by the slaves who worked the ore. Mining slaves worked in very harsh conditions in dark, narrow passages lit only by smokey lamps which made the air foul. They worked in ten-hour shifts, with ten hours off for rest; the strongest handled picks at the ore face, the weaker men or boys transported the ore out of the mine, and women and old men sifted the ore-bearing rock.

In the Laurium silver mines the state claimed ultimate ownership of the metals and leased three- or ten-year mining concessions to individuals (almost always citizens) who could then keep or sell the silver mined by the slaves they bought or hired for the purpose. They probably also had to pay money to the original owners of the land, who may well have created the extraction and ventilation shafts. In fact, many mine operators seem to have had properties in areas with good access to the mine itself. Excavations have revealed many underground shafts and galleries, extensive washeries and strong towers in the Laurium region (similar towers have also been found elsewhere, for example on the island of Thasos). The towers probably indicate the desire for extra security felt by local farmers anxious about the influx of a great many slaves employed in the dreadful conditions of a Greek mine.

Some tens of thousands were employed in this region at peak periods. By far the largest individual holdings of slaves are those mentioned in connection with mining. At the top of the list are the 1000 slaves said to have been hired out by Nicias to work in the silver mines.

Craft industries

Metallurgy and craft manufacture seem to have involved smaller, more closely knit working groups, where for example we commonly find craftsmen with a few slaves working together to produce sculpture or pottery. Many of these operations may be called cottage industries, operating in small houses rather than factories. These houses were often also the residences of the owner and his slaves. In this sense such operations, like the hoplite peasant farms, meet the ideal of the household (*oikos*), a family-size unit which was economically self-sufficient, but in this case in a craft rather than an agricultural context.

Textile production was mostly the work of women within the household. It was the prime domestic function of all wives to work wool themselves in the house, or to supervise the work of their female slaves (see Chapter 5). Women in poorer families might have to risk compromising their reputations by helping outside in the fields, or selling their husband's produce of goods in a small shop, market stall or bar.

However, some manufacturing workshops, such as those owned by Demosthenes' father (see p. 96), were on a larger scale. Many manufacturing slaves, above all in the more urbanized areas of Athens and the Piraeus, lived and worked independently in their shops/houses and were expressly described as 'living apart'. This was also true of the many slaves and freedmen engaged in trading.

This black-figure water-vessel of *c*.520–510 BCE gives an unusually detailed portrayal of a potters' workshop. On the left, a boy hands over a fine completed *amphora*, of the type this particular workshop (the Leagros Group) often produced; a potter is finishing a large storage jar (*pithos*) as it is turned on the wheel by a boy; other jars are carried out for firing, or stand outside. The furnace is stoked, and more fuel is carried to it. In overall charge is apparently the elderly man with the fine stick, presumably the workshop master

SLAVES AND THE IDEOLOGY OF WORK

The constant and visible presence of slave or serf labour in almost all sectors of the city-state economy had a deep and very powerful effect on attitudes to work among the free population of all classes. The presence of large numbers of chattel slaves meant that many of the propertied classes did not need to employ or exploit the free poor. The poorer farmers, craftsmen and retailers all hoped to be in a position to buy slaves of their own. At all costs they would feel it essential to their identity and dignity as freemen and (in most cases) citizens of their polis to avoid engaging in slavish work – in other words working directly and on a long-term basis for the benefit of another. In the words of Aristotle: 'Among the things that are honourable is not working in any vulgar craft; for it is the condition of a free man not to live for the benefit of another' (*Rhetoric*).

There were other related social prejudices concerned with work and its conditions. Farmers (whether leisured or penurious) would look down on craftsmen, who worked, like women or slaves, indoors or in cramped or dangerous conditions. They might also despise the traders who made or grew nothing but, it was alleged, tried to

On this sixth-century Attic black-figure jug by the Amasis Painter we see an adult bearded hunter with his hunting dog bringing his prey, a hare and a fox, for some form of inspection by older men. Hunting, predominantly a leisure activity of richer men, could be justified as providing good training for war. The hare was a choice love-gift from older men to their adolescent beloveds, in the same way as was the cock (see p. 215).

cheat others in cash deals. The leisured classes, who could despise all those poorer than themselves, sneered more vigorously at those citizens engaged in manufacture and trade than at the poorer farmers. But the overwhelming anxiety that might affect all these groups of free men who owned their own farm or business would be that of being labelled a slave. Not to be one's own boss, to be forced to work under another's command and for another's gain was a humiliation, and involved a vital loss of one's freedom. An important consequence of this anxiety was that free hired or wage labour remained very limited, and would be undertaken only by the very poor.

LEISURE AND SOCIAL HARMONY

Wealth was largely seen by the Greeks not as a goal in itself but as a means for enjoying leisure. As ever, the properties classes indulged in the most conspicuous expenditure, setting fashions (and arousing envy) with their hunts and hunting dogs, elegant clothes, houses, furniture, extravagant food, drink, entertaining, sports and gambling. But in many Greek poleis (and as usual Athens and Sparta provide the clearest cases and most of the evidence), attempts were made to control the divisive effects of such élite activities in the interests of greater social cohesion.

In Sparta, the stern ideology of citizen equality sought to mask real social and economic imbalance beneath the supposed uniformity of the messes (see p. 84). Increasingly, though, society failed to match the ideal and the system finally collapsed. In many oligarchies, however, the undisguised gulf between rich and poor must have seemed much greater and would have increased social hostilities accordingly.

The expenditure of the rich

But in Athens, and perhaps to a lesser extent in other democratic states, the laws and the law courts manned by many ordinary citizens (the popular juries, drawn from the panel of 6000 jurymen chosen by lot every year) offered the poor some limited protection against violence and exploitation by the rich. The rich, and especially the politically active rich, were likely to find themselves fairly often before these courts, as part of the normal processes of politics and the constant conflicts between members of the élite. Their chances of winning cases before the juries would increase if they could satisfy them on two points. First, that they could avoid charges of having 'eaten up' their wealth (see p. 96) on excessive amounts of luxurious fish-eating, quality wines, fine carriages or expensive mistresses or boyfriends. Second, that they could demonstrate conspicuous and generous payment of liturgies – that is contributions in both cash and personal commitment to the running of a warship or to the management of many of the state festivals.

Such heavy financial obligations placed severe and unpredictable burdens on the rich, and may have significantly contributed to an increasing involvement in cash markets, and also to individual cases of impoverishment. Yet many of the élite chose to do more than was required in order to claim credit or 'honour' from the democratic electoral and judicial bodies. These complex negotiations of interests between

Symposia-scenes are among the most prevalent subjects for Greek vase-painters, just as many of the vase-shapes were designed for use at the *symposium*. This example, by the Foundry Painter, shows the reclining male guests drinking, playing the game of *kottabos* which involved flicking wine-dregs from their cups at targets, and enjoying listening to, and looking at, the naked pipes-piper (who is probably to be understood to be a slave hired for the evening, and sexually available).

the ordinary people and the wealthy helped to persuade more of the élite to become or remain involved in public life. The liturgies seemed often to generate social cohesion and community spirit too – the ordinary citizens were deeply involved as well in these military and festive activities, as rowers in the triremes and as participants or spectators in festival games, contests and feasts. Many of the Athenian rich, of course, were naturally resentful, and some attempted to buck the system by keeping their wealth fluid and easily concealed in order to avoid their quotas of liturgies, and to spend more on luxuries and sensual pleasures.

Upward mobility

None the less, the Athenian people could also show some indulgence towards such displays of extravagance among the élite, probably because they felt such luxuries were to some extent within their own reach – they found opportunities for social mobility through leisure activities, and a chance to share in some aspects of the 'good life'.

Thanks both to the military needs of the community for fit and trained citizen soldiers, and to the development of large-scale athletic and musical contests at the festivals such as the Panathenaea, a great many ordinary citizens and their sons gained access to the *gymnasia* and wrestling grounds, which became major social gathering places. For the more politically aware or intellectual of the citizens, these became also locations for political or philosophical discussions; Plato's Academy and Aristotle's Lyceum grew alongside such gymnasia. Large numbers of citizens, countrymen as well as city-dwellers, would also have participated in the collective choral singing and dancing at the dramatic and poetic contests which played major roles in the state festivals such as the City Dionysia.

At the highest level of these cultural events – the Panhellenic games at Olympia, Delphi and so on, or the international circuit of actors and choruses which developed at least from the fourth century BCE onwards – major cash rewards and high fame were available to the winners. For example, Olympic victors were honoured with free meals for life at the City Hall in Athens. Furthermore, the all-male atmosphere of the gymnasia and the games, which went with something approaching a cult of the nude male body, aided the cultural acceptability of certain forms of homosexual relationships between young (or not so young) men and youths. From at least the sixth-century BCE onwards, it was regarded as perfectly normal for all men to feel homosexual desire as well as heterosexual; and it was common, especially in the elite classes, for males to pass through two distinct homosexual stages, first, as an adolescent, as a 'beloved', being pursued by young adult men, and then as a young man pursuing a boy or youth. The prime social settings for such meetings were the gymnasia and training grounds.

In these circumstances, athletic (and in some cases amatory) success is likely to have been a route to fame and social mobility for some poor but talented young men. Grumbles occur in élite sources at the triumphs of low-born athletes, and at the growing professionalism and excessively specialized training of athletes. A fifth-century epigram by Simonides, quoted by Aristotle, honoured an Olympic victor in the long-distance race who had previously carried fresh fish from Argos to Tegea in a rough basket on his shoulders; possibly unreliable later sources mention a Glaucus, supposedly a ploughboy from Carystus on Euboea, who won an Olympic boxing victory in 520 BCE, and then was appointed a governor of Camarina in Sicily by the tyrant Gelon (c. 491–78 BCE).

Women and slaves were legally excluded from the gymnastic life. Women, however, played significant roles in many of the state's religious festivals, and organized some festivals entirely on their own, such as a number of rituals to do with fertility in honour of the goddesses Demeter and her daughter Persephone (see pp. 105 and 330), and the more subversive festival, not officially sanctioned by the state, in honour of the beautiful male god Adonis. One may suspect that other female-only networks existed for their leisure activities, though our male-dominated sources allow us to know little of them.

Symposia

The characteristic evening activity of élite circles throughout Greece was the traditional drinking-party, the *symposium*, with its formalized structures: reclining on couches, libations to the gods, drinking wine mixed with water from a shared

Cock-fighting was a very popular sport in Athens, and a pair of fighting cocks appear very frequently in various forms of Athenian art, as here on the shoulder of this black-figure *amphora*, with erect combs and spurs, ready to do combat. The sport was apparently watched by Athenians of all ages and classes, but was perhaps particularly loved by young men, especially those with money and leisure, and a cock was a very popular present for a lover to give to his younger boyfriend. Appropriately enough, cocks were seen as symbols of masculine aggression and sexuality, and the fight showed whether a given cock was a true fighting male or an effeminate coward.

Sex at the symposium

The later stages of a private drinking-party (*symposium*), from which respectable wives and daughters were excluded, were apparently charged with erotic or crudely sexual atmospheres. Extracts from Xenophon's literary recreation of an élite and philosophical symposium attended by Socrates (itself modelled on Plato's more famous *Symposium*) show this, as do lines from a comic narrative from Aristophanes' *Wasps* of an élite symposium which was disrupted by a coarse juror unused to such elegance. Painting, too, represents the erotic revels of such parties.

In Xenophon's work (also called *Symposium*) a party, hosted by Callias, one of the richest Athenians, took place in his house in the Piraeus, and was held to honour his beautiful boyfriend Autolycus for his victory in the boys' all-in wrestling contest at the Panathenaea. The playfully 'intellectual' discussions focused on the nature of love, heterosexual, homosexual and philosophical. Other entertainment was provided, first, by the jokes of the 'scrounger' or 'parasite', Philippus: those with reputations as wits could apparently gain access without invitations to the dinner parties of those richer than themselves; and second, by a troupe of professionals, a Syracusan manager, and his three attractive musician/dancers, two female and one male. This extract is the conclusion of the party. The final remarks, that the guests, aroused by the erotic tableau, either went home to make love to their wives, or determined to get married, must either seem remarkably implausible (given the availability of sex objects at the party on in the city), or else, more probably, an example of Xenophon's rather heavy-handed irony.

> The discussions ended there. Autolycus rose to go for a walk, as it was time for him to do this. His father, Lycon, as he was leaving with him, turned back and said 'By Hera, Socrates, you do seem to me to be a good and fine man'. Then a kind of throne was set up, and the Syracusan came in and said 'Gentlemen, Ariadne will now enter the bridal chamber for her and Dionysus, Dionysus will enter, having drunk with the gods, and will come to her, and then they will have fun with each other.'

> An imitation of the 'wedding night' of the god Dionysus and Ariadne is performed by the artistes to 'Dionysiac' music played on the pipes. When the guests saw that 'Dionysus' was good-looking, and 'Ariadne' was pretty, and that they were not playing at it, but really kissing with the lips, they became all fired up as they watched ... The artistes did not seem to have practised their movements, but it appeared that they were permitted at last to do what they long desired ... When the drinking guests finally saw them in each other's arms and apparently going to bed together, the

bachelors swore they would get married, and the married men got on their horses and rode off to their own wives with the same purpose in mind. Socrates and those who were still left set out with Callias to join Lycon and his son on their walk. And so the drinking-party ended.

(*Symposium*)

In Aristophanes' *Wasps* , the comic hero – an old juror, Philocleon – has been 'cured' of his passion for the courts by his son, and encouraged to go to an élite drinking-party. His activities there are described, first, by one of his slaves, and then by himself, talking to the female 'musician/prostitute' he has left the party with.

Xanthias:
Wasn't the old man the most tiresome nuisance,
and the most drunkenly violent of all the guests?
And yet present were Hippyllus, Antiphon, Lycon,
Lysistratus, Thouphrastus, Phrynichus and his crowd,
but Philocleon was the most insolent of them all by far.
As soon as he was full of all the many good things,
he leapt and frisked about, farted and made mocking jokes,
like a donkey that's gorged on the bran,
and beat me with the vigour of youth, shouting 'Boy, boy'.
...
So he insulted them all in turn like that
making boorish cracks, and adding stories
in the most ignorant way, with nothing to the point.
When he was completely drunk, he left for home,
beating up everyone that he met on the way.

Philocleon:
Come up here my little golden beetle,
keep your hand holding on to my bit of rope
here. Careful, as the rope's a bit rotten.
But still it doesn't mind a bit of rubbing.
You saw how cleverly I stole you away,
when you were just about to suck the guests.
So you should now do a favour in turn to my cock.
But you're not going to do it, nor take it in hand, I know,
but you'll cheat me, and have a big laugh;
you've done that already to many another.

Many Attic vases delight in showing scenes of explicit sexual activities, usually imagined as occurring at the end of symposia; they may be heterosexual or homosexual, and often involve groups as well as couples; assessing the degrees of male fantasy which may be involved is not easy.

mixing-bowl and so on, to accompanying musical, conversational or sexual enter-tainment. Rich men often spent their evenings entertaining friends to expensive fish, wines and women in the smart 'men's room' (*andron*) of their private houses – or moving on to other parties in drunken street processions (*komos*). Such groups of friends who also co-operated together in politics or legal disputes and thus formed political 'clubs' could seem to display attitudes and behaviour contrary to democratic values, or even form a focus of oligarchic plots.

However, many ordinary citizens in Athens and probably elsewhere had sufficient leisure and wealth to drink and dine in their homes, at least occasionally; the inter-nal layout of ground-floor rooms in the egalitarian, standard housing of the harbour town of the Piraeus, developed from the 470s onwards, regularly include a living room, the positioning of whose door suggests that it was designed for a series of reclining couches. That is, a middling Athenian might well have his *andron* too. Such ordinary Athenians also drank in wine shops/bars called *kapeleia* (described as 'the symposia of the poor'), and all Athenians liked occasionally to gamble with dice or at cockfighting contests – which were highly valued as the cock was conceived as a potent symbol of male virility and competitiveness. On more special occasions mid-dling Athenians probably organized their own imitations of the more formal symposia. Such aspirations would have been helped by the sumptuary legislation designed to keep within fixed limits the prices of sympotic entertainers (such as female musicians). All citizens too would have been offered a share in many public feasts and wine-drinkings, some at the end of state festivals such as the City Dionysia or the Anthesteria, some at festivals organized by the smaller, more localized groups such as tribes, demes and *phratries* to which all citizens belonged. Further, many voluntary groups developed (typically called *thiasoi* or groups of *orgeones*), which often combined citizens and non-citizens, and took the form of cult gatherings to worship a god or hero at democratically managed meetings focused on sacrifices, and shared eating and drinking modelled on the symposium.

Through all this wide range of activities, then, open to most or all of the citizens, they were enabled to form friendships, gain supporters and adopt new social iden-tities. Many of these common shared activities had a fairly high intellectual content (such as the many musical contests, and the often challenging and emotionally powerful plays). Though many citizens perhaps acquired, at least by the fourth-century BCE, some basic forms of literacy, enough to read their names on lists or to sign a contract, they participated in the works of what we call Athenian literature primarily by seeing or hearing them performed or recited; Athenian culture remained profoundly an oral culture, even as limited forms of literacy were spread-ing. Very few indeed were in the habit of reading books. Other forms of social enjoyments were less highbrow, such as sport, gambling, drinking and associated party games. But they will all have helped to build social cohesion, as the mass of the citizens came to feel that their life-style included to some extent aspects of the good life previously the preserve of the aristocracy.

(Opposite) Greek boxing could be extremely brutal, and ancient authors comment on the disfigured features com-petitors acquired. Blows were generally aimed at the head rather than the body, and the match proceeded until one competitor was knocked out or conceded victory by raising his index finger. Behind the boxers on this black-figure *amphora* stands the referee, whip in hand, to administer disqualification if need be.

Literature and Performance

COMPETITIVE PERFORMANCE IN CONTEXT

It is 330 BCE. The greatest Athenian orator of all time is standing before a jury of more than five hundred fellow citizens, and an audience of hundreds – perhaps thousands – more. He is defending himself against the eloquent attack on his character, policies and record which has been launched by Aeschines, his political rival. Aeschines used to be a professional actor and learned the art of oratory in the demanding context of the tragic theatre. Now he is putting his verbal dexterity to political use, by speaking against Demosthenes' claim to the civic honour of a golden crown in

recognition of his public services. One of Aeschines' arguments has been that Demothenes' reputation does not bear comparison with those won by the great, dead leaders of the past. In reply to this, Demosthenes makes a memorable speech:

The fourth-century theatre at Epidaurus remains one of the best preserved of all ancient theatres, with near perfect acoustics, showing clearly how the semi-circular seating offered wonderful views of the round *orchestra* (dancing area for the chorus) and the *skene* (stage building). Plays were staged in daylight.

> You should assess a man who is still alive by comparing him with others who are alive, his own contemporaries, in the same way as you make assessments in everything else – as you appraise dramatic poets, choruses and athletes. Philammon did not leave Olympia without a victor's crown because he was weaker than Glaucus of Carystus, or other bygone champions: he was crowned and proclaimed victor because he fought better than the men who entered themselves against him. You, similarly, ought to compare me with the orators of today.
>
> (Demosthenes *De Corona*, 'On the Crown')

In this way Demosthenes also cleverly insinuates a beneficial comparison between himself and Philammon, a much-loved contemporary boxer who was

popular because he gave pleasure to an appreciative public through his great professional competence.

Demosthenes' rebuke is revealing too because it shows that the analogy between adversarial political oratory and athletics arose naturally in the ancient Greek mind. He dwells on the parallel between the assessment of boxing and of oratory. But he implies that the criteria by which dramatic and choral performances are appraised are also comparable.

All these types of exhibition did indeed share certain features, notably performance by specialists in open-air public arenas in front of a large mass of often extremely noisy and critical spectators. Athletes competed in the gymnasium or stadium; oratory was heard in the assembly or law-courts; drama was enacted in theatres.

To successful performers, competitive sport, speech-making and drama brought great prestige. The Greek mind found it difficult to conceptualize a performance of any kind except as an adversarial procedure. Orators, athletes, poets and chorus

members all performed against competitors ('ant-agonists') in an *agon* (originally meaning an athletics competition, from which we get our English word 'agony'). The verb 'to perform' (*agonizesthai*), primarily means 'to engage in a competition'. The term is found in a variety of contexts: combat in battle; the production of a comedy like Aristophanes' *Frogs*; participation in a chariot race at the Olympic games. Even agricultural labour could be turned into a competitive performance. In the *Odyssey*, for example, Homer has Odysseus tell one of Penelope's more importunate suitors that he would like to have a competition with him in hay-harvesting: 'in my hands would be a curving scythe, and in yours another; then we could try our powers together, both of us fasting until late dusk, with no lack of grass to mow'. At Athens the competitive spirit even led to 'Mr Universe'-style contests in manly physique (*euandria*), which seem to have tested both beauty and muscular strength.

Sports, politics and drama

Of all the cultural legacies left by the ancient Greeks, the three which have had the most obvious impact on modern Western life are athletics, democracy and drama. Few individuals today study ancient Greek, and yet most have watched (if only on television) an athletic event, or politicians engaged in democratic debate, or a performance of a play. They may even have seen an ancient Greek play: more ancient plays, especially those of Euripides, are now performed on the commercial stage than at any time since antiquity.

We may not be able to recreate from existing sources as many aspects of ancient Greek society as we would like to, but we have surely shared the tingle of anticipation as champion sprinters await the starting gun (then a trumpet) at the Olympics, or as a politician spars with an eloquent adversary, or as the curtain goes up on a great actor.

For the ancients, excellence in these apparently disparate arenas of public display fell, as Demosthenes emphasized, into the same category. Dramatic, oratorical and athletic performances were public and competitive exhibitions in which success conferred the highest prestige, and failure brought personal disappointment and public ignominy.

When Hippocleas of Thessaly won a running race for boys at Delphi in 498 BCE, the Theban poet Pindar was commissioned by the ruling family of Thessaly, the Aleuadae, to compose an epinician ode (victory song) to commemorate his feat. Hippocleas' success was attributed in part to support from Apollo, in whose honour the Pythian games were held, and in part to his own pedigree:

> Sweet, O Apollo, is the reward for men's work when a god is in action; and it was by your counsels on the one hand that he won the victory, and on the other his inborn inheritance has trodden in the footsteps of his father, who was twice a winner at Olympia in the armour of war.

(Opposite) Euripides' *Medea*, first performed in 431 BCE, was one of the most famous of all tragedies in antiquity, and is one of the most frequently performed today. Its clever, domineering and manipulative heroine is driven to murder her own children in order to spite her husband Jason, who has abandoned her in favour of a younger woman. Here Diana Rigg hatches Medea's horrifying plot.

Divine inspiration

An athletic victory was thought to bring a winner closer to the gods. Contestants usually performed in a sacred sanctuary at festivals held in their honour, so a win was attributed to the inspiration and favour of the god. Often a victor was actually said to be appearing god*like* himself.

The praise in Pindar's ode also encompasses Hippocleas' father, who had once won a victory in the race in armour at Olympia (see below and p. 228). But most of the ode is actually directed at the aristocratic Aleuadae who had commissioned it. The precise nature of Hippocleas' relationship to the Aleuadae (sponsored specialist to wealthy patron? impoverished distant cousin?) is left, perhaps deliberately, vague. But it is clear that both Hippocleas' athletic performance and Pindar's poetic performance are used in an aristocratic family's self-promotion.

It is also clear that to the ancient Greeks performances served to defined boundaries both between man and god, and between man and man. Hippocleas may be assisted by Apollo; but he is also blessed by genetic inheritance and by wealthy aristocratic patrons.

A sense of the role of the divine in performance excellence is also often evident in accounts of song. In the eighth book of the *Odyssey* the Greeks' most versatile hero (Odysseus) is the guest of King Alcinous and Queen Arete of the Phaeacians. Exhausted after an 'epic' three-day swim, Odysseus is refreshed with wine and honoured with a sacrifice and a meal. The banqueters are then entertained by the music of Demodocus. This lyre-playing bard is 'godlike' (*theios*, from *theos*, 'god'): to Demodocus, we are told, 'more than to any other man, the god granted the gift of song', and on this occasion 'the Muse moved him to sing the glorious deeds of heroes'. So the bard is godlike because of his divine gift. Phemius, the other important bard in the *Odyssey*, explains to Odysseus: 'I am self-taught; the god has implanted in my breast all manner of ways of song, and I am worthy to sing before you just as before a god'.

The 'ways of song' comprised the battery of poetic words, formulaic phrases and conventional scenes which the bard in a pre-literate society stored in his memory. The unspecified 'Muse' who inspired Demodocus was, in this oral culture, believed to be the daughter of the goddess Memory. Calling on her was a poet's 'shorthand' for the process whereby he enters the trance-like performance state and strives, by a profound act of concentration, to access his own internal memory bank of poetic language.

ATHLETICS

The Greek view of performance excellence in the different disciplines of oratory, drama and sport being of equal value is demonstrated with special vividness in book eight of the *Odyssey*. In it, Homer interweaves Demodocus' musical performances with discussions of oratory and athletics. The Phaeacians are conducting some athletics contests, including a discus competition. One young man, Euryalus, delivers a nasty speech accusing Odysseus of being a greedy merchant and no athlete. These two accusations are clearly interrelated and grounded in the rhetoric of class distinctions. As Pindar's patrons were so anxious to demonstrate, to practise athletics was virtually synonymous with the possession of wealth, leisure and membership of an aristocratic social élite. Odysseus – illustrious warrior, athlete and king – is not at all amused. He compares Euryalus' conspicuous beauty with his own, less obvious, gifts:

> Stranger, what you have said is not good. You seem like an arrogant man. The gods, I think, do not give all their favours together – physique and sense and eloquence. A man may seem unimpressive in outward appearance, but god beautifies his form with words, and those who look at him feel pleasure as he speaks unfalteringly and with beguiling modesty; he stands out amongst the gathering of people, and as he goes his way through the city they look at him as if at a god.

Euryalus cannot speak well; Odysseus is a great orator – his case is proven.

In the *Iliad* Antenor remembers that 'whenever from his chest he sent forth his great voice, and words like snowflakes on a winter's day, then no other mortal could rival Odysseus'. The great orator's gift, like the athlete's victory and the bard's singing, comes from the gods. In performance the orator, like the athlete and the bard, is transfigured and assumes a divine aspect himself.

As if to stress the parallels between sport, song and speech, Odysseus goes on to refute Euryalus' insinuations more robustly.

> Without removing his cloak he sprang up and seized a discus, a big one and thick, much more massive than the one the Phaeacians used for discus-throwing. He whirled it round, cast it from his hand, and the stone went hurtling. The Phaeacians ... crouched down to the ground as the stone rushed past. It sped swiftly from his hand and exceeded the distance markers of all the others. Athena herself, in the likeness of a man, measured the distances.

With a throw of a discus Odysseus finally establishes his social status, utterly confounding any suspicion that he is a merchant. His worth is measured by Athena herself. Discus-throwing was one of the Greeks' favourite athletics events, immortalized in the famous sculptor Myron's *Discobolus*, 'Discus-thrower'.

The Olympic Games

Discus-throwing was performed at the games in honour of Zeus at Olympia as part of the pentathlon – an event which also included jumping, javelin-throwing, a short foot-race, and wrestling. Other events included several foot-races, ranging from sprints of somewhat less than 200 metres to a long-distance run of about 4000 metres. Among these was the hoplite race, which was originally run in full armour, but by the fifth century participants were required to wear only a symbolic helmet and shield.

The most confrontational events were wrestling, boxing, and the *pankration* – a formidable form of single combat involving both punching and wrestling-style holds. The only banned forms of assault were eye-gouging and biting.

The Olympic Games were the oldest of the Greek games. They are traditionally thought to have been founded as early as 776 BCE. At first they may have been an exclusively Peloponnesian affair, but by the sixth century visitors and participants were coming from far afield, and the judges were called 'the judges of the Hellenes' (*Hellanodikai*) – implying that a truly Panhellenic ethos pervaded the festival.

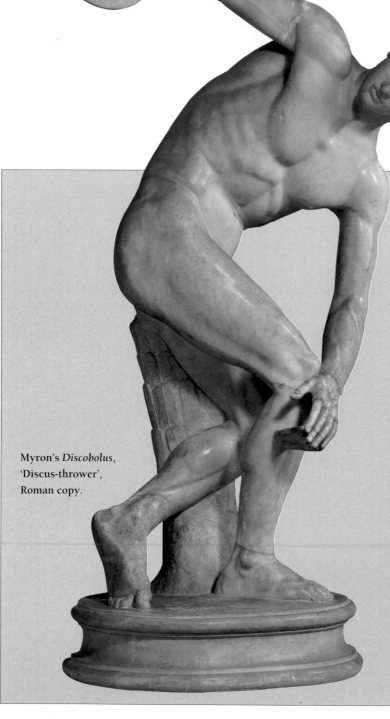

Myron's *Discobolus*, 'Discus-thrower', Roman copy.

Discobolus

Myron made statues of several Olympic victors of the mid-fifth century BCE, but his most famous statue was undoubtedly his discus-thrower. The original was made in bronze, the archaic-style hair, with its innumerable separated curls, and the coiled body entailing an extraordinary degree of artistic and metallurgical virtuosity. When making a throw the ancient athlete stretched the discus out in front of him with his left hand, then transferred it to his right hand and swung his arm back to assume approximately the position depicted in the statue. He then sprang into an upright posture while moving forward on the left foot as he hurled. In a work called *Eikones*, the writer Lucian describes the original statue as 'bent over in the position of the throw, with his head turned back towards the hand that holds the discus, with one leg slightly bent, looking as if he would spring up all at once with the cast'. This is an extraordinarily perceptive account, because the sculpture does indeed imply a sense of strain, physical effort and incipient speed: Myron has chosen to depict the moment of furthest recession and contraction of the limbs – the human spring at its most tightly coiled – just before the actual fling begins.

Indeed, it seems that the popularity of such athletics competitions was a crucial factor in the emergent sense of a collective Hellenic identity in the archaic period. The Olympic Games were to be held every four years, at the height of the summer, for over a thousand years.

(Right) The *hoplitodromos*, or 'race for hoplite soldiers', reflects the original close association between warfare and athletics. It was an event at the Olympic, Pythian and Panathenaic games. Instead of full hoplite armour, competitors wore only a symbolic helmet and shield. The distance was 2 stades – approximately 400 yards.

The Pythian Games

The other great games, called 'Pythian' because they were held at 'Pythian' Apollo's sanctuary at Delphi, were instituted somewhat later, in 582 BCE. They were also held every four years, but the timing was so arranged that the Olympic and Pythian games alternated, meaning that every other year there was a great contest. If the somewhat less ambitious biennial festivals at the Isthmus and Nemea are taken into account, then the Greeks had access to at least one large-scale set of games every calendar year.

There were also important athletics events, in addition to musical and dramatic contests, held at the Athenian Panathenaea – also a quadrennial festival in honour of the city's tutelary goddess. Indeed, many of our best illustrations of both athletic and musical performances are painted on vases originally used as prizes in (or commemorations of) these Athenian competitions.

Martial athleticism

(Previous page) The aim in a wrestling match was to immobilize the opponent in what was called a 'fall'. This entailed either pinning him to the ground or in a hold from which he could not extract himself. Victory was granted to the man who won three out of five 'falls'. Greek myth celebrated the legendary wrestling bouts of the heroes Heracles and Theseus.

Almost all athletic events were tests of martial skill. Although boat-races were held, for example at Salamis, the near-absence of evidence for swimming competitions in classical Greece can probably be explained by the unimportance of swimming to direct combat. Other attested competitive sports are clearly derived from training for the battlefield. For example, the Panathenaea events included the dangerous *apobates* race, which tested agility in dismounting from a moving chariot. A distinctive event at the Panathenaea was the throwing of a javelin at a target while on horseback – a skill with obvious benefits to the trainee cavalryman, as recommended by Xenophon, who wrote two surviving treatises on horsemanship, *The*

Cavalry Commander and *The Art of Equestrianism*. The target was a shield attached to a pole, and the throw was performed at a gallop. The Athenian general Themistocles was even said to have taught his son the acrobatic trick of casting a javelin while standing upright on his horse's back.

The foundation myth of the Olympic Games suggests that chariot racing had always played an important role. Pelops (said to be the founder), who gave his name to the Peloponnese, victoriously competed in a mythical chariot race for the

Delphi Charioteer. Something of the prestige and aristocratic grandeur of a victory in the chariot race is also suggested by the famous bronze sculpture of a charioteer which was dedicated in the sanctuary of Apollo at Delphi a little to the north-west of the god's temple. The statue is particularly important because so few original life-size bronze statues have survived at all from the early classical period. The young man is dressed in the typical charioteer's costume – firmly contained to minimize flapping by bands at the shoulder and waist – and conveys simultaneously a sense of hauteur, intensity and physical control. He was originally one of a whole group of figures, probably including horses, a chariot and a groom. In the chariot there may also have stood an image of the owner and victor, Polyzelus tyrant of Gela in Sicily, for whom this charioteer acted as professional driver. The group was dedicated by Polyzelus to thank Apollo for a victory in the chariot race at Delphi in the 470s BCE and to enhance, amongst the Panhellenic visitors who visited the cult centre, his own reputation and that of his family.

(Previous page) **This Pana-thenaic event seems to have emerged at the end of the fifth century as developments in cavalry training influenced the festival sports programme. On this prize vase, bestowed on a victor, the competitors wear cloaks and one of them wears the *petasos*, a distinctive broad-brimmed hat.**

hand of princess Hippodamia ('Horse-tamer'). The prestige and importance of the chariot race are confirmed repeatedly by the ancient evidence: it is the very first event at Patroclus' funeral games described in the *Iliad* (book 23); and it is in the chariot race at the Pythian games that the heroine's brother in Sophocles' tragedy *Electra* is imagined to have died a particularly aristocratic death.

ORATORY AND DEMOCRACY

Just a few years before Polyzelus dedicated his group of bronzes, Megacles the Athenian was the victor in the chariot race at the same games. Pindar's poem to celebrate the victory, his seventh *Pythian Ode*, is swift to point out that Megacles is one of the famous Alcmaeonid family (see p. 83). 'For what homeland, what household, could you live in and name as more famous for Greece to learn about?' asks the poet. The new democracy at Athens in no way curbed the zeal of prominent well-born families to promote their reputations by competing in the great games. But the birth of democracies in Greece produced a new requirement for basic literacy in citizens, who needed to be able to read laws and names on inscriptions and probably to write their own names. Democracies also meant that speech-making began to rival athletics as a form of competitive public display, and consequently became a skill to be assiduously cultivated by ambitious men of affairs.

In the *Iliad* the right to speak in public (and the ability to do so competently) had clearly been defined as a prerogative of the aristocratic élite. When the commoner Thersites had dared to complain on behalf of the ordinary soldiers at Troy, and had

The messenger speech from *Electra*

The speaker is Orestes' old tutor: it is necessary for him to persuade Clytemnestra, Orestes' mother, that the exiled prince is dead. The speech conveys the sheer excitement of the event – the Pythian Games at Delphi. But it also tells us about the darker, dangerous side of this prestigious sport, especially the hideous mangling of the victim's body when accidents (inevitably) occurred.

For on another day, when at sunrise there was the speedy contest of the chariot horses, Orestes entered the lists with many charioteers ... They took their stand where the appointed judges had sorted them with lots and placed their chariots, and at the sound of the brazen trumpet they darted off. Shouting to their horses, the drivers gripped their reins and shook them loose; the whole course resounded with the clash of rattling chariots: the dust rose up; and all close together they did not spare the use of their goads, each hoping to pass the wheels and the snorting horses of the others; for about their backs and their wheels below alike the breath of the horses touched them with its foam.

And Orestes, keeping his horses near the pillar at the end, each time grazed the post, and giving his right-hand trace horses room he tried to block off his pursuer. At first all had stood upright in their chariots; but then the hard-mouthed colts of the Aenianian, carrying him on against his will, on the turn as they finished the sixth and began the seventh round dashed their foreheads against the chariot from Barce. One driver crashed into and smashed another in a single disaster, and then the whole plain of Crisa was filled with the wreckage of chariots... And when the crowd saw Orestes' fall from his chariot, they cried out with pity for the young man, seeing what misfortunes followed upon such deeds, as at one moment he was borne earthwards, at another with legs skywards, until the charioteers with difficulty checked the horses' career, and released him, all bloody, so that none of his friends that saw him could have recognized his wretched shape.

(Sophocles *Electra*)

made a speech defaming Agamemnon's character, it was Odysseus himself, the great orator of Ithaca, who rebuked him 'and struck his back and shoulders with his [Agamemnon's] sceptre' – the very emblem of inherited excellence and of the divine right of kings. Thersites, bloody and bowed, stayed silent for the rest of the poem.

Yet with the establishment of democracies there came a need for ordinary citizens to be able to understand and assess arguments about policy, if not actually to formulate and deliver complicated speeches themselves.

One corollary of this was certainly to be the gradual emergence of artistic prose and other completely new genres of literature. But even more important to the emergence of prose-writing – whether of speeches (Lysias, Demosthenes), history (Herodotus, Thucydides), or philosophy (Protagoras, Plato) – was the need under the democracies for expertise in oratory. If issues were to be hammered out before a responsive and powerful voting audience, whether in the law-court or the assembly, then the ability to command cogent arguments and sway the citizens' decisions through verbal performance became a requirement in any aspiring orator-statesman.

The Athenians enjoyed rhetorical performances as much as athletics or poetry. The statesman Cleon (himself a notoriously powerful speaker) is said by Thucydides actually to have upbraided the Athenian citizenry for turning the Assembly into a showcase for competitive displays of rhetoric. 'You are simply victims of your own pleasure in listening', he said, 'and are more like an audience sitting at the feet of a professional lecturer than a parliament discussing matters of state.'

There seems to have been some truth in these words: in practice the power and prestige which excellence in oratory now promised to the aspiring politician certainly led at times to the medium superseding the message. It was not unknown for politicians to prosecute one another simply in order to compete against one another verbally in court: the contest between Demosthenes and Aeschines (see p. 219) was almost as much a contest in oratorical ability as in public policy.

Teachers of rhetoric therefore mushroomed at Athens in the late fifth and early fourth century. The most famous of all was the Sicilian Gorgias, whose speeches were full of seductive rhetorical figures, especially rhyme, alliteration, antithesis, and isocolon – a technique whereby clauses of equal or similar length rhythmically balance one another. He specialized in the sophistic art of 'defending the indefensible', and for a fee (in private houses or at venues such as the Panhellenic games at Olympia) he would offer an exhibition piece (*epideictic*) in which to display his brilliantly effective techniques.

One of Gorgias' most famous speeches was the so-called *Encomium of Helen*, an epideictic oration defending in a hypothetical trial the 'indefensible' mythical Helen, who was widely held by most other authors to have been solely responsible for the carnage at Troy. In the opening passage Gorgias programmatically sets out what rhetorical strategies he will adopt, and even an English translation can convey something of the contortion of the word order, and Gorgias' hypnotic use of antithesis, balance, acoustic impact, and clever rhetorical tropes.

The opening of Gorgias' *Encomium of Helen*

The grace of a city is the excellence of its men, of a body beauty, of a mind wisdom, of an action virtue, of a speech truth; the opposite of these are a disgrace. A man, a woman, a speech, a deed, a city, and an action, if deserving praise, one should honour with praise, but to the undeserving one should attach blame. For it is an equal error and ignorance to blame the praiseworthy and praise the blameworthy. The man who says rightly what ought to be said should also refute those who blame Helen, a woman about whom both the belief of those who have listened to poets and the message of her name, which has become a reminder of calamities, have been in unison and unanimity. I wish, by adding some reasoning to my speech, to free the slandered woman from the accusation and to demonstrate that those who blame her are lying, and both to show what is true and to put a stop to their ignorance.

That the woman who is the subject of this speech was pre-eminent among men and women, by virtue and descent, is not obscure even to a few. It is clear that her mother was Leda, and her actual father was a god and her reputed father a mortal, Tyndareos and Zeus, of whom the one was believed to be because he was and the other was reputed to be because he said he was, and the one was the best of men and the other the master of all.

If Gorgias' idiosyncratic style was not to any particular politician's taste, there were alternative ways of learning what was now called the 'art' or 'science' (*techne*) of persuasion. From handbooks like Antiphon's *Tetralogies* one could discover how to anticipate the opponent's arguments and design a speech making use of arguments from probability. Hippias the sophist could teach mnemonic tricks to aid memorization – an essential dimension of performance. And Alcidamas, a pupil of Gorgias, specialized in the art of extemporization; he shrewdly perceived that an elegantly written oration was not enough to guarantee success in performance. He, like Homer's Odysseus, also regarded the brilliant speaker as 'godlike'.

> For who does not know that to speak on the spot is a necessary thing for those who speak in the public assembly, for those who go to law, and for those who make private transactions? Often opportunities for actions fall in one's way unexpectedly, at which those who are silent will seem to be contemptible, but we see those who speak being honoured by the others as if having intelligence that is godlike.

In theory, any Athenian citizen who could afford tuition from the teachers of rhetoric could now tackle other orators in the assembly. Rhetorical performance had come a long way since Odysseus silenced Thersites with Agamemnon's sceptre.

POETRY IN PERFORMANCE

The epic

The earliest surviving Greek 'literature' consists of the written records of orally performed epics composed in dactylic hexameters – in other words the rhythm was based around six lots of two or three syllables, with the stress coming on the first syllable of each. This scheme was the product of an entirely oral society.

The performance context of epic poetry before the sixth century remains a matter of controversy. In the *Iliad* great Achilles himself (half-divine warrior,

(*Opposite*) **Sappho and Alcaeus.** This is a fifth-century vase-painter's depiction of the two most famous lyric poets of Lesbos, Alcaeus and Sappho, imagined perhaps as engaged in an antiphonally performed sung lyric duet: Sappho looks as though she is waiting to respond to a musical approach by her compatriot. They each hold a *barbitos*, a simple form of lyre with a bowl-shaped sound-box and long arms. Plato said of her: 'Some say there are nine Muses: but they're wrong / Look at Sappho of Lesbos; she makes ten'.

speaker and philosopher) is depicted sitting in his tent, apparently with only his friend Patroclus as audience, 'delighting his heart with a clear-toned lyre, fine and elaborately wrought, with a silver bridge', and to its accompaniment 'he sang of the

glorious deeds of warriors'. So it would appear that recitation was not the province of professionals only. Yet the class of epic singers, unlike athletes, seems usually to have been less distinguished. The picture offered by the *Odyssey* is of hired or dependent professional bards singing for their supper in the banqueting halls of kings, as Demodocus sings for the Phaeacians, and Phemius performs in Odysseus' palace. In the poem, bards are socially linked with seers, doctors and carpenters.

Some sources suggest that a specialist 'school' for training epic poets may have existed on the island of Chios. There is also evidence in the *Homeric Hymn to Delian Apollo* that epics were performed at festivals of Apollo on Delos, where 'the long-robed Ionians gather in your [Apollo's] honour with their children and modest wives, and mindfully delight you with boxing and dancing and song, whenever they hold the contest'.

There is in fact no reason why epic poetry – the *Iliad*, the *Odyssey*, and other lays telling of the home-comings of heroes returning from Troy, the siege of Thebes, the adventures of the Argonauts, and the labours of Heracles – should not have been performed in any context where there was a competent performer and a willing audience. And hexameter epic poetry was not the only kind of musical performance which Greeks of the archaic period could enjoy. There were famous composers who worked in the elegiac metre and produced songs for performance, particularly at drinking-parties, to be accompanied by the music of the pipe (*aulos*).

The lyric

There were also poets who composed songs (often love-songs) in a variety of metres, to be performed by a soloist playing the lyre. Solo lyric song was traditionally associated with the eastern Aegean sea, particularly with Mytilene, the chief city of the island of Lesbos, and home of the poets Sappho and Alcaeus.

In mainland Greece in the sixth century BCE the organization of solo musical performances underwent considerable change. The performance of epic began to gravitate towards Athens, which was emerging as one of the most important cities of the late archaic age. The Athenian tyrant Pisistratus is said to have ordered that the Homeric epics be recorded in writing for the first time. Competitions were also established in *citharody* (singing epic and other poetry to the *cithara*, an elaborate lyre), first at the Pythian games and subsequently at the Panathenaea in Athens – where contests also became customary in aulos-playing and singing to the accompaniment of the aulos.

The male monopoly of prestigious competitive performances at public festivals must not obscure the considerable evidence that women were accomplished instrumentalists, and responsible for much of the music-making in ancient Greece.

The same goes for the female aulos-player (*auletris*), a regular fixture at parties. The aulos was a reeded pipe technically more similar to the modern oboe than to the flute, and the Greeks seem nearly always to have played two *auloi* together. In Plato's famous *Symposium*, a legendary drinking-party attended by Socrates and

(Opposite) This work is one of the finest representations of a *citharode*. He is tuning his instrument as he mounts the podium, on which is inscribed in Greek the masculine form of the adjective 'beautiful'. The citharode's costume emphasizes his special status: his mantle is decorated at the edges and on his head he wears a wreath. His cithara is typical of the vase-painters' representations of the professional instruments played in the competitions: it has a flat base, seven strings, and elaborate curlicues on the inner arms, which were part of the mechanism rather than mere ornamentation. Citharody was by far the most prestigious type of performance. The victor won the largest prizes of any of the solo musicians, as well as the highest reputation. One reason was the extreme difficulty of the cithara to master – Aristotle called it a 'professional' instrument unsuitable for general use in education. Attic red-figure, *c.* 475 BCE. Basle.

Aristophanes, it is decided to dispense with the auletris – 'let her play to herself, if she wants, or to the women of the household'. But the sympotic literary context later attracts another auletris. Alcibiades makes a late, inebriated entrance, his head

Women making music. In Plato's *Symposium* the suggestion that the first auletris leave and entertain the women of the household is in itself highly suggestive of the countless unrecorded musical performances by women for women which must have taken place in ancient Greece. This shows a group of women musical performers including an auletris, a dancer and a harpist. It should not be forgotten that the divinity associated with the invention of the aulos was Athena. And yet the god predominantly associated with this instrument was undoubtedly Dionysus: it was the instrument which accompanied choral hymns to him, and also the dramatic performances organized at his festivals.

garlanded with ivy, violets and ribbons; he is, perhaps typically for a late-night Athenian reveller, attended by a woman playing the aulos.

The dithyramb

In classical Athens one of the claims a public man of affairs would be likely to make in any political or legal speech was that he had on one or more occasions sustained the enormous expense, for the public good, of training, equipping, and sponsoring a chorus – a type of tax on the rich known as the *choregia*.

To a Greek, a *chorus* meant a group of people performing a dance accompanied by singing, and the god ultimately responsible for all types of dancing was the wine-god Dionysus. The special danced hymn in Dionysus' honour, to the tune of the aulos, was called the *dithyramb*, a type of performance which remained a prestigious event in the competitions at Athenian festivals throughout the classical period.

Some fragmentary dithyrambs survive: Pindar composed one for the Athenians which invites the Olympian gods to join the dancing at Athens, where 'roses are

A likely visual representation of a dithyrambic chorus is found on this Athenian vase-painting of about 425 BCE (about twenty years earlier than Euripides' *Bacchae*). All the individuals are labelled with ordinary Athenian forenames: the man on the left of the pole who faces outwards and appears not to be singing may well be the *choregus* who has funded the performance. It is surprising that there are only four or five singers (for a dithyramb we might have expected twelve), and little suggestion of dancing. Yet the presence of the aulos player, the absence of theatrical masks, the ivy-decorated pole (ivy was one of Dionysus' chief emblems), the ornate costumes and the garlands combine to suggest that the performance we are viewing is indeed a solemn hymn in honour of Dionysus, which can only mean a dithyramb.

(Opposite) Detail from the Fleischman Choregos Vase. This shows, on the left, a figure dressed in a tragic costume, touching his head in a manner suggesting bafflement, or possibly that he is adjusting his headgear. He is clearly labelled *Aigisthos*, the name of Agamemnon's cousin and Clytemnestra's lover, familiar from several well-known tragedies. He has apparently emerged from the half-open doors on the left of the scene, presumably representing the stage-door. To the right there are three figures already on stage, relatively less tall, and arrayed indisputably in comic masks and costumes. The central man is labelled *Pyrria[s]*, a name often attributed to slaves meaning 'red-haired' or 'ruddy-faced'. He is painted frontally in an arresting posture, standing on a woven object, with one hand held aloft. He may be declaiming or perhaps impersonating a statue. On either side of him are the figures who give the vase its name: an older, white-haired man, and a younger one. They wear identical costumes and masks, and carry identical sticks. Both are labelled *Choregos*; the similarity between them indicates that within the play depicted they both act as chorus-members. The vase-painting therefore illustrates a comedy in which the chorus consisted of chorusgoi, possibly pitting younger choregoi against older ones, for inter-generational conflict between men was a favourite theme of Old Comedy.

In praise of Dionysus

The Asiatic chorus, who have followed the god Dionysus (disguised as a priest) to Thebes, sing of the delights of the Bacchic revel on the hillsides, of Dionysiac costume, music, dancing, and sacrifice in Euripides' *Bacchae*:

What joy there is in the mountains,
    when the worshipper,
wearing his sacred fawnskin, falls to
    the ground
while his companions run on;
he hunts for the blood of the goat that
    is slain, the rapturous
devouring of raw flesh, hurrying on to
    the mountains of Phrygia, Lydia,
the leader of Bromios' [Dionysus']
    rites! Euoi!
The ground is flowing with milk,
    flowing with wine,
flowing with nectar of bees.
The Bacchic one, raising the blazing

flame of the pine torch,
fragrant like the smoke of Syrian
    frankincense,
lets it stream from his fennel-wand;
    with running and dancing
he spurs on stragglers, rouses them
    with his calls,
his soft locks rippling in the wind.
Among the frenzied shouting he
    thunders forth:
'Onwards, you Bacchae, onwards, you
    Bacchae,
sing praise of Dionysus to the deep
    rumble of kettledrums,
sing joyfully glorifying the god of joy,
with Phrygian shouts and calling out,
while the sweet-sounding holy pipe
    rings out in holy playfulness,
in time with you as you climb – to the
    mountain, to the mountain!'

entwined in tresses, and voices ring out in songs to the sound of auloi, and the choruses ring out in honour of diadem-wreathed Semele' (Dionysus' mother).

The dithyramb must originally have been devoted to myths about Dionysus and themes from the rituals surrounding his worship. Probably our best literary source for the kind of material comprising the dithyramb is a tragedy, Euripides' *Bacchae*. Its chorus of Dionysus' worshippers sing repeatedly of their frenzied lives as celebrants of the wine-god, at one with the physicality of nature.

DRAMA

By some mysterious evolutionary process the dithyramb gave birth to the Greeks' three dramatic genres: tragedy, comedy, and satyr drama – all of which were performed in competitions between *choregoi* and the playwrights, each of them sponsored at the great annual Athenian festival of Dionysus, the City Dionysia.

Aristotle said in his *Poetics* that tragedy depicted people as better than they are, and comedy as worse as they are: the dichotomy between tragedy and comedy can be no better illustrated than by the Choregos vase. It was made in a Greek city in Apulia in southern Italy in the early fourth century, and portrayed an exciting performance of comedy, either Old Comedy, the genre associated above all with the name of Aristophanes, or Middle Comedy, which developed subsequently. Scenes of this type on vases from southern Italy used to be associated with an indigenous folk-theatre or farce known as the *phlyax* plays, but this scene almost certainly portrays an exported Athenian comedy, because the choregia was a definitively Athenian institution.

However, what is most fascinating about this vase is the presence, in a scene from a comedy, of an indubitably tragic figure. Every detail of Aegisthus' costume, even down to his cone-shaped hat and high-laced boots, is clearly derived from tragedy. A tragic actor has been introduced directly onto the comic stage.

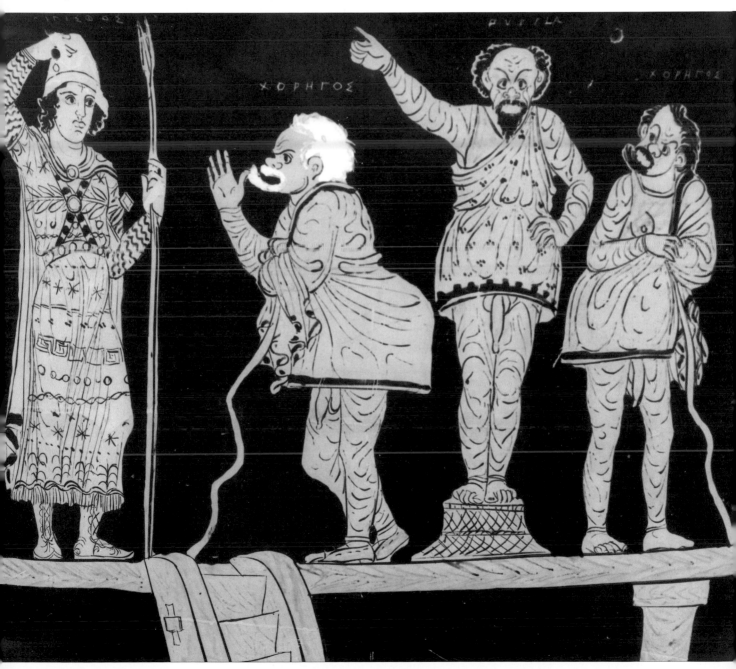

We do not have the comedy which this wonderful scene of genre-confrontation illustrates. Perhaps it was called *Choregoi*. The vase's value lies in its vivid illustration of the Greeks' lively reaction to their theatre. It demonstrates simultaneously the conceptual opposition of beautiful, dignified tragedy with distorted, hilarious comedy; the importance to Greek life of the tension between the two; and the relationship of the production of 'literature' – of theatrical performances – to the civic and economic life of the city-state through the institution of the choregia.

The Pronomos Vase. It portrays two striking figures on the right of the upper level. They represent actors playing Heracles and Papposilenus, the father of the satyrs, respectively. They are depicted as actors holding their masks, thus revealing both their dramatic and true identities to the vase's viewer.

Heracles (a favourite character in satyr drama) is labelled as such and is clearly identifiable from his club and quiver. Papposilenus carries a staff and wears a leopard skin and a woolly costume with tights and sleeves to suggest a furry body. Vase-painters tended to assimilate the faces of actors to their masks. Heracles' mask is not so very different from the head of the actor who plays him: he is a dark, trim-bearded man in his prime, with a broad face, cheerful expression, and a full head of hair.

Papposilenus' mask, on the other hand, bears little relation to the actor playing him: greyhaired, with a much longer beard, and crowned with Dionysiac ivy, this satyr is a creature of the wild. Other actors on the vase wear or bear a variety of masks ranging from that of an attractive young woman to an oriental prince and younger satyrs.

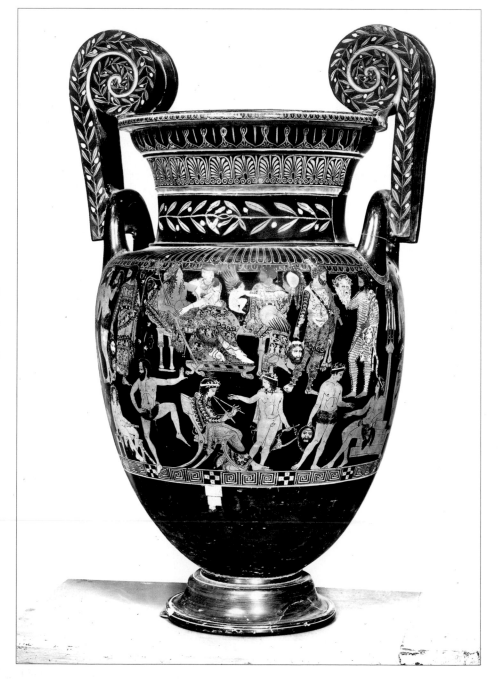

Masks

It is easy to underestimate the impact of drama on the arts in general. For example, it seems that the phenomenon of theatrical masks, the development of techniques for painting them in varied colours (an innovation attributed to Aeschylus), and the experience of watching these walking, talking 'statues' in the theatre facilitated the fifth-century development of realism and naturalism in both painting and sculpture.

One of the best surviving visual illustrations of the masks of drama is provided by the Pronomos vase, an extraordinary Athenian artifact dating from about 400 BCE. It actually relates to the enigmatic genre of satyr drama, of which only one example, Euripides' *Cyclops*, survives.

Satyr drama comically confronted heroes familiar from tragedy with choruses of hairy, ithyphallic satyrs. The Pronomos vase is named after the aulos-player who is depicted and named upon it. It shows on two horizontal levels numerous figures related to a satyr drama who have come to dedicate their masks in the sanctuary of the god Dionysus, presumably in thanks for a victory in the drama contest.

Fragments of an Apulian vase showing theatrical scenery. This illustrates a scene from an unknown tragedy, perhaps one of the several famous lost plays (such as Euripides' *Stheneboea*) in which a married woman fell in lust with her husband's guest or with her stepson. A young woman eavesdrops on a young man in conversation with an older man, while another woman stands on the far right at another doorway.

Scenery

It is also likely that scenery-painting, traditionally an innovation attributed to the tragedian Sophocles, encouraged the Greeks to become skilled in apparently three-dimensional representations of buildings. A fragmentary fourth-century vase, executed using an unusual multi-colour technique found on pottery known as Gnathia ware, bears witness to this. The depiction of the scenery raises an important question about the nature of stage sets in the classical period. Is it evidence that scene-designers painted illusionist three-dimensional palaces onto flat backgrounds? Or is it a vase-painter's attempt, within the limitations of his two-dimensional ceramic 'canvas', to suggest a fully three-dimensional stage building, complete with a projecting wing? Whatever was the case, it is at least clear that techniques were potentially available to the stage designer in the late fifth century to convey the visual appearance of a three-dimensional palace to the audience.

Female roles

Among the most striking aspects of Greek tragedy are the numerous strong roles created for female characters. Perhaps this is why, for example, *Medea* and *Trojan Women* still enthrall us today.

(*Opposite*) **Jane Birkin as Andromache in the National Theatre's 1995 production of Euripides'** *Trojan Women*, called *Women of Troy* in this performance directed by Annie Castledine. After the fall of Troy the widow of the Trojan hero Hector is dragged on to the stage in the chariot of a victorious Greek, holding her baby son Astyanax, the Trojan royal family's last male survivor. He is shortly to be torn from her arms and flung from the city's walls by the Greek conquerors – one of the most heartbreaking events in any ancient tragedy.

Female chorus showing young women engaged in the choral performance of a *partheneion*. *Partheneia* were always accompanied by dancing to the music of the *aulos*. They were especially associated with rituals and festivals preparing young women for marriage. At the end of Euripides' tragedy *Hippolytus*, in which the hero has been the object of his stepmother Phaedra's passion, the goddess Artemis establishes in his honour a ritual and a partheneion to be performed by maidens in posterity: 'Unyoked maidens will cut off locks of their hair for you before marriage, and you will enjoy over a long time the fruits of the greatest mourning of their tears. Always the maidens will be inspired to sing songs about you, and Phaedra's love for you will not fall away nameless and silent.'

Private theatricals of an informal kind in private houses probably used female actors, slaves or hetaerae. At a symposium described by Xenophon the guests were so inflamed by a sexy enactment of Dionysus' seduction of the lovely Ariadne (apparently played by a woman) that 'the unmarried ones swore to take wives, and the married ones mounted their horses and rode off to their wives to take pleasure in them' (see p. 216). Yet tragedy was written and performed exclusively by men, and watched at festivals of Dionysus by audiences overwhelmingly dominated by men. They clearly enjoyed experiencing the emotions tragedy generated through the medium of female impersonation.

The popularity of the female chorus in tragedy can be explained by the long-standing tradition of a choral song for unmarried young women known as the *partheneion* or maiden-song. Pindar composed several, and archaic *partheneia* by Alcman were performed at Sparta. But the strong individual female characters of tragedy are better explained by the idea that ancient Greek audiences found it psychologically and socially appropriate and satisfying to use a mythical female surrogate through whom vicariously to experience the painful tragic emotions of despair, bereavement, vengefulness and sexual obsession.

It is revealing that ancient anecdotes relating to the emotive power of particular tragic performances nearly always concern female roles. The cruel mid-fourth-century tyrant Alexander of Pherae, who thought nothing of burying his enemies alive, had to leave the theatre at a performance of Euripides' *Trojan Women*, because he was ashamed to be seen in public weeping for the sorrows of Hecuba and Andromache. And legendary status attached to the fourth-century actor Polus' impersonation of Sophocles' *Electra*, in the famous scene after she has heard the 'false' messenger speech (see p. 232) and weeps over what she mistakenly believes to be the urn containing her brother's ashes. When Polus took on the role of Electra his own son had recently died. So 'dressed in the sombre robe of Electra, he took his son's urn from the grave, and embracing it as the urn of Orestes, filled everything around him not with representations and imitations, but with real living grief and lamentation. The audience was deeply moved to see the play acted this way.' (Aulus Gellius *Noctes Atticae*, 'Attic Nights'.)

Some ancient thinkers saw the feminine focus of tragedy, especially the cross-dressing it involved, as a dangerous threat to social order. One reason why Socrates banishes tragedy from Plato's *Republic* was that he thought it would encourage effeminacy in both performers and audience. But some vase-painters saw in the moment of transition from a masculine identity to feminine theatrical persona a compelling theme for art.

A discussion of performance in ancient Greek society can be no better concluded than with a look at perhaps the most exciting vase to have been discovered by scholars in recent years, the so-called Cleveland Medea. Standing over fifty centimetres tall, this vessel is remarkable for the stunning impact of the fearsomely coiled yellow dragons drawing Medea's chariot, framed by the circular-spoked 'sun-burst'

(Opposite) The myths relating to Medea were some of the most frequently illustrated by ancient artists, especially after Euripdes' innovational tragedy of 431 BCE. This stunning vase, purchased by the Cleveland Institute of Fine Art in 1991, dates from around 400 BCE. It portrays the end of the play, when the barbarian Medea rides away on the dragon-drawn chariot lent to her by her grandfather Helios, the sun. She is wearing a particularly ornate costume, with embroidered sleeves and imposing oriental headdress. Over the corpses of her children an old grey-haired nurse and male tutor are in mourning; Jason, in the bottom left-hand corner, looks up in horror at his departing wife. Two winged Erinyes, symbols of tragic revenge, gaze down from the upper level.

nimbus. No technique available to the ancient vase-painter could better convey the dazzling effect of the concluding scene of Euripides' famous tragedy, when the Sun's grand-daughter Medea unexpectedly appears *ex machina*. Her distraught husband Jason (in the lower left-hand corner of the vase-painting) has been battering at the entrance of the house, and we expect his infanticidal former wife to emerge from between its doors. Her sky-borne epiphany is thus one of the best prepared surprises in Greek tragedy. It was scenes such as these which made Euripides the most popular and influential of all ancient playwrights, and ensured that his tragedies would be continually revived – both in performance and as literature – right up to modern times.

(*Opposite*) Chorus-men dressing for female roles. The left-hand youth has already donned the calf-length boots and the mask (complete with delicately arranged hair) of an attractive young woman. He now practises the theatrical gestures appropriate to such a role. On the right his colleague has not yet covered his own head and face with the female mask on the floor, and is still putting on his second boot. The scene thus illustrates very precisely the exact moment and process of gender-role transition, and the relationship of that moment with the transformative theatrical mask.

This 'cross-dressing' vase dates from the middle of the fifth century, just a couple of decades before twelve young Athenian men dressed up as a chorus of Corinthian women for the original production of Euripides' tragic *Medea* (431 BCE).

Architecture and other visual arts

CHAPTER 10

Karim Arafat and
Catherine Morgan

Like architecture, sculpture was highly painted; a cast suggests the appearance of this *korē* ('girl' in Greek, but in the sense of a sculptural type, the word is a modern usage) of *c.*530 from the Athenian Acropolis (height 1.17 metres/ 3 feet 11 inches). Korai provide valuable evidence for dress, hairstyles and jewellery. This is the 'Peplos' Kore, named after her Doric dress, which is more simply folded than the elaborate and more widely used Ionic garb. While such statues were usually generic representations of young women, it has been suggested that some may represent goddesses, and that the Peplos Kore may in fact be Artemis. A metal spike arising from the head of this and other archaic statues bears an ornament of uncertain form. This ornament was known as a *meniscus* or 'little moon', and may have been crescent-shaped or, as restored on this cast, a disc. Its function is unclear, although Aristophanes, in his comedy *Birds* of 414 BCE, suggests a bird-scarer for the statue's protection. Indeed, he has the judges in the play warned by the birds:

But should you the prize deny us, you had better all prepare,

like the statues in the open, little copper disks to wear;

Else whene'er abroad you're walking, clad in raiment white and new,

Angry birds will wreak their vengeance, spattering over it and you.

IN WHOSE IMAGE? PERCEPTIONS OF GREEK ART

Imitation of the art and architecture of ancient Greece is pervasive in most countries with a classical tradition. Often inspiration is of a general kind, such as the many-columned facade of the British Museum. Or a specific ancient feature may be recalled: the same building's main entrance is modelled on the north door of the Erechtheum on the Acropolis of Athens, perhaps the most finely detailed of all ancient buildings. The Erechtheum dates from the later fifth century BCE, and is named after Erechtheus, a mythical King of Athens, whose 'well-built house' Athena enters in Homer's *Odyssey*. The Erechtheum is also one of the most copied, adapted, and quoted buildings, at least since Roman times, when the nearby small circular temple to the cult of Rome and its emperor, Augustus, faithfully copied its delicate mouldings.

But the ancient Greece which has held such fascination for artists and designers is often an illusory one, created in error and sustained by repetition. We are accustomed to seeing ancient marbles unpainted, and for that reason, sculptors and architects from the Renaissance onwards have made us accustomed to bright white marble. But we know from vestigial traces of paint that ancient sculptures and buildings were highly coloured. We know much about the colours used, and the techniques of applying them, but it is hard for us to imagine the impression the painted marbles must have made. But in modern Greece, one can often stand in front of newly cut unpainted marble in the full light of the sun – there will be no doubt of the benefit of restraining the glare by paint.

Traditionally, the art and architecture of fifth-century Athens have been the focus of popular and scholarly interest. This is a legacy of the extent and quality of the surviving buildings and sculpture of that period, especially from the Acropolis of Athens. But Greek art has a distinctive character in each period, and a different appeal to its many and varied viewers. We should guard against the unwitting assumption that those who lived and worked in one period – defined not by them- selves but by modern scholars – knew their place in a process of evolution identified and named only once it is over. Each age used the

(Above) The most famous feature of the Erechtheum on the Acropolis of Athens are the finely garbed women acting as columns. Although today known as *caryatids*, the build- ing inscriptions refer to them only as *korai* or 'girls'.

(Left) They are repeatedly imitated, from the villa of the emperor Hadrian at Tivoli in the second century CE to the facade of a late-nineteenth- century Athenian house, pictured here.

advances of the earlier in accordance with its own requirements and preferences. In many respects the classical period is the culmination of the process; but its predecessors are not mere midwives assisting its birth.

Thus the imitators of classical art and architecture have been (in some cases unwitting) purveyors of an inaccurate view of the forms on which they base their work. What, then, is the truth?

THE SOURCES: PIECING TOGETHER THE PAST

The sources may be divided into two categories: the remaining artifacts (from tiny potsherd to massive temple) and the literary sources. Most of the art and architecture which survives is fragmentary, and much more besides is lost. Of the fragments, survival in some form may be brought about by, for example, building pottery sherds into the surface of a newly constructed road or by re-using blocks for new constructions. For example, in Sicily, the cathedral at Syracuse is built round the temple of Athena of *c.*480. There are myriad such examples, ancient and modern: blocks already cut and shaped were too valuable to waste.

Natural causes account for much loss. Numerous earthquakes and landslides are attested in our sources – for example, the Parthenon suffered earthquake damage within six years of its completion, and again most recently in 1981, some 2400 years later. Olympia was all but destroyed by two earthquakes in the sixth century CE; Delphi suffered most extensively in 373 BCE, and has done so again in this century.

Ancient building blocks, sculptures, statue bases, tripod bases, and inscriptions can all be found built into the walls of this Byzantine church at Orchomenus in Boeotia. Particularly prominent are the two rows of column drums. Such re-use saved time and money, and continued a long tradition: the most famous example is the use of archaic sculptures for the defensive wall thrown up round Athens by Themistocles immediately after the Persian Wars (see p. 65). Similarly, architectural members from the archaic Acropolis buildings can still be seen today, built into the mid-fifth century north wall of the Acropolis.

(Left) Boulders which demolished reconstruction work in the sanctuary of Athena, known either as *Pronoia* (Forethought) or *Pronaia* (Before the Temple), at Delphi during a landslip in 1905. Like much of Greece, Delphi suffered several earthquakes in antiquity, notably in 373 when the temple of Apollo *(above)* was destroyed.

A wooden statuette from Samos of the *xoanon* type (later seventh century). Literary sources often refer to wooden statues, but few survive, mostly from water-logged sites. The style of this statuette is 'Daedalic' (see p. 263).

'No wonder that the temple of Artemis was burned down, since the goddess was busy bringing Alexander into the world', wrote Plutarch of the burning of the temple of Artemis at Ephesus on the night of the birth of Alexander the Great in 356. Such famous incidents are just the best publicized of the many losses to fire. Temples in particular were especially vulnerable, since wood was used extensively in Greek architecture, at all periods for much of the construction of the roof, but also for columns in the earliest temples. An example is the temple of Hera at Olympia, built in the early sixth century with wooden columns which were apparently gradually replaced in stone as they wore out. As late as *c.*173 CE, Pausanias recorded that 'in the back chamber one of the two pillars is oak'. In addition, oil stored in temples and other buildings was highly inflammable, and could also be hazardous when used in lamps: Pausanias again tells us that the temple in the Argive sanctuary of Hera 'was burned down through Chryseis, the priestess of Hera, having fallen asleep, when the flame of the lamp caught the wreaths'.

Wood not only burns, it also decays, so much of what we know of its use is inferred from the remains of stronger materials. We hear from ancient writers of simple statues known as *xoana*, which were mostly wooden. An ancient editor of the fifth-century tragedian Sophocles tell us that in his play *Xoanophoroi* ('Xoanon-carriers') 'the gods carry out from Troy their own xoana'. A few examples of small-scale wooden statues have survived, mainly from waterlogged sites. And some wooden plates have survived – less spectacular than the statues and temples, but a useful glimpse of daily life.

Besides natural causes there was destruction wrought by man, some incidental (in warfare, for example), much of it intentional. Materials such as bronze or marble were often consigned to the kiln for re-use: indeed, the low survival rate of classical free-standing sculptures is mainly because most were made of bronze. Old buildings may have been demolished simply to make way for new; or the motivation may be ideological or religious, such as the damage to many of the most prominent pagan sites in the early Christian period. This era also saw the tearing apart of many buildings. This was partly for building stone, but also for lead: ancient buildings did not use mortar, and their blocks were kept in place with the help of clamps, usually of iron; since iron oxidizes in the air, these clamps were cladded with lead to prevent air reaching them, and it was this valuable lead which proved all too tempting a target.

Ancient writers on art need to be approached with caution, since most wrote long after the period of the art they describe, such as Pliny the Elder and Pausanias of the first and second centuries CE respectively. They each had their own reasons for writing. When we read Pliny on bronze or marble statues, we should remember that his main interest was in metallurgy and geology rather than in art. Pausanias' extensive description of what he saw on his travels in Greece *c*.150–175 CE is the best-surviving example of a *periegesis*, a literary form of travel-writing. These writers, and others like them, used previous accounts of the art and architecture of Greece, and lists of artists and their works compiled by previous visitors. Such writings are primarily constructed around individual artists and their achievements, often with a considerable biographical emphasis. With all their shortcomings, they represent the best-surviving part of an extensive literary tradition now, like so much of the art with which it was concerned, long lost.

Above all, such ancient accounts are distinguished by a bias towards what may be called the public arts of sculpture, architecture and wall- or panel-painting. Architecture and its attendant sculpture would have been commissioned by the authority of the day – whether a tyrant or a democratic state – which probably also determined its themes. Its display would have been public, and the expenditure on it considerable. So too most free-standing sculpture, and, in the classical period, wall-painting.

Vase-painting is an art to which modern scholars give great prominence because of the vast quantity of surviving examples. The commonness of pots, both painted and unpainted, their virtual indestructibility, and the generally predictable development of their shapes and of the decorative techniques and styles used on them have ensured for them an important place in histories of ancient art. Yet painted pots are not mentioned in extant literary sources. This is an enormous imbalance: on one hand, public arts like painting, which are much discussed in the sources, are almost entirely lost; on the other, vase-painting is an art-form of a much more private nature, a smaller-scale art whose products, many of which survive, could as easily rest unseen in the home as be conspicuously dedicated in a sanctuary. Pots were clearly less expensive to produce than sculpture or architecture, and were therefore more widely accessible. The scenes painted on them, including many aspects of daily life, bring us closer than those of other art-forms to the interests and preoccupations of the inhabitants of the areas which produced them. Thus the lack of references to painted pottery in our literary sources inevitably means that we must be aware of the limits of such sources, especially the top-heavy view of society which they offer us. All written sources are themselves artifacts, and require the same rigorous scrutiny as would be applied to any humble potsherd.

BEGINNINGS AND EARLY DEVELOPMENT:
THE EARLY IRON AGE (*c*.1050–700)

To trace the development of art through the historical period, it is necessary to go back to the Early Iron Age. This is a period of greater regional individualism than perhaps any other – for example, on the Greek mainland the buildings of the period were primarily made of mudbrick between a stone base and, usually, a thatched

Potters and potting

Potters and pot-painters operated at a humbler level than sculptors and architects, who would usually work to commission, and often used costly imported materials (clay being available in most regions of Greece). Often potter and vase- or pot-painter would be the same, as the two inscriptions illustrated in this panel suggest. Sometimes they would sign their work – perhaps simply taking pride in it, but more likely as a form of advertisement, all the more necessary in

a competitive commercial environment. Indeed, there are many signs that potters and vase-painters attempted to outdo each other. It is perhaps in the potter and vase-painter that we are closest to the artist as an ordinary individual, through inscriptions – many of them referring to the potters and painters themselves – and through depictions of potters at work. Pottery workshops seem to have consisted of extended families, and the scenes they represented often reflected the everyday concerns of ordinary people. They show rituals and rites, but also water-collecting, drinking, dancing, athletics, marriages, death and other daily activities.

By comparing signed works, we can deduce the characteristics of each vase-painter's style, and attribute unsigned vases. The method was pioneered by Sir John Beazley (1885–1970), who studied vases of the lowest, as well as the highest, quality.

(Left). Part of the neck of a small Corinthian oil-jug (from around the mid-seventh century). The painter has first covered it in black paint, then painted three rosettes in white paint. The first two are neatly executed, but he has made a mistake on the third and, in an all too human gesture of frustration, crossed it out.

(Left). Part of a late archaic red-figure vase showing an inscription naming Myson as both potter and painter.

(Opposite). In writing 'Oikopheles painted and potted me', the artist has proudly named himself twice. But the word 'me' shows that it is the cup itself which is addressing us, much as the statuette of Manticlos (see p. 262) had done.

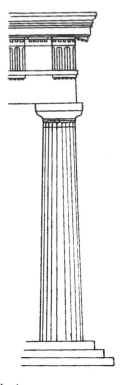

Ionic

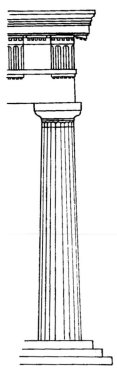

Doric

roof; while the islands (notably Crete) built entirely in stone, reflecting locally available material, and favoured flat roofs (perhaps to conserve rainwater). The most elaborate extant building is at Lefkandi on Euboea of c.1000, a typically apsidal (horseshoe-ended) construction with a veranda and a central row of columns supporting the roof. Its uniqueness is one reason why its function is disputed – it is thought to be either a house converted to a hero-shrine for its owner, or a purpose-built shrine in the form of a house. The difficulty of assigning function – whether domestic, cultic, or a combination of the two – is characteristic of this period.

Stone-carving was still elementary, and no large-scale statuary survives. Bronze was used from the tenth century for tripods and small-scale figurines cast from moulds. These figurines, from sanctuaries such as Olympia, occasionally represent warriors, but mostly horses and other quadrupeds. These are stiff, angular forms, very like those depicted on the vases of the period. As early as the ninth century, complex filigree and granulation were used for jewellery. Wood was also widely used then, as later, for construction of roofs and for supports in mudbrick walls. But neither architecture nor sculpture attains anything like the importance they have in our record and understanding of later periods.

In contrast, painted pottery can be called a major art form in the eighth century, probably for the only time in its history, largely due to the small but striking group of large pots from mid-eighth century Athens. These were mostly used as grave-markers and decorated with stiff, unarticulated silhouette figures participating in elaborate funerals and battles set amid the angular maeander patterns (popular already for over a century) which give the style its modern name of 'Geometric'. There had been precedents for painted figures on Athenian pots. The earliest is a horse, preceding by a century or so the first human figure, a female mourner of the mid-ninth century. Suddenly, c.770, our first figure-scenes appear – a battle, a sea-fight, a *prothesis* (the laying out of the dead). As well as the lying-in-state of the body, we have its removal for burial, or *ecphora*, an appropriate scene for a vase which would stand over the grave (see p. 81).

Now begins the interest in narrative which was to be so characteristic of the Greeks and to inspire so much of their finest art and literature. Now too we have the first identifiable 'hands', the artists who painted the vases, beginning with the Dipylon Master, so named following the discovery of the work which first identified him in the cemetery beside the Dipylon Gate in Athens. These are recognized by the individual traits, akin to the distinctiveness of handwriting. By assessing the careers of vase painters we can deduce much about potters' workshops, above all the later ones of archaic and classical Athens, although the method has been successfully applied to many other schools, most extensively archaic Corinthian. The first signature of a potter, a name ending in '-inos', comes from a Late Geometric krater from Pithecousae (Ischia, in the Bay of Naples).

As the earliest manifestations of two of the most significant phenomena of Greek art – and of all later art derived from it – the birth of narrative and the identification of 'hands' are of inestimable importance. But for now, Athens was to make only a beginning, as the initiative in these areas passed to Corinth.

THE ARCHAIC PERIOD (*c*.700–480)

The eighth and seventh centuries saw extensive Greek contacts with the East – previously limited to areas such as Euboea and Crete. The result was an influx of imported artifacts to the mainland, and the widespread appearance of eastern motifs in Greek art. This 'orientalizing' phase of the seventh century is manifest all over the Greek world, and gave rise to changes in many local styles.

Corinth is especially prominent in this period. It had founded many colonies in the second half of the eighth and the early seventh centuries, and its position on the Isthmus has much to do with its prominence, placed as it is between East and West. The ruling Bacchiad aristocracy was succeeded by the Cypselids (*c*.650–580), who, like many tyrants, seem to have been active patrons of art. Archaeological evidence matches literary in showing that Corinth brought to new peaks the arts of architecture, painting and sculpture.

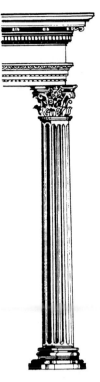

Corinthian

History tells us comparatively little of seventh-century Athens and Attica: an exception is the ill-fated attempt at tyranny – a phenomenon at its heyday in this period – by Cylon, whose failed assault on the Acropolis in the 620s is mentioned by Herodotus and Thucydides. Archaeologically, too, we know less of Athens in this period: its most distinctive product was the Protoattic style of pottery, but even that was strongly influenced by the art of Corinth and East Greece. So the early part of the archaic period sees Athens less inventive and influential than it had been before; but in the later seventh and sixth centuries there was to be an unprecedented flowering of Athens and its art, while Corinth's economic power, and artistic inventiveness, declined.

Architecture

At Corinth a temple, probably dedicated to Apollo, was built *c*.680. It consisted of a cella, a rectangular room designed to house the cult statue, and the core of all later Greek temples. The walls were at least partly stone with wooden beams for strength. The roof sloped down at both ends in the manner of a 'Chinese' roof, rather than being pitched like later temples which had the familiar triangular pediment. The Corinth temple was partly painted, the interior of the cella stuccoed and decorated with rectangular panels of black and red, the roof covered in terracotta tiles alternating in vertical rows, five yellow to one black.

Nearby, the temple of Poseidon at the Isthmus of Corinth, built around the mid-seventh century, is much better preserved and continues these developments. This is the first mainland temple known to have had walls made entirely of stone; these were stuccoed and partly painted with figures as well as patterns. Some sixteen tons of its terracotta rooftiles survive, and experimental archaeology has shown that a team of seven people could make the requisite number of tiles in about two years.

The metopes *(right and opposite top)* of developed Doric architecture are anticipated in these terracotta panels *(opposite middle and bottom)* from Thermum in Aetolia of *c.*630 (*c.*0.88 x 0.99 metres/2 feet 11 inches x 3 feet 3 inches). They were slotted into the upper part of the temple of Apollo, perhaps between the triglyphs familiar on later buildings. The clay is Corinthian; the motifs are from the Corinthian repertoire; and the style is characteristic of Corinthian art, reflecting the pre-eminence of Corinth at this period.

The temple at the Isthmus was probably peripteral: that is, it had the surrounding colonnade, which is perhaps the most distinctive feature of Greek temples. It is among the earliest known mainland examples, but its columns, which would have been wooden, no longer survive.

(Right) Metope (*c.* 560) from the Treasury of the Sicyonians, representing Castor, Pollux and Idas. According to Theocritus' *Idyll* XXII, Castor and Pollux abducted their cousins Hilaera and Phobe (who were to marry Idas and Lynceus) from their wedding. In the resulting fight, Lynceus killed Castor, but was then killed by Pollux who was saved from Idas by a thunderbolt from Zeus and brought to Olympus.

The elaborately painted terracotta panels of the temple of Apollo at Thermum in Aetolia show Corinthian influence in style, technique and subject-matter. These are forerunners of the developed metopes which alternated with the triglyphs in the Doric order of Greek architecture. The first preserved example of the developed Doric order is the temple of Artemis built *c.*580 on the island of Corfu, significantly a colony of Corinth. It bears on both ends the earliest known pedimental sculptures, featuring the fearsome Gorgon who turned to stone those who looked at her – imagine, then, the intimidating effect of approaching a temple under the gaze of a stone Gorgon of some 3 metres/10 feet in height.

Once the basic form of the Doric temple is established, it develops mainly in details and regional variations. We know from the remains of the temples on the Acropolis of Athens, including the predecessor of the classical Parthenon, that by the end of the archaic period architecture had become a sophisticated and mathematically precise skill. Although these trends reach an unparalleled level in the Periclean temples of the mid-fifth century, above all the Parthenon, recent scholarship has made clear the quality of the archaic architecture destroyed by the Persians.

North-west Asia Minor and Lesbos have produced most of the so-called Aeolic capitals, seventh and sixth century forerunners of the Ionic order which developed around the mid-sixth century on large temples at sites like Samos and Ephesus, the latter 55 x 115 metres (181 x 378 feet). The period of use of Ionic for temples on the mainland was yet to come, although it was used to striking effect on the treasury of the island-state of Siphnos at Delphi. Treasuries were state repositories at the Panhellenic sanctuaries, and part of their purpose was to show off a city's wealth and artistic prowess. Built *c.*525, that of Siphnos was the most elaborately decorated of all treasuries, with a series of sculpted relief friezes in the Ionic tradition, and highly ornate carved mouldings, as well as the Doric trait of pedimental sculpture. It also featured sculpted standing figures of women, each with detailed costume and headdress, flanking the entrance in place of columns, precursors of those found in the classical Erechtheum.

Sculpture

Key developments in this period concerned scale and material. Increasing confidence in handling stones led from small statues in soft stones to the appearance of sculpture in hard stones around the mid-seventh century. Orientalizing statuettes were familiar from the later eighth century, in materials such as terracotta and ivory; and in bronze the stiff warrior and animal figurines of the Early Iron Age were succeeded by more adventurously posed animal and human figures.

But large-scale bronze-working did not develop until the later sixth century, and most archaic sculptural developments occurred in stone.

The first truly Greek sculptural style is known by its modern name of Daedalic, after Daedalus, traditionally the first Greek artist, most familiar to us for his mythical flight from Crete with his ill-fated son Icarus. The Daedalic style covers approximately the last three quarters of the seventh century, and is characterized by small plank-like, frontally-oriented figures with triangular faces flanked by inverted wedges of hair. This is part of the orientalizing trend, with inspiration derived from such sources as Eastern statuettes of fertility goddesses. The style occurs in many media – terracotta figurines, heads attached to vases, bronze statuettes, gold jewellery – and is widespread in the Greek world, with no clear origin, although possibilities are Crete and the north-east Peloponnese, perhaps specifically Corinth. But the future of Greek sculpture did not lie in small-scale works, nor in soft stones. Rather, it lay in the harder medium of marble, widely available in the Greek world, and increasingly skilfully worked as the Greeks developed a range of tools to make fullest use of it. Harder stone allows finer carving, and once it began to be used, sculpture developed apace.

From the beginning, the main interest lay in the human figure, especially the male, who could by social convention be depicted naked and thus afforded the sculptor the opportunity to explore the representation of musculature. 'Kouros' is the modern conventional name for the statues of the standing naked male, facing forward, hands by sides, and left foot forward, produced from the late seventh to the early fifth century. The word *kouros* means 'youth', and these are idealized depictions of young men in their prime and, particularly in the case of the early examples, well over life-size. On occasion there may be a name on a statue base – one asks the viewer to 'stay and mourn at the monument for dead Croesus whom violent Ares destroyed, fighting in the front rank' – but the statues themselves represent a generalized ideal of youth and beauty. The Kouros is to some extent derived from Egyptian sculpture, although it rapidly assumes a distinctively Greek form (see p. 49). While Kouroi appear primarily in cemeteries – where they must have presented an almost ghostly appearance to passers-by – their female counterparts, the draped Korai, were mainly votives, found in sanctuaries.

These two types constitute the real beginnings of the Greek exploration of three-dimensional representations of the human body, with drapery often a means of articulating rather than hiding the body. They are found widely across the Greek world. Other free-standing sculptures include seated figures, such as those along the processional Sacred Way to the oracular site of Didyma in the territory of Miletus in Asia Minor. We may assume that dedicating such statues conferred prestige from the status of some of the donors: one proclaims 'I am Chares, son of Cleisis, ruler of Teichioussa. The statue is for Apollo'. There were also riders, such as the Rampin Rider from the Acropolis of Athens, dating from *c*.550. He has exceptionally finely carved beard and hair, and is wearing a wreath, suggesting that he was a successful

(Opposite) **This bronze statuette of *c*.700–675 (over 20 centimetres/8 inches tall) was dedicated at Thebes with the following inscription engraved on its legs: 'Mantiklos offers me as a tithe to Apollo of the silver bow; Phoebus [Apollo], give me some pleasing favour in return'. A hole is visible at the front of its head, and another at its top; these are probably for a helmet, which means that the statuette is unlikely to represent Apollo, who was not generally a martial god (except in Sparta).**

competitor in the games. Also from the Acropolis, and dating slightly earlier, comes a splendid Moschophorus, or calf-bearer, carrying the animal across his shoulders. This is justly admired as a work of art, but it also represents an everyday event in that the calf on the shoulders of Rhonbos (as the inscription on the statue's base suggests the figure is called) is being taken for dedication and slaughter.

Relief sculpture was also developing, for example on the bases of some Kouroi, or the pediment of the temple of Artemis on Corfu mentioned earlier. A series of limestone pedimental sculptures from the sixth century Acropolis of Athens is richly painted and attests to the city's growing prosperity. These early architectural sculptures often bear symmetrical – one might say heraldic – designs, and often employed local myths. At Delphi, as we have seen, the treasury built by Siphnos was adorned with fine relief sculpture. Near it stood the slightly later Athenian treasury, a Doric building with sculpted metopes showing adventures of Theseus and Heracles, both Athenian heroes (the former by birth, Heracles by adoption) used to promote the glory of Athens.

Vase-painting

Corinth saw the invention, near the end of the eighth century, of black-figure, a technique of vase-painting in which the silhouette employed in the Geometric period was enlivened by incision and red and white paint. In the Protocorinthian period (c.720–620), the Corinthians quickly saw and exploited the potential of black-figure, realizing that figures could now overlap, that individual features could be defined, and that colour produced a livelier scene. Much Corinthian vase-painting was small-scale, requiring fine control of the graver and brush. As at all periods, quality varies, but around the mid-seventh century Corinth had reached one of the peaks of Greek art in a small series of vases produced by a few painters. These are distinguished for their immense detail, their complex compositions, and their fine potting. The more typical vases of this period are of lesser quality, but nonetheless bright and lively, featuring processions of strutting creatures both real – lions, goats, bulls and boars – and imaginary, such as sphinxes and sirens. The latter, like the ornaments scattered in the background of Corinthian vases, are derived from the East, another manifestation of the orientalizing tendency noted above. By contrast with contemporary Athens, there is a lack of religious imagery or human narrative, and Corinthian vases are relatively uninformative about daily life (an exception on p. 170).

The succeeding Corinthian period (c.620–550) sees more mechanical vase-paintings, with increasingly ill-drawn animals obediently plodding round the vases. There were, though, still some high quality painters, and the period is by no means one of mere decline. From the mid-sixth century, Corinthian vases featured patterns rather than figures.

One revealing phenomenon of the second quarter of the sixth century was the practice adopted by some Corinthian painters of reddening the surface of their vases before painting them. Corinthian clay is pale by nature, and reddening the

An unusually detailed depiction of daily life, this Athenian *lekythos* of the mid-sixth century (17 centimetres, nearly 7 inches, tall) shows women at the loom (see also pp. 100, 101, 132–5).

surface made vases resemble the warm orange which is characteristic of Athenian clay and helps makes Athenian pots so striking. Paint is based on the clay from which the pot is itself made, and also varies according to region. While Corinthian paint is a dull black, the clay of Attica contains illite, an element which gives Athenian paint its distinctive high lustre. Thus, while Athens and Corinth both used

Corinth dominated the export of pottery in the seventh century, and Athens from the mid-sixth. An Athenian entrepreneur named Nicosthenes, working in the second half of the sixth century, imitated Etruscan native shapes, such as this amphora (*left*), made in bucchero, a local black clay. His workshop created artifacts for sales outside Athens, such as this amphora (*opposite*), and targeted specific cities in Etruria, exporting different shapes to different cities and drawing on Etruscan iconography, such as boxing and symposium scenes familiar from Etruscan wall-paintings. The main frieze on Nicosthenes' amphora shows dancing satyrs and maenads, the companions of Dionysus.

The Acropolis of Athens

'Poor old scrubby Rome sinks into nothing by the side of such beautiful magnificence', wrote Edward Lear in 1848 of the Acropolis of Athens and its ruins. The Acropolis lies in the middle of a plain on a natural plateau with a good water-supply, making it an ideal place for secure settlement. Indeed, it ceased being used as a fortress only in 1831. Three years later King Otho of Greece – seated within the Parthenon on a throne decorated with olive, myrtle and laurel – formally inaugurated its restoration.

Habitation on the Acropolis began in the Neolithic age (c.5000), and Mycenaean activity includes a wall of c.1250–1200, of which part is still visible today. Painted architectural terracottas remain from buildings of some form in the early sixth century, but our first substantial remains are of the second quarter of the sixth century, perhaps related to the reorganization of the city's Panathenaic festival in 566. From this period dates the temple known as the 'Hecatompedon', literally 'Hundred-Footer', probably built on the site of the later Parthenon. Contemporary also is an altar to Athena Nike (Victory), on the site of the classical temple. The later sixth century saw the construction on the north side of the Acropolis of the Old Temple of Athena, which housed the cult of Athena Polias (Guardian of the City). A Doric building, it introduced Ionic elements – porch columns and a sculpted frieze – to Athenian architecture. A series of elaborately painted limestone sculptures adorned a variety of pediments, although their original arrangement and assignment to specific buildings remain uncertain. It is even possible that during these years, Pisistratus and his sons built a residence for themselves on the Acropolis, and some of the remains may have come from such a building.

The establishment of the democracy under Cleisthenes from 508 led to a greater concentration on the Agora, the area of political rather than religious activity. But building continued on the Acropolis in the decade from c.490 with the beginning of construction of the predecessor of the Parthenon. This had reached a height of two or three column-drums when it was destroyed by the Persians in 480–479. Some of these drums, and other architectural elements from the pre-Parthenon, can still be seen in the wall built round the Acropolis in the mid-fifth century. Although the pre-Parthenon was far from complete, we know that it represented the first use on a large scale in Attica of marble, of Ionic elements, and of refinements. In these respects, it was a forerunner of the classical Parthenon, which occupied almost exactly the same site.

All this was swept aside by the Persian destruction. The classical Acropolis made fullest possible use of the resulting open space. Construction began soon after the mid-century, delayed

(*Left*) **A drawing by C. P. Stevens of the Propylaea Gate, with the Parthenon behind, as it would have looked in the fifth century.**

(*Opposite top*) **A model of the Acropolis on the eve of the Persian invasion.**

(*Opposite bottom*) **A model of the Acropolis at its most developed.**

for a generation while Athenian fortunes recovered from the Persian wars. Another delaying factor was perhaps the Oath of Plataea, whereby the Athenians and their allies swore after the Persian wars that 'Of the shrines burnt and overthrown by the barbarians, I will rebuild none, but I will allow them to remain as a memorial to those who come after of the impiety of the barbarians'.

The approach to the Acropolis – which was from the west – had been by ramp and modest entrance-gate, or Propylon, still unfinished when destroyed by the Persians. Now a more spacious, stepped approach led to the large and complex Propylaea, a gateway built almost as if it were a temple. Its severe Doric exterior, topped by pediments, gives way to softer Ionic inner columns, and one would look up to the patterns painted on its ceiling coffers in blue and gold. To the left lay what may have originally been a dining-room but became known as the Pinakotheke, or art-gallery, hung with paintings on wooden panels of the sort about which our literary sources enthuse so fulsomely. To the right stood the temple of Athena Nike (see p. 274). That the Propylaea was seen as a divinely inspired building is suggested by the comment of Plutarch, that Athena 'was a helper both in the inception and in the completion of the work'.

The Propylaea and Parthenon are deliberately positioned in relation to each other in order to show off the latter to fullest advantage, since as one comes through the Propylaea – now as then – one's first view of the Parthenon is of the north-west corner. Although then a wall between the two would have

blocked the view of much of the Parthenon's colonnade, the upper part with all the external sculpture would have been visible. Coming out of the Propylaea, there would have been a full view of the Parthenon's west front and the long north side. Thus half of the building was visible at first glimpse. In addition, the 'business end' of the Parthenon, as of most Greek temples, was at the east, giving access to the cella and its statue. In order to reach that end, one would have had no choice but to walk down the long side, in the process seeing three-quarters of the building at close hand. Thus, cleverly and irresistibly, the visitor would have been obliged to see 75 per cent of the building's exterior before entering it, a unique opportunity afforded by the topography and fully exploited by the architects.

The last of the fifth-century buildings is the Erechtheum. Extending over and beyond the area of the Old Temple of Athena, its irregular form exemplifies the Greeks' ability to make a virtue of necessity: several long-standing cults had to be accommodated in their established locations, and the ground slopes sharply away on the north, where tall columns contrast with the famous *caryatids* of the south porch. The gracefulness of the caryatids is captured by the mid-nineteenth-century traveller Aubrey de Vere, who wrote that they 'support the projecting cornice on their broad and sedate brows, which in that cornice seem rather to wear a crown than to sustain a burthen'.

Few who have seen the Acropolis can doubt the appropriateness of the verdict of Plutarch, that these buildings 'brought most delightful adornment to Athens and the greatest amazement to the rest of mankind'.

black-figure, there were striking differences in the end product. During the seventh and early sixth century, Corinth had exported more widely than any other centre of manufacture – to its own colonies and beyond. But Athens became the main exporter of painted pottery during the sixth century, at times responding to careful market research (see p. 267). It was at the period when Corinth's share of the export trade was diminishing in the face of Athens' growing success that Corinthian artists began imitating Athenian colouring by reddening their vases. This practice looks, therefore, like a desperate attempt to retain its place in the market by passing itself off as the current favourite.

Black-figure was widely used in the archaic world, with the notable exception of East Greece, but reached probably its finest development during the middle quarters of the sixth century at Athens, when the high quality of painting was matched by the delicate potting. Several of the painters and potters who signed their work have foreign names, perhaps denoting the second generation sons of immigrants, whose parents had been among the foreigners whom Solon is reported to have encouraged to come to Athens. Among them were Lydos, 'the Lydian', and Amasis, a potter, and probably also a vase-painter, with a hellenized Egyptian name.

Around 525, the Athenian potters' quarter invented the red-figure technique, whereby the figures were drawn in outline, the inner details added in lines of varying thickness, and the background filled in with black paint. Engraving was replaced by brushwork. The greater flexibility of the brush allowed greater subtlety, and the exploration of the human figure, and of drapery, preoccupations in vase-painting as in sculpture, gathered new impetus. Although the advances occurred in red-figure, black-figure continued to be produced in quantity until the end of the archaic period. And from now on, Athens dominated production of figured pottery more than in any other period, except perhaps the mid- to later eighth century.

THE CLASSICAL PERIOD (*c*.480–323)

In the thirty years between the Persian destruction and the beginning of the Periclean building programme, Athens had been immensely enriched in several ways: an exceptionally rich seam of silver was discovered and mined at Laurium in southeast Attica in 483–2; public coffers were filled with tribute money from the members of the Delian League (the League's treasury was transferred from Delos to Athens in 454); and systematic quarrying began at Mount Pentelicum, north of Athens. The latter was crucial not only in providing an exceptionally fine-grained hard marble, ideal for the wealth and quality of detail that were to be so characteristic of the Acropolis buildings, but also for its location, just outside the city. Transport of raw materials in the ancient world was very costly. The temple of Bassae in Arcadia, for example, which in 1814 inspired William Haygarth to write that

> Mould'ring and gray, the Doric columns nod
> O'er scattered heaps of massy pediment

Public accountability was a feature of many ancient building projects. Such records are invaluable evidence for the activities and status of craftsmen, as well as for economics and demography. Here some of the accounts from the Erechtheum (*c.*421–406) are publicly displayed. They reveal that half the workers were resident aliens, a quarter slaves and a quarter citizens. The architect was salaried at one drachma a day, other workers were paid by the job: a frieze figure earned 60 drachmas, column-fluting 350 drachmas per 20-foot column. At a pinch, three obols or half a drachma was at the time a living wage.

was substantially built of local stone. Some, however, was carried from Paros some 400 kilometres by sea, and 22 kilometres overland to a height of 1100 metres. The expense and time lavished on architects and sculptors visiting the quarries and choosing suitable blocks would have been saved by the presence of nearby quarries. These circumstances allowed Athens to produce an unparalleled set of buildings, and it did so in unprecedented style. We know much of the processes of setting up the project and of executing it through building records engraved on marble stelae.

With brief interruptions when the Peloponnesian war began to divert funds from the building, the sound of hammer on marble must have resounded from the Acropolis for nearly half a century. So what resulted? By the end of the fifth century, the visitor approaching the Acropolis would first see the Propylaea and, jutting out to the right, the small Ionic temple of Athena Nike. Beyond the Propylaea was the Parthenon, exceptional in width and length, and probably the greatest achievement of Greek architecture. It boasted the most elaborately decorated of all temple exteriors, its pediments unprecedentedly crowded and complex, and, uniquely, all ninety-two external metopes fully carved. Less visible, at the top of the exterior of the cella wall within the outer colonnade was an Ionic frieze of 160 metres (524 feet) in length, and nearly a metre (just over three feet) in height, carved to a maximum depth of about 6 centimetres (2 inches).

Architecturally, the Parthenon is a masterpiece – most obviously in its refinements, the adjustments made by the architect to counteract apparent visual distortions. For example, to prevent vertical columns appearing to lean outwards when viewed from below they actually lean slightly inwards. (It has been estimated that a continuation of the lines of the columns would meet about a mile and a half above the building.) This was not a new technique – it had been used on the predecessor of the Parthenon, destroyed by the Persians – but the precision with which it was carried out, and the extent of the refinements employed, were new. And the practical difficulties involved were considerable. Columns were made up of individual drums dowelled together. If, then, a column was to lean consistently inward, each drum must be cut at a very slightly different angle so that the effect accumulates imperceptibly. With this and other refinements, some 30,000 tons of marble were marshalled to millimetre accuracy.

To the north of the Doric Parthenon, the Ionic Erechtheum (c.421–406) rivalled it in elaboration, but of a fussier, less grand sort – any attempt to rival the Parthenon would be foolhardy, and the different order with its different features provides the perfect foil. But, like the Parthenon, it is executed with extreme care and precision. Building accounts on marble blocks give us detailed information concerning the workers, slave as well as free, on the Erechtheum.

In common with most temples, those on the Acropolis acted as treasuries and repositories of votives, but were primarily designed as integral parts of the sanctuary in which they were situated, and central to its function. The role of the Erechtheum is clear from the many cults housed in its irregular plan – and it must not be forgotten that the area of the temple included a courtyard and altar and not just the physical building itself – including those of Athena, Poseidon and Hephaestus, as well as the grave of Erechtheus himself. But the cult function of the Parthenon is at least in doubt. The cella of the Parthenon was dominated by Phidias' statue of Athena Parthenos, some 40-feet high and made in the technique known as chryselephantine, in which a wooden mast is adorned with ivory head and limbs and clothed in drapery composed of plates of gold shaped in clay moulds. As an innovation in scale, although not in technique (which enjoyed a vogue in the second half of the fifth century), it was entirely appropriate to a building of the elaboration of the Parthenon. But it has rightly been called 'a splendid votive offering rather than a cult image'.

It is to the exterior of the Parthenon that we must return for its 'message': the scale, elaboration and material of the building certainly gave a very effective impression of Athenian wealth and magnificence. And it is precisely the Athenian aspects

This highly imaginative drawing of the Parthenon, made by Benoît Loviot between 1879 and 1881, combines the building's frieze and statue of Athena with the pedimental sculpture of the late archaic temple of Aphaea on the island of Aegina. The owls flanking the apex of the pediment are – alas – fictional, although appropriate as the birds of Athena: 'owls to Athens' was the ancient Greek equivalent of the English 'coals to Newcastle'.

The temple of Athena Nike

'From this point the sea is visible, and it was here, they say, that Aegeus cast himself down and perished'. Thus Pausanias relates the death of the legendary King of Athens, and father of Theseus, who threw himself from the place where the Ionic temple of Athena Nike, or Victory, later stood. Theseus had promised to use white sails on his return if his expedition to kill the Minotaur in Crete had been successful; but, elated by his success, he forgot and kept the black sails that so tragically misled his father. The fact that Aegeus is said to have seen his son's ship approaching Attica in the far distance is striking testimony to

the prominence of the spur of rock on which the temple was to be built. This lies on the right of the Acropolis, and had already had a bastion built on it in Mycenaean times. This natural prominence was fully exploited in the classical period for the smallest of the Acropolis temples, measuring a mere 5.4 x 8.2 metres (18 x 27 feet), and dating probably 427–4.

While an altar of the second quarter of the sixth century is our first evidence for the cult, the defeat of the Persians in 480–479 prompted a growth in the cult of Athena Nike, and her temple sent a clear message to all who approached the Acropolis or looked up from the south and west. By a new regulation of c. 450, Athena Nike's priestess was to be selected democratically by lot from among all Athenian women. Round three sides ran a highly visible parapet embellished in the 410s with a series of panels, each 1.40 metres (4 feet 7 inches) high, bearing exquisite reliefs of Nike, and three of Athena Nike, in varying poses and in finely carved drapery. Nike is the personification of Victory – wingless in Athens, according to Pausanias, 'so that she will always stay where she is'. The message of victory, sent out in bright marble and bronze, could neither be missed nor mistaken. In a culture as visual as that of ancient Greece, simple messages like this could be very effectively disseminated through art. And above the columns, a continuous sculpted frieze represents complementary scenes of Greeks and Persians battling, among them probably the battle of Marathon.

that are most immediately apparent to any visitor: the west pediment, the first one sees, depicted the acquisition of Attica by Athena (the city's patron goddess) through a contest with Poseidon. The myth is not certainly attested before this period, and is seemingly a specifically Athenian one (see p. 112). Among the figures depicted was Cecrops, one of the early kings of Athens, a contemporary of Erechtheus, whose shrine lay opposite. On the east pediment was the birth of Athena. It is, then, a particularly Athenian, rather than generically Greek, thematic programme.

The metopes depicted Greeks fighting orientals, probably Amazons (west); the sack of Troy (north); Gods fighting Giants (east); Greeks fighting Centaurs (south). As depictions of civilization triumphing over barbarism, these have often been interpreted as symbolic of Athenian victory over the Persians. This is surely right to some extent. However, undisguised reference to victory over the Persians was to be found in the major – and publicly sponsored – art of wall-painting. A depiction of the battle of Marathon was commissioned by Cimon for what later became known as the Painted Stoa in the Agora of Athens (c.475–450); and the theme recurs on the Nike temple. In literature also, recent historical events were referred to directly, for example in Aeschylus' *Persians* of 472, which was sponsored by Pericles, under whose leadership Athens later embarked on the public building programme. There is, therefore, no apparent obligation to refer to the greatest events of the recent past obliquely; that seems rather to have been the Athenian preference.

If the decorative themes of the Acropolis buildings were intended to convey to outsiders a repeated and confident statement of Athens' past and of its victory, they would surely have made that point very effectively. But how would the population of Athens have reacted to the buildings? They certainly could not have missed them – even in the enormously greater expanse of modern Athens, they stand out like no others. Would people have agreed with the fine sentiments expressed by Pericles: 'Mighty indeed are the marks and monuments of our empire which we have left. Future ages will wonder at us as the present age wonders now'.

How often would most Athenians have gone up the steep slope to dedicate, or simply to look? Would the prominent walls – some still Mycenaean (c.1250–1200 BCE), but mostly of the mid-fifth century – have diverted their attention from present glories to past conflicts? Would they, in the manner of so many nowadays who live near stately homes or ancient sites, never quite manage to visit? Would they have roundly cursed the endless clink of the hammers and the clouds of marble-dust? Would they have grumbled about the price of food and the waste of money on the buildings? Certainly, they would have been well aware of the striking contrast between the huge and magnificent public buildings and the dull, comparatively uniform private houses (see pp. 89–90).

Elsewhere in mainland Greece, the architectural and artistic adornment of Pan-hellenic sanctuaries, such as Olympia and Delphi, also reached new heights in the classical period. They received dedications – from magnificent temples to humble terracottas – from all over the Greek world. And, like the Acropolis of Athens, they illustrate perfectly the strong link between art and religion, pleasing and placating the gods by dedicating something valuable and beautiful. But making dedications was not only to please the gods, it was an opportunity for conspicuous display to impress your fellow-men, and there was no better way than through elaborate buildings, sculptures, or precious objects.

Architects' skills continued to develop in the later fifth and fourth centuries, with an increasing emphasis on temple interiors. For example, the temple of Apollo at Bassae in Arcadia (built, according to Pausanias, by Ictinus, the designer of the Parthenon) featured the first example of a sculpted frieze inside the cella (now displayed in the British Museum), as well as the first recorded Corinthian capital. At Tegea, also in Arcadia and dating from soon after the mid-fourth century, powerful pedimental and metopal sculptures were matched on the interior by exceptionally fine mouldings – the architect wisely inserted doorstops to ensure that the doors could be opened fully without having to rest against the mouldings and risk damaging them.

On both sides of the Greek world, temples of exceptional size were built: the Doric tradition of South Italy and Sicily produced a good number, most spectacularly the enormous temple of Zeus at Acragas on Sicily, measuring 53 x 110 metres (173 x 361 feet), and still unfinished when the Carthaginians invaded in 406, a century after it had been started.

In Asia Minor, the Ionic order was favoured, as it had been in the archaic period, and the successor to the temple of Artemis at Ephesus was built on the site of the archaic one. In fact Asia Minor employed building traditions not found on the mainland. In large part these reflected the greater role among these Greek states and their neighbours of personal rule and patronage, combined with an ability, by virtue of their location, to mix artistic influences from the Greek world and the East. A fine example is the elaborate tomb architecture of Lycia, notably the Nereid Monument (see pp. 184–5) of the early fourth century, now in the British Museum. This has a tall podium decorated with relief sculpture depicting an oriental king in state, siege scenes and a battle of Greeks and Persians. Columns flank statues, perhaps of Nereids, or of personifications of winds. One of the pediments shows a man and woman enthroned; the other, poorly preserved, a battle. The most elaborate of all such tomb monuments was the one built c.370–350 at Halicarnassus for Mausolus, the ruler of Caria (see p. 72). This building, the original Mausoleum, was of the same basic form as the Nereid Monument, but was vastly greater in scale, some 42 metres (140 feet) high and topped by a huge four-horse chariot. Between its columns were thirty-six statues of the ruling dynasty, from life-size to one and two-thirds life-size. More adorned one of the steps of the podium. The sculpted friezes which decorated its sides were, according to Pliny, the work of the most famous sculptors of the day, Scopas, Bryaxis, Timotheus and Leochares. Like Phidias' statue of Zeus at Olympia and the temple of Artemis at Ephesus, it was counted one of the Seven Wonders of the world.

(Following pages) A lively representation by Lawrence Alma-Tadema (1836–1912) of 'Phidias and the Frieze of the Parthenon' (1868), an imaginative and colourful reconstruction of work in progress on the Parthenon's painted frieze. It gives a good idea of the bustle and noise that must have been a constant feature of the Agora during the years of building. Alma-Tadema visited Pompeii on his honeymoon in 1863 and was utterly captivated by the beauty of its classical remains. He spent the rest of his life recreating scenes from the ancient world, becoming something of an expert on classical architecture and archaeology through drawings and measurements taken on trips to Greece and Italy. The colours he used may seem rather vivid to us, but ancient sources describe luxurious fabrics left as votive offerings in striking shades, for example 'frog green'.

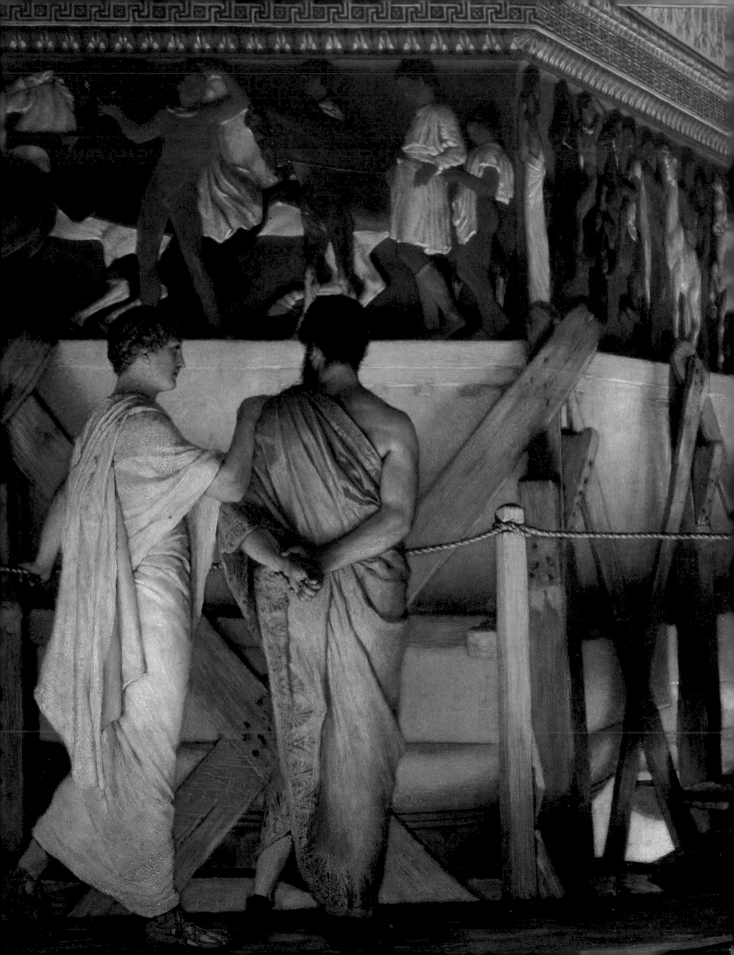

Free-standing sculpture

From the late archaic period, bronze became the favoured medium for free stand-ing statues since, because of its greater tensile strength, sculptors were now able to produce figures in freer poses than had been possible with marble. Parts of the figure were made separately and joined, each constructed around a moulded wax core with a terracotta covering into which the molten bronze would be poured as the wax melted and poured out. The vulnerability of bronze to re-use and decay means that we have very few originals (see pp. 229 and 350) and are reliant on literary sources and Roman copies for detail.

Arguably the leading sculptor of the human body in the fifth century was Poly-clitus of Argos. He was most famous for the Doryphorus, or spear-bearer, also known as the 'Canon', after the title of Polyclitus' account of the statue and its mathematics. It established new proportions for the human body, and its great influence is indicated not least by the many derivations from it in contemporary and later relief sculpture and vase-paintings. Later, another sculptor, Lysippus of

A sixth-century Boeotian terra-cotta of a man sawing wood. The ancient Greek word *architektōn* meant literally 'master carpenter'.

Sicyon (around the mid-fourth century), reduced the Polyclitan proportion of head to body from 7:1 to 8:1. This resulted in a taller-looking, slimmer body. Lysippus is said to have made some 1500 bronze statues, an impossible number given that each could take up to a year. Probably he was the designer rather than actual maker.

Perhaps the most famous of all Greek sculptors was Praxiteles, but he remains a shadowy figure. Even his origin is uncertain. There is reason to think there was a younger Praxiteles – perhaps a grandson – and it is possible that some of his works (for example, the Hermes and baby Dionysus at Olympia) were erroneously attributed to the more famous one. Praxiteles, who had a much more fluid style than previous work, creating sinuous, curving figures (the so-called Praxitelean 'S'-curve), is credited with re-introducing the use of marble and with introducing the female nude to life-size sculpture. He used as a model for his famous Aphrodite of Cnidus his mistress, Phryne, who notoriously 'in the festival of the Eleusinians and in the festival of Poseidon took off her robes in view of all the Greeks' (see pp. 108–9).

Chryselephantine statues of a little after the mid-sixth century have been found in fragments at Delphi. Otherwise, this most luxurious of sculptural media – used on the most lavish scale for the Athena Parthenos – remains known to us only through descriptions, and a few pieces of workshop debris from Olympia. It was there that the most famous example of the genre was housed, the massive seated cult-statue sculpted by Phidias for the temple of Zeus soon after he had created the Parthenos. While the surviving workshop débris does not belong to the Zeus, it does give an indication of technique. Pausanias – who says of the statue that 'the god himself bore witness to Phidias' artistic skill' – relates that in front of the statue stood a pool of oil to create humidity and prevent the ivory from cracking. A pool of water did the same for the Parthenos in Athens. Maintenance of such prestigious statues was both an obligation and a privilege; at Olympia the descendants of Phidias himself were appointed to the task and called *phaidruntai*, or 'polishers'. Not everyone was impressed, though: the second-century CE satirist Lucian cynically suggested the viewer should 'take a peep inside and what have we? One tangle of bars, bolts, nails, planks, wedges, with pitch and mortar and everything that is unsightly, not to mention a possible colony of rats and mice'.

Before leaving sculpture, it is worth considering the many thousands of terracottas, often finely painted, found throughout

Two jointed dolls of the fourth century from the sanctuary of Demeter and Persephone in Corinth. Such small terracotta figurines were easy to make and cheap to purchase as dedications or toys. These may have been dressed and dedicated to the two goddesses by young girls.

the Greek world. The tradition of terracotta manufacture had been a continuous one since the Early Iron Age (and it had Mycenaean predecessors). According to Pliny, the coroplast's art had been introduced to Magna Graecia from Corinth; certainly, the two areas shared a highly developed skill in terracotta working, which continued to flourish for architectural sculpture in the West, where hard stone and marble were not readily available. But it is fitting that we end this section with far humbler pieces, children's toys from Corinth (see previous page).

Vase-painting

> Gods chase
> Round vase
> What say?
> What play?
> Don't know
> Nice though

Louis MacNeice's verse wittily conjures up the scene on a Greek vase viewed from a cultural distance. Painted pottery was a humbler, more accessible, art, and consequently a much better indicator of what the average citizen was interested in than the magnificent buildings and sculptures which were commissioned with an eye to impressing outsiders and citizens alike. Of course, much pottery was not painted, and among the scenes which were painted appear a good number of activities we would expect to be restricted to the élite. Prime among these was the self-indulgent symposium, or drinking-party, favoured by young aristocratic males in the late archaic period and commonly represented on Athenian pottery of the time. But there are scenes of everyday activities more widely practised: craftsmen at work – potters (p. 209) and metalworkers (p. 90); or tradesmen – a cobbler (p. 147) or a fish-seller (p. 197). Women, as they did in the archaic per-

(Below, and opposite top and bottom) Terracotta drinking-cup (*rhyton*) in the shape of a cow's hoof, from Attica *c*.470–60. This is a charming example of a more humble painted art, showing scenes from rural daily life and, perhaps, an element of humour.

iod, appear mainly in subordinate roles: as playthings at the
symposium, filling water-jugs at the fountain, or inside
the home, perhaps playing with wool-baskets or at the
loom, or preparing for marriage (see Chapter 5).

Eye-catching among the red-figure vases of the
classical period are the stately products of artists like
the Berlin Painter, named after the location of perhaps
his most famous vase, whose mastery of anatomy combined with his artistic skill to produce some of the finest
studies of the human figure yet made. And in the second
quarter of the fifth century, a group of vase-paintings
took their inspiration from contemporary wall-paintings – now lost to us, but described by Pausanias
among others – to depict heroic themes with
many figures disposed at different levels. Later
fifth-century vase-painting developed in
two directions. One was characterized by
extremely precise, fussy drapery – the
vase-painting equivalent of the sculptures
of the day, especially of the temple of Athena
Nike (see p. 274). The other style was grander,
achieving realistic depictions, but with
greater economy.

Red-figure was not the only
vase-painting technique of this
period. The other prominent one
was white-ground, in which figures are painted on a white slip – a
thin solution of clay – with which the
vase has been previously covered.
White-ground technique had been used
sporadically from c.520 on a variety of
shapes, especially cups in the early
classical period. But for the
second half of the fifth century,
it was mostly restricted to
lekythoi, oil-vases with a
variety of uses. The
white-ground exam-
ples were usually
funerary, contain-
ing oil to be used in

the burial ceremony and then often being buried with the dead. The white gave a neutral background on which it was possible to paint a wider range of colours than the bright orange clay allowed, and now we have blue, green, red, yellow. Although

Painting

A reconstruction of the facade of Philip II's tomb at Verghina, showing the painted frieze.
(See also pp. 50–1.)

The prominence of painting in our written sources is not matched by its survival rate, so much of our understanding of Greek painting depends on how we interpret these sources. A reconstruction of part of the Painted Stoa's decoration is the most recent interpretation of many drawn from Pausanias' description, and probably the most accurate, since it draws on figures from contemporary vases for both individuals and groups. However, we need to be aware that sources can be written in a rhetorical fashion, often delighting in 'compare and contrast' biographies: for example, two classical painters are contrasted, Agatharchus as a quick painter, Zeuxis as slow; the mid-fourth century sculptor and painter Euphranor said that the Theseus painted by his rival Parrhasius had been fed on roses, while his own was fed on meat'.

The Painted Stoa at the edge of the Agora of Athens (c.475–450) was decorated by three famous painters: Micon, Panaenus, and Polygnotus. The Stoa was part of Cimon's improvement of Athens, and he and Polygnotus are said to have been friends, hence Polygnotus' inclusion of a covert portrait of Cimon's sister in the painting. The subjects depicted in the Stoa (such as the fall of Troy, the fight of Greeks and Amazons, and the battle of Marathon) typify the weighty themes usually employed on such buildings.

Private houses were not painted with figures, a rare exception being the house of Alcibiades, who 'once imprisoned the painter Agatharchus in his house until he had adorned it with paintings'. Agatharchus is said to have painted theatrical scenery for Aeschylus (see p. 243), an example of the association with prominent men of the day which reflects the high social status enjoyed by many ancient painters.

There was a close association of painting with public architecture. For example, the paintings from the temple of Poseidon at the Isthmus of Corinth of the mid-seventh century – the best preserved of the few archaic paintings we have – would probably have been commissioned by the ruling family of Corinth. They were painted on the exterior of the cella walls on a stucco background in a wide range of colours, with figures (of some 12 inches in height) and patterns closely comparable to those on Corinthian vases of the mid-seventh century.

From Verghina, the tomb of a Macedonian ruler, perhaps Philip II, illustrates the close identification between state and ruler which was to be characteristic of the Hellenistic world. The frieze on the facade depicts a hunt in a forest, perhaps showing Philip and his son Alexander the Great. The most complex composition of any surviving painting, it features figures in a variety of poses set at different levels and distances from the foreground, along with a variety of colours – brown, orange, blue, green, violet and purple.

Paintings like those in the Painted Stoa in Athens, or in the Pinakotheke (art-gallery) of the Propylaea on the Acropolis (see p. 269), were executed on whitened wooden panels. We know from remains in a Hellenistic stoa at Delphi that panels could be hung on a frame, secured by pegs. However, none of the panels themselves survives. In fact, the only paintings on wood which we possess are a series of plaques (see pp. 206–7) of c.540–500 from Pitsa near Corinth, the largest 6 by 12 inches, considerably smaller than the classical panels must have been. The Verghina paintings use both true fresco and secco; elsewhere, encaustic was used, in which pigments were mixed with heated wax, a technique also used for statuary and architecture.

the colours have worn off many of them, some spectacular examples remain. The
fragility of the colours renders them unsuitable for the rigours of normal use, but
ideal for burial vases. The white-ground lekythoi are unusual among Greek vases

An Athenian white lekythos (95 centimetres/3 feet 2 inches tall), c.410–400. Designed to contain oil, and decorated with funerary scenes in a broad range of colours against a white background, these were the most characteristic funerary vases in fifth-century democratic Athens (contrast p. 81). This is exceptional in size, some three times the average; in technique, being covered completely in white; in the use of shading and perspective; and in the range of colours, notably violet.

(Opposite) Part of one of the first Greek mosaics, from a house at Eretria, on the island of Euboea. It is dated c.360, partly by potsherds used in its construction. The pattern is formed by pebbles set into the mortar, and some examples use a preliminary sketch, exactly like that used on red-figure vases. Around the central palmette-and-sunburst tondo are symmetrically opposed scenes of a lion attacking a horse and a caped hero confronting griffins (mythical beasts, part lion and part eagle, favoured as a heraldic symbol by royalty).

in that their iconography almost always reflects their purpose. Where myths are depicted on them, they are usually related to death; but more often we see burial mounds and monuments hung with ribbons and dedications. Above all, those depicted are ordinary Athenians – notably women – grieving, crying at the tomb, bidding farewell.

The fourth century was a period of economic decline for Athens, and its painted pottery generally reflects this, coming to a halt around 320. But a last efflorescence of high-quality Athenian vases around the mid-century produced some of the finest of all depictions of the human body, a sense of volume acutely rendered with few lines.

By contrast, the fourth century in South Italy was a period when several local schools of vase-painting flourished. And on the Greek mainland, the mid-fourth century saw the emergence of pebble mosaics, with examples at the Cerameicus of Athens, Sicyon, and Eretria. But the greatest concentration, and highest quality, appear nearer the end of the fourth century in Macedonia, specifically the royal capital of Pella (see p. 71). Also from Macedonia came the first preserved classical wall-paintings, found at Verghina. So at the very end of the classical period art was moving in a different direction – a change of balance of artistic power and patronage not unrelated to the shift in the balance of political power. The story continues away from the centres we have been discussing in this chapter towards the art of the Hellenistic period. But that is for another time.

CHAPTER 11 — *Philosophy and Science*

Lesley Dean-Jones

Sources

The extant texts of the pre-Socratic philosophers are fragmentary, sometimes literally so, but mostly because, much later on, shorter or longer passages from the earliest works were excerpted by ancient scholars producing compilations (or tracts of their own) from the vast resources of the ancient libraries. These proved so popular that they were preserved by copying and recopying and the earlier philosophers' complete texts were allowed to perish. A further consequence is that it is sometimes difficult to identify when the compiler is quoting, paraphrasing or interpreting the philosopher's original text.

The opposite is the case with Plato. There is every indication that we have everything he ever wrote for publication, and a good deal published under his name which he did not write. Because of the reverence in which his texts have been held since their first appearance we have excellent manuscripts for all his works, and disagreements over his meaning usually have very little to do with minute textual discrepancies and more to do with the context of the individual work in which a particular passage appears.

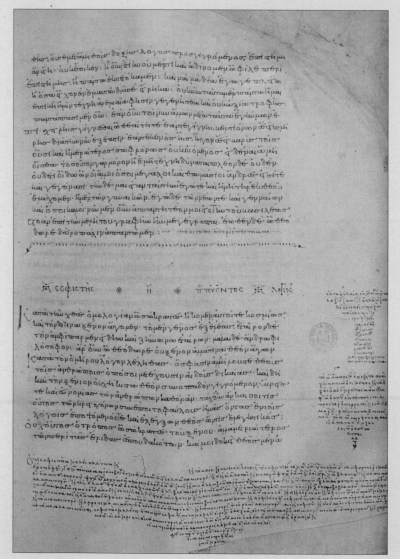

The situation is different again with Aristotle. His works were divided into two categories – the *exoteric* (intended for general publication), and the *esoteric* (notes he used in lecturing his students in the Lyceum). Only the esoteric works have survived, and the unpolished nature of the texts has led to enormous debate over the meaning of almost every passage. Passages from Aristotle also tend to be discussed in the light of other parts of the Aristotelian corpus as well as within their own context because it is generally agreed that Aristotle, more so than Plato, was aiming at a thoroughgoing philosophic system. But this only compounds the problems of interpretation as Aristotle frequently changed his ideas on various points and sometimes leaves an earlier passage beside an apparently contradictory later one.

The frustrations and limitations are obvious; scholars can be diametrically opposed to one another not only on the validity of one or another philosopher's ideas, but also on what he meant, and sometimes even on what he said. This is not to imply there is no consensus of opinion on any segment of early Greek philosophy, but it is a caveat against assuming that anything is cut and dried.

The earliest Greek theories about the nature of the world were framed as myths and divine revelations to poets and *mantics*, or prophets. At the beginning of the sixth century BCE, however, there was a gathering conviction that people could understand the

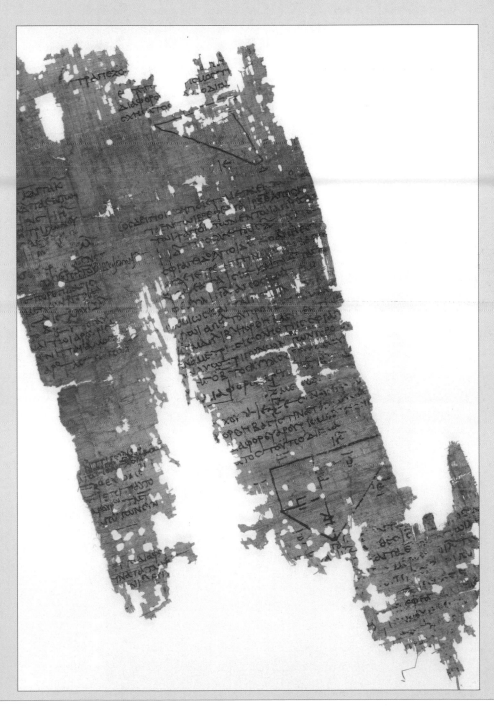

Plato's works were never at risk of being lost because they were so venerated by his immediate followers and all later philosophers. (*Opposite*) This is a page from a ninth-century manuscript of his dialogue the *Sophist*. The smaller writings in the margins are annotations by a medieval scholar and are typical of many manuscripts. Sometimes these *scholia* could be accidentally incorporated into the main text when it was being recopied, which is one way the original words of even a very well preserved text can be thrown into doubt. The writings that have survived from antiquity have done so mostly because they have been copied and recopied over and over. Occasionally, though, fragments of papyri that were discarded in antiquity are recovered, such as this geometrical papyrus (*left*) from the Hellenistic period, deriving from works which are otherwise lost. Sometimes, indeed, complete new works are discovered, as was the case with the papyrus called the *Anonymus Londiniensis*, discovered in 1892, which greatly increased our knowledge about ancient medicine.

forces that governed the world through the exercise of reason with no recourse to the supernatural – a type of thinking often called *natural philosophy*. This new dimension of Greek thought was first documented in Ionia (the coast of modern Turkey, at that time colonized by the Greeks), and the development is sometimes called the Ionian revolution.

Two important contributing factors in this revolution were leisure and wealth, allowing some Ionians time for reflection and contemplation. It also helped that Ionia's wealth came from trade with the ancient and learned cultures of Babylon and Egypt. But clearly other societies had had similarly thriving economies and did not develop the Greek fascination with trying to explain the world rationally.

An acknowledgement of the extent of Babylonian astronomy and of the use the Greeks made of it serves well to illustrate what was revolutionary about Greek natural philosophy. Babylonian astronomers had been observing and recording certain celestial phenomena for about a millennium before the first Ionian thinkers began to speculate upon the nature of the world. This had enabled them to predict certain celestial events and to begin to develop a mathematical system to aid in this prediction. The Babylonians were interested in the heavens because they believed they portended the future of individual kings and kingdoms on this earth. They were not interested in *why* a lunar eclipse would take place at a certain time, only *that* it would. They were not led to debate what the heavens must be like to produce such phenomena but to detecting what the heavens said the gods held in store for humans.

That the Greeks used Babylonian astronomical data (and similarly Babylonian and Egyptian mathematical observations and perhaps some medical knowledge) for the former type of inquiry is due in part to two quintessentially Greek institutions.

The first is the nature of the Greek priesthood. Unlike Babylon, Egypt and most other early civilizations, priests in Greece were not viewed as repositories of recondite wisdom. So there was no powerful vested interest in stifling any incipient secularization of the forces of nature. The second is open debate – the forerunner of democracy. Greek thinkers who wished to have their theories accepted by others had to frame them in a way that was amenable to public, rational discussion. So five reasons – wealth, leisure, trade, weak priesthood and open debate – go a long way to explaining the Ionian revolution. But ultimately we will never fully understand why it was that at the beginning of the sixth century BCE the Greeks conceived the hugely optimistic conviction that humans could understand, explain and perhaps even manipulate the workings of the natural world.

Western science and philosophy developed from a fundamentally empirical basis. The earliest Greek philosophers took the existence of this world as given and were concerned to explain why it was the way it was. But they also operated on an assumption that knowledge was of the real and eternal. Because things in the world are constantly changing, what they looked like at any given point was not what they 'really' were. Knowledge of the world, then, necessitated identifying a fundamental stuff that remained constant behind all the changes.

This endeavour would today be considered more properly the domain of science than philosophy, but the earliest stages of the Western tradition of both disciplines are intertwined. As philosophers, the early Greek thinkers relied on speculative theorizing rather than structured observations and experiments to test and demonstrate their theories. However, they believed that their theories could be shown to be correct by reference to commonly observable phenomena, and that competing theories could be objectively refuted by reference to the same sort of phenomena. Initially Greek thinkers used such observations sporadically when it supported their cause, and the concept of deliberately devising ways to try to undermine a theory in order to prove its truth never developed in Greek science. But by the end of the classical period there emerged disciplines (notably medicine and astronomy) in which theories were expected to take account of as much empirical evidence as possible, and some were supported by procedures which could be repeated at will with predictable results – rudimentary experiments. This type of observational methodology grew in time to be considered almost the antithesis of philosophical inquiry, but its roots lay in the same conviction that human reason could comprehend the order behind the changes in the world. The application of the term 'philosophy' to the systematic inquiry and theorizing about knowledge, being, the nature of the divine, morality, et cetera, also developed at the end of the classical period, largely under the influence of Plato – though Pythagoras was said to have originally coined the term to designate his devotion to learning.

THE MILESIANS

Thales

Thales was the first philosopher on record. He was active in the Ionian city of Miletus at the beginning of the sixth century BCE (he is said to have been a merchant), and is credited with the hypothesis that water was the underlying reality behind the world. His reasons for thinking this could have been that water was the only substance appearing in the world naturally in liquid, gaseous and solid state, or that all life was dependent upon water, but unfortunately we do not know for certain how he reached this conclusion.

It would seem that Thales viewed the world (water) as a living, generative thing in itself because he cites no external forces that would either have created it, or destroyed the things on it. He argued that even apparently inanimate things could contain soul (i.e. a self-moving life-force), citing the attractive properties of magnets and amber as an indication of this. But most rocks do not have even this minor indication of self-moving ability. If Thales meant to imply that all rocks did somehow contain soul, his citation of the properties of a magnet as support is a good example of the way Greek philosophers could use empirical observation without taking into consideration all

Thales of Miletus is considered to have been the earliest Greek philosopher. Although there was an apocryphal story of his absent-mindedness (he is said to have fallen down a well while star gazing), the historical Thales appears to have been very practical. He is said to have given advice on politics (advising the Ionians to have a single deliberative council) and engineering (dividing a river in two to make it fordable) and to have used his knowledge of predicting weather by the heavens to make a fortune in olives. He is also said to have predicted an eclipse.

its ramifications. On the other hand, if he was differentiating animate rocks from the inanimate variety he leaves unexplained how the life-principle water could become such an inanimate substance or how, once it had, it could regenerate itself.

Anaximander

Anaximander was also a resident of Miletus and a younger contemporary of Thales – possibly his pupil. He argued that the fundamental stuff of the world was the 'unlimited' (*apeiron* in Greek). It was infinite spatially and temporally, but it was also 'limitless' in that it could never be bounded by having a portion of it separated off – as could be done with water, for example, by putting some in a cup. In this respect it could not be identified with any naturally occurring substance. In Anaximander's world the water and the cup were both equally, and continuously, *apeiron*. Thus, though the *apeiron* was still a stuff, it could be apprehended only by the intellect. From this stuff 'seeds' of contraries, such as hot and cold, became separated off by eternal motion. Once these contraries were in existence the principles of justice and necessity brought about the creation of worlds by making them 'pay recompense' to each other, causing differentiation and change within a world. A world was destroyed when the contraries paid recompense to the *apeiron* for their initial creation by being reabsorbed into it. The conception of 'seeds' as the beginning of generation suggests Anaximander may have thought of the *apeiron* as a living being, for it is not clear that he considered necessity and justice to be agents or forces external to the stuff itself. They are never discussed as being spatially, temporally or metaphysically distinct from the *apeiron*.

Anaximenes

Yet a third Milesian, Anaximenes, active in the third quarter of the sixth century BCE and possibly the pupil of Anaximander, reverted to a naturally occurring stuff as his fundamental reality – it was air. As support for this he cited the ease with which air can oscillate between two of the most fundamental opposites – hot and cold. Blow on the hand with pursed lips and the air is cold; breathe with the mouth wide and the air is warm. He thus argued that all substances in the world – which were generally considered to be colder than air – were brought about by air being progressively condensed (into wind, clouds, water, earth, stone). Fire, the one substance considered warmer than air, was produced when air was rarefied. In this way Anaximenes made the first attempt to explain qualitative change along quantitative lines, though he still does not identify an agent of change, again probably because he thought of air as animate.

XENOPHANES

Xenophanes of Colophon was also born in Ionia *c*.570, but later settled in southern Italy. He accepted the view of the natural philosophers that the world was brought about by some formless stuff taking on form. However, he proceeded to ask not about the stuff, but about the force – god – that acted upon it to bring about change. He became famous for having pointed out that most cultures depict their gods in their own image, saying that if horses could fashion likenesses of gods they would resemble horses. So Xenophanes thought that the traditional views of gods could not be correct because they lacked a necessary absoluteness which would place them beyond the contingencies of this world. Instead, he proposed a deity, one and ungenerated, which governed everything by pure thought while remaining itself immovable.

Xenophanes' god is probably to be thought of as transcendent, but we do not know if he made clear exactly how it related to the things of this world. He may not have attempted to explain the relationship. This is because while the deity itself is real and eternal, and therefore a possible object of knowledge, Xenophanes thought human views about the changing things in this world could be no more than an opinion. This does not mean that he believed observation and reason could not advance knowledge; his view of the nature of god, after all, was posited on the existence of a rationally ordered world, and he himself argued that the presence of ocean fossils far inland suggested that oceans had once stood where now there was dry land. But to know this absolutely was the province only of the divine.

PYTHAGORAS AND PYTHAGOREANISM

Pythagoras, a late sixth century BCE contemporary of Xenophanes, was, like him, an Ionian (from Samos), who later settled in southern Italy. There, at Croton, he established a community bound not only by a shared philosophy based on reason, but also by religious beliefs. From the earliest formation of this community any advances that were made in Pythagorean doctrine were attributed to Pythagoras himself, so it is very hard to discern the earliest form of Pythagoreanism amid reports about its later accretions.

The two defining factors of Pythagoreanism are its mysticism and its concern with mathematics. Many of the beliefs which governed the ethical and moral behaviour of Pythagoreans, such as their belief in the transmigration of souls after death (they thought souls could pass into other bodies, including the bodies of animals, which led to the exclusion of meat from their diet), were based on mysticism rather than reason and are not easy to reconcile into a unified whole with their philosophical theories.

Pythagoras. That the square on the hypotenuse of a right-angled triangle was equal to the sum of the squares on the other two sides was a fact known to Babylonian mathematicians and engineers centuries before Pythagoras' name was given to the theorem. The Greeks called it 'Pythagoras' theorem' because they believed he had been the first to develop a visual proof demonstrating the truth of the theorem, though that proof has not survived.

The Pythagoreans believed that 'all things are number'. Traditionally this conviction arose from Pythagoras' observation that the difference in pitch between two notes on a harmonizing scale could be expressed as a mathematical ratio. For example, the highest note in an octave could be produced by halving the length of the string on the lyre which had produced the lowest note in the octave. Hence the relationship between the highest and lowest notes in an octave is represented by the ratio 2:1. The ratios between the fourth and fifth notes and the lowest note in an octave are 4:3 and 3:2 respectively. From this point the Pythagoreans went on to investigate a variety of numerical phenomena, largely in the geometrical field. They used number to express the creation of things, starting from a point and building up to objects: 1 was a point; 2 a line; 3 the simplest plane figure (a triangle); 4 the simplest solid (a tetrahedron) et cetera. More complex three-dimensional objects and abstract concepts were correlated with higher numbers. The forging of most of these correspondences can seem to have been a matter of caprice, the correlation of human with 250 for example. But in other instances, for example the correlation of justice with the number 4, they did give cogent reasons why certain numbers went with certain things and concepts, and their general belief was, presumably, that knowledge of the number of everything would lead to a knowledge of how everything related to everything else and so to a full understanding of the cosmic order.

Pythagoreanism gives no indication of what it is that the numbers were ordering, but it acknowledged that there could be no such thing as number (that which imposes form or limit) if there were not also something to be numbered. So the phenomena of the world came about through the interplay of two basic opposites – limit and unlimited – though it was only the limit – number – of a thing which could be known.

At some point in the fifth century a Greek, possibly a Pythagorean, made the discovery of incommensurables – in particular that the relation between the side and the diagonal of a square could not be expressed as a relation between whole numbers. The problem had, in fact, been known to the Babylonians in the form of the difficulty of rendering the square root of 2 in numerical terms, but their purposes had been served by using an approximation of its value. The Greeks, in response to the same problem, eventually developed a geometrical proof demonstrating the *impossibility* of expressing the number. That the ratio between two such closely related entities as a square and its diagonal could not be expressed as the proportion between two integers was a serious challenge to the claim that the universe could be understood by learning the numbers of things and the correspondences between them. The implications of this for the Pythagorean theory are demonstrated in the legend that divine displeasure caused the drowning of Hippasus, the Pythagorean who revealed the existence of incommensurables.

Nevertheless, the purity and the eternal nature of the relationships between numbers in mathematics, geometry and harmony were taken up by Plato, who saw mathematics as foreshadowing the purity of the knowledge of reality itself.

HERACLITUS

Heraclitus was active in another Ionian city, Ephesus, in the early fifth century BCE. What we have of his philosophy is preserved in discontinuous, deliberately obscure maxims, so it is difficult to see how all the elements of his system fitted together, but like his predecessors he believed there was an eternal rational order behind all the changes in the world. Heraclitus uses the word *logos* to refer to this order. There was an *order* in the universe which was the *cause* of things being in *proportion* and which could be understood by *reason* and expressed in human *speech*. The italicized words could all be translated by the Greek term *logos*, and Heraclitus seems to have all the connotations in mind whenever he uses the word.

One aspect in which Heraclitus' *logos* differed sharply from the theories of his predecessors was in claiming that it was the plurality of things and the tension between opposites which gave the world its unity, eternity and existence: the essence of the world, its *logos*, was change. He uses images to express this: a bow exists only because the string and the wood are pulling in opposite directions; life would have no meaning if death did not exist to mark it as a specific type of state; there could be no up without a down. In short, A could not exist if its opposite (not-A) did not also exist to give it meaning. In Heraclitus' *logos* there is no room for a single, fundamental, undifferentiated stuff.

Fire, though, does have special status in Heraclitus' thinking. Although there was never a time when everything was fire (nor, did he think, would there be), he believed everything could ultimately be 'exchanged' for fire. But this exchange was always carried out 'in measures', so that at any given time there was always the same proportional amount of the various things in the world – in this way the eternity of the world and the *logos* was maintained. Fire came by its special status for Heraclitus, in part at least, because it was more clearly an agent of change than any other substance and so at times came close to being identified with the physical manifestation of *logos* as cause. Because people participate in *logos* (reason) only when they are alive and warm, Heraclitus thus identified the immortal soul with the 'fiery' part of humans.

Heraclitus had no problem claiming it was possible to *know* a changing world once he had established that *change* was what was real and eternal about the world and had identified an agent of change – the fiery *logos* – albeit somewhat ambiguously. In these circumstances, change itself confers identity upon things as they are 'kindled and extinguished in measure'. Heraclitus' statement, 'Upon one who steps into the same river different waters at different times flow', does not deny the possibility of stepping into the same river twice, as it is sometimes paraphrased. It says that if the river did not change it would not be a river. If humans did not pass through all the stages of life from birth to old age they would be something else other than humans.

PARMENIDES

Parmenides of Elea (in southern Italy) was a younger contemporary of Heraclitus, and was active during the first half of the fifth century BCE. Like every Greek thinker who preceded him, he began from the premise that what can be known is real and eternal. He was, however, the first to deny that the things of this world had any share in this reality. He set himself the task of explaining not the existence of change but the nature of existence. His commitment to the absolute nature of reality may have been influenced by Xenophanes.

He begins by distinguishing two *paths* of thought. The one that must be followed, the Path of Truth, declares, '*is*, and *not to be* is impossible'. The path that must be rejected declares, '*is not* and *not to be* is necessary'. This strategy is a rejection of Heraclitus' claim that the existence of A necessarily implies the existence of some other thing which A is not, specifically its opposite. Parmenides is taking *Being* as the object of his inquiry, and it is manifestly absurd to say '*Being* is not', i.e. to deny the existence of existence. Nor is the phrase 'is not' made possible by the introduction into the Path of Truth of qualities or identities which are to be denied to *Being*. Parmenides viewed the relationship as reciprocal, and if they were to be denied to *Being* so was existence denied to them and hence there was no place for them on the Path of Truth.

This does not mean Parmenides makes no negative statements about Being – but things that *are not* cannot be the objects of knowledge. One cannot know or speak about *not-Being*.

For Parmenides, then, only sentences consonant with '*Being is*' are true. For example, '*Being* is eternal' is one such because *Being* can never not be. Similarly, the statement '*Being* is continuous, indivisible and homogeneous' is also true because nothing else can exist to sunder it from itself. Parmenides views *Being* as finite since he considers finiteness an aspect of perfection and self-sufficiency, but there is nothing which bounds *Being*. In particular there is no void, so *Being* is immovable.

Although he never followed the impossible path of *is not*, Parmenides did follow the Path of Seeming, which employed both *is* and *is not* to explain what gave rise to pervasive mortal opinions about the world. He appears to have developed a fully-fledged theory of the origin of the universe generated from the contraries *light/dark* and *dense/rare*, all the while maintaining that the perceived world is not real and is therefore unknowable. We do not have much information about this part of Parmenides' theory, and – naturally enough, since even its originator did not vouch for its truth – it does not seem to have been very influential in later Greek philosophy.

Parmenides' legacy was to make Greek philosophers question how to combine reason and experience in examining the nature of reality; and also how, without invoking the paradox of the existence of *not-Being*, to explain the occurrence of divisibility and motion. From his first attempts at deduction or abstract logical reasoning flowed the later Socratic elenchus, mathematical proof, Platonic theory and Aristotelian logic.

Among Parmenides' followers were Zeno of Elea and Melissus of Samos (both active in the mid-fifth century BCE). Together, this group is referred to as the *Eleatics*. Zeno and Melissus developed new arguments in support of their teacher's view of reality as an indivisible unity, and particularly in support of the view that motion was impossible and only seemed to take place. Because, before any distance could be covered, half of it had to be covered, and in turn half of this distance had to be covered and so on, with the distances concerned converging on, but never reaching, zero, so no distance could ever be covered. In one famous illustration of the paradox Zeno argued that Achilles could never catch up with a tortoise which had started ahead of him.

EMPEDOCLES

Empedocles was born *c*.492 and hailed from Sicily. Like his southern Italian neighbours Xenophanes and Pythagoras, he was interested in religion and mysticism. He accepted Parmenidean logic that what *is* must always be, i.e. it cannot undergo qualitative change. But he insisted also on the primary empirical observation of the Ionians that this world has a relative reality. He achieved this by explaining the process of change in the world as the continuous separation and recombination of four unchanging but, contrary to Parmenides, divisible elements – earth, air, fire and water – in differing proportions. In contrast to Thales' and Anaximenes' systems, water was never *not-water*, and air never *not-air*, but mixed together in different amounts they could give the appearance of different materials.

Empedocles also included two forces in his system, more clearly non-corporeal than Heraclitus' fire/*logos*, to explain why combination and separation should take place at all. He called the two forces *Love* and *Strife*. under the influence of *Love* all the elements combined; under the power of *Strife* they separated. The universe itself, Empedocles argued, oscillated between complete *Love* – when all the elements were combined in a homogeneous and undifferentiated whole – and complete *Strife*, when they were strictly separated from each other. A variety of objects were created by the combination and separation of these elements as they travelled between the two poles, from *Love* towards *Strife*. The objects formed in this way were a matter of chance, and only those which were viable survived.

Empedocles, then, returned to the speculative materialism of the Ionians, but with great advances in the theory of causation. Explaining the phenomenon of change by proportional mixture of a number of basic elements rather than by qualitative change of a single substance was to remain the foundation of science for two and a half millennia, and for a considerable portion of that time the accepted elements (earth, air, fire and water) were Empedoclean. More importantly, Empedocles clearly differentiated between stuff and force. His thinking had a strong influence on subsequent Greek thought.

ATOMISTS

The original developer of the *Atomist* theory was Leucippus in the mid- to late fifth century BCE, but its more famous proponent was Democritus – a slightly younger contemporary of Socrates. However, as Atomism was, like the theories of

Empedocles and Anaxagoras, almost a direct answer to Parmenides, it is essentially pre-Socratic.

Like Empedocles, the Atomists combined an acceptance of Parmenidean logic on the nature of *Being* with a conviction that this world was produced from such *Being*. The Atomists agreed with the Eleatic argument that what *is* has to be eternal, indivisible, unchanging and homogeneous, but they believed there was an infinite number of these entities – the atoms, literally things which could not be cut. A plurality of such entities could exist in the Atomists' system because they rejected Parmenides' claim that *not-Being* could not be; void was necessary to allow for motion. Only by admitting the existence of three things Parmenides had rejected (plurality, void and motion) could *Being* produce this world.

(Right) Democritus is said to have found the follies of the human race humorous and by the time of Cicero at the latest had earned the nickname 'The Laughing Philosopher'. Confirmation of his measured response to life is found in his ethical fragments which record such sentiments as, 'The life without festival is a long road without an inn', and 'More men become good through practice than by nature'.

Atoms differed in size and shape and were eternally in motion. They clashed together randomly but sometimes, in the infinity of time, produced viable combinations that led to the generation of worlds such as ours. Combining in different proportions and configurations, the atoms produced all the phenomena in our world, including the *secondary* qualities of colour, smell and taste. (Touch was a function of atomic shape and therefore a *primary* quality.) Anything formed by the conjunction of atoms would ultimately be destroyed because of the admixture of void which would allow two atoms, however tightly united, to be sundered, either through blows from external atoms or through an object's own internal atomic motion.

Taking account of appearances in this world could lead one to the truth because the qualities of things were sensed by the soul, which was itself a material, perishable body formed from small round atoms (as was fire). These experiences were true in that they were real movements of the atoms in the soul, but they were not necessarily a true reflection of the way things were. To reach the eternal truths of atoms, void and motion, one had to use rational cognition – another function of the material soul – and argue from the visible to the invisible.

ANAXAGORAS

Like Empedocles and the Atomists, Anaxagoras of Clazomenae (born *c*.500 BCE and active primarily in Athens) said change resulted from shifts in the proportions of a number of things rather than from qualitative change of one stuff, but he argued there were no things in the world (such as elements or atoms) that were more real and eternal than any other. There was, he said, a portion of everything in everything. Earth looks like earth because it has more earth than anything else, but it also contains a portion of every other material in the world. This is why seeds planted in the earth can grow into grass, corn and trees. The material in the earth is recombined in different proportions to produce the material of the plants. In turn these are eaten by animals and the materials recombine to form blood, bones and hair. Throughout the series of changes there always remains some of everything in everything, so when an animal dies its body recombines with the earth. Anaxagoras insisted that matter was infinitely divisible and, however small a piece of matter became, it always had a piece of everything in it. 'Pure earth' was a mere abstraction.

Order was imposed on the separation and recombination of the various materials in the world by the action of *nous*, 'mind'. This was apparently a non-corporeal force that was everywhere in the world,

but it is unclear how Anaxagoras deployed it other than to explain that the world was ordered rationally.

THE SOPHISTS

In the mid-fifth century the rights and obligations of both individuals and entire societies began to supplant speculation about the physical world as the major topic of philosophical debate. There had been a long tradition of ethnographic thought. (The first geographer/ethnographer, Hecataeus, was a Milesian contemporary of Anaximander and Anaximenes.) It provided a wealth of data showing that concepts of the good life varied widely from culture to culture without necessarily exciting any adverse consequences. On what basis, then, could one decide what really constituted *aretē*, 'excellence' or 'virtue' in human life? Originally the term *aretē* was taken to cover excellence or virtue in many areas of human endeavour. It was only after Aristotle that the term was applied almost exclusively to moral excellence, thanks largely to what Socrates began.

A conjectural reconstruction of the map that accompanied Hecataeus' description of the world in two books, one devoted to Europe and one to Asia (in which continent he included North Africa). He believed the world was a disk surrounded by Ocean and divided into four quadrants, on an east–west axis by the Mediterranean and Black Seas and on a north–south axis by the Ister and the Nile. Although Herodotus ridicules much of Hecataeus' geography he takes a great deal of ethnographic information from him, especially about Egypt. Herodotus tells us that in a meeting with an Egyptian priest Hecataeus boasted of being able to trace his lineage back through sixteen generations (to a god), only to have the priest counter with a pedigree of 345 generations!

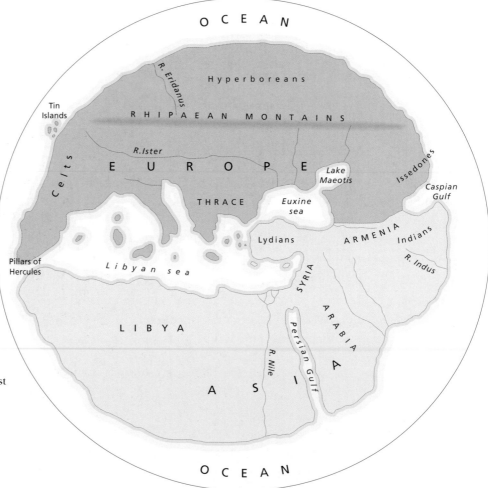

The issue had special significance at Athens, owing to its new-found prominence in the Mediterranean after the Persian Wars. Men who concerned themselves with the theoretical side of these issues, largely non-Athenian, were attracted to Athens. They were given the appellation *Sophists*, 'teachers of wisdom'. Earlier philosophers may, of course, have been considered wise (Thales was counted one of the Seven Sages), but their theories did not hold out the promise of practical application. By claiming to be able to teach *aretē* the Sophists attracted not just pupils or followers, but paying customers.

Many of these customers wanted to learn not only how to choose the best course of action in their own lives, but also how to influence public policy in the debates of the Assembly. Some Sophists obliged by offering to teach not only *aretē* but also, independently of the content of their theory, how best to frame an argument to convince an audience of the correctness of a position – the skill of rhetoric (see p. 232). Many sophistic theories on the nature of moral virtue, which in several cases argued it was acceptable for the strong man to place his own needs and desires above those of the polis, were unpalatable to traditional Athenian sensibilities anyway; but the Sophists' concern with forms of argument made traditional Athenians doubly suspicious that their followers were taught to aim for power rather than truth. By the end of the fifth century, the term Sophist had lost much of its original dignity and meant rather one who through argument could make a self-serving position, which even he knew was false, appear stronger than the truth. Such training was obviously a threat to the Athenian democracy.

Yet, although most of our evidence about sophistic thought derives from hostile sources (primarily Plato, no friend of Athenian democracy himself) we can see in some of their theories the seeds of the Western humanist tradition in ethics and politics. Protagoras, for example, argues that no individual or society can identify an absolute justice to which all societies should be held. Whatever laws a society as a whole takes to be just *are* just for that society, a form of relativism. A 'wiser' man within a society may have 'more valuable' ideas on what is just, but unless he can peaceably persuade the society to adopt his laws they do not constitute 'truer' justice. Protagoras would, of course, consider himself one of the 'wiser' men with 'more valuable' ideas.

SOCRATES

Socrates was a native Athenian. Like the Sophists he was concerned with moral virtue, but unlike them he did not claim to know what it was; his search for an answer led him to show that the Sophists did not know either. He did this by applying the assumption of the early natural philosophers that knowledge is of the real and eternal, thereby contradicting Protagoras' claims for relativism. If virtue can be known, all the different forms it takes in this world are simply manifestations of an underlying eternal unity. To know virtue was to be able to give an account or definition of it that would hold true at all times and in all places. If people could not do

The death of Socrates

In 399 BCE, a small majority of Athenians in a jury of 501 were persuaded to vote against Socrates on charges of introducing new gods and corrupting the city's youth. The defence which Plato presents Socrates as making in his *Apology* ('Defence') is anything but apologetic, and if Socrates said as much it may have disposed some otherwise neutral jurors to vote against him.

Since Socrates refused to change his way of life or go into exile, the only way to rid Athens of his presence was to execute him (there were no long-term prisons). Because a festival of Apollo was underway at the end of the trial he could not be put to death straightaway, so he was held for a time in a prison close to the court-house in the Agora. This building has recently been identified. There are a series of cells opening off a central passageway, one of which has a tiled floor and a drain as if it was used for ablutions. This would be the room to which Socrates withdrew and bathed just before his execution. In one corner of the room, which controlled the entrance (presumably the jailer's room), there was a compartment in the wall filled with *aryballoi*, small jars used for perfumes and drugs. Executions in Athens were carried out by giving the prisoner a carefully pre-measured lethal dose of hemlock.

One of the most interesting objects in the building was a statuette (see p. 304) which was found in the courtyard. It very much resembles other representations we have of Socrates and it is interesting to speculate how soon after the death of Socrates the Athenians repented of their decision and offered such memorials to him.

Although he lived a life that was not without influence, it was the manner of his death and the effect it had on Plato that caused Socrates to be venerated as the perfect philosopher – one who single-mindedly pursues truth and knowledge for their own sake and is willing to pay the ultimate sacrifice rather than abandon that pursuit.

In the Uffizi 'The Death of Socrates' by Charles Alfonse Dufresnoy (1611–68) shows the death of the philosopher in heroic style (see also p. 354). During his imprisonment Socrates engaged daily in philosophical conversations with his followers, and in the *Phaedo* Plato portrays him on the day of his death discussing the possibility of the soul's immortality and drinking the hemlock with a complete lack of concern for death. However, contrary to the impression conveyed by Plato and Dufresnoy, the effects of a fatal dose of hemlock are excruciatingly painful; the poison, coniine, causes paralysis of the nervous system.

Socrates may originally have earned his living as a sculptor, the profession of his father Sophroniscus, but he renounced any profession early in life in preference for spending his time questioning other Athenians, often prominent men, about their views on courage, justice and other virtues. He developed a form of argument called the 'Socratic elenchus' by which he led his interlocutors to refute themselves, showing that their beliefs on a single subject were contradictory. Socrates was physically unprepossessing to the point of ugliness, and this in conjunction with his poverty led to him being a figure of fun for Athenians who did not appreciate the power of his intellect. On other young Athenians his effect was spellbinding; Plato tells us that Alcibiades (see p. 158) had (unfulfilled) erotic designs on Socrates.

this, claimed Socrates, they did not know virtue; in fact they were in the same state of ignorance as Socrates – except that Socrates was aware of his own ignorance and could therefore be said to be wiser. Being able to produce a list of examples of virtue, or even always to have behaved virtuously, did not mean a person knew what virtue was. If people could not explain what it was that made their actions virtuous there was no guarantee they would behave virtuously in all future situations.

Although virtuous action did not guarantee knowledge, Socrates argued that knowledge of virtue entailed that one would act virtuously because nobody does wrong willingly. Doing wrong injured a person's soul – the real person inside the body – and as nobody would willingly injure themselves, nobody would willingly do wrong; in fact the only reason anybody ever did wrong was because they did not know true virtue. Once they had this knowledge they would be virtuous. Socrates' aim in his discussions (he did not claim to teach and accepted no fee) was to divest his listeners of their belief that they knew what virtue was and to turn them to searching after the true, eternal nature of virtue.

Despite these noble aspirations Socrates was forced to drink hemlock by the Athenian state. Doubtless this was partly because, in the minds of his contemporaries, he was associated with the Sophists, because he challenged traditional ideas about virtue, and had taught a few oligarchic traitors (such as Alcibiades and Critias) who had been part of the Socratic circle before pursuing the sort of political life Socrates criticized so roundly. But some men would also have seen Socrates' own message as a threat to civic unity. In Greek society virtue had always been a publicly bestowed quality. To tell people that their virtue could come only from philosophical inquiry, not socially mandated mores, struck at the cohesiveness of society.

PLATO

Plato's introduction to philosophy at the hands of Socrates led him to believe that philosophy was best conducted in the form of questioning with a fellow-seeker after knowledge. Hence Plato wrote his philosophic works in the form of dialogues between two or more people, one of whom was usually Socrates. The earlier dialogues are known as the *Socratic* or *aporetic* dialogues because like the original Socrates they leave the reader in a state of *aporia* – at a loss for any positive idea about the nature of virtue. Gradually, though, Plato began to place some of his own positive doctrines about virtue in the mouth of Socrates; these works are known as the *middle dialogues*. In the *later dialogues* he criticized many of these positive doctrines.

Being Greek, Plato accepted the principle that if virtues were to be the objects of knowledge they must be real and eternal. In the middle dialogues he placed these eternal realities in a transcendental realm, claiming that this world was only a world of appearances because what was virtuous seemed to shift so much. To this extent he was influenced by Eleatic arguments on existence, but unlike Parmenides he did not deny this world all contact with reality. For Plato there had to be some reason the world had the appearance it had. This is why he rejected the Empedoclean and Atomist theories that the world came into being through chance conjunctions of eternal elements or atoms, and in one of the middle dialogues he has Socrates ridicule Anaxagoras' theory of *nous*, because, he says, it does not explain why things are the way they are, only how.

Plato's Theory of Forms or Ideas

Plato explained that this world is ordered the way it is because the things of this world 'partake' in the transcendental realm of real, eternal being – although he never specifies what he visualizes this 'partaking' relationship to be. According to him, the reason so many people can recognize, for example, particular actions as virtuous without knowing the real and eternal nature of virtue is that their souls (or part of their souls) also existed in the transcendental realm before they were born. So when they see any particular thing on this earth 'partaking' of a *Form* (the true, unchanging thing behind the idea of, for example, 'virtue', 'good' et cetera), their souls recognize, some more dimly than others, the reality (or *Form*) through the image. This is known as Plato's Theory of Forms.

Plato argued that the only way to be truly virtuous was to struggle toward a knowledge of the real and eternal virtues in this life, using particulars to begin with, but gradually moving through more and more abstract knowledge (including the Pythagorean mathematical truths) until finally the true philosopher could contemplate the real and eternal virtues in their transcendental purity. This could be achieved only with a pure soul, the real and eternal part of a human.

As the scion of a distinguished Athenian family Plato would have been expected to pursue a political career. But after the horrors of the Thirty (in which his uncle Critias – an erstwhile follower of Socrates – played a prominent part), and the execution of Socrates by the restored democracy he renounced all active participation in Athenian political life. He retained a great interest in political theory and in 366 BCE began an attempt to apply his theory by shaping the young Dionysius II of Syracuse into a philosopher king. The experiment was a complete failure, ending with the assassination of Dion – Dionysius' uncle and Plato's close friend – in a conspiracy supported by Callippus, a follower of Plato sent to aid Dion. After this Plato made no more forays into political activity and at the end of his life, when he once again constructed an imaginary ideal state, he made the sovereign power the law, to which the rulers too were subject.

Roman mosaic of the Academy, found near Pompeii in the first century CE. In *c.* 380 BCE Plato began to teach in the gymnasium in the grove sacred to the hero Academus, situated just outside Athens. He later bought a piece of land in the area, built himself a house and used this and its grounds as his school. The Academy, as it was called, had a religious centre in a shrine to the Muses, and Plato may have been influenced both in organizing his followers into a coherent group and in giving his group a religious focus by his respect for Pythagoras. The Academy expanded and had continued influence under a succession of leaders (though not Aristotle, who started his own school, the Lyceum) until it was shut down by the emperor Justinian in 529 CE.

In many of his dialogues Plato talks of the soul as having three parts: the best part the intellectual, the worst the appetitive, and between them the spirited. A philosopher had to control his spirit and appetites completely by the use of intellect, having as little to do with the appetites as possible, in order to achieve true knowledge.

Once having contemplated the *Forms*, philosophers would be armed with the knowledge not only of how best to live one's life, but also how to govern a society so that it too was as good as possible. The nature of such knowledge (immediate personal contemplation of the *Forms*) meant that philosophers could not write it down, for example as laws, and leave the actual governing of the city to someone else. For Plato, philosopher-kings served the same function in the just/virtuous city as the intellect did in a just/virtuous person: to rule the spirited and appetitive elements of the population.

Plato felt that attention to all three elements (spirit, intellect and appetite) was necessary for the perfectly virtuous city because, just as no individual philosopher could survive if he did not eat and drink when absolutely necessary, no city could survive if it did not have an 'appetitive' section of the population concerned to produce the necessities of life. Neither could it defend itself against attack if it did not have spirited individuals acting as soldiers. As in a virtuous individual, so in a just city, the ruling and spirited elements worked in concert and had little to do with the appetitive element.

Later in life Plato himself came to criticize his own Theory of Forms – though it is not clear he ever gave it up entirely. One problem was that if partaking in the *Form Man* made a man a man, what made the *Form Man Man*? Did it 'partake' of itself, or of yet another *Form*? This possibility of an infinite regress was called the 'third man argument'.

There was also the problem of the range of things that must exist in the transcendental realm if particulars in this world were to be understood as images. Was there, for instance, a *Form* for mud? Plato's dissatisfaction stemmed from insisting on a dichotomy between what is real, eternal and knowable on the one hand, and the transient appearances of this world on the other, whilst at the same time wanting the former to impose order on the latter. His greatest pupil was to resolve the conflict by denying the dichotomy.

ARISTOTLE

Aristotle was born at Stagira in Chalcidice. At seventeen he went to Athens to study at Plato's Academy. He too believed knowledge had to be of the real and the eternal, and that the real and eternal imposed order on the world, but unlike Plato he located reality and eternity within worldly things. Despite their constant change, he argued that the types of those things remained the same. And it is these types, the Aristotelian *forms*, which are the real and eternal objects of our knowledge. For him, *form* was one of the *four causes*, or reasons, why the world is the way it is. Aristotle's causes were *form, matter, efficient* and *final cause*.

For Aristotle, forms could never exist independently; they had always to be sub-stantiated in matter, the second of the four causes. Like forms, matter was real and eternal and could not exist independently; it had always to exist in conjunction with a form, and this conjunction was called a substance. It was the form which made a substance knowable; pure matter could never be known because by defini-tion it was not a *type* of thing. The instant it was given even the most basic form of the four elements – earth, air, fire or water – it became a type of thing, and it was this type which was knowable.

This made form the superior cause, though matter was just as necessary to a sub-stance. Forms themselves could be ranged hierarchically – a substance with a less complex form could be utilized as matter for a more complex form; for example, clay was the matter of bricks, bricks the matter of houses, and so on. The more complex forms were thought of as superior because they motivated the production of the sim-pler substances. The reason clay, which has the potential to become brick, becomes brick is because bricks in turn have the potential to become a house, so it was for the sake of a house that bricks were made. It is the potential, more complex form which explains the existence of the simpler, actual substance. The agent which turns the potential form into an actual substance acting as matter is the efficient cause, and the reason the potentiality is actualized is the final cause. So, to explain the existence of a house Aristotle would say that a builder (*efficient cause*) built bricks and wood (*matter*) into a house (*form*) for the sake of shelter (*final cause*).

For Aristotle, living beings were the substances *par excellence* in the sublunary realm (the terrestrial part of the universe below the moon) both because they had the most complex forms and because their formal, final and efficient causes coa-lesced. The efficient cause of an animal was the animal form in the father. The form of an animal is the sum of all the functions it could perform (including reproduc-tion), and its final cause was to actualize its potentiality by performing all these functions, in other words by being fully its form.

However, Aristotle did not think all reality was immanent in the things of this world. He believed the purest and best reality existed in the superlunary realm where, like living beings in this world, the heavenly bodies were self-moving and had no end beyond realizing their potential. However, unlike things of this world, the heavenly bodies were also eternal in their own right because they were com-posed of pure *aether*, the only immortal conjunction of form and matter, something which could not exist in the sublunary world where substances were composed of the four Empedoclean elements.

Aristotle conceived of the universe as a number of concentric spheres. The earth lay at the centre surrounded immediately by spheres of water, air and fire. The fur-ther outlying spheres carried the stars and planets around the earth; and finally the outermost sphere held the fixed stars. Beyond these lay the primary *Unmoved Mover*. This is the 'god' of the Aristotelian universe because it is the ultimate explanation for all change and movement within it. It does not move because it is pure form. It

Plato and Aristotle

Plato had been one of the younger members of the Socratic circle, and after the death of his teacher he took it upon himself first to record the nature of Socrates' teaching and later to elaborate it into a positive doctrine. His answer to the conundrum of why people could recognize virtue when they had such a hard time saying what it was, was to suggest the existence of transcendental *Forms* beyond the confines of this world, which all souls saw before being incarnated upon this earth. Particular instances of virtue were recognized as such because they partook in these *Forms*, of which humans retained a dim memory. True knowledge of the *Forms*, though, could belong only to philosophers who had spent their lives in arduous pursuit of the truth, divorcing themselves as far as possible from the particulars of this world. It is these transcendental *Forms* Plato is indicating by pointing upwards in Raphael's famous painting 'The School of Athens'.

Aristotle studied under Plato at the Academy and won his respect. It is said Plato called him 'the Mind' and refused to start his lectures until he was present. But in Raphael's painting Aristotle is pointing down. This is because he made his *forms*, the eternal realities that could be known, immanent (or inherent) in the particulars of this world. Although for Aristotle knowledge of the heavenly bodies was ideally the best sort of knowledge, knowledge of the inner workings of an ant, for example, was surer knowledge, and lent itself to an understanding of nature in its entirety.

> Inasmuch as it is possible for us to obtain more and better information about things here on the earth, our knowledge of them has the advantage over the other [eternal things]; ... though there are animals which have no attractiveness for the senses, yet for the eye of science, for the student who is naturally of a philosophic spirit and can discern the causes of things, Nature which fashioned them provides joys which cannot be measured.
>
> (Aristotle, *Parts of Animals*)

(*Opposite*) 'The School of Athens' (1509–11) by Raphael (1483–1520), showing the philosophers engaged in disputation beneath the arching ceiling of a great basilica. Whereas Plato points upwards, Aristotle, more down-to-earth, points downwards

(Opposite) Womb Amulet. Among the most popular magical amulets were those depicting the womb as an upside-down jar locked underneath by a key. Whether the key was meant to prevent conception by locking the semen out, or miscarriage by locking the fetus in, or perhaps to curtail extended uterine bleeding, cannot be determined. Its function may have depended on the desire of the wearer. The fact that the locked womb could be accompanied by one or more figures carrying cornucopias suggests that such amulets were thought to be effective in matters other than the purely medical.

contains no matter and so is always fully actualized. It has no potentiality, so there is nothing prior to it. It moves the universe by acting as an ideal, inspiring other entities to actualize their potential. The matter from which the heavenly bodies are constituted can never undergo alteration. However, because they are formed of matter they exist in space and time and therefore have the potential for movement. They actualize this movement in the trajectory of a circle, itself the symbol of eternity. Living beings are motivated to find sustenance in order to achieve their full potential, and are then further motivated to reproduce other individuals of their species to achieve the potential of species eternity.

Humans were the highest form of living being on this earth because they possessed intellect, or *nous*. To actualize their distinctively human potential, therefore, individuals had to engage in intellectual activity. However, because they were not pure form, like the primary Unmoved Mover, they also had to actualize their other potentialities – but always, of course, under the guidance of *nous*. The virtuous life required a certain amount of material well-being in order to be able to achieve these potentialities, and accordingly Aristotle's ethics have been accused of being an apology for traditional mores which assessed the success of a man's life by his wealth and adherence to social values, but this is to miss the central position of intellectual activity in Aristotle's ethical system and the fact that all other action took place in accordance with it. Aristotle was attempting to systematize and explain morality – to turn it into a 'science' of ethics.

THE EMERGENCE OF SCIENCE

The earliest Greek philosophy had been fundamentally empirical in that it assumed the world existed. Sometimes philosophers would use observations of this world to support their view of what it 'really' was – for example, Anaximenes' observation that compressed air blown through pursed lips was cooler than rarefied air blown through an open mouth; and Xenophanes' appeal to sea fossils found inland (see p. 292). But there was no systematic collection of data before Aristotle.

Medicine

However, the Greeks had begun amassing a large body of empirical data in the area of healing long before the beginnings of natural philosophy. A record of what measures seemed to have worked in which circumstances was seen to be necessary if they were not to be totally helpless in the face of disease.

Healing before the fifth century, though, was hardly a science. The measures which were thought to work were just as likely to involve incantations and magical amulets or appeals to the healing god Asclepius as herbs, diet or regimen, and there was no interest in investigating the nature of the human body, disease itself, or why the measures worked.

By the time of Hippocrates in the mid-fifth century BCE, however, the development of a scientific form of medicine can be identified which incorporated the principles of natural philosophy. It eschews magic entirely. Gods themselves could restore health only in accordance with natural laws, and these laws could be learned and applied by humans. Hippocratic medicine (the term is used to cover most of the rational medicine we know of in the fifth and fourth centuries) uses some traditional forms of healing, but only those that can be explained with reference to theories of the human body and disease.

Medicine was also differentiated from natural philosophy as a science because practitioners believed knowledge about the objects of medical study (disease and the human body), rather than being the product of one man's intellectual theorizing, had grown over time and could be improved through further empirical observation. The purpose of many of the medical treatises of the period was simply to record such observations. Moreover, the truth of a medical theory could be demonstrated or disproved by the results of its application to a series of different bodies – a source of knowledge not available to theorists speculating about the cosmos.

It is also in early Greek medicine that 'scientific method' takes its first faltering steps beyond passive observation of the world. For example, one anonymous treatise suggested the first simple experiment: leave a jar of water out overnight to freeze, let it melt the next day and you will find that some of the water has been lost. This was an experiment because it was phrased as something to be done deliberately to see what would happen, and the results were repeatable.

However, the author used it to support his theory that snow was harmful for humans to drink because the finest parts of water were separated off by freezing leaving only the heavy 'muddy' parts behind. He did not consider or test alternative explanations for the reduction in the volume of water after freezing.

Another anonymous Hippocratic author recommended cutting open a goat's head to prove his theory that epilepsy was caused by an excess of phlegm in the brain. The Greeks likened the behaviour of goats to that of epileptics, and the author assures his readers that if they were to open the head of a goat they would find the brain excessively wet and foul-smelling. We do not know how often, if ever, the author followed his own recommendation. Not only did no early medical writer dissect a cadaver, human or animal, but the Hippocratics made very little use of what was known about animal anatomy from sacrifices, et cetera, in their treatises. This was doubtless partly because they did not conceive of the bodies of quadrupeds as all that similar to those of humans, but more importantly their primary interest was in disease as it was manifest in the human body. The study and knowledge of symptoms were considered the cornerstone of medical expertise, not a knowledge of normative anatomy and physiology.

In the fourth century, Aristotle – though he did not dissect human bodies – did initiate the methodical dissection of animals, and urged others to do likewise. He

Humoral theory and bloodletting

The Greek scientific theory of health held that the body was formed from a variety of components, usually conceived as fluids or *humours*. A body was healthy when its humours were balanced in the correct proportions; diseased when they were unbalanced by inappropriate diet or exercise, injury or foul air (*miasma*). Originally there were a variety of humoral theories,

but eventually phlegm, bile, black bile and blood became established as the canonical four humours. When a patient fell ill, a doctor would frequently proceed by letting blood. This was not because Greek doctors considered blood a pathological humour itself but because they believed that at a certain point in an illness a pathological humour could be separated off into the

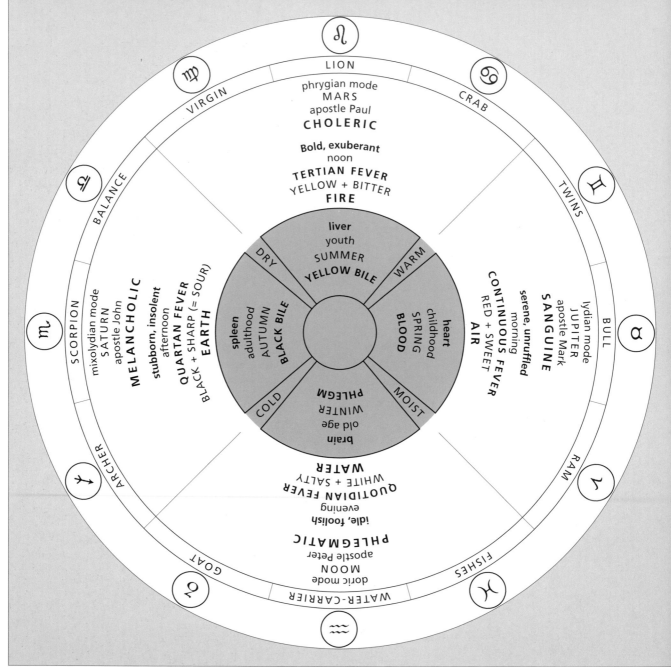

(Below) A scene from an Athenian doctor's surgery around the time of Hippocrates, painted on a perfume vase. As well as making house-calls a physician would see patients in his surgery. Here he is about to make an incision into a patient's arm. He may also be about to employ the cupping instrument which is hanging on the wall behind him. Any blood which is drawn will fall or be emptied into the bowl at the feet of the patient. (Left) A relief depicting bloodletting instruments; the cupping instruments stand either side of the box of bleeding tools. (Opposite) The green ring shows the Hippocratic correlations with the humours (yellow bile is warm and dry and associated with youth and summer, etc.). Galen further elaborated this schema (yellow ring), and it was added to again in the Middle Ages (white ring). It is from this period that we derive the four character types: sanguine, phlegmatic, choleric (from the Greek *chole*, bile) and melancholic (from the Greek *melan*, black + *chole*).

blood vessels. A good doctor had the ability to decide when, where, and how much blood could be drawn to ensure the pathological humour was thereby removed from the body. If a doctor felt a large amount of blood needed to be drawn, in order to prevent uncontrollable bleeding which he had no way to staunch, he would make only a small incision and then place a heated cupping instrument over the cut. As the air in the cup cooled and condensed it drew the blood through the cut by vacuum, but the bleeding would stop when the cup was removed. Bloodletting and cupping were used as forms of therapy right up to the nineteenth century.

thought an understanding of animal form, which could be gained only from examining the internal structure of actual bodies, afforded an insight into the design and
order of Nature itself. Moreover, although contemplation of and knowledge about
the heavenly bodies were superior, the fact that animals were more immediately
accessible to our senses made knowledge about them more reliable.

Living beings were important to the speculative side of Aristotle's philosophy –
particularly his ontology and epistemology – because he viewed them as the best
sublunary examples of substances. However, he also had a passionate interest in
the study of biology for its own sake. Over the course of his life he accumulated

prodigious notes on the behaviour, life-cycle and structure of hundreds of animals. On the basis of his observations he was able to go a long way towards a classification of animals ordered hierarchically from the least complex animals (sea-cucumbers) to the most complex (humans). He was also able to demonstrate that there was a system running through all animal structure; for example, some animals have a bowel and no bladder but no animal has a bladder and no bowel; or again, animals which lack upper front teeth all have several stomachs. Many of these similarities we would attribute to the animals sharing a common ancestor, but Aristotle believed that all species were fixed eternally by Nature in the form that was best for each. So the disposition of no upper front teeth and several stomachs in camels, sheep, deer, et cetera, enabled them better to digest the thorny, woody diet to which they were exposed.

Galen

Galen of Pergamum (129–216 CE) was active at Rome in the second half of the second century CE. He earned a great reputation as a doctor among his contemporaries and was court physician to three emperors (Marcus Aurelius, Commodus and Septimius Severus). He was also one of the most prolific writers of all time, and his extensive corpus continued to be the foundation of all branches of rational medicine for thirteen centuries after his death.

His father Nikon had originally intended that Galen should be a philosopher, and Galen's early training was in arithmetic, logic and grammar. However, when Galen was sixteen Nikon had a dream urging him to make his son a doctor. From then on Galen studied with the great teachers of medicine in Pergamum, Corinth and Alexandria, but his early training and continued interest in philosophy greatly influenced his career as a doctor.

Although he was writing more than five centuries after the deaths of Hippocrates and Plato, Galen took these two as the greatest authorities on medicine and philosophy respectively and wrote a treatise *On the Doctrines of Hippocrates and Plato* to demonstrate how they cohered with each other and the truth. His debt to Plato is shown principally in his teleology. He believed that the regularity of the universe showed that it had been designed by a supreme creator and that everything in it, and therefore everything in the body, had a purpose. In Hippocrates he believed he had found an advocate for establishing knowledge of the anatomy and physiology of the body and all its parts as the foundation of medicine.

Galen believed that the use of theory and logic was indispensable to medicine and to this extent he falls into the 'Dogmatist' camp of Greek medicine. However, Galen was more conscious than many other Dogmatists of the importance of experience and empirical testing in validating theories and inferences. He frequently performed public dissection and vivisection of animals (he never dissected a human cadaver) to illustrate his theories. As a scientist, then, Galen was closer to Aristotle than to either Plato or Hippocrates, though he does not acknowledge Aristotle's influence over him to the same extent.

Galen's medicine can be seen as reuniting the disciplines of philosophy and science. Diffused through the lens of his corpus the medicine, philosophy and science of classical Greece continued to exert influence on Western medicine until the Renaissance.

The fathers of medicine and pharmacology as they appear in a fifteenth-century manuscript by Giohanne Cademosto. Clockwise from the top left are: Asclepius, Hippocrates, Avicenna (Ibn Sina), Rhazes (ar-Razi), Aristotle, Galen, Macer, Albertus Magnus, Dioscorides, Mésué (Yuhanna ibn Masawayh), and Serapion. Ancient Greece has a good share of the credit for the founding of modern medicine. Galen, particularly, based his procedure on observation and explanation. His diagnostic methods included palpation, pulse-taking and occasionally the examination of urine.

He regularly performed dissections and vivisections before audiences of prominent Romans. In one of his most celebrated demonstrations he exposed the structures in the neck of a live boar and showed how the boar's bellowing could be silenced by pinching the laryngeal nerve descending from the brain. This supported Galen's claim that human consciousness (manifest most perfectly in speech) was located in the brain, not the heart as Aristotle had argued.

Aristotle's observations were not mistake-free. Many of the mistakes he made seem to us to be clearly avoidable and to have been the product of baseless theorizing rather than empirical observation. For example, his claim that the mammalian heart had three chambers seems to have resulted from his belief that the life-principle was situated in the heart and should have a single, central locus. Distortion of observation by expectation, though, is a hazard of scientific research even today, and to acknowledge that Aristotle made such mistakes is not to lessen his scientific achievement in gathering and organizing the data in his natural history.

Astronomy

Astronomy is the second science that can be said to emerge from philosophy by the end of the fourth century. Eudoxus, a younger contemporary of Plato, was able, with a fair amount of success, to account for the apparent movement of the stars, planets, sun and moon around the earth; the different speeds at which these bodies appeared to move; the predictable change of positions of the bodies relative to each other at different seasons of the year, and the periodic apparent backwards movement of the planets. His achievement is the more outstanding because it was predicated on a central, stationary earth and on the belief (inherited from Plato) that heavenly bodies could move only in a circle. He used complex mathematical and geometrical calculations to construct a system of concentric spheres between the sphere of the fixed stars and the central, stationary earth all moving at different, but in each case uniform, speeds. The movements of each of the five known planets were explained by positing four concentric spheres for each of them – and three for the sun and moon, because he did not have to account for any backwards motion.

The more outstanding medical and astronomical discoveries of the Greeks were made in later periods, but the essential aims and methods of these sciences were laid down in the fourth century BCE. Inquiry in areas that are more commonly thought of as philosophy today (epistemology, ontology, metaphysics, ethics, et cetera) also continued apace after Aristotle under new innovators such as Epicurus, Zeno and the Stoics, and the 'Academic' heirs. The legacy of Plato and Aristotle in particular is still strongly felt in modern philosophy. A.N. Whitehead stated, 'the European philosophical tradition … consists of a series of footnotes to Plato.'

There were, of course, many more aspects to Greek philosophy than have been detailed here, and some of them – for example, ethics, or even political theory – might seem more immediately relevant to our own concerns than ancient Greek speculations about what the world 'really' is. But for the earliest Greek thinkers there could be no knowledge of anything without a knowledge of the fundamental reality of the world, and the various branches of their philosophies cannot be appreciated without an understanding of what they took this reality to be.

Thomas Kuhn (in his book *The Structure of Scientific Revolutions*) has remarked, 'only the civilizations that descend from Hellenic Greece have possessed more than the most rudimentary science'. This can be traced ultimately to early Greek theories about the nature of reality. Concepts such as causation, non-corporeality and purpose did not spring fully formulated from the mind of the first philosopher, but Thales' assumption that something he saw in this world could help him, a human, understand the cosmos is the seed that blossomed into the Western scientific method.

A fifteenth-century miniature showing Nicole Oresme at work on his *Traité de l'Espère*, which was related to his commentary on Aristotle's *On the Heavens and the Earth*. Before him stands an armillary sphere. Eudoxus' system of concentric spheres was eventually rejected in favour of a theory involving epicycles and eccentric circles which was able to account more economically for more astronomical phenomena. It was still believed, however, that each of the heavenly bodies moved round a stationary earth with uniform circular motion, the moon marking the circle closest to the earth and the fixed stars marking the outer limits of the celestial sphere. The second century-CE astronomer Ptolemy used a complex instrument called an armillary astrolabe – a skeletal celestial globe with hoops (*armilla* in Latin) marking the paths of the heavenly bodies within the sphere – to determine the relative positions of heavenly bodies in their circular trajectories. Armillary spheres continued to be used even after Copernicus' heliocentric theory was established because of Plato's doctrine, first given practical application by Eudoxus, that the motion of heavenly bodies must be a uniform circle.

CHAPTER 12

Richard Buxton

Religion and Myth

Of all the buildings which survive from antiquity, none conjures up an image of 'the glory that was Greece' more effectively than the Parthenon on the Athenian Acropolis. Reproduced on a million postcards, Athena's majestic temple beckons the viewer into an apparently perfect world of gleaming marble (see p. 268). Its sculptural decorations – many removed by Lord Elgin and still, controversially, to be found in the British Museum in London – complement the picture. Some of the carvings evoke the triumph of youthful, civilized Lapith heroes (Greeks from Thessaly) over their semi-bestial opponents, the centaurs; the frieze depicts various groups in Athenian society – young horsemen, elders, girls bearing the implements of sacrificial ritual – whose orderly procession glorifies both the goddess Athena and, by extension, the idealized Athenian community of which she was the divine patron.

The Athenian Acropolis from the air. Dominating the site is the Parthenon, a temple dedicated to the city's patron deity Athena in her guise as Virgin (*Parthenos*).

When looked at from another angle, however, Athena's temple may elicit a rather different response. The Parthenon came into being at a time when Athens was exercising an increasingly imperialist stranglehold over its subject states, whose tribute in money and in ships was a crucial factor in facilitating Athens' massive public works programme in the mid-fifth-century. Moreover the city of Athens, despite the idealist imagery on the Parthenon, in reality fell well short of being a paradise for all. The temple itself was constructed in large part by slave labour. And although in name Athens was a democracy, in fact public decisions were taken exclusively by adult, free, citizen males. Women and resident foreigners indeed had their place in the great ceremony of the Panathenaic festival, but when the smoke from the sacrifice of a hundred sheep and oxen cleared, members of these social groups returned to their predominantly acquiescent or marginal role in Athenian society (see chapters 4 and 5).

Thinking about the Parthenon inevitably raises central questions about Greek social life: questions about power, about collective self-image, about the relative status of different groups. That there should be such a close relationship between religious and social issues is no coincidence. The religion of the Greeks was so embedded in their society that the idea of a separable 'church' and 'state', so fundamental to other religious traditions, would have been wholly meaningless in an ancient Greek context. (The situation had been no different in Bronze Age – or Minoan – Crete, where the so-called 'palaces' were centres of cult as well as of administration.) This embeddedness means that we even have to ask ourselves whether a separate entity called 'Greek religion' can be identified at all. So just how pervasive were the behaviour and attitudes which we are inclined to describe as 'religious'?

THE SCOPE OF THE SACRED

Within the anthropomorphic world of Greek polytheism, divinities proliferated. Pride of place went to major gods and goddesses such as Zeus, Hera, Artemis, Hermes, Aphrodite and Apollo. Most of these were linked with a special area of activity. Aphrodite, for example, was associated with sexual pleasure; Athena with the use of technical skills; Hermes with movement across boundaries ... These associations were often further broken down by epithet: so Hermes might be, amongst many possibilities, Hermes 'Of the Door Hinge' or Hermes 'Conveyor of Dead Souls'. In addition to the pantheon of the greatest divinities, lesser but still potentially crucial figures were revered – for example Eileithyia, goddess of childbirth, or Boreas, the North Wind. Personifications like Desire (*Himeros*) and Victory (*Nike*) were also venerated, as were heroes, who resembled the gods in that they were powerful, but differed from them in that they had died – indeed, a hero's cult typically centred on his grave.

Taken together, the divinities and heroes constituted neither a perfectly integrated system nor a disorganized chaos, but an open grouping of contrasting and complementary powers. Its composition and characteristics varied from place to

The so-called 'Ludovisi throne' (perhaps originally part of an altar) depicts the birth of Aphrodite from the sea-foam. According to mythology, she grew from the genitals of the sky-god Ouranos, which had been severed and thrown into the sea by his son Kronos. This violent deed was committed while Ouranos was sexually united to Gaia, the Earth goddess. Aphrodite was thus the distillation of sexuality.

place, in keeping with the pluralism of belief which was a fundamental characteristic of Greek society.

Mortals expressed their respect for these suprahuman entities through rites, at festivals. Sacred acts rather than pious beliefs were the root of Greek religion. Festivals gave life its rhythm. Calendars varied from city to city, but everywhere it was common practice for the names of months to be derived from divinities (*Heraios* from Hera; *Hestiaios* from Hestia, goddess of the hearth), or from festivals (*Thesmophorion*, from Demeter's festival).

Sacred ceremonies also marked out time-spans longer than a calendar year. For example, athletes from all over the Greek world trained to meet every four years to compete for honour within the precinct of Zeus at Olympia in the Olympic Games. Private as well as public life was also dramatized in ritual. At birth a newborn baby was ceremonially carried round the hearth, sacred to Hestia. Marriage and death were also marked by ritual. There were other rites which gave rhythm to the life of a Greek individual, for example the Anthesteria, a spring festival of Dionysus. This represented a memorable turning-point in the lives of very young children. It was based around the broaching of the new wine, an act accompanied by a ritual in which the whole community drank together – including, for the first time, three-year-olds, each of whom received a little jug. Such jugs have been found, very poignantly, in the graves of infants who died too young to participate in their first Anthesteria.

Wherever Hellenic civilization extended, sanctuaries where festivals were celebrated were found in a variety of types of location: city-centres (the Athenian Acropolis, Apollo's sanctuary in Corinth); sites outside major population centres but under the control of a neighbouring polis (Hera's shrine near Argos); inter-urban sites drawing their pilgrims from many different communities (Olympia, Delphi), and so on.

The symbolic focus of a sanctuary was almost always a sacrificial altar. There may have been other sacred features too – a spring or a cave, for instance. But the most impressive attribute was usually a temple, the dwelling-place of the divinity. Few visual manifestations of Greek culture can compare with such breathtaking constructions as the temples at, say, Bassae (Arcadia), Paestum (southern Italy) or Agrigentum (south-central Sicily) – each the product of immense artistic ingenuity, physical effort and financial commitment. But it is not only on such a grand scale that sanctuaries provide evidence of Greek religious mentality. Archaeologists have unearthed huge numbers of votive offerings presented by ordinary people to their local deities, in gratitude for a favour received or in hope of a future blessing. 'I am the dedicated property of Hera in the plain', runs the inscription on a bronze axe from southern Italy; 'Kyniskos the butcher dedicated me as a tithe of his work'.

At the Anthesteria wine-festival, young children were given miniature wine jugs. This one shows a toddler sitting on a potty. To the right is a push-cart, and in the child's hand is another toy, perhaps a rattle. In fact infant and perinatal mortality in classical Greece was very high: perhaps no more than one in three newborns survived its first year. Naming of newborns was regularly postponed for some days after birth out of respect for the high risk of death. Some of these miniature jugs were interred with infants who died well before reaching Anthesteria age.

Greek sanctuaries, which look empty to the modern traveller, were in antiquity full of votive dedications. These cemented a reciprocal relationship between worshipper and god. The logic of the gift was either: 'You helped me before, so now I make this offering to you', or: 'I make this offering to you now, so that you will help me in the future' (see p. 263). We do not know which alternative applied to this small bronze statuette (from near Mount Lycaeum in Arcadia) of a shepherd holding a fox. His cap and cloak are typical clothing for a shepherd, but the role he is cast in here seems to be that of a hunter (as in the scene on p. 210).

Festival and sanctuary formed a framework for living, but interaction with the sacred reached far beyond the time of festivals and the space of sanctuaries. Whatever men or women did, their activity was relevant to the sphere of influence of one or more of the gods. If you were to put adultery before married fidelity, you would be choosing Aphrodite in preference to Hera (as Paris and Helen did); to unleash the dogs of brutal war was to follow the path of Ares; burglars – and those who wished to keep them out – prayed to Hermes. Almost wherever one looks, the opposition between sacred and profane looks blurred. There were three interesting areas in which 'religion' overlaps with other practices – law, warfare and medicine.

Law

It was standard procedure for anyone appearing in court, or entering upon a period of public office, to bind himself with an oath sworn by the gods. Demosthenes tells us that before beginning his year of duty, an Athenian juror had to swear 'by Zeus, Poseidon, and Demeter, and shall invoke destruction upon himself and his household if he in any way transgresses this oath, but he shall pray that if he keeps his oath there may be many good things for him'. By explicitly invoking them as potential avengers, oaths drew the gods into all kinds of human activities with which they would otherwise have been unconcerned, from domestic disputes to interstate treaties.

War

Religion impinged on warfare in countless ways. Commanders of armies often saw themselves as walking in the symbolic footsteps of divine or heroic predecessors. Before leading an expedition across to Asia Minor, the Spartan king Agesilaus wished to sacrifice at Aulis, following the example of Agamemnon at the outset of the Trojan War. And Alexander of Macedon regarded himself variously as Achilles, Heracles and Dionysus (in increasing order of divinity).

If mythology played its part in war, so did ritual. To begin an expedition or a battle without conducting preliminary sacrifices was unthinkable. Sacrifice by no means guaranteed success, but *failure* to sacrifice would inevitably lead to defeat. To ignore unfavourable omens was also unwise. When Alexander went ahead and attacked the Scythians against the advice of his seer, the normally resilient constitution of the general succumbed immediately to diarrhoea. So the anticipated reaction of the gods to the conduct of campaigns was a constant factor in the practice of war. But there was always room for manoeuvre and negotiation. The Spartan commander at the battle of Plataea (479 BCE) circumvented a series of unfavourable sacrifices by praying directly, and successfully, to Hera. In a later military crisis Xenophon, a leader of the expedition of the Ten Thousand mercenaries in Asia, sacrificed day in, day out, until he obtained the appropriate prognosis (401 BCE).

Medicine

Opinions today differ, even among medical practitioners, about how far medicine is a 'rational' activity. There was a comparable debate among the Greeks. In a passage from the Hippocratic treatise *On the Sacred Disease,* the author criticizes the views of those who, unlike himself, see divine causation lying behind certain seizures: 'They make a different god responsible for each of the different forms of the complaint. If the patient acts like a goat, and if he roars or has convulsions involving the right side, they say that the Mother of the Gods is responsible. If he utters a higher-pitched and louder cry, they liken him to a horse and blame Poseidon. If the patient should be incontinent of faeces... Enodia [a form of the goddess

One situation which commonly led to the making of a dedication was recovery (either already accomplished, or hoped for) from illness. Many sanctuaries have yielded votive representations of parts of the body, presumably because these were the organs afflicted. The marble relief illustrated here was found in the shrine of the healer-hero Amphiaraus at Oropus in Boeotia. Patients 'incubated', that is slept in the sanctuary in the hope of receiving a dream which would miraculously effect a cure. Centre-right is the man who made the offering, Archinus, asleep on a couch. A snake, symbol of the hero's curative powers, is licking the patient's shoulder. To the left is what Archinus dreamt – the hero touching and curing him. The figure on the far right probably represents Archinus yet again, this time in the role of worshipper.

Hecate] is the name ascribed ...' So it is clear that religion was invoked in diagnosis. But it is equally clear that not everyone accepted divine causation as a way of explaining disease, although probably the majority of Greeks did – there are numerous myths told of individuals whose transgressions led the gods to punish them by madness, blindness or dumbness. It was reasonable to assume that if the gods could cause illness, they could cure it, so sanctuaries of healing divinities flourished in many places. None was more famous than the shrine of Asclepius at Epidaurus, which continued to attract patients until the fifth century CE. At this ancient Lourdes, the sick slept in a special enclosure in the hope of being granted a dream which might bring about a cure.

The range of tones which people might adopt in imagining the gods was great. At one end of the spectrum was profound awe, famously embodied in Homer's description, in the *Iliad*, of the wrath of Apollo, provoked by the dishonouring of his priest:

> So he spoke in prayer, and Phoebus Apollo heard him,
> and strode down along the pinnacles of Olympus, angered
> in his heart, carrying across his shoulders the bow and the hooded
> quiver; and the shafts clashed on the shoulders of the god walking
> angrily. He came as night comes down and knelt then
> apart and opposite the ships and let go an arrow.
> Terrible was the clash that rose from the bow of silver.
> First he went after the mules and the circling hounds, then let go
> a tearing arrow against the men themselves and struck them.
> The corpse fires burned everywhere and did not stop burning.

In other contexts, however, the approach was one of downright hilarity. Homer treats the lame and cuckolded god Hephaestus as an object of mockery. But it is Athenian comic drama which most boisterously presents the gods as absurd. In Aristophanes' *Frogs* the god Dionysus was portrayed as embodying a number of all-too-human frailties, not least a cowardice which afflicted him, copiously and visibly, in the bowels. Yet *Frogs* was staged at the Lenaea, one of Dionysus' own festivals, at which a place of honour was reserved for the god's own priest. This will seem paradoxical only if we equate divinity with perfection. The Greeks made no such equation. To exploit the comic side of the gods was not felt to undermine their authority, since that comic side was so clearly only one manifestation of the divine being. What, then, could possibly constitute blasphemy?

CITIZENS AND OTHERS

The death of Socrates and the absence of blasphemy
'Socrates does wrong because he corrupts the young, and also because he does not duly acknowledge the gods whom the city recognizes, but introduces other demonic beings' (quoted from Plato's *Apology*). The conviction and execution of

(*Opposite*) **Zeus' amorous adventures lent themselves to comic treatment, as on this South Italian vase. To the right is Hermes, identifiable by his hat and wand. The ladder which Zeus is holding will give him access to the object of his affections (perhaps Alcmene, mother of Heracles), visible in the window above. The style of this representation has been thought to echo a type of dramatic farce characteristic of southern Italy, but it may rather preserve traces of the fifth-century Athenian comedies of Aristophanes and his contemporaries, which we know were performed in South Italy.**

Sacrifice

At the heart of Greek religion was the ritualized killing, butchering, cooking and eating of an animal. Victims, almost always domesticated, varied from the humble fowl, goat or pig to the more highly valued ox. The choice depended on what was prescribed by sacred law for a particular deity or occasion (and to some extent, of course, on the means of the worshipper). In this vase-painting, many of the essential components of the ritual are visible. A god, Hermes, is present through the medium of his potent statue. In the centre is the altar, over which meat is being roasted (a second spit leans on the right). To the left, a man pours a libation, allowing drops of wine to fall onto the fire. The youth second from the left bears a basket. Before the killing, the basket had contained grain, beneath which the sacrificial knife had been hidden.

This image shows just one moment. In reality the drama of sacrifice had a meticulously structured plot. During the prologue the protagonists – priest, victim, participants – entered in procession and assembled round the altar. Suspense mounted as the action entered its most crucial phase (thanks to a trick): the pure water sprinkled onto the head of the victim made it nod in 'assent' to what was to follow. Without delay the beast was stunned; then the knife was plunged into its throat. As the blood spurted onto the altar, women uttered a ritual scream to mark the climax. The dénouement consisted of an elaborate process of carving, roasting and sharing; the distribution of portions was made either by lot or according to the relative status of the participants.

In view of the explanatory and exploratory functions of Greek myths, it is not surprising that stories were told to make sense of sacrifice. The archaic poet Hesiod connected the origin of the rite with the moment when a gulf opened up between humans and gods. Once upon a time, the Titan Prometheus had tried to deceive Zeus. He set out two portions of a slaughtered ox, to be divided between mortals and gods. One portion comprised the delicious flesh and innards covered with an unappealing ox-paunch; the other was a heap of bones, disguised with a beguiling layer of fat. With the ambiguity so beloved of myth, Zeus both saw through the trick and made the 'wrong' choice. Ever since, sacrifice has been in honour of the gods, but to the alimentary benefit of humanity.

Both the ritual and the myth used to interpret it involve the drawing of distinctions. At each sacrifice, some persons and groups were included, others excluded. For those who did participate, the size and quality of portions varied. Implied in the sacrifice is another distinction: between domesticated animals, which were sacrificed, and wild animals, which as a rule were not. In the myth, gods and mortals were sharply demarcated.

And the role of sacrifice in communal self-definition had yet another dimension. Socio-religious groups whose beliefs did not correspond with those of their fellow-citizens – such as members of the Orphic and Pythagorean sects (said to have been founded by the mythical singer Orpheus and the philo-

sopher Pythagoras) – sometimes articulated their differences in terms of sacrificial practice. In rejecting the community's central ritual of animal blood-sacrifice, they were making a conclusive statement of self-marginalization.

Sacrifice at an altar – the central act of Greek religion – is here depicted on a mixing-bowl.

the Athenian philosopher (see pp. 302 and 354) on this charge continue to provoke debate. Why did the restored democracy *really* put him to death? Because some of his pupils had been implicated in the discredited oligarchic and pro-Spartan regime of the Thirty Tyrants? Because the city of Athens, catastrophically defeated by Sparta, was a prey to superstitious fear and so felt threatened by religious impropriety? Because Socrates – who argued that the gods were not interested in the lavishness of a sacrifice, only in the justness of the sacrificer – was undermining sacrifice as traditionally practised? Probably all three factors played a part. One thing is certain: Socrates was not put to death because he had transgressed against a Panhellenic prohibition on 'blasphemy' – for there was no such prohibition. When an earlier philosopher, Anaxagoras, was ejected from Athens, his unorthodoxy (teaching that Helios, the sun god, was merely a lump of incandescent stone) was no barrier to his being welcomed back with honour into his native city of Lampsacus. Socrates lost his life because of a particular cluster of political circumstances obtaining in the Athenian polis of 399 BCE.

The Sun god, Helios, was closely connected with the island of Rhodes. According to a myth, told by among others the lyric poet Pindar, Helios chose Rhodes as his special preserve even before the island rose from the sea. As this Rhodian coin illustrates, Helios became the symbol of the community where he was revered. He was also the grandfather of Medea, hence his key role in the concluding scene of Euripides' *Medea* (see p. 249).

Religious participation

The trial of Socrates illustrates how decisive a city's control over religious matters might be. The polis was not, it is true, the only arbiter of cult. Some cults were associated with the household, others with a specific family or descent-group (*genos*). But by and large the state had the final say. Priests and priestesses held office not because they belonged to a professional and vocational cadre, but because they were appointed by the community. As in other matters of the state, a stranger (*xenos*) would not be appointed to such a post and would be debarred from participation in at least some rites of the host state. Polis and religion were scarcely separable, as is symbolized by the many coins on which a state was represented by its leading deity or hero.

Yet participation in civic cult was not entirely restricted to the *politai* – the adult, male, free, citizen population. At the Eleusinian Mysteries, for example, initiation was available not only to free, citizen men, but also to women, slaves and some non-Greeks (provided they could understand the Greek language). Some festivals, such as the Thesmophoria (for Demeter), celebrated in many parts of the Greek world, were for women only. At the Anthesteria, slaves (the ultimate non-citizens) and young children (not citizens until they reached the age of about eighteen) participated in the drinking-rite. At the Kronia, which centred on a carnivalesque festival of reversal, slaves and their masters were temporarily placed on the same level or had their normal roles reversed.

Nevertheless, cults often did mark out social distinctions of all kinds. For example, non-Greeks were excluded from the oracles of Trophonius and Amphiaraus (at Delphi, on the other hand, they were admitted). But during the procession at the Athenian Panathenaea, resident foreigners had the honoured role of bearing specified offerings – a way of symbolizing the fact that such foreigners were distinct from the host community, yet also integral to it. At a festival for Demeter celebrated on

The painter of the interior of this Attic white-ground cup (see p. 283) has graphically suggested the round-dance of a female chorus, accompanied by a woman playing the *auloi* (double-oboe). The flames on the altar (top) show that a sacrifice is taking place. To the right of the altar is a basket, evidently containing bands of wool, perhaps like the one displayed as an offering above the basket. Woolworking is women's 'rightful' task: the whole image conveys a sense of social and religious harmony.

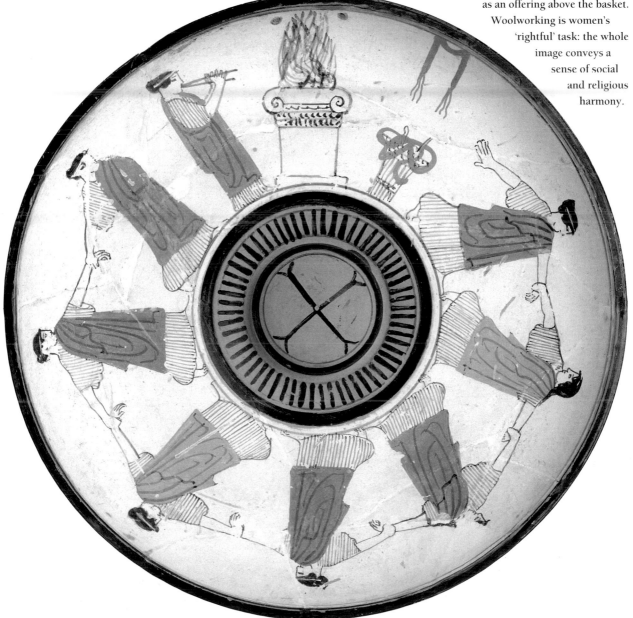

the island of Mykonos, foreign women had to be initiated before being allowed to take part, but no such restriction applied to citizen women.

A particularly striking example of ritual exclusiveness is provided by the Olympic Games. Not only could women not compete, they could not even *watch*. (Any female intruder would, it was stipulated, be hurled from a nearby cliff.) However, the great Games had a female counterpart. Every four years at Olympia there was an athletic festival in honour of Hera, organized by a community of sixteen women, in which the main event was a race between virgin girls. Unfortunately our evidence for Hera's event is minimal compared with the wealth of data about the games in honour of Zeus.

Greek youth and initiation

To gain a broader understanding of the role of cult in Greek society, it will be useful to focus on three social groups which were in different ways distanced from the centre of the polis: the young, women and slaves.

It has become a commonplace amongst historians of ancient Greece that the twin goals of girls' upbringing were marriage and childbirth, whereas boys' education aimed at preparing them to be citizens and especially warriors. At least in the area of religion, this generalization is well founded.

Throughout Greece there was a custom of participation by young women in choral song and dance (see chapters 5 and 9). Some of the songs (from as early as the seventh century BCE) have survived, and they confirm that the values prized in the archaic period correspond closely with those recommended to young women by Aristotle three centuries later: 'beauty, stature, self-control, and industriousness without meanness'. Another tradition in some places involved small groups of girls temporarily living away from their families in the service of a female divinity (Artemis at Brauron and Hera at Corinth, for example). During this time they might be obliged to carry out tasks such as weaving, in obvious preparation for their future role as wives. Another custom required such girls to have their hair cropped. This symbolized their temporary marginalization (making them resemble those other marginals, slaves and mourners), as a prelude to their later return into society as wives and mothers. Since the girls are often specified as of noble birth – that is, they did not constitute the whole of a given age-group – it may be the case that an initiatory rite of passage which at one period *did* apply to an entire age-group became in later times 'diluted', so as to involve only a select few.

Initiation certainly played an important part in the upbringing of boys. In fourth-century Crete youths who, having spent a period performing menial service for aristocratic adults in *andreia* ('men's houses'), were then grouped into 'herds', whose activities focused on learning how to fight. Eventually, during the 'Undressing' festival, these adolescents cast off the shabby garb which they had been obliged to wear during their training, and took on the mantle of adulthood (literally and symbolically).

In other parts of Greece similar sorts of rites of passage occurred. For instance, in Sparta young men underwent a period of 'secret service' (*krupteia*) during which their behaviour contrasted in virtually every way with what would later be expected of them as fully-fledged hoplites. They were encouraged to use trickery, roaming the countryside at night in order, it was said, to terrorize the subjugated population of Messenian helots. Athenian youths spent a period at the end of their adolescence guarding the frontiers, before returning to the centre of civic life to swear their hoplite oath of loyalty to the polis. Common to these forms of military organization is that the ultimate goal – assumption of the role of warrior – is preceded by a liminal phase of exclusion-plus-reversal, a pattern which anthropologists and historians have identified in numerous other cultures. In Greek practice, moments of transition were marked by rites and festivals.

The role of women in Greek religion

For a society in which women played almost no public part, it is perhaps puzzling that they were so prominent in religious activities. There were many female divinities (Hera, Athena, Aphrodite, Demeter ...) and mythological heroines (Medea, Antigone, Clytemnestra, Penelope ...) as well as numerous 'women-only' festivals (see p. 105). So how are we to interpret women's exceptional 'visibility' in religious matters?

Certain female religious duties were, of course, not a contradiction of women's usual social role, but a confirmation of it. The classic example is female dominance of funerary ritual, which sits perfectly with the prevailing notion that the *continuity* of the community lay principally with women: through honours paid to the dead, the memorialized past lived on. There are other examples. The Thesmophoria, in all its regional variations, featured a dramatized progress from abstinence (sexual and nutritional) to a resumption of normal eating and a celebration of fertility. But there was one ritual activity which seems more difficult to reconcile with the restrictions normally placed upon female licence: the worship of Dionysus.

Numerous vases depict women in an obviously trance-like state, in close proximity to wild nature. Often these *maenads* (raving women) are in the company of Dionysus, the ecstatic god (*ekstasis* meaning 'standing outside oneself'). The behaviour evoked by such images is potently described by Euripides in his play *Bacchae* ('The Bacchants'), in which denial of the divinity of Dionysus by a group of aristocratic Theban women provokes the god into driving them mad. On Cithaeron, the neighbouring mountain, an orgy of violence culminates in the tearing apart of King Pentheus by these crazed Bacchants, led by Pentheus' own mother Agaue. This story raises the intricate question of the relationship between myth and ritual, since there are many correspondences between the Euripidean narrative (and others like it) and a ritual enacted in many Greek cities. In his *Periegesis* (in the second century CE), Pausanias reports that a group of women ran raving in honour of Apollo and Dionysus above the clouds on the peak of Mount Parnassus.

Another festival which explored the relationship between Dionysus and women was the Agrionia (*agrios* means 'wild'). As celebrated in the Boeotian city of Orchomenus, this festival involved the ritual pursuit of women by a man; a closely parallel myth speaks of the Minyads, women from the same city, whose rejection of Dionysiac worship led them to insanity and finally infanticide. Since Greek myths often bring out the latent meaning of the rituals which they accompany, it is significant that the myth of Pentheus and the myth of the Minyads both portray mothers who kill their own offspring – the ultimate negation of woman's societal role.

How do these ritual practices relate to the mythical narratives? The crucial difference is that, whereas after the *mythical* infanticide the women might even lose their humanity altogether – the Minyads were metamorphosed into birds or bats – the women who followed the mountain-walking *ritual* resumed their everyday lives until the next festival two years later. Such rituals offered women a powerful release from domesticity. But it was a *temporary* release. If it had a more lasting impact on women's perception of their everyday lives, it is not an impact we can detect.

Religion and slaves

There was no 'slave religion'. Slaves might sometimes participate in the cults of the household where they lived, and they were admitted to certain public cults such as the Eleusinian Mysteries, the Anthesteria and the Kronia (see p. 331). They might seek asylum in temples, which were also, in later times, locations for proclamations of emancipation. They could pray and curse as a free person could (indeed, it seems that slaves were particularly inclined to such invocations, because of their powerlessness). But what all these possibilities illustrate is the subordination of slaves to the religion of their masters. Nor is this surprising, given the chattel status which slaves commonly had in Greece, with the exception of Sparta (see below).

There is nothing comparable to the paradox of women's experience. Women were both of and not of the polis; slaves were simply *not* of it. Myth seems to confirm this. By and large, Greek myths, which love to explore the ambiguities and contradictions in experience, have little to say about the status of slaves – although mythical slaves can be noble as well as contemptible. Tragedy, in particular, dwells on the pity and horror of the transition from free to slave, as in the case of the widows and orphaned daughters depicted with such pathos in Euripides' *Trojan Women*. But the institution of slavery is a given, a function of the plot, rather than something to be examined in itself as a moral or social problem.

The one major exception seems to have been Sparta, where the social situation differed radically from that in most parts of Greece. There the slave population had a marked and threatening degree of cohesion, consisting as it did of helots, subservient

(Opposite) **With the power of Dionysus inside her, a maenad became uncannily close to the raw world of nature. The figure depicted here (on the inside of a white-ground cup) has her hair bound with a coiled snake, wears a panther-skin tied round her neck, and grasps the hind leg of another panther. In her other hand is the Dionysiac wand (*thyrsus*), its end wreathed with ivy, the god's sacred plant.**

but potentially (and sometimes actually) rebellious native Greeks who were kept in check by the 'true' Spartans, the Spartiates. The French historian Pierre Vidal-Naquet has pointed out that here and there in the mythical tradition we can glimpse a story which allows 'rule by slaves' as a theoretical, albeit fantastic possibility. For example, in one legend the city of Tarentum in southern Italy was said to have been founded by a group descended from the union between Spartan women and slaves. Here, a myth makes explicit through fantasy a possibility latent in Sparta's real political situation. In the quite different state of affairs obtaining in, say, Athens, such a possibility was, it appears, inconceivable, even in the imaginary world of myth.

MYTHS AND THE NATURE OF DIVINITY

The Greeks had no equivalent of the Christian Bible, no revealed truth which could be interpreted but not contested. So sacred narratives have played quite different roles in the cultures where these two religions have been practised. Christians tell stories which fill out the revealed record by detailing the lives of saints and martyrs, but the fluidity and open-endedness characteristic of Greek reflections on gods and heroes are denied them. Greek myths wove in and out of experience – both everyday experience and the experience of ritual – and mythical accounts of the world very often conflicted with one another. One important reason is that the myths were told in different contexts: by nurses and mothers to children; by epic, tragic, lyric and comic poets to their audiences; by painters and sculptors to their patrons and viewers. As the contexts vary, so do the messages. For example, Dionysus appears as a brutal avenger or a cowardly buffoon, according to whether the narrative is tragic (see p. 333) or comic (see p. 327). Nevertheless, in spite of this variety, a number of general observations can be made.

To begin with, the Greeks had no Devil. True, gods may be repellent, as in Aeschylus' description of the Furies at the beginning of his play *Eumenides* : 'they are vile: they snore repulsively; their eyes ooze a filthy discharge...'. They may be destroyers, like the Aphrodite who punishes the chaste hunter Hippolytus by making his stepmother Phaedra fall in love with him – an event which brings agonizing death to the one and suicide to the other. But the gods are not simply *evil*. The powers they represent are necessary to the running of the world, even if those powers are sometime exercised in ways which humans find cruel or baffling.

Bound up with this is a paradox. The gods stand as arbiters of the moral order, and may take action when certain fundamental transgressions are committed. Thus when Lycaon (Wolf Man) invites the gods to a banquet and serves up to them the flesh of a human child, Zeus ejects him from humanity by turning him into a wolf. But the gods are behind not just the moral order – they are behind everything, irrespective of morality. Indeed the gods themselves perpetrate 'immoral' deeds of every kind: Kronos castrates his father Ouranos; Zeus overthrows his father Kronos; Hermes steals the cattle of his brother Apollo; Ares and Aphrodite commit adultery at the expense of the cuckolded Hephaestus ...

The same paradoxical mixture of behaviour applies to heroes, who may be involved either in defending humanity and upholding morality – as when Heracles in his Labours eradicates the beasts which threaten civilized life and rescues his family from the clutches of the wicked tyrant Lycus (another Wolf) – or in transgressing boundaries and infringing moral norms (as when Heracles slaughters his wife and children in a fit of madness sent by Hera). A resolution of this paradox is not hard to find: an important role of divinities and heroes in Greek belief is to test out the limits of proper human conduct, sometimes by enforcing norms, sometimes by breaking them.

Another paradox built into the nature of the suprahuman beings of Greek myth is the fact that they are in part like humans, and in part wholly alien to them. A good example is the goddess Thetis. Her glittering wedding to the mortal hero Peleus took place on Mount Pelion, the festivities being crowned by the presence of the

Niobe rashly boasted that, whereas Leto, mother of Apollo and Artemis, had only two children, she herself had many. On this fifth-century Attic red-figure *krater*, Leto's children demonstrate their superiority by slaughtering Niobe's.

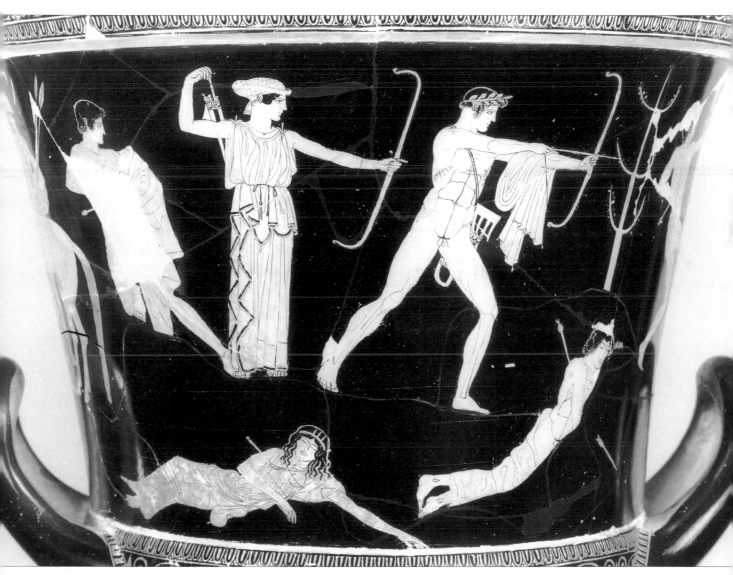

One aspect of Heracles was his defence of humanity against lawlessness and monstrosity. Here (*right*) he combats one of the man-eating horses of Diomedes (the head and arm of its last victim are hanging out of its mouth). But Heracles also committed monstrous crimes, one of which was to kill his children in a fit of madness. In this illustration (*below*) he is on the point of hurling his son onto a makeshift pyre of burning furniture.

Olympian deities themselves. In due course a son was born: Achilles. The relationship between this peerless hero and his mother is one of the most touching details in the entire *Iliad*, rendered the more poignant by the anticipation felt by both of them of Achilles' early death. Thetis' repeated sensing of his grief, her gentle words

of comfort to him, recur like a tender *leitmotiv* at key moments in the plot. All this is profoundly human. And yet Thetis is no ordinary mother, but a nymph and a daughter of Nereus, a great god of the sea. When courted by Peleus, her reaction to his advances was (according to Apollodorus, a mythographer probably to be dated to the early Roman empire) to turn herself 'now into fire, now into water, and now into a beast'. Again and again in Greek mythology we meet this essential duality of the gods – human-like, yet also incommensurate with humanity.

When a mortal married a goddess, he sometimes got more than he bargained for. Here Peleus attempts to hold Thetis fast, in spite of the lion and snakes which have sprung to her defence.

One consequence of this duality was the difficulty faced by humans in deciphering the divine will. How could one determine the views of these uncomfortably unpredictable beings? The commonest way of trying to peer beyond the limits of mortality was by consulting an oracle. Apollo's shrine at Delphi was the most prestigious, but there were others, such as that sacred to Zeus and Dione at Dodona.

But oracles were not foolproof guides to the future because they involved the interpretation of the words of a god by a mortal. Catastrophic misunderstandings of oracles became part of Greek tradition, and were elaborated in historical and mythological accounts (in so far as the two can be distinguished). The historian Herodotus records the fateful oracle given to the Lydian king Croesus: if you attack the Persians, you will destroy a great empire. (He did: his own.) The plots of tragedies frequently turn on oracular predictions, which enable the dramatist to illustrate the gap between human and divine knowledge. No hero's fate was more notorious than that of Oedipus, who learnt from Apollo's priestess at Delphi that he was to kill his father and marry his mother, and, in attempting to avoid the prediction, fulfilled it.

The oracle of the talking oak

Remote and isolated in the mountainous north-west of Greece, in a broad valley below Mount Tomarus, nestles Dodona, site of one of the most famous oracles of antiquity. This lovely place attracted pilgrims for well over a thousand years. The object of their pilgrimage, the shrine of Zeus and his consort Dione, centred on an oak tree. Inquirers received answers through the mediation either of soothsayers or of priestesses called 'Doves'. The god's response was given when the oak tree 'spoke'. There were various explanations of how it spoke: through the rustling of its leaves; through the calls or flight of the doves which lived in its branches; through the sound emitted by a ring of bronze cauldrons encircling it which touched when the wind blew...

Thanks to the work of Greek archaeologists, most recently Sotirios Dakaris, we have a wonderful opportunity to see the sort of religious activity which centred around this shrine. The sanctuary has yielded thousands of inscribed strips of lead (tablets) bearing ques-

tions put by inquirers at the oracle. These strips were rolled up, marked for identification, and handed in to the god's human representatives. These representatives later gave the answer, without divulging the contents of the original inquiry. Some of the questions concern public matters, as when the people of strife-torn Corcyra (modern Corfu) asked to what god or hero they should sacrifice and pray 'in order to be in agreement with each other for their good'. But it is the private enquiries which reveal most. Marriage, parenthood, health, personal property – these are the concerns which prompt people to make the often long and difficult trek to Dodona. Someone called Thrasybulus wanted to know to which god he should sacrifice if his eyesight was to recover. Agis was puzzled about those blankets and pillows which he has lost: did someone steal them? More personal still is the anxiety of one questioner: 'Am I the father of the child which Annyla has

'The Dodoneans ask Zeus and Dione whether the god has sent the heavy winter because of some individual's impurity.' Fourth-century BCE.

Yet such dramatic stories as those of Croesus and Oedipus demonstrate the tendency of the Greek tradition to select and emphasize certain aspects of experience – in this case, those aspects which spring from the distinction between humans and gods. In real life, oracles were no more threatening, and no more (or less) misleading, than the astrological predictions so avidly read in the modern world. Like those predictions, they responded to the actual needs of real people.

INTERPRETING THE SACRED

Each generation remakes the Greeks in its own image. In few areas are such assumptions so tenacious as in the interpretation of ritual and mythology. For example, a persistent undercurrent in readings of Greek religion has been a tendency to see the Greeks as having sporadically anticipated the truths of Christianity. The *Hymn to Zeus* by the Hellenistic philosopher-poet Cleanthes ('So I will praise you, and always sing of your power. The entire universe which moves round the Earth follows where you lead it, and is willingly mastered by you...') has been seen as a precursor of

Most of the questions addressed to the Dodona oracle were prompted by anxiety of one kind or another. Many of the enquiries relate to childlessness. On this tablet, which dates back to *c.* 500 BCE, a man called Hermon wants to know what god he should pray to in order to get useful children from his wife Kretaia. The tablet is written in the Corinthian alphabet, in the style known as *boustrophedon*, 'like an ox ploughing', i.e. the first line is written left to right, the second right to left, the third left to right, and so on.

conceived?'. Such requests, the product of major or trivial crises in individual lives, bring us for a moment very close to the Greeks, as a counter-weight to the many religious practices and attitudes which hold them at an unbridgeable distance.

Magic

Where are my magic charms? Wreathe the bowl with fine crimson wool so that I may bind a spell upon my love, who treats me so badly ... Tomorrow I will go to Timagetus' wrestling-school to see him, and will reproach him for treating me so; but now I will bind him with fire-spells ... Hail, grim Hecate, and to the end attend me, and make these drugs of mine as potent as those of Circe or Medea or golden-haired Perimede.

Simaetha, the woman whose emotions are explored in this Hellenistic poem (*Idyll* 2) by Theocritus, makes use of techniques which have often been regarded as belonging to the underside of Greek civilization. The terms 'magic' and its close relative 'superstition' are sometimes used in a strongly normative way, in opposition to the more highly valued 'religion' and 'science'. Yet, as far as Greece is concerned, it would be quite misleading to suggest that magic was a wholly separate area. Greek life, geared as it was to competitive situations, produced many strategies for self-protection and self-assertion, in parallel with the enormously pervasive ethic of 'help friends, harm enemies'. Some of these strategies used procedures to which the term 'magic' can quite reasonably be applied: amulets (worn for protection against disease); curse tablets;

love-charms; spells for invoking the presence of a deity ... Far from being a wholly distinct way of negotiating with the sacred, such strategies were seen merely as extensions of ordinary religious practices. Simaetha's invocation of Hecate is eminently comparable with the earlier poet Sappho's prayer to Aphrodite, uttered in a similar situation of imagined lovesickness. 'Free me from my cruel love-anguish,' pleads Sappho, recalling the goddess' promise in a similar crisis once before: 'Who must I persuade *this* time to love you, Sappho? ... Even if she flees, soon she shall pursue you; though she refuses your gifts now, soon she shall give them; though she loves you not, soon she *shall* love you, even against her will.'

Magical procedures were by no means exclusively the province of the less respectable, the down trodden, or/and women. A lead doll, about 6 centimetres tall (c.400 BCE), with its own little coffin, was found in a grave in the Cerameicus district of Athens. Its hands are bound behind its back. On the right leg is inscribed the name 'Mnesimachos'; on the coffin is a list of names, including that of Mnesimachos, followed by the words 'and whoever else is a *xyndikos* (fellow-participant in a law suit) with him, or a witness'. Burial in a grave is a common location for such objects, probably because it was believed that the ghost of the dead person might be an agent for the execution of the curse: the deceased would transmit the curse to the gods of the Underworld, the agents who might put it into effect. In this case the curser was doubtless an opponent of Mnesimachos in a law suit, that is, a citizen man – women being disqualified from active public participation in law suits (see p. 107). At just this period a man called Mnesimachos did indeed figure in a legal case for which the orator Lysias wrote a speech. This may be pure coincidence; but it is at any rate a useful symbol of the lack of division between Greek daily life and the world of magic.

This miniature lead doll (*opposite*), together with the words inscribed on its container (*left*), was designed to act as a curse. The lead used came from Laurium.

The 'mystery' cult at Eleusis, celebrated in honour of Demeter and her daughter Persephone, centred on the notion of renewal. In this drawing (based on a red-figure vase), renewal of nature's growth is expressed through the person of Triptolemus, the hero who brought corn to human beings. Seated on a winged cart, he is flanked by Demeter and Pherephatta (an alternative name for Demeter's daughter).

monotheism. The 'Mystery religions', exemplified in the rituals practised at Eleusis, have seemed to some a higher or more spiritual dimension of paganism, in virtue of their serious concern with the fate of the soul after death. But such a pick-and-choose approach ignores the fact that, for the Greeks, practices which have sometimes been differentiated as 'high' and 'low' co-existed: animal sacrifice and 'spiritual' prayer shared many common characteristics as they tried to cope with the uncertainties of the future; 'superstitious' magic might be practised by the very same individual who was initiated into the supposedly 'higher' Mysteries of Eleusis. Instead of regarding the Greeks as pagans who occasionally showed inklings of something finer, most students of Greek religion now concentrate on how ancient ritual and myth were integrated both with each other and within a wider social context.

Of course, this approach incorporates its own assumptions. To place emphasis on the role of marginal social groups is to borrow a perspective common amongst contemporary historians of religion (and amongst historians *tout court*). To look at Greek religion from a largely synchronic point of view follows an approach, again by no means unusual today, which interests itself less in the origins of religious phenomena than in their interrelation. And to look at how religion constituted a way of creating meanings – meanings which might help the worshipper/ believer/ myth-teller to cope with the anxieties and joys and perplexities of being alive – this is one possible way of understanding Greek religion, though by no means the only one. But it does have the important advantage of showing how it might once have made perfectly good sense to pray to Athena, or to fear the wrath of Apollo.

Legacy

CLASSICISM

For the purposes of this book, the word 'ancient' refers chiefly to those Greeks who lived in the *classical* epoch of the fifth and fourth centuries BCE. 'Classical' in this sense (meaning not just excellent but paradigmatic and canonical) is a coinage of the early seventeenth century. As applied to ancient Greece, the term originally referred above all to Greek art and architecture. But the concept of a classical canon first appeared in Greece itself.

In Athens, during the 330s, the leading politician Lycurgus persuaded the Athenian Assembly to vote that proof texts of the surviving plays of three long dead Athenian tragedians should be officially copied and kept in the state's public archives. In this way he was recognizing and preserving Aeschylus, Sophocles and Euripides as classic authors. The sustained impact and influence of such works from antiquity through to modern times are what has gained for all Greek (and Latin) texts the title 'Classics'.

Of course, one of the major pitfalls of defining an era as 'classical' is that what comes after it seems somehow diminished or downgraded. That indeed has been the fate of the *Hellenistic* era (c. 323–30 BCE) that followed. The term was invented in the nineteenth century by the German scholar Johann Gustav Droysen. He wanted to convey the distinction between a purely Greek or Hellenic civilization and a civilization which, thanks to the conquests of Alexander the Great, was a fusion of Greek and non-Greek oriental elements.

Unlike many of his successors, Droysen did not view this Graeco-oriental fusion negatively. Rather, he saw the Hellenistic era as the indispensable precondition for the spread of Christianity – the world's first truly universal religion. Had it not been for the hellenization of the Jews of Palestine, he argued, the Christian Gospel would have remained tied to its Levantine social origins. But since the first Christians were already hellenized, the Gospel could be spread quickly around the considerable Greek-speaking world in Greek.

By the first century CE, moreover, that world had been incorporated into the eastern half of the Roman empire. Hence the crucial evangelistic role played by St Paul. He was a hellenized Jew from Tarsus, in what is now southern Turkey. But he was also a Roman citizen who, in dire straits, could 'appeal unto Caesar' for the right to a proper trial. This dual identity gave him and his teaching great mobility across a huge territory.

Scholars who did not share Droysen's messianic vision of historical predestination often saw the Hellenistic era very differently, and much more pessimistically, as a falling away from the standards of

Winged Victory of Samothrace (from the Sanctuary of the Great Gods). This is one of the most powerful icons of Hellenism today, thanks to its prominent display in the Louvre in Paris. It comes from a long tradition of Greek sculptures of the Goddess of Victory, traceable back to the seventh century. But to show her in the act of alighting on a warship, to reproduce that ship life-size in monumental stone, and to endow the Goddess with such a combination of power and grace – these are genuinely Hellenistic achievements.

classical Greece – in visual art and literature no less than in politics and government. They also thought that even the Greeks of the Hellenistic era and the early centuries CE must have thought the same way too because they themselves seemed to look back to the classical era as a golden age. Of course, all such interpretations are highly subjective. Creative originality is as much knowing how to make something new out of one's heritage and influences as it is doing something for the very first time.

From papyrus to print

Ancient Greeks wrote, painted or scratched texts on a wide variety of materials – wood, wax, pottery, lead, stone, bronze and papyrus prominent among them. For everyday personal use broken potsherds were probably the commonest medium, though the percentage of Greeks who were fully and regularly literate was probably never very high. Pairs of wooden tablets covered with wax that could be folded and tied together served for more private communication. Our 'paper' is derived from the Greeks' word for a writing material in use solely at the luxury end of the market, *papyrus*.

The principal and almost the sole ancient source of papyrus was always Egypt. Reeds were cut into thin strips, dried and then glued in such a way that one surface presented a smooth platform for inscribing in ink with a quill pen. The unusually dry climatic conditions in Upper (southern) Egypt have permitted the survival of large numbers of ancient papyrus texts, which are grouped by scholars into two broad classes: literary and documentary.

Occasionally, papyrus texts have survived outside Egypt – a famous example from Derveni in northern Greece contains religious texts of the untypical Orphic sect: among other variations from Greek norms Orphics refused to practise animal blood-sacrifice. But these survivals are unfortunately quite exceptional.

The next best thing, an imprint from a literary papyrus, has been found at Ai Khanum in what may originally have been the library of a palace located at the far eastern extremity of the Greek, or Hellenistic Greek, world. Ai Khanum ('Moon Woman') in Afghanistan was perhaps the ancient Alexandria-in-Sogdia. The papyrus original seems to have carried an Aristotelian philosophical text carefully transcribed in the early third century, little more than a generation after the death of Aristotle himself, whose own great library in Athens found its way eventually to the Egyptian Alexandria. One of our greatest losses of original papyrus texts, however, is from the Museum and Library in damply urban and often destroyed Alexandria.

Papyrus texts were traditionally in the form of rolls – the Latin term *volumen* gives us our 'volume'. The longest extant example measures 22 feet. Between the second and fourth centuries of the Common Era, rolls began to give way to the *codex*, in which papyrus leaves were gathered together in book-like form. This seems to have been a specifically Christian innovation.

The link between papyrus and print in the chain of transmission of ancient literary texts was the late antique and medieval manuscript. Made of parchment (a corruption of *pergamena charta*, or 'paper from Pergamum') and copied in monkish or

Archimedes is shown bestriding a flat earth, which in turn is floating on water, as Thales had suggested. This is an illustration to an edition of the mathematical works of the great third-century BCE Syracusan scientist, printed in Venice in 1503.

LITERATURE AND CRITICISM

The history of Greek literature is often said to be a continuous one from Homer (roughly the end of the eighth century BCE) to the present. But it would be more accurate to speak of a continuous tradition of Greek texts. The idea of texts as literature also has a history, and that history begins only in the Hellenistic period, in Alexandria. Euripides exceptionally was said to have had something of a private

(*Above*) Papyrus, second century CE, from Oxyrhynchus in Egypt, bearing part of Sophocles' satyr-play *Trackers*, on which Tony Harrison based his *The Trackers of Oxyrhynchus*.

(*Left*) These miniatures of the tenth century illuminated a text originally composed in the first century BCE, a commentary by the physician Apollonius of Citium (on Cyprus) on the Hippocratic treatise *On Joints*.

royal *scriptoria* (writing-rooms), such manuscripts were enormously expensive to produce in both labour and materials, and the choice of ancient texts to copy was made with this very much in mind. From the thirteenth century, paper – a Chinese invention brought to Western attention by Arab traders – was quite commonly used for the production of Greek manuscripts.

Printing by movable type was a Chinese invention made long before its independent re-invention in the West during the fifteenth century. Within half a century of Gutenberg's biblical breakthrough in Germany, printers in Italy, driven by the demands of the humanist scholars of the Renaissance, were producing printed texts of both Greek and Latin classical authors.

library, consisting of texts on papyrus rolls. Aristophanes presumably had one too, unless his memory was prodigious even by the highly developed mnemonic standards achievable in a largely oral culture. But papyrus was expensive, and 'books' (papyrus rolls) were very rare. That was still the case in the time of Aristotle, almost a century later, although he, like his predecessors Isocrates and Plato, needed texts not only for personal use but also as teaching aids in his school (see p. 307).

In the Hellenistic era, Aristotle's personal collection – as opposed to the holding of the Lyceum school – was transformed from a collection of texts into literature. According to tradition, it found its way into the library of Alexandria, the Royal Library attached to the Museum (literally 'shrine of the Muses') established early in the third century BCE by Ptolemy I (see p. 11). Here Aristotle's collection was classified and catalogued, alongside the host of other texts that poured into the Egyptian capital, both solicited and unsolicited. Two of the categories defined by scholars such as the librarian–poet Callimachus and the textual critic Aristarchus were what we would call literature and literary criticism.

Laocoön and his sons. Copy, perhaps early first century CE, by three Rhodians – Hagesander, Polydorus and Athenodorus – of one or more original(s) from perhaps c.200 BCE. Laocoön was a Trojan priest who tried to warn his countrymen against the Greek 'gift' of the Trojan Horse; he and his sons (two, according to Vergil's *Aeneid*) are shown at an altar enveloped by giant sea serpents sent by gods hostile to Troy. Pliny (see p. 255) described a Laocoön group in the palace of Titus. In 1506 this sculpture, closely matching Pliny's description, was excavated in Rome, under the gaze of Michelangelo.

The Alexandrians were by no means interested only in literature. In fact, in Ptolemaic Alexandria during the last three centuries BCE were laid the foundations of Western learning in all the major branches of intellectual endeavour – from literature to astronomy, from medicine to historiography. The polymath Eratosthenes of Cyrene is perhaps the best single illustration of the intellectual fervour and creative ferment of the age. Nicknamed 'Beta', because he was placed second in every sphere and discipline of learning, his achievements include both a remarkably accurate estimate of the Earth's circumference and a challenge to the historical authenticity of Homer – show me, he said, the cobbler who sewed the bag in which King Aeolus shut up all the winds, and *then* I'll believe in the literal truth of the *Odyssey*! This reminds us that Scepticism in the technical sense, a philosophical school, was one of the Hellenistic era's major formal contributions to philosophy.

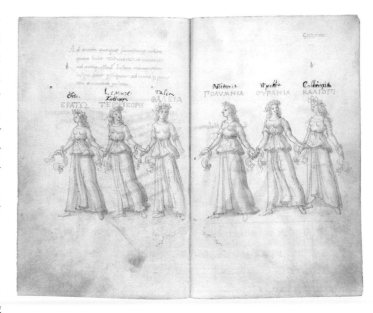

Cyriac of Ancona's drawings of the dancing women on a fourth-century BCE frieze-block from the gateway of the sanctuary of the Great Gods, Samothrace, do at least convey the spirit of the originals, although he was mistaken in his assumption that the women depicted were Muses (see p. 352).

THE COMING OF ROME

Very few people, then or since, have been prepared to embrace entirely Eratosthenes' robustly sceptical attitude to 'the Poet'; least of all the Romans – the first true connoisseurs of Greek (including Hellenistic) culture. In step with their military and diplomatic conquest of the Greek-speaking world, the Romans displayed a passion for acquiring Greek culture and artifacts. How better to appropriate Hellenism than by attaching themselves to the Homeric tradition of mythical pedigrees? After all, weren't the Romans lineally descended from Homer's Aeneas, himself the son of Aphrodite (known to them as Venus)?

A nice example of Rome's homage to Greek art is recorded by the antiquarian Pliny the Elder, who died in 79 through a surfeit of scientific curiosity (he was overcome by fumes from the eruption of Vesuvius, which he was observing at too close quarters). He wrote a *Natural History*, the earliest surviving reference guide to, among other things, ancient sculpture and painting. In it he declared that 'a work superior to any painting or bronze' was a marble group of three figures depicting Laocoön, Trojan priest of Apollo, and his two sons. The three sculptors were Greeks, from Rhodes, but their work as described was to be found in the palace of the future Roman emperor Titus (reigned 79–81 CE).

Another way of bringing Greece to Rome, besides commissioning Greek artists, was to appropriate Greek artifacts. Lucius Mummius, conqueror of Greece in 146 BCE, became notorious for the extent of his largely indiscriminate plunder, which he would probably have justified as the spoils of war. Revealing of Roman taste in a different way was the transfer in unknown circumstances of a Greek marble pedimental composition of the high classical era from its original site to the temple of Apollo Sosianus, built at Rome in the Campus Martius during the 20s BCE under the first Roman emperor Augustus.

Augustus actually wrote his memoirs in Greek, and in the Greek-speaking half of his empire he was worshipped in the conventional Hellenistic manner as a god-king. But in Rome he was careful to distance himself from Greekness, and especially from worship of himself as divine. Through the epic poetry of Virgil and in other ways Augustus publicly fostered the cult of those gods to whom he attributed Rome's – and his – good fortune in emerging so happily from decades of civil war. Chief among these gods were Mars and Venus (his personal ancestress, so he claimed), and Apollo, who had helped him win the decisive battle of Actium over Antony and Cleopatra. In the fourth book of Virgil's *Aeneid* the Carthaginian queen, Dido, is meant

Rome's Greece

It is to the Romans and their empire that we chiefly owe the preservation of Hellenism. Horace described the hellenization of Roman culture as 'captive Greece taking her fierce conqueror captive and introducing the arts to rustic Latium'. But, according to Virgil, it was Jupiter himself who had taught the Romans that they were 'to spare those who had been subjected and war down the stiff-necked resisters'. The Romans' adoption of Greek high culture, in other words, was accompanied by a good deal of physical brutality to Greeks who were less than eager to become Roman imperial subjects – and by a good deal of plundering.

Greek statues were especially prized by the Roman conquerors. For the most part, however, what has survived are not the Greek originals, often in bronze, but Roman copies in marble that could be multiply reproduced. Occasionally, though, and by accident, the looted originals have come down to us, none being more magnificent than the two over life-size bronze statues of the mid-fifth century BCE fished out of the sea off Riace in Calabria only a few decades ago. Happily for us, the ship carrying them from Greece to Rome was wrecked en route.

One theory has it that these masterpieces were from the hand of Phidias, originally part of a victory dedication at Delphi made by the Athenians in commemoration of their victory at Marathon. True or not, Phidias would surely have been astonished by the use to which one of the Riace bronzes was put soon after its discovery *(right)* in an Italian soft-porn cartoon magazine. 'Forbidden to minors', indeed.

Greek literature, too, the Romans as a rule consumed with a will, producing their own equal, some would say superior, versions of many genres of writing. But the theatre was an aspect to recall Cleopatra. In Augustan propaganda the Graeco-Macedonian Queen was por-trayed as the incarnation of the barbarian and decadent Orient – in opposition to himself, the latter-day reincarnation of the pious and utterly Roman Aeneas.

BYZANTIUM, OR THE NEW ROME

With the establishment of Constantinople as a second capital in 330 the Roman empire's centre of gravity shifted eastwards, and Rome and Italy fell relatively into decline. The demise of the Roman empire in the West in 476, the religious split between Catholicism and Eastern Orthodoxy, and then the conquest of what remained of the Byzantine empire by the Ottoman Turks in 1453 had the effect of erecting a near-impermeable cultural barrier between East and West, with Greece on the Eastern side. The cultural Renaissance of Europe in the fifteenth and six-teenth centuries was therefore not primarily a rediscovery of ancient Greek but of ancient Roman culture and civilization. Yet there were exceptions.

of Greek culture which the Romans, though they admired and imitated it, were slow to make their own. Greek drama, especially comedy, was introduced to Italy in the fourth century and had reached Rome by the third, but it did not overshadow native Ital-ian pantomiming and farces in popularity, and acting remained a profession of dubious respectability, barred by law to Roman citizens – hence the shock and outrage when an emperor, Nero, seemed in traditionalist Roman eyes to degrade himself by per-forming as a Greek-style actor. One of his advisers, Seneca, more acceptably wrote as opposed to acted in tragedy.

It was a sure mark of Rome's suspicion of Greek theatrical cul-ture that a permanent stone theatre was not constructed in the capital itself until the middle of the first century BCE. Shortly before then, however, a Roman official had followed the usual practice of employing a punning device on coins that bore his name – his sur-name being Musa, he enterprisingly had his issues illustrated with masks depicting the Muses of both Tragedy and Comedy.

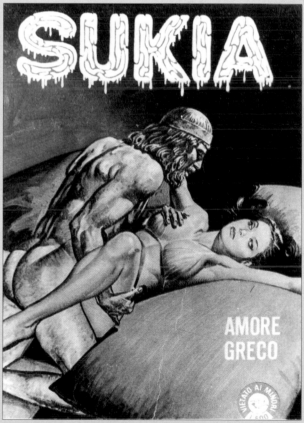

One of the extraordinary and beautiful Riace bronzes (*facing page*), **and one of the more unusual representations of it** (*above*). (*Left*) **The Musa silver coins.**

RENAISSANCE

The Italian merchant Cyriac of Ancona spent the best part of thirty years during the first half of the fifteenth century travelling through Italy, Greece and the eastern Mediterranean. His drawings of Greek antiquities (see p. 349) and his copies of Greek inscriptions provided the Renaissance with its only significant glimpse of ancient Greek material culture. He was not, however, a slavishly faithful recorder of what he saw. For example, the profiles and proportions of the columns in his drawing of the Parthenon's west front are completely awry, and he represented its pedimental sculpture in accordance with Italian Renaissance preconceptions. He did rather better, to our eyes anyhow, when he visited the sanctuary of the Great Gods on Samothrace, the source also of the 'Winged Victory'.

SCIENCE

The preceding examples of the Greek legacy have been drawn mainly from the Arts, in accordance with the modern distinction between the Arts and the Sciences. The ancient Greeks, however, would have recognized no such distinction, any more than did the leading intellectuals of the Renaissance (or the Enlightenment). Of course, there are profound differences between Greek and modern science. It is from Greek *physis* ('nature') that our word 'physics' is derived. But to describe, for example, the discovery of the top quark, the sixth and last of the subatomic particles predicted to exist by current theories of the structure of matter, as the completion of a project of scientific enquiry initiated by Greeks would be problematic.

Nevertheless, there are also important continuities. If science as an enterprise tries to discover and explain the phenomena and regularities of the empirical world, in the belief that natural laws are uniform in space and time, then the ancient Greek 'enquiry into nature' (*historia physeos*) was indeed science. The Greek attitude to the natural world of (for example) Democritus does anticipate the predominantly non-religious scientific attitude of the Renaissance and early modern West. There is some poetic justice in the Greek ancestry of much of our scientific terminology. For example, as Primo Levi remarks in *The Periodic Table*, the *yl* of ethyl, methyl and so on, is derived from Greek *hyle* or 'matter'.

ANTI-CLASSICAL REACTION

Not all Renaissance and early modern thinkers, however, felt equally indebted to the ancient Greeks and Romans. John Locke was no doubt not alone in believing that a classical education left something to be desired:

> When I consider what an ado is made about a little Latin and Greek, how many years are spent in it, and what a noise and business it makes to no purpose, I can hardly forbear thinking that the parents of children still live in fear of the school-master's rod, which they look on as the only instrument of education, [just as they think] a language or two to be the whole business.

Denial of the overriding importance of a shared classical heritage paralleled the sharp religious and political divisions of the seventeenth century.

Consider its views on democracy. Leading Renaissance and early modern thinkers often approved republican liberty, or at any rate freedom from absolutist despotism. But they were for the most part by no stretch of the imagination democrats in an ancient Greek sense. Many would have preferred a dictatorship, even if it were less than entirely benevolent, to the rule - over them – of the masses. One such was Thomas Hobbes, whose first published work was the first translation of Thucydides into English directly from the Greek (rather than via a Latin version). At the end of his life he claimed that it was Thucydides who had taught him how much wiser was the rule of one man than giving power to the mob.

On the other side, perhaps John Milton's *Areopagitica*, addressed to Parliament in 1644, was the nearest anyone got at the time to espousing ancient Greek democratic ideals of full freedom of public political speech. The title-page carried a quotation in translation from the *Suppliant Women* of Euripides:

> This is true Liberty when free born men
> Having to advise the public may speak free,
> Which he who can, and will, deserv's high praise,
> Who neither can nor will, may hold his peace;
> What can be juster in a State than this?

ENLIGHTENMENT

In the European and American Enlightenment movements of the eighteenth century 'philosopher' came to be used in something like the original Greek sense of

Trophies of the philosophic tourism of the eighteenth-century Grand Tour include this portrait bust of one of the greatest of ancient philosophers, Marcus Aurelius, who, though a Roman emperor, wrote his Stoic *Meditations* (literally *Eis Heauton* or *To Himself*) in Greek.

The foreground of this drawing (1751–53) by James 'Athenian' Stuart (1713–88) of the Acropolis is dominated by the Tower of the Winds, a first-century BCE clock still standing (but no longer working) today. Stuart managed to incorporate a replica of it in a 1760s folly he designed for the ancestral estate of Lord Lichfield at Shugborough in Staffordshire, England. It, too, has stood the test of time.

'The Death of Socrates' (1787) by Jacques-Louis David (1748–1825). In *Phaedo*, Plato puts into the mouth of Phaedo, who was with Socrates as he drank, these words:

Soon the jailer ... entered and stood by him, saying: 'to you, Socrates, who I know to be the noblest and gentlest and best of all who ever came to this place, I will not impute the angry feelings of other men, who rage and swear at me when in obedience to the authorities I bid them drink the poison – indeed, I am sure you will not be angry with me; for others, as you are aware, and not I are to blame. And so fare you well, and try to bear lightly what needs be – you know my errand'. Then bursting into tears he turned away.

Later, when Socrates raised the cup to his lips and drank off the lethal dose of hemlock, Phaedo relates:

... hitherto most of us had been able to control our sorrow; but now when we saw him drinking, and saw too that he had finished the draught we could no longer forbear, and in spite of myself my own tears were flowing fast; so that I covered my face and wept, not for him, but at the thought of my own calamity in having to part from such a friend. Nor was I the first; for Crito, when he found himself unable to restrain his tears, had got up, and I followed; and at that moment, Apollodorus, who had been weeping all the time, broke out in a loud and passionate cry which made cowards of us all. Socrates alone retained his calmness.

sophistes (before it acquired its pejorative overtones) – to mean a wise and cultured man or, more narrowly, an intellectual. One common cultural practice was philosophical travel.

As the eighteenth century progressed, it became more and more the thing for a cultured young gentleman to embark on a Grand Tour of the classical lands – at first to Rome, later and less frequently (for practical rather than other reasons) to Greece and the Aegean.

Perhaps the most visible and enduring result of the Grand Tour was a passion for classical architecture expressed in the development of neoclassicism. No one did more to stimulate the Greek Revival than the Scot James Stuart, 'Athenian' Stuart as he became known. Together with Nicholas Revett he spent the years 1751–3 sketching and measuring what were later (in some cases very much later) published as *The Antiquities of Athens*. Their visit coincided with the beginnings of an important shift in northern European and (rather later) North American classical interest away from Rome towards Greece. The pioneer art-critic of this movement was the German Johann Joachim Winckelmann, though he never actually set foot in Greece and based his views on copies of Greek sculpture in Rome.

This new interest in Greece was by no means disinterested, however. Museums and private collectors wanted classical art, while the primary aim of Stuart and Revett was to provide usable models for British neoclassical architects. Indeed, Stuart was himself commissioned to design replicas of several ancient monuments.

Besides architecture, the neoclassical movement also embraced both painting (including ceramics, like those made at Josiah Wedgwood's famous 'Etruria' factory – it was thought that the Athenian vases then being uncovered in Etruria were local Etruscan products) and sculpture. Perhaps the greatest of neoclassical painters in

France was Jacques-Louis David, court artist to Napoleon. The emperor exploited the taste for classicism by having himself represented alternatively as Alexander the Great or Julius Caesar. But David was also a sophisticated painter of Greek themes, and 'The Death of Socrates' (see p. 302) is one of the most famous of all his canvasses. Truly, as Gibbon had remarked of David Hume in 1776, David's Socrates died the death of a philosopher.

ROMANTICISM

It was in Edinburgh, 'Athens of the North', that Hume breathed his last, and it is in Edinburgh today for half of every year that Antonio Canova's second 'Three Graces' (1815–19) is now publicly displayed. Winckelmann had insisted that Greek sculpture of the finest (classical) period was inimitable, but Canova's flair and technique enabled him to create more than passable imitations of Hellenistic sculpture.

At the very time that they were being carved, the fate of even more controversial sculptures from a genuine Greek temple was being settled: the Elgin – or Parthenon – marbles. These had been removed from the Acropolis by the seventh Earl of Elgin in 1801. They were eventually bought by the Trustees of the British Museum in 1816 for what was then a king's ransom of £35,000 – though they had cost Elgin twice that amount just to ship them back to England. Byron (in his 'The Curse of Minerva' and elsewhere) expressed the rage of the philhellenes at the spoliation.

> Yes, 'twas Minerva's self; but, ah! how changed
> Since o'er the Dardan field in arms she ranged!
>
> ...
>
> 'Mortal!' – 'twas thus she spake – 'that blush of shame
> Proclaims thee Briton, once a noble name;
> First of the mighty, foremost of the free,
> Now honour'd *less* by all and *least* by me:
> Chief of thy foes shall Pallas still be found.
> Seek thou the cause of loathing? – look around.
> Lo! here, despite of war and wasting fire,
> I saw successive tyrannies expire.
> 'Scaped from the ravage of the Turk and Goth,
> Thy country sends a spoiler worse than both.'
>
> ...
>
> She ceased awhile, and thus I dared reply,
> To soothe the vengeance kindling in her eye:
> 'Daughter of Jove! in Britain's injured name,
> A true-born Briton may the deed disclaim.
> Frown not on England; England owns him not:
> Athena, no! thy plunderer was a Scot'.

Debate as to the proper location of the marbles continues vigorously to this day.

'The Three Graces' (1815–19) by Antonio Canova (1757–1822). Before being 'rescued for the nation [Britain]' in 1995 by private charity (at a cost of almost £8 million) when they came up for sale and aroused international interest, the Graces had stood in James Wyatville's Temple at Woburn Abbey, England. After a long period of disfavour during the various modern art movements of this century, Canova's flawless classicism is again finding an appreciative public – and market. Canova, one of the first neoclassicists, spent time in London studying the Elgin marbles.

Athenaeum Club, London. The response of the Committee of the Athenaeum Club to the arrival of the Elgin Marbles was to commission for its exterior decoration a Wedgwood-style version of the Parthenon frieze.

(*Below*) Hiram Power's 'Greek Slave' (1843). The extreme aestheticization of Hiram Power's 1843 marble sculpture of a nude female 'Greek Slave' represented 'passionless perfection' to Elizabeth Barrett Browning, but conveys something more like a barely sublimated voyeurism to our eyes.

VICTORIAN VALUES

The Victorians' wholehearted appropriation of Hellenism presented them with some cultural problems. On the one hand, Greece was – in politics and education as well as in literature and the visual arts – the constant point of reference and standard of value. On the other hand, a veil had to be drawn over certain aspects of ancient Greek culture that did not cohere easily with Victorian Christianity. Above all, Greek sexuality, and especially homosexuality, was found highly problematic. One solution was to represent supposed scenes of real life in a style as far removed from earthy realism as possible.

On the other hand, what some late Victorians appreciated about the Greeks was precisely what they took to be their uninhibited and unorthodox sexual attitudes and behaviour. For example, Oscar Wilde's novel *The Picture of Dorian Gray* (published in 1890, the same year as the English term 'homosexuality' is first recorded), can be seen as a coded exploration of Greek pederastic love. Some of Aubrey Beardsley's graphic drawings offer an exuberantly heterosexual counterpart.

MODERNISM: REVOLUTION AND REACTION

Both Wilde and Beardsley, who famously collaborated on Wilde's play *Salome*, were primarily concerned to depict those aspects of human behaviour or social mores that convention repressed or ignored. In that respect, at least, there was common ground between them and later artistic revolutionaries, such as Pablo Picasso. He, it has been said, introduced not one but four separate revolutionary changes in twentieth-century painting – often in reaction against a sterile and fossilized academic classicism. Even Picasso, however, was unable to kill classicism, and he did not himself entirely avoid the use of classical imagery to express or wrestle with his deepest personal, professional or political feelings. The bull-man Minotaur preoccupied him especially during the dark night of fascism and totalitarianism in the 1920s and 1930s.

Without the efforts of the Titan Prometheus, who had to resort to deceiving Zeus in order to steal fire for humans' benefit, there would have been no possibility of technological progress – and so no possibility of casting bronze statues. In the nineteenth century, Prometheus held a particular attraction for thinkers of the radical left, among them Shelley and Karl Marx. Today, however, he has become an acceptable icon for the captains of industry.

Another curiously mechanical modern appropriation of the classical Greek achievement is the Parthenon replica to be seen in Nashville, Tennessee. In a different class is Ricardo Bofill's freshly designed new National Theatre of Barcelona, but its neo-classicism has aroused a chorus of disapproval orchestrated by Spain's avant-garde post-modernist establishment.

POST-MODERNISM?

Far more to their taste, presumably, would be the work of their compatriot Francesc Torres, who returns to the classical past in a far less straightforward and far more playful way than Bofill. For example, to an exhibition labelled 'Re-Writing History' Torres contributed 'Oikonomos', a two-channel video installation of which the famous fifth-century bronze Zeus or Poseidon from Artemisium formed the central focus.

(*Above*) **Aubrey Beardsley's graphic skills as a draughtsman were rarely put to more dramatic use than in his series of drawings inspired by Aristophanes'** *Lysistrata.* **Commissioned by Leonard Smithers, they appeared in a limited edition of the play he published in 1896.**

(*Left*) **The Nashville Parthenon. The attempted replica of the Parthenon in Nashville, Tennessee, may be 'just one of the unsung attractions of Music city, USA' (as a tourist advertisement has it). But opinions differ on the validity of such reconstructions.**

(*Above*) **Outside the Rockefeller Center in New York stands a bronze statue of Prometheus, fire in hand. Appropriated here as an unambiguous symbol of technological progress, in other renditions the Titan has served to question the divine dispensation of life on earth for humankind.**

(*Above right*) **Picasso's 'Minotaure', 1933. Picasso, as a Spaniard for whom the bull had a special appeal as a symbol for the beast in man, was a natural choice as illustrator of the cover of the first issue of Albert Skira's magazine *Minotaure*. This appeared in 1933, the same year as Hitler's seizure of power.**

'Oikonomos' reveals how enriching for the artist can be the possibility of seeing and judging one's own culture's idioms and language in the light of other languages and idioms. It thereby reminds us sharply that the classical Greek tradition, if it is to continue, cannot be something fixed and static but must be constantly subject to reinvention. As the contemporary writer Juan Goytisolo has urged, relativism in the sense of 'a plurality of perspectives and experiences' allows 'a much sharper perception of the original elements and features in one's own culture, and healthily affirms the personal principles of the creator of the fashions of contemporary society'.

Such multicultural relativism, rather than a sterile academic classicism that seeks merely to embalm the oldest dead white European males and their achievements, must be the ambition of all who value and love ancient Greece.

Reference guide to
The Cambridge
Illustrated History of
Ancient Greece

Who's Who

Achilles son of the mortal Peleus and immortal Thetis whose anger at being dishonoured by Agamemnon forms the theme of Homer's *Iliad*.

Aeneas Trojan hero, son of Anchises and Aphrodite (Virgil's Venus), noted for rescuing his father from the Sack of Troy and becoming a founder of Rome.

Aeolus god of the winds, which he enclosed in a bag and gave to Odysseus as he returned from Troy, only for his jealous sailors to let them out again.

Aeschines fourth-century Athenian politician, chief opponent of Demosthenes, whose career ended with failure in a major prosecution of an associate of Demosthenes 330.

Aeschylus *c*.525–456, tragedian, said to have written ninety plays, seven surviving (or six, if *Prometheus Bound* is not his).

Aesop reputed sixth century, Aesop was a slave on Samos, none of 'his' fables certainly authentic.

Agamemnon legendary king of Mycenae, commander-in-chief of the Greek expedition against Troy, his murder by Clytemnestra (his wife) and her lover Aegisthus forms subject of first play in the *Oresteia* trilogy of Aeschylus, 458.

Agathon *c*.447–400, Athenian tragedian, Plato's *Symposium* was set at a party to celebrate his first victory as a tragic poet at the Lenaec in 416.

Agave mother of Pentheus whom she destroyed in a Bacchic frenzy horribly dramatized in Euripides' *Bacchae*.

Agesilaus II king of Sparta *c*.400–360, for a time one of the most powerful figures in mainland Greece but presided over Sparta's decline and fall.

Alcaeus *floruit c*.600, lyric poet of Mytilene, Lesbos, active in domestic politics.

Alcibiades *c*.450–404, ward of Pericles and most brilliant if most wayward of his successors, disgraced by treachery, rehabilitated, disgraced again and eventually murdered.

Alcidamas fourth century rhetorician noted for claiming that 'God had made no man a slave' and thereby supporting the liberation of the Messeuian Helots.

Alcmaeon of Croton (South Italy) early fifth-century physician, pioneered theory that the brain not heart was seat of intelligence.

Alcman lyric poet of Sparta, *floruit c*.600, most famous for inventing the genre of the Maiden Song, choral lyrics sung competitively by girls on the verge of marriage.

Aleuadae an aristocratic house of Thessaly which in the Persian Wars abandoned the Greek cause and defected to Persia.

Alexander of Pherae Thessalian tyrant, murdered 358, failed to restore the position achieved by his predecesor Jason.

Alexander the Great born 356, pupil of Aristotle *c*.343, reigned 336–323; assumed father Philip's role and completed conquest of Persian empire before early death at Babylon prevented consolidation of a new imperial system.

Amasis sixth-century pharaoh of philhellenic inclinations, conquered in 525 by Cambyses of Persia (see Cambyses).

Amazons mythical race of female warriors, one of whom (Penthesilea) was killed by Achilles, another (Antiope of Hippolyte) was mother of Hippolytus.

Ammianus Greek historian of the fourth century CE who wrote in Latin and celebrated the pagan emperor Julian.

Anaxagoras of Clazomenae *c*.500–428, natural philosopher famous or notorious for holding that the sun was not divine but a red-hot mass of stone rather larger than the Peloponnese. He was perhaps prosecuted at Athens for impiety.

Anaximander first half sixth century, Milesian natural philosopher in line of Thales, conceived of universe as a cosmos in balance.

Anaximenes first half sixth century, Milesian natural philosopher, possibly pupil of Thales, who postulated air as the governing principle of the cosmos.

Andromache wife of Hector, with whom she shares a famous scene in the *Iliad*, taken captive and as a slave to Greece by Achilles' son Pyrrhus.

Antalcidas *floruit* fourth century, Spartan general and diplomat, eponym of Peace with Persia in 386.

Antigonus/Antigonid dynasty Macedonian dynasty named after Antigonus the One-Eyed which ruled Macedon and Greece after Alexander the Great's empire was carved up.

Antipater Macedonian noble, made regent of Macedon and Greece during Alexander's Asiatic campaign.

Antiphon Athenian oligarchic politician, rhetorician and perhaps philosopher, mastermind of 411 coup but executed for treachery.

Antisthenes *c*.445–360, pupil and friend of Socrates, but founder of School later called *Cynic* (from Greek for 'dog').

Apelles *floruit* fourth century, originally of Colophon, later court painter to Philip and Alexander of Macedon at Pella.

Aphrodite wife of the lame craftsman god Hephaestus but lover of the war god Ares, her special concerns were erotic attraction and sexual gratification.

Apollo archer-god, god of healing, of music, of intellectual activity, full brother of Artemis.

Apollodorus pseudonymous – author of a compendium of Greek myths 1–2 CE.

Apollonius of Citium *c*.90–15, Alexandrian physician and author of extant commentary on the Hippocratic treatise 'On Joints'.

Archelaus King of Macedon 413–399, unifier of territory but assassinated.

Aratus *c*.315 to before 240, author of verse version of Eudoxus' *Phaenomena*.

Archilochus of Paros and Thasos early seventh-century iambic poet of Paros, then Thasos; composer of passionate erotica and political invective.

Archimedes *c*.287–212, inventor, especially mathematical, and astronomer, died fighting Romans in defence of his native Syracuse.

Ares god of war, adulterous lover of Aphrodite in Homer, not very widely worshipped.

Aristagoras tyrant of Miletos, *c*.505–496.

Aristarchus Samian astronomer, dated by his observation of the summer solstice of 280 and famed for his heliocentric hypothesis of the universe.

Aristides *c*.525–467, Athenian general famed for justice of his original assessment (478/7) of tribute in cash or kind for allies of Athens in Delian League (see Glossary).

Aristophanes *c*.445–385, author of over forty comedies, eleven extant, both master of political Old Comedy and inaugurator of Middle Comedy of manners.

Aristotle 384–322, originally of Stagira, son of court physician to Philip of Macedon's father, pupil of Plato, teacher of Alexander, founded own Lyceum School *c*.335; some 500 titles known, thirty treatises extant, especially biological, zoological and political.

Artemis hunter goddess of the wild margins and of adolescent transition from childhood to adulthood, perpetual virgin, twin sister of Apollo.

Artemisia of Halicarnassus Greek queen of outstanding prowess on Xerxes' side at Salamis, 480, glowingly written up by compatriot Herodotus.

Asclepius worshipped both as hero and as god, patron divinity of healing (especially through dreams).

Aspasia of Miletus, associate of Socrates and famous, or notorious, for being partner of Pericles, whom she was forbidden to marry by his own Athenian citizenship law of 451/0.

Athena daughter of Zeus, notorious for the unusual mode of her birth (fully armed from her father's head), goddess of craft skills and practical wisdom, also a perpetual virgin associated with the male sphere of war.

Atossa daughter of Cyrus the Great of Persia, wife of Darius I of Persia.

Augustus 63BCE–CE14, first Roman emperor, who included Greece in the Roman Empire under the name of 'Achaea'.

Bacchus Alternative name (in Latin form) for Dionysus.

Bacchylides c.510–450, of Keos, relative of Simonides, lyric poet of victory odes and dithyrambs.

Biton one of a pair of mythical or legendary brothers (see also Cleobis) who dragged their priestess mother to her religious shrine a distance of some 8 kilometres and fell asleep and died, possibly sixth century.

Boreas god of the north wind, worshipped (e.g. at Athens).

Brasidas Spartan general of Peloponnesian War, best known for detaching from Athens the city of Amphipolis, where he died in battle against Cleon in 422.

Callias Athenian politician and diplomat of immense wealth, brother-in-law of Cimon but collaborated with Pericles, negotiating favourable peaces both with Persia (c.450) and with Sparta (445).

Callicrates *floruit* fifth century, co-architect of Parthenon, also worked on Nike shrine on Athenian Acropolis.

Callimachus third century, scholar-poet originally from Cyrene, produced first catalogue of Alexandria Royal Library, credited with more than 800 works and proverb ' a big book is a big bore'.

Callisthenes c.380–327, of Olynthus (destroyed by Philip 348), kinsman and co-author of Aristotle, official historian of Alexander, but executed by him for alleged treason.

Cambyses Great King of Persia 530–522, died in suspicious circumstances after adding Egypt to the Persian empire.

Cecrops legendary king of Athens regarded by the historical Athenians as their archetypal ancestor figure.

Cephisodotus fourth-century Athenian sculptor, father of Praxiteles.

Charon of Lampsacus fifth-century historian, work mostly lost, also produced list of Spartan officials.

Chilon mid-sixth-century Spartan ephor (elected official), sometimes included in lists of Seven Sages.

Cicero 106–43, Roman politician, orator and philosopher, letter-writer extraordinary, whose main correspondent Atticus resided in Greece.

Cimon c.510–450, son of Miltiades of Marathon, Athenian politician and general, mainly responsible for early development of Delian League, fell out with Pericles over policy towards Persia (aggressive) and Sparta (pacific).

Ciriaco de' Pizzicolli/Cyriacus of Ancona 1391–1452, merchant and humanist who first introduced ancient Greek visual art and culture to the Renaissance.

Cleanthes successor of Zeno as head of the stoic school of philosophy, author of an extant 'Hymn to Zeus'.

Cleisthenes (i) of Sicyon, tyrant c.600–570 (ii) of Athens, c.565–505, maternal grandson of (i), credited – or debited – with founding the Athenian democracy 508/7.

Cleobis brother of Biton (see Biton).

Cleomenes King of Sparta c.520–490, a central figure in Herodotus' *Histories*.

Cleon leading Athenian politician in succession to Pericles (died 429), cordially detested by Thucydides for whose exile he was probably responsible and savagely lampooned by Aristophanes (especially *Knights*, 424), died in battle 422.

Cleopatra 69–30, the famous Cleopatra VII, last of the Graeco-Macedonian Ptolemies to rule Egypt following Alexander's conquest, defeated with Antony by Octavian/Augustus at Actium in 31, committed suicide.

Cleophon leading Athenian democratic politician of the late fifth century, assassinated in 405 right at the end of the Peloponnesian War.

Colaeus sixth-century Samian merchant reputed to have made a killing on the Spanish run.

Conon c.450–389, Athenian admiral, fled to Euagoras on Cyprus after decisive defeat at Aegospotami, 405, redeemed himself by defeating Sparta at Cnidos, 394, as admiral funded by Persia.

Cratinus Athenian comic poet, older contemporary and rival of Aristophanes, whose *Clouds* he beat with his swansong *Flask* in 423.

Cresilas *floruit* c.450–420, bronze sculptor from Cydonia on Crete but most famous for helmeted bust of Pericles, worked also at Delphi.

Critias c.460–403, older relative of Plato, leader of pro-Spartan junta of Thirty Tyrants, wrote works in praise of Sparta in both verse and praise.

Croesus proverbially wealthy ('rich as Croesus') king of Lydia c.560–546, philhellenic ruler of Greek cities including Ephesus (whose Artemis temple he adorned), defeated by Cyrus.

Cylon would-be dictator of Athens, c.620, but his coup failed despite – or because of – support from his father-in-law Theagenes (q.v.).

Cypselus/Cypselid dynasty tyrant dynasty of Corinth founded by Cypselus c.650 (see also Periander).

Cyriac of Ancona see Ciriaco de' Pizzicolli.

Cyrnus addressee, possibly fictional, of many homoerotic verses by Theognis (see Theognis).

Cyrus II, Great King of Persia c.559–30, founder of Achaemenid empire, liberator of Jews from Babylon.

Darius I Great King of Persia c.520–486, second founder of Achaemenid empire, quelled Ionian Revolt 499–4 but his forces failed at Marathon 490.

David, Jacques-Louis 1748–1825, classically trained painter famous for his classical (e.g. 'Death of Socrates') and classicizing works.

Demeter earth-mother goddess, one of the twelve Olympians particularly associated with the fertility of women.

Democritus c.460–?385, of Abdera, wrote ethical, mathematical, and musical treatises, but most famous for his 'atomist' theory of physical universe.

Demosthenes 384–322, Athenian politician and forensic orator of genius, led Athenian and Greek resistance to Philip and Alexander of Macedon, ultimately without success.

Dexileos of Athens young cavalryman born 414, killed near Corinth in late 390s.

Dido legendary queen of Carthage who failed to halt Aeneas on his mission to found Rome.

Diodorus Siculus *floruit* c.60–30, Sicilian Greek 'universal' historian ('universal' meaning what the Greeks took the whole human world to be, i.e., the known Greek world), compiler of 'Library of History' beginning with early Greece using, for example, Ephorus.

Diogenes of Sinope c.400–325, Diogenes the Cynic, noted for his unconventional lifestyle (for example, sleeping in the open in a large pottery storage-jar, masturbating in public) and *bons mots*.

Dione wife of Zeus at Dodona, or rather a female version of Zeus, worshipped in north-west Greece.

Dionysius I Tyrant of Syracuse 405–367, kept Greek Sicily free of Carthaginian control, patron of Plato, winner of crown for tragedy at Athens.

Dionysus god of illusion and ecstasy, especially through wine and drama.

Draco *floruit c.*620, author of earliest Athenian laws, later – unfairly – believed to have been 'written in blood', i.e. to stipulate capital punishment for all or most defined crimes.

Eileithyia goddess of childbirth, invoked to ease pains of childbirth and parturition.

Elgin, Lord (1766–1814) controversial ambassador to the Ottoman emperor who (depending on viewpoint) stole or removed to safety many Parthenon marbles.

Empedocles *c.*492–32, of Acragas in Sicily, author of two hexameter poems, *On Nature* (originator of four-element physical theory) and *Purifications* (religion).

Epaminondas died 362, Theban general and (Pythagorean) philosopher, most famous for defeating Sparta, 371 and 362, and enabling foundation of Messene and Megalopolis.

Ephialtes assassinated 461, opponent of Cimon, principal author of democratic reforms of 462/1 maintained and developed by Pericles.

Ephorus of Cyme fourth century, 'universal' historian of Greece post-Trojan War, possibly pupil of Isocrates.

Epicurus 341–270, founder of the Epicurean school of philosophy preaching tranquillity as the greatest good, born on Samos of Athenian parentage.

Eratosthenes *c.*275–195, like Callimachus originally from Cyrene but made his name at Alexandria, multi-talented chronographer, literary critic and geographer.

Erechtheus mythical king of Athens transformed into a hero and worshipped as such in the Erechtheum.

Erinna fourth-century woman poet, place of origin uncertain, best known for her 300-line *The Distaff*.

Etruscans people of central Italy between Tiber and Arno rivers, origin uncertain, of great political and cultural importance before rise of Rome.

Euagoras *c.* 435–374/3, King of Salamis on Cyprus, host of Conon and resister of Persia; awarded honorary Athenian citizenship.

Euclid *floruit* 295, mathematician and astronomer, his thirteen books of *Elements* (plane geometry, theory of numbers, stereometry) have remained foundational.

Eudoxus *c.*400–347, of Cnidus, much travelled mathematician, astronomer and geographer, best known for influential theory of movements of heavenly bodies.

Euhemerus *floruit c.*300, utopian novelist, proposed that Greeks' gods had originally been human rulers.

Euphranor *floruit c.*370–330, painter and sculptor, commissioned to decorate Stoa of Zeus in Athenian Agora with history paintings.

Euphronius *floruit c.*515–480, pioneering Athenian red-figure vase-painter, for one of whose works, found in Etruria, the Metropolitan Museum in New York was prepared to pay one million dollars.

Eupolis late-fifth-century Athenian comic poet and major rival of Aristophanes; first play produced 429, won at least four victories, but only fragments survive.

Euripides *c.*485–406, tragedian, nineteen of whose approximately eighty attributed plays survive. He was much ridiculed by comic poets in lifetime but the most popular of the 'Big Three' tragedians after his death. He died at Pella, capital of Macedon, where he had written *Bacchae*.

Galen 129–*c.*200 CE, of Perganum, physician to the Roman emperor Marcus Aurelius, author of many, massively influential medical treatises, especially on anatomy and physiology.

Gelon Tyrant of Syracuse 485–78, defeated Carthaginian invasion at Himera, 480, allegedly on same day as battle of Salamis.

Gibbon, Edward 1737–1794, author of the most influential work of ancient history in the English language, *The Decline and Fall of the Roman Empire* (6 vols, 1776–88).

Gorgias *c.*483–375, of Leontini on Sicily, one of four 'ancient Sophists', charmed Athenian Assembly 427, influential teacher and exponent of rhetoric.

Guicciardini, Francesco 1483–1540, of Florence, pioneer modern historian (*Storia d'Italia*, 1494–1532).

Harmodius beloved of Aristogiton with whom in *c.*514 he killed brother of Athenian tyrant Hippias; the pair were the first to receive official honorific statues in Athenian Agora.

Hecataeus of Miletus *floruit c.*500, politician and geographical historian, author of *Journey Round the World* to whom Herodotus was much indebted.

Hecate chthonian (earth) divinity capable of inflicting terrible harm when conjured by

magic and witchcraft but also associated with initiatory mystery cults, often worshipped at crossroads.

Hector son of Priam and Hecuba, husband of Andromache, whose death and burial form the climax of the *Iliad*.

Hecuba mother of Hector, wife of Priam, taken into captivity as slave after the fall of Troy, subject of Euripides' *Hecuba*.

Helios god of the sun but little worshipped except most notably at Rhodes.

Hellanicus second half of fifth century, of Mytilene on Lesbos, historian used – and abused – by Thucydides, author of first *Atthis* (local history of Athens).

Hephaestus lame craftsman god conceived by his mother Hera without a male partner, created miraculous automata, the shield and other armour of Achilles, and Pandora.

Hera sister-wife of Zeus, associated in human worship especially with assistance to married women and patronage of cities (e.g. Argos).

Heracles the universal Greek hero, son of Zeus and a mortal woman (Alcmene) most famous for the Twelve Labours but also credited as a founder of the Olympic Games.

Heraclides Ponticus fourth century, from Heraclea on Black Sea, pupil of Plato's Academy narrowly defeated in contest to succeed the Master in 347.

Heraclitus *floruit c.*500, aristocrat of priestly family from Ephesus, famed for his enigmatic obscurity and author of some of the most quoted sayings ('everything flows', 'you can't step twice into the same river').

Hermes son of Zeus and the nymph Naia, as the messenger god capable of moving and meditating between human and divine sphere, worshipped in the form of a pillar, sproting an erect phallus.

Hermias of Atarneus died 341, tyrant of Atarneus, perhaps semi-Hellenic eunuch, pupil of Plato and former guardian of Aristotle's wife.

Herodotus *c.*484–25, of Halicarnassus, pioneer historian, in exile became citizen of Thurii.

Hesiod *floruit c.*700, didactic poet, author of *Works and Days* and *Theogony*.

Hestia one of the twelve Olympians, goddess of the hearth, sworn to perpetual virginity.

Hieron I Tyrant of Syracuse 478–67, in succession to Gelon, defeated Etruscans at Cumae, 474, patron of Simonides and Pindar.

Hieronymus of Cardia *c.*364–260, soldier and administrator in period of the wars of Alexander's Successors, historian of years 323–272.

Hipparchus *floruit* second half second century, born Nicaea but spent much of life at

Rhodes, transformed Greek astronomy from a theoretical to a practical science, only extant work a commentary on the *Phaenomiena* of Eudoxus and Aratus.

Hippias (i) of Athens, tyrant 527–510 in succession to father Pisistratus (ii) of Elis, later fifth century, ancient Sophist and polymath, for example credited with fixing date of first Olympiad to (our) 776.

Hippocrates of Cos *c.*460–380, founder of medical school, attributed with sixty treatises comprising the 'Hippocratic Corpus'.

Hippodamia daughter of legendary king of Pisa (near Olympia) whose hand was at last won when Pelops cheated and defeated her father in a chariot race.

Hippodamus fifth century, of Miletus, town-planner and utopian political philosopher, redesigned Peiraeus and designed new city of Rhodes on orthogonal 'Hippodamian' plan.

Hippolytus son of Theseus and an Amazon woman, devoted to the virgin goddess Artemis, whose rejection of his stepmother Phaedra's amorous advances led to his destruction, dramatized tragically by Euripides.

Homer claimed by many Ionian cities, 'blind Homer' may or may not have flourished in in the eighth century and been responsible for combining and developing long oral traditions into the two monumental epics that bear his name.

Hyperbolus most influential Athenian popular leader after Cleon, ostracized *c.*417, murdered 411 in exile at Samos.

Hyperides 390–22, Athenian orator, pupil of Plato and Isocrates, consistently anti-Macedonian in politics.

Ibycus later sixth century, originally of Rhegium, lyric poet at court of Polycrates.

Ictinus co-architect of Parthenon, also credited with Hall of Initiation at Eleusis and Apollo's temple at Bassae.

Isis Egyptian goddess 'mistress of the house of life' warmly embraced by Greeks and Romans from the Hellenistic era on, especially since she was thought to offer personal salvation in a better afterlife.

Isocrates 436–338, speechwriter, conservative pamphleteer and founder of Athens' first institute of higher studies, with special attention to rhetoric, pupils may include Ephorus and Theopompus as well as Hyperides and others.

Jason Tyrant of Pherae *c.*380–70, for a brief time the most powerful ruler in Greece, methods anticipating those of Philip of Macedon.

Kronos Titan, father of Zeus and Hera, husband of Rhea, brutally emasculated by his son who replaced him as chief god.

Laertes father of Odysseus who retired to make way for his son to rule Ithaca.

Laocoön Trojan prince and priest who objected to bringing the Greeks' Wooden Horse within the walls of Troy, killed along with his sons by two great serpents (a scene famously represented by the marble group now in the Vatican).

Lapiths a Thessalian Greek people who in mythology engaged in a ghostly battle with Centaurs when their king Pirithous invited them to his wedding.

Leonidas I king of Sparta, died heroically at Thermopylae 480.

Leucippus second half of fifth century, reportedly from Elea (South Italy), jointly credited with Democritus as originator of the atomist theory of matter.

Livy probably 59 BCE–CE 17, author of what was considered the definitive history of Rome under the Kings and the Republic (753 BCE–CE 9) in 144 books of which thirty-five survive.

Lucian born CE*c.*120 of Samosata on the Euphrates, author of up to eighty works, most charcteristically the literary dialogues that blend comedy with philosophy.

Lycurgus (i) of Sparta, possibly mythical lawgiver credited with establishing all main components of Sparta's military, social and political regime, laws all unwritten (ii) of Athens, *c.*390–24, orator, statesman and financier, turned Athens' fortunes around in 330s and 320s.

Lysander died Haliartus 395, Spartan admiral, key player in Sparta's Peloponnesian War victory, but clashed with former beloved, Agesilaus, over post-war policy.

Lysias *c.*459–380, of Syracusan origin and hence metic at Athens, speechwriter and orator, of whose *c.* 200 speeches thirty-five survive.

Lysippus fourth century, of Sicyon, hugely prolific sculptor most famed for portraits of Alexander.

Magi Median priesthood.

Mardonius nephew and son-in-law of Darius.

Mausolus hellenized sub-satrap of Caria 377–53/2, based on Halicarnassus, where his sister-widow built for him the original Mausoleum embellished by leading Greek sculptors.

Medea granddaughter of Helios and daughter of a King of Colchis (in modern Georgia) who helped Jason acquire the Golden Fleece but was deserted by him and exacted revenge by (according to Euripides) murdering their two children.

Medes people related to and regularly confused with Persians despite clear differences of language and religion.

Melissus fifth century, philosopher-admiral, led Samos in revolt against Athens 441, follower of Parmenides.

Menander *c.*342–292, principal author of New Comedy, famed for super-realism of characterization, pupil of Theophrastus.

Menelaus brother of Agamemnon, husband of Helen of Troy, with whom he shared a tomb and a cult near Sparta.

Meton later fifth century, Athenian astronomer, calculated nineteen-year luni-solar calendrical cycle, observed summer solstice datable to 27 June 432.

Micon first half fifth century, Athenian painter and sculptor, contributed to the Stoa Poikile ('Painted Portico') at Athens and fashioned a victor-statue at Olympia, father of a painter daughter.

Miltiades *c.*550–489, Athenian general whose strategy carried the Battle of Marathon, but earlier a tyrant in the Thracian Chersonese and vassal of Persia.

Mnesicles architect of the Propylaea, built in marble on Athenian Acropolis 436–432.

Mummius, **Lucius** as Roman consul in 146 quelled revolt by Greeks of the Achaean League ending resistance to Roman rule, sacked and looted Corinth, shipping many artworks to Rome and Italy.

Muses nine goddesses who patronized respectively the arts of epic poetry, history, flute-playing, choral dancing, lyric poetry, tragedy, comedy, hymns, and astronomy.

Myron *floruit* mid-fifth century, Athenian sculptor in bronze best known for his 'Discus-thrower' (Roman copies only).

Nearchus *floruit* 334–*c.*312, boyhood companion and later admiral of Alexander, account of his voyage down the Indus in 326 later used by Arrian (second century CE).

Nereus old sea-god, son of Pontus ('the Sea'), praised for his righteousness by Hesiod and Pinder, wrestled unsuccessfully with Heracles.

Nestor aged ruler of Sandy Pylos who went on the Trojan expedition mixing sound practical advice with rambling anecdotage.

Nicias (i) *c.*470–413, hugely wealthy slave-owning Athenian politician and general, defeated and killed on expedition to Sicily proposed by Alcibiades that he had opposed (ii) fourth century, Athenian painter, master of chiaroscuro.

Odysseus eponymous hero of the *Odyssey*, son of Laertes and husband of Penelope, famed for his craftiness which saw him safely through twenty years of absence from his kingdom of Ithaca and countless life-threatening adventures.

Oedipus mythical son of a king of Thebes who killed his father and, thanks to his cleverness in solving the riddle of the Sphinx, married his mother and fathered children who were also his brothers and sisters.

Orgeones members of a religious society devoted to the *orgia* (rites) of a particular god or hero.

Ouranos divine personification of 'Sky', consort of Gaia ('Earth') castrated by their son Kronos.

Oxyrhynchus Historian early fourth century, Athenian historian who continued Thucydides' unfinished history, identity unknown (Cratippus?) and work recovered only on papyri from Oxyrhynchus in Upper Egypt.

Panaetius *c*.185–109, Stoic philosopher from Rhodes, influential at Rome before becoming head of the Stoic School at Athens in 129.

Pandora both earth goddess and the first human female, fashioned by Hephaestus, inflicted as curse on mortals by Zeus.

Papposilenus father of the Satyrs, imaginary part-animal male creatures who formed the retinue of Dionysus.

Parmenides born *c*.515, of Elea (hence 'Eleatic' School), expounded his monist philosophy in long hexameter poem.

Parrhasius *floruit* 430–390, of Ephesus but became Athenian, painter and author of treatise on painting.

Patroclus intimate friend of Achilles with whose father Peleus he had taken shelter after accidentally killing a play-fellow, killed at Troy thanks to Apollo.

Pausanias Spartan regent, commanded victorious Greek forces at Plataea 479, starved to death on suspicion of treason *c*.470.

Pausanias of ?Magnesia *floruit* 160s–170s, religious traveller and antiquarian author of ten-book *Guide to Greece* preserving much lore and fact about classical Greece.

Peleus mortal husband of immortal Thetis whose wedding was attended by many gods and goddeses, father of Achilles.

Pelopidas *c*.410–364, Theban politician and commander, especially of Sacred Band, worked closely with Epaminondas.

Pelops eponym of the Peloponnese ('Island of Pelops'), father of Atreus, worshipped as a hero at Olympia, served as food to gods by father Tantalus.

Pentheus son of Agave, grandson of Cadmus, king of Thebes, torn to pieces by his mother in a Bacchic frenzy.

Periander tyrant of Corinth *c*.625–585 in succession to his father Cypselus, handed down both as an archetypally wicked ruler and as one of the Seven Sages.

Pericles *c*.495–29, Athenian democratic statesman, financial expert and commander, hugely influential *c*.450–30, connected especially with imperial building programme.

Persephone daughter of Demeter and Zeus, also known as Core ('Daughter', 'Girl'), abducted to the underworld by her wicked uncle Hades.

Perses brother of Hesiod and formal addressee of his *Works and Days* didactic poem.

Phaedra Cretan princess married to Theseus and stepmother of Hippolytus for whom she conceived an incestuous passion with tragic consequences.

Pheidon king or tyrant ruler of Argos, either mid-eighth or early-seventh century, credited with military and monetary innovations.

Phidias *c*.490–30, Athenian sculptor in bronze, marble and wood embellished with gold and ivory, fashioned cult-statues of Zeus at Olympia and Athena Parthenos at Athens, perhaps responsible for entire sculptural programme of Parthenon, associate of Pericles, disgraced for alleged theft of gold meant for Athena's statue.

Philammon son of Apollo, legendary musician and poet associated with Pythian Games in honour of Apollo at Delphi.

Philetas of Cos *c*.330–280, of Cos, influential scholar-poet.

Philip II ruled Macedon 359–336, conquered most of Greece, planned invasion of Persia but assassinated during daughter's wedding.

Philistus *c*.430–356, Syracusan, follower of Dionysius I, author of thirteen-book *History of Sicily* in Thucydidean manner.

Philocrates Athenian politician and diplomat, eponymous author of peace with Macedon 346 that Demosthenes soon persuaded Athens to repudiate.

Phocion 402/1–318, conservative Athenian politician, elected General forty-five times, but ended by endorsing Macedonian-imposed oligarchy and so was condemned to drink hemlock.

Phrynichus *floruit c*.510–476, pioneer Athenian tragedian, fined for reminding Athenians of their sorrows in his *Capture of Miletus* 493.

Pindar 538–*c*.445, Theban praise-singer, author of four books of epinician (victory) odes for victors at Olympic, Pythian (Delphi), Isthmian, and Nemean Games.

Pisistratus *floruit c*.560–27, three times tyrant of Athens, longest 545–527, promoted lavish

public works and Athenocentric cultural and religious programmes.

Plato *c*.427–347, pupil and disciple of Socrates, founded Academy *c*.385, all known dialogues extant together with some probably falsely attributed.

Pliny the Elder CE*c*.23–79, polymath and author of both history and the extant thirty-seven-book *Natural History*, killed by the eruption of Vesuvius.

Plutarch *c*.46–120 CE, of Chaeronea, author of over 200 works, of which the seventy-eight *Moral Essays* and fifty biographies (most of them paired Greek–Roman) survive.

Polus late fifth century, pupil of Gorgias and principal character in Plato's *Gorgias*.

Polybius of Megalopolis *c*.200–120, historian in forty books of the rise of Rome to 'universal' empire.

Polyclitus *floruit* mid-fifth century, of Argos, sculptor and fellow-pupil with Myron, best known for *Doryphoros* ('Spear-bearer').

Polycrates tyrant of Samos *c*.535–522, crucified for plotting agaisnt Persia, patron of artists, craftsmen, poets and engineers.

Polygnotus *floruit* 480–50, of Thasos, painter famed for work in Athens (especially Painted Stoa) and Delphi, none surviving.

Polypaides

Poseidon one of the twelve Olympians, god of the sea, earthquakes and horses, in literature famous for persecuting Odysseus.

Praxiteles *floruit* 370–30, Athenian sculptor in both marble and bronze, chiefly notorious for first nude Aphrodite cult-statue and liaison with prostitute Phryne ('Toad').

Priam husband of Hecuba, king of Troy at the time of its destruction, father of fifty sons, including Hector and Paris.

Procopius first half of sixth century CE, historian of the emperor Justinian (527–565), including his scurrilous *Secret History*.

Prodicus later fifth century, of Keos, 'ancient Sophist' with special interest in language.

Prometheus Titan, tricked the gods into feasting on the bones and fat of sacrificial animals, while men ate the meat, for which Zeus punished men by withdrawing fire, which Prometheus stole back, so Zeus inflicted on mankind Pandora.

Protagoras *c*.490–20, of Abdera, 'ancient Sophist', wrote at least two treatises including *On the Gods* in the preface of which he expressed agnosticism, possibly democratic in politics and author of first constitution for new city of Thurii 444–3.

Ptolemy I *c*.367/6–283/2, founder of Ptolemaic kingdom and dynasty of Egypt as 'Successor' of

Alexander, founded Museum and Library at capital Alexandria, wrote apologetic history.

Pyrrhon c.365–275, of Elis, founder of Sceptical School of philosophy.

Pythagoras *floruit* 530, originally of Samos but settled in exile at Croton (South Italy), founder of quasi-religious community avoiding animal blood-sacrifice, preoccupied with number theory and astronomy.

Pytheas late fourth century, of Massalia, explored waters of northern Europe, including circumnavigation of Britain.

Revett, Nicholas see Stuart, James.

Sallust c.86–35, Roman politician and historian of the moral decadence of the late Republican era.

Sappho late seventh century, of Eresus on Lesbos, poet and perhaps pedagogue, her homoerotic lyrics have given us 'Lesbian'.

Scopas *floruit* 370–30, of the marble island of Paros, noted for expressiveness of his sculpture, employed on Mausoleum.

Seleucus/Seleucids Hellenistic dynasty, based on Antioch, founded by Seleucus I Nicator ('Conqueror') c.358–281, terminated by Pompey in 64.

Semonides seventh century, of Samos and then Amorgos, verse author of both local Samian history and prolonged misogynistic invective.

Seven Sages a body of varying composition, including Chilon of Sparta, Solon and Thales.

Simonides c.556–468, of Keos, relative of Bacchylides, praise-singer most famous for epigrams, for example on Athenian dead at Marathon and Spartan dead at Thermopylae.

Socrates 469–399, Athenian philosopher of unorthodox ethical and religious views and anti-democratic political outlook, satirized by Aristophanes in *Clouds* 423, convicted of impiety 399, never wrote a word of his teaching.

Solon *floruit* 594, Athenian poet-politician, chosen Archon to resolve grave crisis, passed laws that mostly superseded those of Draco.

Sophocles c.496–406, Athenian tragedian and sometime politician, credited with 123 plays of which seven survive (the last, *Oedipus at Colonus*, produced posthumously).

Sostratus later first century, leading surgeon at Alexandria and author of zoological works to be ranked only after those of Aristotle.

Speusippus c.407–339, relative and successor of Plato as head of Academy 347.

Stesichorus c.630–553, lyric poet, originally from South Italy but spent most time at Himera, Sicily.

Stuart, James 1713–88, English architect nicknamed 'Athenian Stuart' who with Nicholas Revett produced accurate drawings and measurements in their *Antiquities of Athens* (1762–1814).

Tacitus c.55–120 CE, Roman politician and historian, famous for excoriating analysis of the despotism of the first Roman emperors CE 14–96.

Thales c.625–547, of Miletus, natural philosopher and Sage, alleged to have predicted solar eclipse of 585.

Theagenes late seventh century, tyrant of Megara and father-in-law of Athenian Cylon.

Themistocles c.524–459, Athenian admiral and statesman, guiding spirit of Greek resistance to Persia 480–79, laid foundations of Athens' naval power, ostracized c.471 and ended days as honoured pensioner of Persian Great king.

Theognis probably sixth century, author of elegiac verses of conservative political tendency, many addressed to one Cyrnus.

Theophrastus c.371–287, originally of Eresus, pupil and successor of Aristotle as head of Lyceum, founder of systematic botany, author of collections of laws and customs, and of *Characters*.

Theophylact Simocatta first half seventh century CE, Egyptian Greek historian covering reign of Byzantine emperor Maurice (582–602).

Theopompus fourth century, of Chios, conservative and splenetic historian, including fifty-eight-book *Philippica* based on career of Philip of Macedon.

Theramenes executed 404/3, oligarchic Athenian politician involved in both the 411 and 404 coups.

Thespis sixth century, Athenian actor and composer credited with founding tragedy as a genre (hence 'Thespian').

Thetis sea-nymph goddess, daughter of Nereus, wife of Peteus, mother of Achilles.

Thrasybulus died 389, Athenian democratic statesman and admiral, leader of resistance to Thirty Tyrants.

Thucydides c.455–400, historian and general, exiled 424 for failing to preserve Amphipolis, wrote unfinished history of Peloponnesian War (431–411).

Timaeus c.356–260, of Tauromenium, Sicily, but wrote *History* at Athens in at least thirty-eight books, combining Greek with Roman history and the first to use Olympiads for dating.

Timoleon c.365–34, Corinthian, distinguished himself in Sicily for overthrowing the Syracusan tyranny and defeating a Carthaginian army.

Titus Roman emperor CE 79–81, son of Vespasiaa, notorious for affair with the Jewish Berenice.

Virgil 70–19, originally from Mantua, client of Maecenas, under whose auspices he composed the patriotic Roman epic the *Aeneid* celebrating Augustus' rule as a golden age.

Winckelmann, Johanne Joachim 1717–68, German archaeologist and art-historian, published pioneering study of Greek art based on study of Roman copies (1764).

Xenophanes c.570–478, originally of Colophon but spent most of life in Sicily, philosopher-poet with interests ranging widely from ethics to natural history to theology.

Xenophon c.428–354, Athenian, conservative pupil and disciple of Socrates, soldier of fortune and writer of history, biography, ethics, romance and technical treatises.

Xerxes Persian Great King 486–65, son of Darius I whose project of Greek conquest he failed to complete.

Zaleucus seventh century, lawgiver of Italian Locri, reputedly the earliest to have his laws written down.

Zeno (i) of Elea, c.490–54, philosopher, formulated paradoxes in support of Parmenides (ii) of Citium, c.333–262, philosopher of Phoenician origin who founded the Stoic School (named after the Painted Stoa) at Athens.

Zeus chief deity of the Greek pantheon, lord and father of the Olympian gods and goddesses, in origin a sky-god but with all-encompassing powers.

Zeuxis *floruit* 430–390, originally of Heraclea in South Italy, later of Athens and Pella, famed for an Eros mentioned in Aristophanes' *Acharnians* 425.

Glossary

acropolis high city, citadel.

agoge Sparta's state education.

agora civic centre, marketplace.

alphabet, Greek borrowed from Phoenician, with addition of signs for vowels, probably in eighth century.

Amphictyonic League representatives of mainly central Greek communities chosen to oversee sanctuary of Delphi and Pythian Games.

amphora double-handled storage or transport jar of clay or bronze, especially for oil or wine.

antefix ornament of terracotta placed in front elevation of temple.

Aphetairoi a category of social inferiors in Crete.

apobates man dressed in heavy armour who jumped on and off chariots in athletic competition.

archaic period conventionally c.700–500 or 480.

arche see oligarchy

archon civic official.

aristocracy rule (*kratos*) of the so-called best men (*aristoi*).

aristoi see aristocracy

Attic adjective of Athenians, as in script, dialect or territory

Attica home territory of Athens, c.1000 square miles/2400 square kilometres.

BCE, CE Before Common Era, Common Era.

black-figure vase painting technique whereby figures are represented in applied black paint on red ground.

boule council

Bronze Age conventionally c.3000–1100 in Greek world.

calendar see **months**.

caryatid supporting pillar of temple in form of young girl with basket serving as column-capital.

Centaurs mythical creatures half-man half-horse, generally noted for lust, violence and greed for alcohol, though Chiron who raised Achilles was a wise exception.

Chalcidian Confederacy politico-military unit of cities of Chalcidice of which the capital was Olynthus.

chora countryside, rural territory of a polis (see polis).

choregus Athenian impresario, wealthy citizen required to finance a dramatic chorus for a festival.

chorus song, dance, group of singers/dancers (for example, twelve in a tragic chorus at Athens).

chryselephantine of especially luxurious statues, adorned with ivory and gold over a wooden core, such as Phidias' Zeus at Olympia and Athena Parthenos at Athens.

classical period conventionally c.500/480–323/300.

coinage most Greek cities had their own coinages, usually in silver and for small change in bronze; coins were worth what the metal they contained was worth, so units of coinage (e.g. stater, mina, talent) were also units of weight.

comedy singing and revelry, formally introduced as dramatic form in Great Dionysia (see Great Dionysia) 486.

cult religious worship of a deity (god or goddess) or hero (semi-divine personage) or other superhuman phenomenon (e.g. personified Fear).

Dark Age transitional era between the Bronze Age and the Archaic period in Greece, characterized by material impoverishment, c.1100–800.

Delian League imperial alliance dominated by Athens, 478–404, founded to resist Persia but exploited by Athens e.g. to fight Sparta in Peloponnesian War.

deme parish, ward, village of Athens and Attica.

democracy literally, sovereign power of the *demos* or People (see *demos*).

Demos people, citizen body, common people.

Dicasterion People's Court, jury.

diolkos stone trackway across Isthmus of Corinth, constructed c.600 under Periander, for transporting ships and/or cargoes between Corinthian and Saronic Gulfs.

dithyramb ritual song sung by chorus in honour of Dionysus.

Dorians ethnic division of Greeks, based – as Ionians – on dialect and some distinctive customs.

Doric Order architectural order of temples distinguished chiefly (like Ionic) by form of column and column-capital (cushion-shaped).

drachma monetary unit, literally a 'fistful' of six *obols* (see *obol*).

East Greece convenient name for Greek world on seaboard of Western Aziz from Bosporus to coast opposite Rhodes.

ecclesia assembly, primary political gathering of citizens.

Eleusinian Mysteries state controlled initiatory cult in honour of Demeter and Persephone at Elensis in Attica.

Epicureanism philosophical doctrine and way of life founded by Epicurus, preaching tranquillity of mind as the highest good for man.

epiklēros only daughter with no surviving brothers who acted as vehicle transmitting her father's property to his son-in-law, her husband.

ethne 'peoples' (e.g. Aetolians) organized in a political framework looser and less centralized than the *polis*.

genos descent-group, civic corporate body.

granulation technique of decorating jewellery by dropping tiny lumps of precious metal to form granules.

Great Dionysia annual religious festival at Athens in honour of Dionysus of Eleutherae, scene of dithyramb, tragedy, comedy and satyr-drama.

Hellas the Greeks' own name for the concept, more notional than actual, of the whole Greek-speaking world.

Hellenes the name by which the Greeks called themselves.

Hellenistic Age conventionally from death of Alexander, 323, to death of Cleopatra, 30.

helot native Greek serf-like subject of Sparta.

hetaera expensive prostitute, courtesan, usually free in status.

hoplite heavily armed Greek infantryman.

hubris violation of another's status with malevolent intent.

Ionians see Dorians.

Ionic Order architectural order of temples with distinctive volute-capitals on columns which also have bases.

isonomia equality of status and privilege under the laws.

Koine Eirene 'Common Peace', meaning a peace treaty to which all Greeks were in principle party whether or not they had participated in the swearing of the oaths, first in 386.

krater mixing-bowl of clay or bronze, used especially in the symposium.

kylix drinking-goblet of clay or metal with high-swung handles.

Lacedaemon (i) official name of polis of Sparta (ii) territory of Sparta, *c*.3000 square miles/8000 square kilometres.

League of Corinth a politico-military alliance of most mainland and island Greek states (except Sparta) formed by Philip of Macedonia in 338.

liturgy financing a chorus (see *choregus*) or *trireme* (see *trireme*) at Athens.

logos word, speech, reason, account.

metic more or less permanently resident alien with certain rights but more disabilities compared to citizens.

metopes associated with triglyphs to form frieze in the Doric order (pp. 260–1).

mina unit of currency equivalent to 100 *drachmas* (plural *mnai*).

months Greek cities each operated their own version of a luni-solar calendar, though some month names (e.g. Heraios) were common to more than one city.

Mycenaean Period alternative name for Late Bronze Age in mainland Greece, *c*.1600–1100.

mystai initiates, for example in Eleusinian Mysteries (see Eleusinian Mysteries).

Nereids sea nymphs, named after Nereus (see Who's Who).

obol monetary unit, derived from *obelos*, 'spit'. There were six obols in one drachma (see *drachma*).

oikos household, both property and human family members.

Old Comedy best defined practically as the comedies produced at Athens during the fifth century, notably by Cratinus, Eupolis and Aristophanes.

oligarchy rule (*arche*) of the (wealthy) few (*oligoi*).

oligoi see oligarchy

Olympia sanctuary of Olympian Zeus, site of quadrennial Games.

Olympiad method of time-reckoning according to four-year periods between Olympic Games.

Orphism an eccentric set of religious beliefs and practices, associated with Orpheus as founder, practised by marginal sects and expressed in its own literature.

ostracism enforced exile from Athens for ten years, decided by counting names of 'candidates' inscribed on *ostraka*, potsherds.

peer polity interaction the modern idea that city (*polis*) would endeavour to keep up with *polis* in a process of mutually stimulating emulation.

Peloponnese 'Island of Pelops', landmass linked to central Greece by Isthmus of Corinth.

Peloponnesian War war between Athens and Sparta and their respective allies, 431–404 with intervals.

phlyax a type of farcical play developed in South Italy in the fourth century, often illustrated on South Italian vase painting.

phratry literally 'brotherhood', social and religious association.

phyle 'tribe', often artificial political sub-unit.

Plataea small Boeotian town on borders of Attica, site of decisive land battle of Persian Wars, 479.

polis city (state), city (urban centre) see also peer polity interaction.

politeia citizenship, constitution (for example, democracy).

potsherd (also pot shard) a broken piece of ceramic material found on an archaeological site; the Greek for 'potsherd' is *ostrakon*, whence 'ostracism'.

praise-singers professional poets who composed odes celebrating athletic victories at the great games (e.g. Pindar).

Propylaea monumental marble gateway to Athenian Acropolis, 430s, designed by Mnesicles.

protoattic seventh-century style of Athenian vase painting preceding the emergence of Athenian black-figure.

protocorinthian late-eighth and seventh-century style of Corinthian vase painting preceding Corinthian black-figure.

Pythia oracular priestess of Apollo at Delphi.

red-figure style of vase painting in which the figures are 'reserved' in the red of the clay and slip, and the background is painted in added black.

Sacred Band crack Theban infantry force of 300, consisting of 150 homosexual pairs, founded 378.

satrap Persian viceroy.

satyr horse-goat-man mythical familiar of Dionysus (see Who's Who).

satyr-drama humorous drama with satyrs as chorus, composed by tragedians at Athens as addition to three tragedies.

Second Sophistic modern term with some ancient authority for the period *c*.60–230 CE characterized by the declamations of Greek *rhetores* (orators).

South Italy area from Bay of Naples south, also known in Latin as Magna Graecia ('Great Greece'), colonized by Greeks from mid-eighth century.

stade see stadion.

stadion one length of athletic racetrack, *c*.200 metres.

stasis a 'standing' apart, so faction, civil war.

stater unit of currency equivalent to two drachmas.

stele slab, marker stone with inscribed text and/or carved relief.

syllabary script the units of which denote syllables not individual letters (e.g. Linear B).

synoecism 'housing-together' (see *oikos*), so unification of villages to form centralized political community.

talent measure of weight and monetary value, originally Babylonian; equals 6000 drachmas.

Thebes chief polis of the Boeotians.

Thermopylae site of unsuccessful but heroic resistance led by Sparta to Persian land invasion, 480.

thetes as a general term meant hired labourers, but at Athens specifically the lowest of the four economic property-classes of citizens.

Thirty Tyrants self-appointed Athenian junta of extreme oligarchs, 404–3.

triglyphs see metopes.

trireme three-banked, oared warship.

tyrant illegitimate, absolute ruler by usurpation and force.

white-ground style of vase painting in which the background is painted white, and against which stood out the red or black figures.

Chronology

c.3000–1000 Minoan civilization

c.1600 Mycenaean period (to c.1150)

c.1400 Destruction of Cnossus

c.1250 Destruction of Troy

c.1100 Dark Age (to c.900/800)

c.1050 Migrations to Asia minor
(to c.800/700)
Dorian migration

776 (trad.) Foundation of Olympic Games

c.750 Greek alphabet
Euboeans settle Ischia and Cumae

c.735–715 Sparta conquers Messenia

c.700 Homer
Hesiod

c.700 Introduction of hoplite fighting

c.620 Dracon's laws at Athens

c.600 Development of trireme
Invention of coinage
Thales of Miletus

594 Solon's laws at Athens

c.550 Achaemenid Persian empire founded
(to 330)

c.546 Cyrus of Persia defeats Croesus of
Lydia

545 Tyranny at Athens of Pisistratus and son
(to 510)

508 Cleisthenes introduces democratic
reforms at Athens

c.505 Sparta's Peloponnesian League formed
(to c.366)

499 Revolt against Persia of Ionians and
others (to 494)

490 Battle of Marathon

480 Second Persian invasion (to 479)

478 Athens founds Delian League (to 404)

462 Democratic reforms at Athens of
Ephialtes and Pericles

460 'First' Peloponnesian War (to 446)

c.449 Peace of Callias

447 Parthenon begun (completed 432)

446 Thirty Years' Truce between Sparta and
Athens (actually to 431)

431 Peloponnesian War (to 404, with
interruptions)

421 Peace of Nicias (to 414)

418 Battle of Mantinea

415 Athenian expedition to Sicily (to 413)

404 Spartan hegemony (to 371)

401 Expedition of the '10,000' to Asia
(to 400)

399 Death of Socrates

395 Corinthian War (to 386)

386 King's Peace

c.385 Plato founds Academy

378 Athens founds Second Sea-league
(to 338)

371 Thebans defeat Spartans at Leuctra
Theban ascendancy in Greece (to 362)

362 Second Battle of Mantinea
First Common Peace (?)

359 Accession of Philip II of Macedon
(to 336)

346 Peace of Philocrates

338 Battle of Chaeronea
Foundation of League of Corinth

336 Accession of Alexander the Great (to
323)

335 Alexander orders destruction of Thebes

c.335 Aristotle founds Lyceum

334 Alexander invades Persian empire (to
323)

331 Foundation of Alexandria
Battle of Gaugamela

323 Revolt of Greeks against Macedon (to
322)

322 Deaths of Demosthenes and Aristotle
End of Athenian democracy

301 Battle of Ipsus
death of Antigonus founder of Antigonid
dynasty of Greece

c.300 Zeno founds Stoic school

283 Death of Ptolemy I founder of Ptolemaic
dynasty of Egypt (to 31) and of
Alexandria Museum and Library

281 Seleucus founder of Seleucid dynasty of
Asia assassinated

280 Achaean League refounded

263 Eumenes I succeeds Philetaerus as ruler
of Pergamum kingdom

244 Agis IV king at Sparta (to 241)

238 War of Attalus I for mastery of Asia
Minor (to 227)

235 Cleomenes III king at Sparta (to 222)

224 Antigonus III invades Peloponnese,
founds Hellenic League (to 222)

223 Antiochus III succeeds Seleucus III
(to 187)

222 Battle of Sellasia

221 Philip V succeeds Antigonus III (to 179)

215 Alliance of Philip V and Hannibal of
Carthage

211 Alliance between Aetolia and Rome
initiates First Macedonian War (to 205)

200 Second Macedonian War (to 197)

196 Rome declares Greek independence

194 Rome evacuates Greece

192 Syrian War of Rome against Antiochus
III (to 188)

171 Third Macedonian War (to 168)

168 Battle of Pydna, end of Antigonid
dynasty

148 Macedonia becomes Roman province

147 Achaean rising against Rome (to 146)

146 Sack of Corinth, Achaea becomes Roman
protectorate

31 Battle of Actium

27 BCE–

CE 14 Reign of Octavian/Augustus

330 Foundation of Constantinople

1453 Fall of Constantinople to Ottoman
Turks

Synopses of Plots

Alcestis

Euripides (438). Not a tragedy but a melodrama substituted for the usual satyr-play. Alcestis, wife of Admetus, king of Pherae (Thesaly), volunteers to die in place of her husband whose death Apollo has postponed only on condition that another dies in his place. Heracles opportunely rescues Alcestis from Hades and restores her to her chastened husband.

Anabasis

Xenophon (early-mid fourth century). In 401 Xenophon joined up as a mercenary on the side of the young Persian pretender Cyrus in his attempt to overthrow the latter's elder brother, Great King Artaxerxes II. Cyrus was killed in battle and the mercenaries' leaders were treacherously murdered, but somehow the '10,000', with Xenophon among their new leaders, managed to escape from the heart of Asia back to Greek civilization. The *Anabasis* ('journey up country') was Xenophon's interested version of that stirring tale.

Antigone

Sophocles (?441). Antigone, daughter but also sister of the late Oedipus, defies the order of the new king of Thebes, her uncle Creon, not to give proper burial to the corpse of her brother Polynices, condemned by Creon as a traitor. When Creon discovers her defiance, he sentences her to death by incarceration, her betrothed (Creon's son) commits suicide, as does Creon's wife.

Apology

Plato (early fourth century). In 399 Socrates was condemned to death and executed for the public crimes of impiety and corrupting the youth. Socrates appears not to have made a good job of his self-defence speech (*apologia*), so his most distinguished pupil did the job for him, posthumously. Another disciple, Xenophon, did likewise, but the two speeches are chalk and cheese, Xenophon's probably staying closer to the historical actuality than Plato's.

Acharnians

Aristophanes (425). The earliest Aristophanes' eleven surviving comedies is one of his several 'peace' plays. The hero (whose name is revealed well on in the play to be Dicaeopolis, 'Just City'), frustrated that the Athenians will not make peace with Sparta – this is the seventh year of the Peloponnesian War – makes a private peace with the Spartans on his own account, inviting any Athenian who desired the return of the blessings of peace (mainly drink and sex) to join him.

Bacchae

Euripides (406). The last known of Euripides' more than a hundred tragedies, written while he was in self-imposed exile at the Macedonian court, and first performed posthumously. Pentheus, king of Thebes, refuses to recognize the power of Dionysus, which has infected many women of Thebes including his own mother Agave. Persuaded to go into the wilds to watch the women in their Bacchic frenzy, he is captured by them and torn limb from limb. Too late Agave realizes what she has done, as Pentheus had been too slow to come to terms with raw Dionysiac power.

Clouds

Aristophanes (423). The first (and, as usual, only) performance of this comedy was not a success; so dispirited was Aristophanes by its failure that he rewrote it some five years later, and it is the rewritten version that we have. Its chief target is the novel education associated with the Sophists, most of whom were not Athenians. But to give it a local flavour Aristophanes somewhat unfairly cast Socrates as the archetypal Sophist. Provided he was paid enough, this caricatural Socrates was prepared to teach the pupils at his 'Thinkery' to make the bad or weaker argument appear to be the good or stronger, the height – or depths – of immorality. The play is named after its chorus of divine Clouds, just some of the newfangled divinities that Socrates and his pupils worship in preference to the old gods. The play in our version ends with the *auto-da-fe* of the Thinkery.

Dyscolus

Menander (316). An Athenian called Cnemon, the 'grumpy old man' who gives the comedy its title, prefers to live in isolated rural border-country rather than enjoy the fruits of Athenian urban civilization. With him lives his only daughter, for whom a young man called Sostratus falls and seeks her hand. Her father Cnemon is reluctant to lose the equivalent of a skivvy, but is won over when Sostratus saves his life after he falls down a well.

Electra

Euripides (c.420). Sophocles (c.414–411). Two tragedies named after the elder daughter of Agamemnon and Clytemnestra survive. Euripides introduces a novel twist by making Electra the wife of a nobly born but impoverished farmer, who has to work with her hands, as he does with his, to get a living. Another difference between the two versions is that whereas in Euripides Electra recognizes her returning brother Orestes straight away, Sophocles delays the recognition (*anagnorismos*) to the final third of the play and indeed makes it a key aspect of the drama. In both tragedies, however, brother and sister conspire to avenge their murdered father Agamemnon by murdering their murderess-mother in her turn.

Ethics and Politics

Aristotle (c.330s). Three works entitled 'Ethics' attributed to Aristotle have survived, but the most important is the *Nicomachean Ethics* (so called because Aristotle addressed it to his son Nicomachus). It forms a prelude to the *Politics*. In the *Ethics* Aristotle seeks to discover the highest good for man, and decides that it is the happy life of active political virtue. In the *Politics* he argues that such a life is to be, and indeed can only be, lived in the *polis* or Greek city, since that is mankind's naturally ordained destiny. But besides philosophy, the *Politics* also contains an enormous amount of empirical historical detail, the fruits of the researches of himself and his pupils in his Lyceum institute for advanced studies.

Ecclesiazusae

Aristophanes (?392). In this the last of his three extant 'women-plays' a group of Athenian citizen wives successfully conspire to 'pack' a meeting of the (legally) male-citizen-only Assembly and secure a majority vote to transfer the direction of the city to the women. But the new order is to be not only feminist but also communalist – all goods are to be shared in common, including beautiful young men, who are to be compulsorily available to any women who desire them, in descending order of age and ugliness. A fantasy, literally a travesty, but perhaps also a distorted reflection of a certain feminism (and communalism) abroad in the real post-War Athens of the depressed (3)90s.

Frogs

Aristophanes (405). The famous 'brek-ek-ek-ek koax koax' refrain of the Frog chorus was but byplay compared to the main plot and the main chorus (consisting of Eleusinian Mystery initiates). Athens is in crisis – who is to save her? Dionysus, patron of the Lenaea festival at which the comedy was shown, has the bright idea of going down to Hades to bring back a tragic poet, since poets were supposed traditionally to be public teachers of wisdom. After hearing a debate (*agon*) between Aeschylus and Euripides, Dionysus in his wisdom (such as it is) decides for the older, more traditional Aeschylus.

Hippolytus

Euripides (428). This was Euripides' second go at the Hippolytus myth. Hippolytus, son of Theseus and an Amazon, stepson of Phaedra, is devoted to chastity, hunting and – therefore – the goddess Artemis. Phaedra conceives an unholy sexual passion for her stepson, a secret which is betrayed to him by a nurse. Rejected, Phaedra commits suicide. Theseus, getting hold of the wrong end of the stick, utters a terrible curse on his son, who is destroyed by a monster sent from the deep by Poseidon. But shortly before expiring Hippolytus tells Theseus the truth and father and son are reconciled.

Iliad

Homer (? c.700). The *Iliad* is the fruit of a centuries-long tradition of oral epic verse. Whether there was a single 'monumental' composer called Homer, or not, the brilliance of this epic lies in its focusing of the action around a single theme, the anger of the peerless but doomed Achilles. The Greeks have gone to fight Troy to recover Helen of Sparta, wife of Menelaus, adulterously seduced by Paris son of Priam, king of Troy. The Greek army is led by Menelaus' brother Agamemnon, lord of Mycenae, mainly because he is the most powerful Greek king. Achilles, cheated as he sees it by Agamemnon of his rightful prize of war, the beautiful Briseis, skulks within his tent, relenting only to the extent of allowing his intimate comrade Patroclus to go out and fight in his stead wearing his own armour. Patroclus' death, however, changes his mind. Equipped with a magnificent new suit of armour fashioned by Hephaestus, craftsman to the Olympian gods, Achilles slays Troy's main champion, Hector, another son of Priam. The climax of the epic comes, not with the fall of Troy, but with the restoration of Hector's body by Achilles to his grieving old father Priam, one of the greatest reconciliation scenes in all literature.

Lysistrata

Aristophanes (411). This, the first comedy to be named after a female lead, was staged in the same year as *Thesmophoriazusae* (below). Lysistrata's fictional name is probably a pun on that of the real priestess of Athena, Lysimache. Like Dicaeopolis in *Acharnians*, she wishes for peace with Sparta, but being a woman chooses a different route: a sex strike of Athenian wives, to be co-ordinated with wives from the other side. The tactic is a brilliant success, though just to make sure the men do make peace, Lysistrata and her gang also seize the Athenian Acropolis and get control of the city's war chest (stored in the Parthenon). The play ends in reconciliation – between husbands and wives as well as Athenians and Spartans – and mutual joyous celebration.

Medea

Euripides (431). Euripides had dealt with Medea in his very first play, twenty-four years earlier, but this is his definitive, and novel, treatment. Medea, a non-Greek princess and sorceress from the far eastern end of the Black Sea, has crucially aided Jason in his quest to secure the Golden Fleece and returned with him to Greece, only to be deserted for a Greek princess from Corinth. In dire revenge Medea kills the two children she has had with Jason – a twist to the myth first introduced here by Euripides. In a further bizarre twist Euripides allows Medea to escape upwards to heaven at the end of the play, making her virtually divine.

Odyssey

Homer (? *c.*700). Like the *Iliad*, this is the outcome of a long tradition of oral epic which derives its dramatic coherence and impact from the focus on one hero. Odysseus' return from Troy to Ithaca is destined to take ten years, as long as it had taken the Greeks to capture Troy in the first place. The story is not told sequentially but in a series of complicated recapitulations and flashbacks. The wily Odysseus' hair-raising adventures by land and sea are counterpointed by his wife Penelope's steadfast and no less wily resistance to demands for her hand from 108 suitors. At the climax the disguised Odysseus together with his loyal son Telemachus and slave swineherd Eumaeus exact a terrible revenge on the suitors.

Oeconomicus

Xenophon (mid-fourth century). The title probably means 'Discourse on Estate-management', though it could also mean 'The Estate-manager'. The estate (*oikos*) in question is a large one in the countryside of Attica based on the labour of slaves in both fields and house. Socrates engages in dialogue chiefly with one Ischomachus, and between them they expose the ideal economic and moral conduct of such an enterprise (in reality open only to a tiny handful of very rich Greeks).

Oresteia

Aeschylus (458). A genuine trilogy with a single theme running through it, the vengeance of Orestes on his mother Clytemnestra for her murder of his father Agamemnon on his return from Troy. In the first of the three plays, *Agamemnon*, the murder of the eponym is accomplished by the strongly masculine Clytemnestra. In the second play, *Libation-bearers* (*Choephoroe*), Orestes' revenge is accomplished, with help from his sister Electra. In the third, *Eumenides*, Orestes is pursued by the divine Furies (Erinyes) who avenge kindred murder, but escapes from Argos

to Athens where he is put on trial before the newly constituted Areopagus presided over by Athena. Apollo leads for Orestes' defence, the jury is hung, but Athena takes the side of Orestes who is acquitted. Simultaneously the defeated Erinyes are tamed into the Eumenides ('Kindly Ones') and worshipped thereafter as such at Athens.

Phaedrus

Plato (early fourth century). A Socratic dialogue in which Socrates engages with Phaedrus in discussion and critique on the subjects of love and rhetoric. Unusual care is taken to set the scene in the landscape of Athens and its immediate surrounds, but unlike other such contextually located dialogues (see *Protagoras*) *Phaedrus* has no narrator.

Protagoras

Plato (early fourth century). Can virtue be taught? That is the question, posed by Socrates to Protagoras of Abdera, a leading Sophist and thus a teacher who taught young members of the Athenian upper class for a (hefty) fee. Protagoras, not surprisingly, answers the question in the affirmative, whereas Socrates seeks to show that all Protagoras can possibly teach are skills and techniques, above all sophistical (our word comes from the Greek for Sophists) debating tricks.

Republic

Plato (early fourth century). Formally a Socratic dialogue, but by far the most complex and elaborate example of that genre. Alternatively entitled 'On Justice', the *Republic* (in Greek *politeia*) presents Socrates questioning a series of imaginary interlocutors, including two of Plato's real-life brothers, as to what justice is. The ultimate goal is ethical, but in Plato's Greece ethics and politics were inseparably intertwined (see *Ethics and Politics*, above), so Socrates goes looking for justice 'writ large' in the city (polis) before seeking to identify it in the individual human soul (*psyche*). The paradoxical conclusion reached is that, unless true (i.e. Platonic) philosophers become rulers of their cities, or city rulers become (Platonic) philosophers, true justice will be never be realized in the actual everyday world. The dialogue is as important for its assumptions and methods as for its utopian conclusion. It should be read together with the *Laws*, where in an altogether more down-to-earth and utilitarian spirit Plato sets about establishing the legal as well as moral framework of a proposed new city foundation (to be established notionally on Crete).

Symposium

Plato (early fourth century). The Athenian tragic playwright Agathon has won his first victory, at the Lenaea festival of 416, and to celebrate he invites some of his closest associates, including Socrates, to a symposium or drinking-party. Such is the dramatic scene for this text, which runs the theoretical gamut of possible variations on human love, or rather sexual desire (*eros*). Not so much a dialogue, more a theatrical performance, the *Symposium* boasts among many delights a speech by Aristophanes, in which he tries to explain by a charming myth why some people are more homo- than heterosexually inclined, and an impromptu intervention by a disgracefully drunken Alcibiades. There is also an effective speech by a respectable and intelligent woman, Diotima; since her presence would not have been countenanced at a real-life symposium, she marks out the artificiality and literariness of the whole proceedings.

Theogony

Hesiod (? *c.*700). Hesiod of Ascra in Boeotia wrote two extant long poems in the epic hexameter metre of Homer, the *Theogony* and the *Works and Days* (see below). In the former, drawing on oriental as well as Greek myth, he sought nothing less than to give an account of how the world had come to be as it was, a sort of Greek Genesis. That he succeeded triumphantly is shown not only by the poem's survival but also for instance by Herodotus' reference to Hesiod as having (with Homer) 'described the gods for the Greeks, giving them all their appropriate titles, offices and powers'.

Thesmophoriazusae ('Women at the Thesmophoria')

Aristophanes (411). The second of Aristophanes' 'women-plays' to be staged in 411, probably at the Dionysia festival. At the Thesmophoria, a festival in honour of Demeter for married citizen women only, the celebrants discuss how to get their revenge on Euripides for revealing through his tragedies the truth about their sex – that they are drink- and sex-mad. A relative of Euripides infiltrates the gathering, in drag, but is exposed and held captive until Euripides himself appears and promises not to abuse the women's 'honourable sex' ever again.

Trojan Women

Euripides (415). The only surviving member of a trilogy of plays on the theme of Troy, the *Trojan Women* strikes a consistently downbeat note. The chorus is composed of ordinary women of Troy, who like the famous speaking characters – Hecuba, Andromache, Cassandra – are about to be shipped off to Greece as captive slaves. Helen (treated almost as an honorary Trojan woman) is represented sympathetically in comparison to the conquering male Greeks. In contrast to the *Iliad*'s portrayal, the women's fate is seen entirely from their point of view, an uncomfortable viewpoint for an audience many of whom will have just taken part in the real-life enslavement of the women of Greek Melos.

Wasps

Aristophanes (422). 'Wasps' is how Aristophanes represents the play's chorus of ordinary Athenian citizens who form the juries in the People's Court, because they love nothing better than to sting defendants, i.e. find them guilty and preferably condemn them to death. One such supposedly typical juror, Philocleon ('Cleon-lover'), is the comedy's antihero, so named so that Aristophanes can take a (further) swipe at the leading democratic politician of the day. The plot consists in showing how his son Bdelycleon (roughly 'Cleon-hater') eventually succeeds in curing his father of his jury-mania.

Works and Days

Hesiod (? *c.*700). This hexameter poem takes its name from its second main part, which is a sort of farmer's almanac detailing what should or should not be done on the farm at the various seasons of the year. The first part is a morality tale addressed notionally to the poet's miscreant brother, Perses, warning him and his aristocratic patrons that divine retribution is sure to strike them in the end no matter how prosperous they may now appear to be. It is here that Hesiod includes his famous degenerative myth of the 'ages' or 'generations' of mankind: gold, silver, bronze, heroic and – the dispiriting present – iron.

Further Reading

General Works

Parker, R *Miasma*. Oxford: Clarendon Press 1983 (reprinted with new preface 1996).

Parker, R *Athenian Religion: a History*. Oxford: Clarendon Press 1996.

INTRODUCTION: *THE GLORY THAT WAS GREECE?*

Browning, R (ed.) *The Greek World. Classical, Byzantine and Modern*. London & New York: Thames & Hudson 1985.

Burn, AR *Pelican History of Greece*. Harmondsworth: Penguin, latest reprint 1996.

Cartledge, P *The Greeks. A Portrait of Self and Others*. Oxford: Oxford University Press 1993 (revised edition 1997, 2nd edition 2002).

Dover, KJ *The Greeks*. London: BBC Books 1980.

Etienne, R & F *The Search for Ancient Greece*. London & New York: Thames & Hudson 1992.

Lévêque, P *Ancient Greece. Utopia and Reality*. London & New York: Thames & Hudson 1994.

Levi, P *Atlas of the Greek World*. Oxford & Amsterdam: Phaidon 1980.

Morris, IM (ed.) *Classical Greece. Ancient Histories and Modern Archaeologies*. Cambridge: Cambridge University Press 1994.

PART I: *THE WORLD OF GREECE*

Chapter 1: *History and Tradition*

Cartledge, P *The Greeks. A Portrait of Self and Others*. Oxford: Oxford University Press 1993 (revised edition 1997, 2nd edition 2002).

Crawford, M (ed.) *Sources for Ancient History*. Cambridge: Cambridge University Press 1983.

Finley, MI *Ancient History. Evidence and Models*. London: Chatto & Windus 1985.

Finley, MI *The Use and Abuse of History* 2nd edn London: Chatto & Windus 1986.

Fornara, CW *The Nature of History in Ancient Greece and Rome*. Berkeley, Los Angeles & London: University of California Press 1983.

Grant, M *The Ancient Historians*. London & New York: Routledge 1970/1995.

Loraux, N *The Invention of Athens. The Funeral Oration in the Classical City*. Cambridge, MA: Harvard University Press 1986 [1981].

Thomas, R *Literacy and Orality in Ancient Greece*. Cambridge: Cambridge University Press 1992.

Thomas, R *Herodotus in Context: Ethnography, Science and the Art of Persuasion*. Cambridge: Cambridge University Press 2000.

Vidal-Naquet, P *The Black Hunter. Forms of Thought and Forms of Society in the Greek World*. Baltimore & London: Johns Hopkins University Press.

Chapter 2: *Environment*

Cherry, JF, Davis, JL & Mantzourani, E *Landscape Archaeology as Long-term History: Northern Keos in the Cycladic Islands*. Los Angeles: UCLA Institute of Archaeology 1992.

Foxhall, L 'Greece Ancient and Modern – Subsistence and Survival' *History Today* 36 (1986) 35–43.

Gallant, TW *Risk and Survival in Ancient Greece: Reconstructing the Rural Domestic Economy*. Cambridge: Polity Press 1991.

Garnsey, P *Famine and Food Supply in the Graeco-Roman World: Responses to Risk and Crisis*. Cambridge: Cambridge University Press 1988.

Isager, S & Skydsgaard, J-E *Ancient Greek Agriculture*. London & New York: Routledge 1992.

Jameson, MH, Runnels, CN & van Andel, TH *A Greek Countryside: the Southern Argolid from Prehistory to the Present Day*. Stanford: Stanford University Press 1994; Cambridge: Cambridge University Press 1995.

Kardulias, PN (ed.) *Beyond the Site: Regional Studies in the Aegean Area*. Lanham, MD: University Press of America 1994.

Murray, O & Price, S (eds) *The Greek City from Homer to Alexander*. Oxford: Oxford University Press 1990.

Osborne, R *Classical Landscape with Figures*. London: George Philip 1987.

Rackham, O 'Ancient Landscapes'. In O Murray & S Price (eds) *The Greek City from Homer to Alexander*, 85–111.

Rackham, O 'Observations on the Historical Ecology of Boeotia', *Annual of the British School at Athens* 78 (1983) 291–351.

Snodgrass, AM 'Survey Archaeology and the Rural Landscape of the Greek city'. In O Murray & S Price (eds) *The Greek City from Homer to Alexander*, 113–36.

van Andel, TH & Runnels, CN *Beyond the Acropolis: A Rural Greek Past*. Stanford: Stanford University Press 1987.

Wells, B (ed.) *Agriculture in Ancient Greece*. Stockholm: Paul Åströms Förlag 1993.

Chapter 3: *Peoples: Who were the Greeks?*

Bernal, M *Black Athena. The Afro-Asiatic Roots of Classical Civilization*, 2 vols (of 4). London: Free Association Press 1987–91.

Boardman, J *The Greeks Overseas. Their Early Colonies and Trade*. London & New York: Thames & Hudson 1999.

Chadwick, J *The Decipherment of Linear B*. Cambridge: Cambridge University Press 1967/1990.

Chadwick, J *The Myceneaean World*. Cambridge: Cambridge University Press 1976.

Graham, AJ *Colony and Mother City in Ancient Greece*. Manchester: Manchester University Press & Chicago: Ares 1964/1983.

Dickinson, O *Mycenaean Greece*. Cambridge: Cambridge University Press 1994.

McDonald, WA & Thomas, CG *Progress into the Past. The Rediscovery of Bronze Age Greece*. Minneapolis: University of Minnesota Press 1990.

Vermeule, ET *Greece in the Bronze Age*. Cambridge, MA: Harvard University Press 1964/1972.

INTERMEZZO: *HISTORICAL OUTLINE*

Andrewes, A *The Greeks*. London: Hutchinson 1967 = *Greek Society*; Harmondsworth: Penguin 1971.

Austin MM, *The Hellenistic World*. Cambridge: Cambridge University Press 1981.

Burn, AR *The Lyric Age of Greece*. London: Arnold 1960/1978.

Davies, JK *Democracy and Classical Greece* 2nd edn Glasgow: Fontana 1993.

Dillon, M & Garland, J *Ancient Greece. Social and Historical Documents from Archaic Times to the Death of Socrates*. London & New York: Routledge 1994.

Green, P *A Concise History of Ancient Greece to the close of the Classical Era*. London & New York: Thames & Hudson 1974.

Green, P *From Alexander to Actium. The Hellenistic Age* Berkeley, Los Angeles & London: University of California Press 1990/1993.

Harding, P *From the Peloponnesian War to the Battle of Ipsus*. Baltimore: Johns Hopkins University Press & Cambridge: Cambridge University Press 1985.

Murray, O *Early Greece* 2nd edn Glasgow: Fontana 1993.

Powell, A *Athens and Sparta. Constructing Greek Political and Social History from 478 BC*. London & New York: Routledge, 2nd edn 2001.

Powell, A (ed.) *The Greek World*. London & New York: Routledge 1995.

Snodgrass, AM *Archaic Greece. The Age of Experiment*. London: Dent & Berkeley/Los Angeles: University of California Press 1980.

Walbank, FW *The Hellenistic World* 2nd edn Glasgow: Fontana 1992.

PART II: *THE LIFE OF GREECE*

Chapter 4: *Rich and Poor*

Cohen, D *Law Violence and Community in Classical Athens*. Cambridge: Cambridge University Press 1995.

Connor, WR *The New Politicians of Fifth-Century Athens*. Princeton: University Press 1971. [reprint Indianapolis: Hackett, 1992 with new preface]

Davies, JK *Wealth and the Power of Wealth in Classical Athens*. New York: Arno 1981.

Dover, KJ *Greek Popular Morality in the Time of Plato and Aristotle*. Oxford: Blackwell 1974.

Hunter, VJ *Policing Athens: Social Control in the Attic Lawsuits 420–320 BC*. Princeton: Princeton University Press 1994.

Morris, I *Death Ritual and Social Structure in Classical Antiquity*. Cambridge: Cambridge University Press 1992.

Murray, O & Price, S (eds) *The Greek City from Homer to Aristotle*. Oxford: Oxford University Press 1990.

Ober, J *Mass and Elite in Democratic Athens. Rhetoric, ideology and the power of the people* Princeton: Princeton University Press 1989.

Osborne, R *Demos: the Discovery of Classical Attika*. Cambridge: Cambridge University Press 1985.

Ostwald, M *From Popular Sovereignty to the Rule of Law*. Berkeley & London: California University Press 1986.

Rich, J & Wallace-Hadrill, A (eds) *City and Country in the Ancient World*. London & New York: Routledge 1991.

Ste. Croix, GEM *The Class Struggle in the Ancient Greek World*. London: Duckworth; Ithaca: Cornell University Press 1981 [corr. impression 1983].

Whitehead, D *The Demes of Attica, 508/7 – ca. 250 BC*. Princeton: Princeton University Press 1986.

Chapter 5: *Women, Children and Men*

Blundell, S *Women in Ancient Greece*. Cambridge, MA: Harvard University Press 1995.

Cameron, A & Kuhrt, A (eds) *Images of Women in Antiquity* 2nd edn London & New York: Routledge 1993.

Cantarella, E *Pandora's Daughters: the Role and Status of Women in Greek and Roman Antiquity*. Baltimore & London: Johns Hopkins University Press 1987.

duBois, P *Centaurs and Amazons: Women and the Pre-History of the Great Chain of Being*. Ann Arbor: University of Michigan Press 1982.

duBois, P *Sowing the Body: Psychoanalysis and Ancient Representations of Women*. Chicago & London: University of Chicago Press 1988.

Fantham, E et al. *Women in the Classical World*. New York & Oxford: Oxford University Press 1994.

Foley, HP (ed.), *Reflections of Women in Antiquity*. New York, London & Paris: Gordon & Breach 1981.

Garland, R *The Greek Way of Life*, London & Ithaca: Duckworth & Cornell University Press 1990.

Golden, M *Children and Childhood in Classical Athens*. Baltimore & London: Johns Hopkins University Press 1990.

Greene, E (trans. modified), 'Sappho, Foucault, and Women's Erotics'. *Arethusa* (1996).

Halperin, DM, Winkler, JJ & Zeitlin, FI (eds), *Before Sexuality: The Construction of Erotic Experience in the Ancient Greek World*, Princeton: Princeton University Press 1990.

Hawley, R & Levick, BM (eds), *Women in Antiquity: New Assessments*. London & New York: Routledge 1995.

Humphreys, SC *The Family, Women and Death* 2nd edn Ann Arbor: University of Michigan Press 1993.

Just, R *Women in Athenian Law and Life*. London & New York: Routledge 1989.

Keuls, E *The Reign of the Phallus: Sexual Politics in Ancient Athens*, revised edn Berkeley, Los Angeles & London: University of California Press 1993.

Konstan, D (ed.) *Documenting Gender: Women and Men in Non-literary Texts* (special issue of *Helios* 19), 1993.

Peradotto, J & Sullivan, JP (eds) *Women in the Ancient World: the Arethusa Papers*. Albany, State University Press of New York 1984.

Pomeroy, SB *Goddesses, Whores, Wives, and Slaves: Women in Classical Antiquity*. New York: Schocken 1975.

Pomeroy, SB (ed.) *Women's History & Ancient History*. Chapel Hill & London: University of North Carolina Press 1991.

Rabinowitz, NS & Richlin, A (eds) *Feminist Theory and the Classics*. New York & London: Routledge 1993.

Reeder, ED (ed.) *Pandora: Women in Classical Greece*. Baltimore & Princeton: Walters Art Gallery & Princeton University Press 1995.

Schmitt-Pantel, P (ed.) *A History of Women in the West I: From Ancient Goddesses to Christian Saints*. Cambridge, MA & London: Harvard University Press 1992.

Sealey, R *Women and Law in Classical Greece*. Chapel Hill & London: University of North Carolina Press 1990.

Snyder, JM *The Woman and the Lyre: Women Writers in Classical Greece and Rome*. Carbondale, IL: Southern Illinois University Press & Bristol: Classical Press 1989.

Winkler, JJ *The Constraints of Desire: the Anthropology of Sex and Gender in Ancient Greece*. New York & London: Routledge 1990.

Zeitlin, F *Playing the Other: Gender and Society in Classical Greek Literature*. Chicago & London: University of Chicago Press 1996.

Chapter 6: *Power and the State*

Bruit-Zaidman, L & Schmitt-Pantel, P *Religion in the Ancient Greek City*, trans. P. Cartledge. Cambridge: Cambridge University Press 1992.

Camp, JM *The Athenian Agora. Excavations in the Heart of Classical Athens*. London & New York: Thames & Hudson 1986.

Cartledge, P *Sparta and Lakonia. A Regional History 1300–362 BC*. London, Henley & Boston: Routledge 2nd edn 2001.

Cartledge, P & Spawforth, A *Hellenistic and Roman Sparta. A Tale of Two Cities*. London & New York: Routledge 1989.

Ehrenberg, V *The Greek State* 2nd edn London: Methuen 1969.

Finley, MI *Democracy Ancient and Modern* 2nd edn London: Chatto & Windus 1985.

Finley, MI *Politics in the Ancient World*. Cambridge: Cambridge University Press 1983.

Forrest, WG *The Emergence of Greek Democracy 800–400 BC*. London: Hutchinson 1966.

Hansen, MH *The Athenian Democracy in the Age of Demosthenes*. Oxford: Blackwell 1991, 1999.

Jones, AHM *Athenian Democracy*. Oxford: Blackwell 1957/1978.

Lintott, AW *Violence, Civil Strife and Revolution in the Classical City 750–330 BC*. London & Sydney: Croom Helm 1982.

MacDowell, DM *The Law in Classical Athens*. London & New York: Thames & Hudson 1978.

Moore, JM (ed.) *Aristotle and Xenophon on Democracy and Oligarchy* 2nd edn London: Chatto & Windus 1983.

Sinclair, RK *Democracy and Participation in Athens*. Cambridge: Cambridge University Press 1988.

de Ste. Croix, GEM *The Class Struggle in the Ancient Greek World*. London: Duckworth & Ithaca: Cornell University Press 1981 (corr. impression 1983).

Chapter 7: *War and Peace*

Cargill, J *The Second Athenian League: empire or free alliance?* Berkeley, Los Angeles & London: University of California Press 1981.

Garnsey, P & Whittaker, CR (eds) *Imperialism in the Ancient World*. Cambridge: Cambridge University Press 1978.

Hanson, VD *Warfare and Agriculture in Ancient Greece*. Pisa: Giardini 1983, 1998.

Hanson, VD *The Western Way of War*. New York: Oxford University Press 1989, 2000.

Hanson, VD *The Other Greeks. The Family Farm and the Agrarian Roots of Western Civilization*. New York: Basic Books 1995.

Hanson, VD (ed.) *Hoplites. The Classical Greek Battle Experience*. London & New York: Routledge 1991.

Lazenby, JF *The Spartan Army*. Warminster: Aris & Phillips 1985.

Meiggs, R *The Athenian Empire*. Oxford: Oxford University Press 1972.

Rich, J & Shipley, G (eds) *War and Society in the Greek World*. London & New York: Routledge 1993.

Ryder, TTB *Koine Eirene*. Oxford: Oxford University Press 1965.

Snodgrass, AM *Arms and Armour of the Greeks*. London & New York: Thames & Hudson 1967/1981.

de Ste. Croix, GEM *The Origins of the Peloponnesian War*. London: Duckworth & Ithaca: Cornell University Press 1972.

Chapter 8: *Work and Leisure*

Burford, A *Land and Labor in the Greek World*. Baltimore & London: Johns Hopkins 1993.

Dover, KJ *Greek Homosexuality*. London: Duckworth 1978; 2nd edn Cambridge, MA: Harvard University Press 1989.

Finley, MI *Ancient Slavery and Modern Ideology*. London: Chatto & Windus 1980; Harmondsworth: Penguin 1983.

Fisher, NRE *Slavery in Classical Greece*. London: Duckworth 1993.

Gallant, TW *Risk and Survival in Ancient Greece*. Cambridge: Polity Press 1991.

Garlan, Y *Slavery in Ancient Greece*. Ithaca: Cornell University Press 1988.

Garnsey, P, Hopkins, K, & Whittaker, CR (eds) *Trade in the Ancient Economy*. London: Chatto & Windus 1983.

Garnsey, P *Famine and Food Supply in the Graeco-Roman World*. Cambridge: Cambridge University Press 1988.

Hanson, VD *The Other Greeks: The Family Farm and the Agrarian Roots of Western Civilization*. New York: Basic Books 1995.

Kyle, DG *Athletics in Ancient Athens*. Leiden: EJ Brill 1987.

Lissarrague, F *Aesthetics of the Greek Banquet*. Princeton: Princeton University Press 1990.

Millet, P *Lending and Borrowing in Ancient Athens*. Cambridge: Cambridge University Press 1991.

Murray, O (ed.) *Sympotica. A Symposium on the Symposion*. Oxford: Oxford University Press 1990.

Osborne, R *Classical Landscape with Figures: The Ancient Greek City and its Countryside*. London: George Philip 1987.

von Reden, S *Exchange in Ancient Greece*. London: Duckworth 1995.

Sallares, R *The Ecology of the Ancient Greek World*. London: Duckworth 1991.

Whitehead, D *The Ideology of the Athenian Metic*. Cambridge: Cambridge Philological Society 1977.

Whittaker, CR (ed.) *Pastoral Economies in Classical Antiquity*. Cambridge: Cambridge Philological Society 1988.

Wood, EM *Peasant-Citizen and Slave: The Foundations of Athenian Democracy*. London & New York: Verso 1988.

Chapter 9: *Literature and Performance*

Gardiner, EN *Athletics of the Ancient World*. London: Macmillan 1930.

Harris, HA *Greek Athletes and Athletics* 2nd edn Bloomington: University of Indiana Press 1966.

Neils, J (ed.) *Goddess and Polis: The Panathenaic Festival in Ancient Athens*. Princeton: Princeton University Press 1992.

Poliakoff, M *Combat Sports in the Ancient World*. New Haven: Yale University Press 1987.

Tzachou-Alexandri, O *Mind and Body: Athletic Contests in Ancient Greece*. Athens: Ekdotiki Athenon 1989.

Kennedy, G *The Art of Persuasion in Greece*. Princeton: Princeton University Press 1963.

Vickers, B *In Defence of Rhetoric*. Oxford: Oxford University Press 1988

Worthington, I (ed.) *Persuasion: Greek Rhetoric in Action*. London: Routledge 1984.

Walsh, GB *The Varieties of Enchantment: Early Greek Views on the Nature and Function of Poetry*. Chapel Hill, NC & London: University of North Carolina Press 1984.

Barron, JP & Easterling, PE (eds) *The Cambridge History of Ancient Literature: Greek Literature* (Vol. 1). Cambridge: Cambridge University Press 1985.

Comotti, G *Music in Greek and Roman Culture*. Baltimore & London: Johns Hopkins University Press 1989.

West, ML *Ancient Greek Music*. Oxford: Oxford University Press 1992.

Cartledge, P *Aristophanes and his Theatre of the Absurd*. reprint Bristol & London: Duckworth 1999.

Csapo, E & Slater, WJ *The Context of Ancient Drama*. Ann Arbor: University of Michigan Press 1995.

Easterling, PE (ed.) *The Cambridge Companion to Greek Tragedy*. Cambridge: Cambridge University Press 1997.

Green, JR *Theatre in Ancient Greek Society*. London: Routledge 1994.

Taplin, O *Comic Angels and other Approaches to Greek Drama Through Vase-Painting*. Oxford: Oxford University Press 1993.

Zeitlin, FI *Playing the Other: Gender and Society in Classical Greek Literature*. Chicago & London: University of Chicago Press 1996.

Chapter 10: *Visual Arts*

Amyx, DA *Corinthian Vase-painting of the Archaic Period*. Berkeley: University of California Press 1988.

Brommer, F *The Sculptures of the Parthenon*. London: Thames & Hudson 1979.

Cook, RM *Greek Painted Pottery* 3rd edn London: Routledge 1997.

Coulton, JJ *Ancient Greek Architects at Work*. Oxford: Oxford University Press 1977/1988.

Dinsmoor, WB *The Architecture of Ancient Greece* 3rd edn London: Bell 1950.

Hurwit, JM *The Art and Culture of Early Greece, 1100–480 BC*. Ithaca, NY: Cornell University Press 1985.

Jenkins, I *The Parthenon Frieze*. London: British Museum Press 1994.

Lawrence, AW *Greek Architecture* 4th edn New Haven, CT: Yale University Press 1983.

Mark, I *The Sanctuary of Athena Nike in Athens. Architectural Stages and Chronology*. Oxford: Oxford University Press 1993.

Pollitt, JJ *The Art of Ancient Greece: Sources and Documents*. New Haven, CT: Yale University Press 1965/1990.

Robertson, CM *A History of Greek Art*. Cambridge: Cambridge University Press 1975.

Robertson, CM *The Art of Vase-Painting in Classical Athens*. Cambridge: Cambridge University Press 1992.

Sparkes, BA *Greek Pottery*. Manchester: Manchester University Press 1991.

Spivey, N & Rasmussen, T (eds) *Looking at Greek Vases*. Cambridge: Cambridge University Press 1991.

Stewart, A *Greek Sculpture: an Exploration*. Berkeley, CA: University of California Press 1990

Chapter 11: *Philosophy and Science*

Fraenkel, H *Early Greek Poetry and Philosophy*. English trans. Oxford: Blackwell 1975

Guthrie, WKC *A History of Greek Philosophy*. 6 vols. Cambridge: Cambridge University Press 1962–80.

Robinson, JM *An Introduction to Early Greek Philosophy*. Boston, MA: M.I.T. Press 1968.

Kirk, GS, Raven, JE & Malcolm Schofield *The Presocratic Philosophers*. Cambridge: Cambridge University Press 1983.

Kerferd, G *The Sophistic Movement*. Cambridge: Cambridge University Press 1981.

Santas, GS *Socrates: Philosophy in Plato's Early Dialogues*. London: Routledge 1979.

Annas, J *An Introduction to Plato's Republic*. Oxford: Oxford University Press 1981.

Prior, WJ *Unity and Development in Plato's Metaphysics*. London: Routledge 1985.

Shorey, P *What Plato Said*. Chicago, IL: University of Chicago Press 1933.

Vlastos G, (ed.) *Plato: A Collection of Critical Essays – I: Metaphysics and Epistemology & II: Ethics, Politics and Philosophy of Art and Religion*. Garden City, NY: Doubleday 1971.

Ackrill, JL *Aristotle the Philosopher*. Oxford: Oxford University Press 1981.

Grene, D *A Portrait of Aristotle*. Chicago, IL: University of Chicago Press 1967.

Lloyd, GER *Aristotle: The Growth and Structure of His Thought*. Cambridge: Cambridge University Press 1968.

Lloyd, GER *Early Greek Science, Thales to Aristotle*. London: Chatto & Windus 1971.

Lloyd, GER *Science, Folklore and Ideology. Studies in the Life Sciences in Ancient Greece*. Cambridge: Cambridge University Press 1983.

Chapter 12: *Religion and Myth*

Bremmer, J *Greek Religion*. Oxford: Oxford University Press 1994.

Bruit-Zaidman, L & Schmitt-Pantel, P *Religion in the Ancient Greek City*, ed. P. Cartledge. Cambridge: Cambridge University Press 1992.

Burkert, W *Greek Religion: Archaic and Classical*. Oxford: Blackwell 1985 [1977].

Buxton, R *Imaginary Greece*. Cambridge: Cambridge University Press 1994.

Carpenter, TH *Art and Myth in Ancient Greece*. London & New York: Thames & Hudson 1991.

Easterling, PF & Muir, JV (eds) *Greek Religion and Society*. Cambridge: Cambridge University Press, 1985.

Edmunds, L (ed.) *Approaches to Greek Myth*. Baltimore: Johns Hopkins University Press 1990.

Faraone, CA & Obbink, D (eds) *Magika Hiera*. New York: Oxford University Press 1991.

Gordon, R (ed.) *Myth, Religion and Society*. Cambridge: Cambridge University Press 1981.

Graf, F *Greek Mythology*. Baltimore: Johns Hopkins University Press 1993.

Lloyd, GER *Magic, Reason and Experience*. Cambridge: Cambridge University Press 1979.

Mikalson, JD *Athenian Popular Religion*. Chapel Hill: University of North Carolina Press 1983.

Versnel, HS (ed.) *Faith, Hope and Worship*. Leiden: Brill 1981.

Versnel, HS (ed.) *Inconsistencies in Greek and Roman Religion*. 2 vols. Leiden: Brill 1990–93.

Vidal-Naquet, P *The Black Hunter*. Baltimore & London: Johns Hopkins University Press 1986 [1983].

EPILOGUE

Clarke, G (ed.) *Rediscovering Hellenism. The Hellenic Inheritance and the English Imagination*. Cambridge: Cambridge University Press 1983.

Dover, KJ (ed.) *Perceptions of the Ancient Greeks*. Oxford: Blackwell 1992.

Finley, MI (ed.) *The Legacy of Greece. A New Appraisal*. Oxford: Oxford University Press 1981.

Haskell, F & Penney, N *Taste and the Antique. The Lure of Classical Sculpture 1500–1900*. New Haven & London: Yale University Press 1981.

Jenkyns, R *The Victorians and Ancient Greece*. Oxford: Blackwell 1980.

Rawson, ED *The Spartan Tradition in European Thought*. Oxford, Oxford University Press 1969/1991.

Reid, JD *The Oxford Guide to Classical Mythology in the Arts* 2 vols. Oxford: Oxford University Press 1994.

Richard, CJ *The Founders and the Classics*. Cambridge, MA: Harvard University Press 1994.

Roberts, JT *Athens on Trial. The Antidemocratic Tradition in Western Thought*. Princeton: Princeton University Press 1994.

Taplin, O *Greek Fire*. London: Channel 4 Books 1989.

Tsigakou, F-M *The Rediscovery of Greece. Travellers and Painters of the Romantic Era*. London & New York: Thames & Hudson 1981.

Turner, FM *The Greek Experience in Victorian Britain*. New Haven: Yale University Press 1981.

Biographies

Susan E. Alcock

Susan E. Alcock is Professor of Classical Archaeology and Classics in the Department of Classical Studies at the University of Michigan. She holds a B.A. degree from Yale University, and M.A. and Ph.D. degrees from the University of Cambridge. Research interests include landscape archaeology and the archaeology of imperialism. Her most recent archaeological fieldwork has been as co-director of the Pylos Regional Archaeological Project in Messenia, south-western Greece. Professor Alcock was recently awarded a MacArthur Fellowship by the John D. and Catherine T. MacArthur Foundation.

Karim W. Arafat

Dr Karim Arafat is a Reader in Classical Archaeology at King's College London and author of *Classical Zeus: a Study in Art and Literature* (Oxford, 1990), and *Pausanias' Greece: Ancient Artists and Roman Rulers* (Cambridge, 1996). He has participated in excavations in Greece, Albania and Russia, and is currently preparing the archaic pottery from the sanctuary of Poseidon at Isthmia for publication.

Richard Buxton

Richard Buxton is Professor of Greek Language and Literature at the University of Bristol, where he has taught since 1973. He was educated at King's College, Cambridge, and subsequently at the Ecole des Hautes Etudes in Paris. He has worked and published on a number of aspects of antiquity, especially the relationships between ancient Greek society and the literature and mythology which it produced. In addition to many articles published in several languages (including Greek and Japanese), his principal publications are: *Persuasion in Greek Tragedy* (Cambridge, 1982), *Sophocles* (Oxford, new edition 1995) and *Imaginary Greece* (Cambridge, 1994). He has also edited *From Myth to Reason? Studies in the Development of Greek Thought* (Oxford, 1999) and *Oxford Readings in Greek Religion* (Oxford, 2000).

Paul Cartledge

Paul Cartledge is Professor of Greek History, Chairman of the Faculty of Classics, and a Fellow of Clare College at the University of Cambridge. He took his undergraduate and doctoral degrees at the University of Oxford. He is co-editor of the monograph series Key Themes in Ancient History (Cambridge) and Classical Inter/Faces (Duckworth), and is a member of the editorial boards of the journals *Dialogos* (Hellenic Centre, King's College London), *POLIS*, and *History of Political Thought*. Publications include most recently *The Greeks: Crucible of Civilization* (BBC Worldwide, 2001) and *Spartan Reflections* (Duckworth/University of California Press, 2001). He is currently preparing studies of Greek political thought from Homer to Plutarch, and of ancient Greek social and economic history.

Lesley Dean-Jones

Lesley Dean-Jones is Associate Professor of Ancient Greek Literature in the Department of Classics at the University of Texas at Austin. She specializes in both ancient medicine and women in antiquity. Her first book, *Women's Bodies in Classical Greek Science*, was published by Oxford University Press in 1994. She is also the author of several articles on Greek medicine, history and philosophy. She received her B.A. in Classics from University College London, and her Ph.D. from Stanford. In 1989–90, she held a fellowship from the American Council of Learned Societies, and in 1990 she was a Fellow at The Institute for the Humanities at the Unversity of Michigan at Ann Arbor.

Nick Fisher

Nick Fisher is Professor of Ancient History at Cardiff University. He has published *Aeschines: Against Timarchos, Introduction, Translation and Commentary* (Oxford, 2001), *Hybris, a Study in the Values of Honour and Shame in Ancient Greece* (Aris & Phillips, 1992), *Slavery in Classical Athens* (Duckworth, 1993), *Social Values in Classical Athens* (Dent, 1976), and numerous articles on Greek political and social history.

Edith Hall

Edith Hall is Leverhulme Professor of Greek Cultural History at the University of Durham, and Co-Founder and Co-Director of the Archive of Performances of Greek and Roman Drama at the University of Oxford. Her books include *Inventing the Barbarian: Greek Self-Definition through Tragedy* (Oxford, 1989), *Medea in Performance, 1500–2000* (with Fiona Macintosh and Oliver Taplin, Oxford, 2000), and *Greek and Roman Actors* (with P. E. Easterling, Cambridge, 2002).

Marilyn A. Katz

Marilyn A. Katz is Professor of Classical Studies at Wesleyan University in Middletown, Connecticut. She is author of articles on epic poetry, the historiography of Ancient Greece, sexuality in Ancient Greece, and women in Ancient Greece. Her book, *Penelope's Renown: Meaning and Indeterminacy in Homer's Odyssey*, was published by Princeton University Press in 1991. She is currently at work on manuscripts on *Women and Ideology in Ancient Athens*, and on *Women and the Polis in Ancient Greece*.

Catherine A. Morgan

Dr Catherine Morgan is a Reader in Classical Archaeology at King's College London and author of *Athletes and Oracles: the Transformation of Olympia and Delphi in the Eighth Century BC* (Cambridge, 1990). Her publication of the Mycenaean settlement and Early Iron Age sanctuary at Isthmia is forthcoming (Princeton University Press). She also has excavated in Greece, Albania and Russia.

Acknowledgements

ix*t*, 242, 348, Archivi Alinari; ix*b*, The Earl of Pembroke and the Trustees of the Wilton House Trust; xiii, 46*t*, 109, Kunsthistorisches Museum, Vienna; xv, 2, 3, 10, 38, 41, 43, 58–59, 71, 72, 152, 191, 221, 229, 304, 322, 338, 340, 350, Ancient Art & Architecture Collection; xvii, 162, Ny Carlsberg Glyptotek; xvi, Dave Bartruff/Corbis-Bettmann; xviii, reproduced by courtesy of the Trustees, The National Gallery, London; xii*l*, courtesy of the National Portrait Gallery, London; xi*r*, courtesy of the Hyde Collection; xx–1, 20, 217, The J. Paul Getty Museum, Malibu, California; 5, from Petworth House, National Trust; 6, 65*b*, 66, 67*t*, 82, 111, 130, 132–133*t*, 147, 166, 183, 198*l*, 266, 267, 270, 330, 344, 351*l* © British Museum, London; 7, Museo Etrusco, Vaticano; 8, Graeco-Roman Museum of Alexandria; 15, © Geospace/Science Photo Library; 16, 17*t*, 21, 22, 23, Susan Alcock; 17*b*, 250, Museum of Classical Archaeology, Cambridge; 18–19, Denver Art Museum Collection/photo: Lloyd Rule; 25, courtesy of Harold Koster; 27, courtesy of the Halieis Excavation Publication Committee; 28, photo by Otto Nelson; 31, Manchester City Art Galleries/J.W. Waterhouse: *Hylas and the Nymphs*, 1997; 33, Daniel Schwartz Photography/Lookat Photos; 36–37, Bildarchiv Foto Marburg; 42, Hulton Getty Picture Collection; 44, 316, Bibliothèque Nationale; 47*t*, Sofia, National Museum of History; 47*b*, © Bildarchiv Preussischer Kulturbesitz, Berlin, 1997/photo: Ingrid Geske-Heiden; 48, Cairo Museum; 49*r*, William E. Nickerson Fund, courtesy, Museum of Fine Arts, Boston; 49*l*, The Metropolitan Museum of Art, Fletcher Fund, 1932 (32.11.1) photograph by Schecter Lee; 50, Manolis Andronicos; 51*t*, Archaeological Museum of Thessaloniki (photo: Archaeological Receipts Fund); 51*b*, courtesy of the Archaeological Museum of Thessaloniki; 52, 143, © The Manchester Museum/University of Manchester; 54–55, 69, 91, 184–185, 210, 230–231, 323, Michael Holford; 57, © the British School at Athens Archives; 62, 171*t*, Cliché, Ecole Française d'Athènes (© EFA, Emile SERAF); 65*t*, 157, 254, 342–343, Deutsches Archäologisches Institut-Athen; 67*b*, 245, Soprintendenza Archeologica per L'Etruria Meridionale; 68, Henri Stierlin; 74–75, 123, 339, © Bildarchiv Preussischer Kulturbesitz, 1997/photo: Ingrid Geske-Heiden, Staatliche Museen zu Berlin-Preussischer Kulturbesitz Antikensammlung; 79, Rheinisches Landesmuseum Trier; 80, Thera Museum; 81, 190, 203, Hirmer Fotoarchiv; 83, 262, Francis Bartlett Collection, courtesy, Museum of Fine Arts, Boston; 86–87, Museum für Kunst und Gewerbe, Hamburg, Inv. no. 1984.488 (photo: Angelika Paul); 88, courtesy of Archaeological Receipts Fund, Athens; 89, Deutsches Archäologisches Institut-Istanbul; 90, 195, © Bildarchiv Preussischer Kulturbesitz, Berlin, 1997/photo: Ingrid Geske; 94, © Sonia Halliday Photographs; 95, Martin von Wagner Museum, Universität Würzburg/photo: K. Oehrlein; 98–99, Museum für Kunst und Gewerbe, Hamburg, Inv. no. 1981.173 (photo: Maria Thrun); 100, The Metropolitan Museum of Art, Rogers Fund, 1906 (06.1117); 101, 337, Musée du Louvre/© Photo RMN – Hervé Lewandowski; 102, H.L. Pierce Fund, courtesy, Museum of Fine Arts, Boston (00.330); 103, Makron, Greek, Attic, Kylix (red-figure), about 480 BCE, wheel-thrown, slip-decorated earthenware, Ht. 4 11/32 in. (11cm) (1972.55), The Toledo Museum of Art, Toledo, Ohio, Purchased with funds from the Libbey Endowment, Gift of Edward Drummond Libbey; 104, Staatliche Museen zu Berlin, Preussischer Kulturbesitz Antikensammlung/photo: Eva-Maria Borgwaldt; 106, The Metropolitan Museum of Art, Rogers Fund, 1906 (06.1021.144); 108, William Francis Warden Fund, courtesy, Museum of Fine Art, Boston (63.1246); 113, Alison Franz photo/Photographic Archives, American School of Classical Studies at Athens; 118, Bernisches Historisches Museum, inv. 12227; 119, 131, 148, 315*b*, Musée du Louvre/© Photo RMN; 124, The Metropolitan Museum of Art, Purchase, Walter C. Baker Gift, 1956 (56.11.1); 126, 171*b*, 324, © Bildarchiv Preussischer Kulturbesitz, Berlin, 1997/photo: Johannes Laurentius, 1990, Staatliche Museen zu Berlin-Preussischer Kulturbesitz Antikensammlung; 128, The Metropolitan Museum of Art, Rogers Fund, 1944 (44.11.1); 133*b*, The Metropolitan Museum of Art, Fletcher Fund, 1931 (36.11.4); 134–135 (detail of vase), 265, The Metropolitan Museum of Art, Fletcher Fund, 1931 (31.11.10); 136, Bequest of David M. Robinson, © President and Fellows, Harvard College, Harvard University Art Museums (1960.342); 137, courtesy of Antoine Vivenel Museum Collection, Compiègne (no. 1090); 144, 180–181, 260–261, 257*l*, 325, National Archaeological Museum, Athens (photo: Archaeological Receipts Fund); 145, 150*b*, 153, 154, 163, 269, American School of Classical Studies at Athens: Agora Excavations; 146, 306–307, Scala (Museo Nazionale Napoli); 150*t*, 256, Ashmolean Museum, Oxford; 156, Mansell Collection; 159, Archaeological Receipts Fund (Sparta Museum); 165, City of Bristol Museum and Art Gallery/Bridgeman Art Library, London; 167, Cliché Musée du Châtillonnais-Châtillon-sur-Seine/photo: Christian Labeaune; 170, Scala; 175, © The Trustees of the National Museums of Scotland 1997; 176–177, 182, 209, 219, 235, 334, Staatliche Antikensammlungen und Glyptothek, München; 178, Paul Lipke/Trireme Trust; 186–187*b*, The Metropolitan Museum of Art, Rogers Fund, 1930 (30.11.12); 169, The Metropolitan Museum of Art, Gift of Norbert Schimmel Trust, 1989 (1989.281.71); 188, 206–207, Bildarchiv Preussischer Kulturbesitz, Berlin, 1997; 198*r*, 227, courtesy of Rijksmuseum van Oudheden; 199, 353*t*, reproduction by permission of the Syndics of the Fitzwilliam Museum, Cambridge; 197, Scala (Museo Mandralisca Cefalu); 200, 228, 345, Musée du Louvre/photo: © RMN; 202, Bibliothèque Nationale (Cabinet des Médailles); 204, National Museum, Copenhagen, Department of Classical and Near Eastern Antiquities, inv. no. Chr VIII 967/photo: Kit Weiss; 208, courtesy of John Ellis Jones; 215–216, National Museum, Copenhagen, Department of Classical and Near Eastern Antiquities, inv. 13536/photo: Kit Weiss; 222, 244, © Donald Cooper/Photostage; 226, Museo delle Terme, Roma/Scala; 236, Christie's Images; 238, National Museum, Copenhagen, Department of Classical and Near Eastern Antiquities, inv. no. Chr VIII 316/photo: Kit Weiss; 239, National Museum, Copenhagen, Department of Classical and Near Eastern Antiquities, inv. no. Chr VIII 13817/photo: Kit Weiss; 241, The J. Paul Getty Museum, Malibu, California. Photo provided courtesy of Bruce White; 243, Martin von Wagner Museum, Universität Würzburg, photo: K. Oehrlein; 247, © The Cleveland Museum of Art, 1997, Leonard C. Hanna, Jr. Fund, 1991.1; 248, Henry Lillie Pierce Fund, courtesy, Museum of Fine Arts, Boston; 251, 252, 253, 257*r*, 268, 274, 275, Karim Arafat; 265, The Metropolitan Museum of Art, Fletcher Fund, 1931 (31.11.10); 273, Paris, Ecole Nationale Supérieure des Beaux-Arts; 278–279, by permission of Birmingham Museums and Art Gallery; 280, National Museum, Copenhagen, Department of Classical and Near Eastern Antiquities, inv. no. 3888; 281, American School of Classical Studies, Corinth Excavations; 282, 283, The Metropolitan Museum of Art, Fletcher Fund, 1938 (38.11.2); 286, Foto: Antonio Trigo Archivo Fotográfico. Museo Arqueol8.11.2); Eastern 287, courtesy of Ecole Suisse d'Archéologie en Grèce, 288, The Bodleian Library, Oxford, MS.E.D.Clarke 39, fol. 113r; 289, by courtesy of the papyrology Collection, Graduate Library, The University of Michigan; 291, Musei Vaticani Archivo Fotografico; 293, Bulloz/Museo Capitolino, Rome; 298, Archivi Alinari/Museo Capitolino, Rome; 299, Bildarchiv Preussischer Kulturbesitz, Berlin, 1997/photo: Jürgen Liepe, 1992; 302–303, Galleria degli Uffizi, Florence/Bridgeman Art Library, London; 305, © Bildarchiv Preussischer Kulturbesitz, Berlin, 1997, Staatliche Museen zu Berlin-Preussischer Kulturbesitz Antikensammlung; 310–311, Vatican Museum and Art Galleries, Vatican City/Bridgeman Art Library, London; 313, Professor Ann Ellis Hanson, University of Michigan (see also 'The Medical Writers' Woman' pp 309–338 in DM Halperin, JJ Winkler & FI Zeitlin (eds) *Before Sexuality: The construction of erotic experience in the ancient Greek world.* Princeton University Press: Princeton 1990 & A Hanson 'Uterine Amulets and Greek Uterine Medicine' *Medicina nei secoli* 7.2, 281–99, 1995; 315*t*, photo: National Archaeological Museum, Athens; 319, Edimedia/Bibliothèque Nationale; 320, Aerofilms; 326, Museo Gregoriano Etrusco Vaticano/Scala; 331, Edwin E. Jack Fund, courtesy, Museum of Fine Arts, Boston; 328–329, Museo Nazionale, Naples; 338*t*, Hermitage Museum, Leningrad; 338*b*, Museo Arqueologico, Madrid (11094); 341, courtesy of Ioannina Museum; 346 Ann Ronan at Image Select; 347*t*, Papyrus 2068/by permission of the British Library; 347*b*, Firenze, Bibliotheca Medicea Laurenziana, MS. Laur. Plut. 74.7, fol. 198v and fol. 203v; 351*r* © Edifumato, Milan; 349, The Bodleian Library, Oxford, MS. Lat. misc.d.85, fols. 137v–138r; 353*b*, Royal Institute of British Architects: The British Architectural Library; 354, The Metropolitan Museum of Art, Catharine Lorillard Wolfe Collection, Wolfe Fund, 1931 (31.45), photo © 1995 The Metropolitan Museum of Art; 355, 357*t*, courtesy of the Board of Trustees of the Victoria & Albert Museum; 356, Royal Commission on the Historical Monuments of England (RCHME); 356*b*, Private Collection/photo: Bridgeman Art Library, London; 358*l*, Tick Ahearn, New York; 357*b*, courtesy of Lofthouse Enterprises, Hitchin, Herts; 358*r*, Pablo Picasso, Maquette for the cover of *Minotaure*. Paris (May 1933). Collage of pencil on paper, corrugated cardboard, silver foil, ribbon, wallpaper painted with gold paint and gouache, paper doily, burnt linen, leaves, tacks, and charcoal on wood, 19 1/8 x 16 1/8" (48.5 x 41.0cm). The Museum of Modern Art, New York. Gift of Mr and Mrs Alexandre P. Rosenberg. Photograph © 1997 The Museum of Modern Art, New York/© Succession Picasso/DACS 1997.

Index *Italic numerals indicate illustrations*

CAMBRIDGE ILLUSTRATED HISTORY

Ancient Greece

edited by Paul Cartledge

Sumptuously illustrated in colour and packed with fascinating information, *The Cambridge Illustrated History of Ancient Greece* is now available for the first time in a revised paperback edition. Offering fresh interpretations of classical Greek culture, the book devotes as much attention to social, economic, sexual and intellectual aspects as to politics and war. Paul Cartledge and his team ask what it was like for an ordinary person to partake in 'the glory that was Greece'. They examine the influences of the environment and economy; the effect of interstate tensions; the implications of sexuality; the experience of workers, soldiers, slaves, peasants and women; and the roles of myth and religion, art and culture, and science and education. This is a cultural history from the bottom up, which reveals the far-reaching linguistic, literary, artistic and political legacy of ancient Greece, and seeks justification for Shelley's claim that 'we are all Greeks'.

'This is an original and insightful work. Its authors have lucidly synthesized the results of a generation of creative scholarship, and restored the voices of many groups that were often left out of more traditional Greek histories.' *International History Review*

'... a thoughtful portrait of the cultural history of ancient Greece for the general reader ... this is an interesting and handsome book that might bring new students to the field with its updated approach to an ancient culture.' *New England Classical Journal*

'... no one reading this book will fail to appreciate the complexity of ancient Greece as a society, a competitive, high achieving, innovative world ... We have grown up in our understanding of Greeks since the nineteenth century and this book shows how much. A fine achievement.' *History Today*

'A beautiful addition to the *Cambridge Illustrated History* series.' *Religious Studies Review*

Joint winner, Criticos Prize

CAMBRIDGE
UNIVERSITY PRESS

The cover illustration is of 'Dionysus in a warship', from the interior of a drinking goblet by Exekias (sixth century BCE). Reproduced by permission of Staatliche Antikensammlungen und Glyptothek, Munich.

$39.99
ISBN 0521521009
53999
9 780521 571000